The Missing Pill

Dr. John G Ryan MD

Copyright © 2013   Dr. John G Ryan MD

All rights reserved.

ISBN-10:   0988148315

ISBN-13: 978-0988148314

"There is a revolution going on, and this book is proof of it. My work as a channeller is mysterious to many. It's spiritual esoteric information and is mostly laughed at by a community of professionals who believe they "know better." However, for over 24 years KRYON has been giving messages about the potentials of multi-dimensional biological discoveries that will begin to change humanity past 2012. The Missing Pill is just that!

We are all "trained" in a very 3D world to expect certain things in certain ways. It simply is the way things work for us, so it becomes our reality. Both patients and doctors world-wide have participated in a traditional, allopathic chemistry-based consciousness that is about to be changed forever. According to KRYON, this slow awareness will be brought to us by medical Doctors, and not spiritualists.

Dr. John Ryan is one of a handful of medical professionals who has seen this "bridge coming" for years. In this book he presents the concept of how your own consciousness is the missing pill that the body is craving. He outlines a world of quantum-based healing that is non linear, but still understandable. He is one of the few who will begin to demystify the utterly confusing area of New Age energy healing into an integrated idea, and a new healing reality for many.

At last we have the beginning of credible information to help us put together one of the most powerful forces on the planet, and use it... that of Human consciousness. Our bodies are ready, and our DNA is saying "It's about time!" Congratulations Dr. John, for your courage to write this book!"

LEE CARROLL PH.D

AUTHOR & ORIGINAL CHANNEL FOR KRYON

"*Dr. John Ryan's incredible book is a gift to humanity and an essential read for all on the path of integral wholeness of body, mind and spirit. The information is an eloquent discourse on the importance of 'Unity Field Healing' and beautifully provides the means and methods for the trinity of harmony and integration of full DNA in bio energetic transition. Thank you John for this important work and for the open sharing. This is a an important work and truly 'must-read' !* "

JAMES TYBERONN

AUTHOR & CHANNEL FOR ARCHANGEL METATRON

"A Western doctor's persuasive testament to energy healing."

The notion that all matter contains energy and consciousness has been gaining traction in public discourse. Ryan (Harp of the One Heart, 2013) adds credibility to the conversation with scientific examination as well as his own journey of conversion. He reframes the human experience as a biospiritual continuum that runs from subatomic particles to our higher spiritual natures and comprehensively explores that perspective. The scope and length are daunting, but a clear, conversational style, abundant personal anecdotes, and palpable empathy for the reader make even technical or arcane concepts accessible. The treatment of commonly observable phenomena—fundamentals of electromagnetics, DNA, visible sound and vibration, sacred geometry—provides the foundation for the less easily perceived ones, such as the aura, chakras and energy bodies. Ryan addresses the role and limitations of science and explores modes and levels of healing. Key to the book's value is the revealing chronicle of his own awakening to intuition and energetic healing, which accelerated during his medical studies. His grounding in logic and science remains firm, a stance that lends credence to his more unconventional practices and may especially appeal to those new to energy work. In his view, healing has moved from curing a condition to restoring balance with the self, environment and spirit. The means for achieving this balance, he explains, is embracing the spiritual and giving it suitable expression in the physical. That is the thrust of current human evolution, he contends. It is also the goal of his Unified Field Healing technique. As with the discussions that precede it, he introduces it without hype or pressure. Don't park your brain at the door is the consistent message. As his life demonstrates, logic and the physical coexist with the intangible.

"AN IMPRESSIVE PRIMER ON THE ROLE OF ENERGY AND CONSCIOUSNESS IN THE PHYSICAL WORLD AND HUMAN HEALING."

KIRKUS REVIEWS

DEDICATION

I dedicate this work to my parents, John Francis Ryan and B. Frances Ryan. Their supreme dedication in providing their family with a loving, noble and honorable start is my greatest asset in life.

DR JOHN G RYAN MD

TABLE OF CONTENTS

PART I
INTRODUCTION — 1

1 INTRODUCTION — 3
   WELCOME — 3
   AN ORIENTATION — 5

2 SCIENCE, MEDICINE AND NEW CONSCIOUSNESS THINKING — 13
   INDEED A FEW SHORTCOMINGS — 13
   WHILE WAITING FOR SCIENCE — 21
   A MEDICINE OF THE FUTURE — 29

3 WHAT AND WHY NOW? — 33
   JOIN (OR KEEP RIDING!) THE WAVE — 33
   2012 AND BEYOND — 35
   LUCKY 13 — 46

4 ONE MAN'S STORY — 63

PART II
ENERGY, CONSCIOUSNESS AND THE HUMAN ENERGY SYSTEM 111

5	LIFE AS AN ENERGY AND CONSCIOUSNESS BASED REALITY	113
	The Energetic Nature of Life	115
	Energy Basics	120
	Energy Fields	128
	DNA	131
	Consciousness and Intelligent Design	138
	Cymatics, Sacred Geometry and Crop Circles	142
6	THE HUMAN ENERGY FIELD AND BIOSPIRITUAL CONTINUUM	151
	Introduction	151
	The Aura	156
	The Energy Bodies	158
	The Physical body	161
	The Etheric Body	166
	the emotional Body	170
	the Mental Body	187
	Higher Energy Bodies	198
	The Four Body Model, The Soul and The Higher Self	200
7	CHAKRAS, ENERGY FLOW AND KUNDALINI	205
	Chakras	205
	Nadis	233
	Kundalini	235

PART III
HEALING   247

8	**THE HEALING UNIVERSE**	249
	Healing Defined	249
	Responsibility and Healing	264
9	**HEALING - THE 4 BODY MODEL**	277
	Etheric Healing	278
	Psychoemotional Healing	289
	Emotional Healing	295
	Mental Healing	309
	Spiritual Healing	330
10	**DEEP BIO-SPIRITUAL TRANSFORMATION**	347
	All Things Ego	350
	Peace Consciousness	396
	The Spiritual Ego	406
	Coming Home:	409
	The Body as a Temple	410
11	**UNITY FIELD HEALING**	413
	Unity Field Healing	414
	The Origin of Unity Field healing	416
	The Inaugural Vision	417
	The Story Evolves	420
	New Information Arrives	422
	The sharing Begins	423
	Synthesis	424
	The workings	426
	Sessions	432
	An Exercise of Introduction	436

PART III
HEALING (CON'T)

12	SUPPORTIVE TOOLS, INFORMATION AND GRACE	439
13	IN CLOSING	467
	BIBLIOGRAPHY	471
	FIGURES & REFERENCES	475

AKNOWLEDGEMENTS

I love to read the acknowledgement section of a book. It reveals so openly the influences, which have been present in the life of an author, and what they hold dearly in their mind and their heart.

The list of influences is large in my life, for like you, I have been the grateful benefactor of so many human and spiritual influences. Each one has played a role in molding me, in one way or another, into the person I have become today. Yet, my first acknowledgment goes to you. This is for having the courage and curiosity, as well as the openness of spirit, to entertain a single word in this book. For you to consider it as worthy of a moment of your precious life is an honor.

I dedicate this work to my parents, John Francis Ryan and B. Frances Ryan. From a humble beginning in maritime fishing families, off the rugged coast of Newfoundland, they gave opportunity to seven wonderful children. They saw us each as the focus of their most important responsibility and support. Their desire for the self-defined success of each of us is one of the cardinal reasons I am anything close to who I am today.

I would also give honor to my siblings, their spouses and my vast dynasty of nieces and nephews. They have each inspired me and supported me in an endless variety of ways through my sojourn to date. The playfulness of Jim, the quiet reserve of my brother Leonard, the wisdom and nurturance of Joan, the angelic kindness and absolute non-judgmentally of Angela, the curiosity and will of Randy and the unbridled inspiration of Michael - have all inspired me through the years. The wonderful luck I have had in the assignment of siblings and spouses has not escaped my awareness or my love.

I give honor to the friends, acquaintances and apparent foes of my life. Each is treasured, each in their respective beauty, love and lessons. To my dear friends Joe, Susan and Robert for their beauty of spirit, and to my dear friend Tracey for anchoring the world – Thank you.

To Michael, my partner, thank you for keeping me inline with hard-pressed logic, yet never ceasing to inspire me by the beauty of your heart – a heart that knows life is enriched, in fact created by sharing, loving and forever expanding its reach.

To my vast array of teachers in medicine, in energy healing and in life – I will be eternally grateful.

And finally to two of the greatest loves of my life – my first great dane Nexus and my current great dane, Miah. Together they have kept vigil so I may never lose sight of the true power of peace, presence, kindness, playfulness, a non-judgmental nature, and forgiveness. They have shown my very active mental nature and sensitive emotional being, the importance of being both true to the moment, and always, to my heart.

Namaste.

DISCLAIMER

The information in this book is not a substitute for medical care. The information including ideas, suggestions, techniques and other material is for general and educational purposes only. This information is not intended to represent medical or psychological advice and should not be used for medical diagnosis, cure, treatment or healing in the western medical convention.

This information is not intended to create a patient-physician relationship, or any other type of professional relationship between the reader and the author. It should not be considered a replacement for consultation with a personal health care professional. If you have any questions or concerns about your health, please consult your personal health care provider or providers.

Energy-based healing and biospiritual transformative techniques promote harmony and balance to relieve internal restrictions to support the body's ability to heal. It is widely demonstrated as an effective complement to, but not a substitute for, conventional professional medical care.

Understand you will be introduced to energy healing processes and spiritually oriented information in your exposure to the material in the book. Energy healing, energy healing modalities, Energy Medicine, biospiritual transformation, vibrational healing and energy techniques are terms used to refer to a variety of alternative and complementary treatments, which rely on the manipulation of the human energy fields, thoughts, beliefs and emotions of the body. Although energy techniques have promising benefits, they have yet to be fully researched by the western medical establishment and western psychological agencies.

The author and publisher accept no responsibility for use or misuse of the information contained within. No liability or claim for injury, loss or health consequence, which may be perceived to occur from the usage of material in this book against the author or publisher, is recognized as valid. By reading the material, you agree to release, indemnify and hold harmless the author and publisher of this material.

A SPECIAL WORD OF THANKS

I am deeply grateful to a few dear friends who played a great role
of support during the editing and development of this book.
To each of you I offer my heartfelt thanks – not simply for your support,
but your presence in my life:

Michael Donovan

Joan McMurrer

Angie Lapointe

PJ Clarke

Angela Quirk

Denise Leitch

Rock Lafontaine

Janet Little

Nancy Voestermans

Tineke Colijn

James Tyberonn

Lee Carroll

DR JOHN G RYAN MD

PART I

INTRODUCTION

DR JOHN G RYAN MD

CHAPTER 1

INTRODUCTION

Faith, hope and love remain, but the greatest of these is love.
1 Corinthians 13[1]

WELCOME

The book you now hold in your hands is an orchestra of thought, a composition reflecting the integrative bio-spiritual odyssey of healing. And, like in an orchestra, there are many contributing facets. Yet, in many ways it is a simple book - a book of human hope, scientific progress, spiritual faith but ultimately, inspired love. The maestro of healing, the fanner of the flames of transformation, always returns to this source. For in the deepest recesses of our being – that is our nature. The sooner we return to the truth of this promise, the sooner we understand what "healing" truly means.

Human healing is a vast and complex topic. Yes, there are many scientific and spiritual concepts to examine when we speak of healing. However, the hope "to heal" from anything addresses a deeper yearning. It is not simply to feel better or to eradicate an illness. It is a visceral awareness of the human condition, and the desire to find what we know is possible as a human being, and as a human race. It is a desire to reunite with the state of being whole, individually and collectively, from which healing can blossom.

When we speak of healing in modern day, our faith to heal lies much in science. This faith is not totally misplaced, for science achieves marvelous things. Science, however, remains limited in many ways in its capacity to provide healing. Why? Science does not yet fully grasp the spiritual nature of reality, the bio-spiritual spectrum inherent in life, or the energetic nature of the human experience. We shall explore these ideas intimately.

If science fails when healing is sought, faith turns for many, to spiritual pursuits. And again, many elements of healing are found in our longstanding spiritual traditions. Yet ironically, spiritual wisdom is found in all healing, even scientific healing, if we look deeply. All healing wisdom emerges from a deeper spiritual intelligence and wisdom, whether we first acknowledge this or not.

Hence the quest to heal may involve science and it may involve spirituality. However, no matter what tools are used in healing endeavors, the greatest force of healing ever known lies in the *conscious* spirited human being. Understanding the profound truth in this simple statement is the threshold on which humanity now sits. And as a conscious spiritual being, the power to heal profoundly lies within you.

The mystical understanding that every human is a functional "spiritual consciousness" and "organized system of energy" is at the threshold of being scientifically introduced. Humanity is in the process of uncovering the "consciousness" foundation of life. And this is occurring, not simply through spiritual teachings, but in many ways through science and the quantum frontier. As this happens, a gentle spiritual awakening is occurring in the hearts and minds of millions of human beings alive on the planet today, and consequentially, the human race will never be the same.

As we probe deeply into healing, consciousness and the energetic nature of reality – we uncover a mystery. We come to understand that it is a willingness to assume our worth as spiritual beings, love authentically, and live wisely as responsible co-creators with spirit, which sets the stage for deep healing. This incites a personal biospiritual transformation – and what many believe will be the greatest transformation known to mankind.

So how does a person make sense of this? It is my intent that the book you are about to read presents a clearer understanding of your "human" nature, your deeper nature as a "spiritual being", and the energetic bridge that spans this sometimes seeming abyss. With this foundation of knowledge, it will be a little easier to navigate the waters of energy and consciousness based healing, and feel comfortably footed in an awakening world.

In whatever state you consider your life to be at present - wonderfully creative and superbly amazing, or, in need of great healing attention – there is always a fuller spiritual potential available within you. I would love to accompany you, as you take these next steps. Join me on a journey as we travel through the foundational precepts of energy and consciousness based or "spiritual" healing. It is not a passive journey. It is a catalytic adventure to further awaken the marvelous healing potential found in developing a deeper connection with your spiritual roots.

I trust the book will offer knowledge, experience, and an integrated understanding of healing. Yet, I hope these words ignite hope, inspire faith and facilitate your journey not just to heal – but to self realize in love's nature. May they not only deepen your conscious realization, but also your real-life manifestation, of a promise-filled potential seeded within you.

An Orientation

A Million Paths to Oneness.

If you are anything like me, hope and faith have visited at the strangest moments in life. This may even be such a time in your journey, and what draws you to read this book. However, hope and faith visit not only in times of crisis, but live constantly within us. As attributes of consciousness, they can serve as beacons in uncertain, confusing or fearful times. Yet, they also serve to provide resilience, strength and transformation in times of wellbeing. So, in whatever space you find yourself today – there is still an expanding magnificent power waiting to manifest more fully through you. If our time together fans the light that burns as your true nature – I confess – I will be pleased.

As a stimulus to read this book, one may be seeking physical, psychological, or social healing. Perhaps, you may be interested in helping others in their healing journey. Or, you may be simply curious to learn. All are appropriate points of departure. Yet I must caution you that we will discuss frankly many spiritual concepts with no unwarranted reserve. This will be natural for many but perhaps uncomfortable for others. I encourage you to simply open your mind and your heart – for it will all make sense if you give things a chance to sink in.

Whether you are religious, spiritual, agnostic or atheistic – is of limited significance. God, in however you understand the term, is reported not to judge human beings the way human beings judge God, or each other. That has been my experience. I am pretty confident that God is indifferent to the words we use to describe him or her - but is infinitely keen on the intention and the love we manifest in our lives by any name. Your spiritual and energetic nature is truly as real and available to you, however you see yourself – as long as you are willing to open up and to acknowledge love as relevant and assume your spiritual worth. The intent is therefore to help build a stronger relationship between your conscious self, your spiritual potential and your manifest life.

In the upcoming pages we will unite from our diverse paths, to explore together, both ancient and emerging knowledge. We will explore concepts of energy medicine and spiritually inclusive healing. We will also explore the intimate relationship of your very real spiritual nature, and your energetic nature, with the healing potential it provides. We will then turn our attention to new tools that are beyond our 3D concepts of healing, even modern energy healing - perhaps even for the most energy savvy among you! And along the journey, we will explore a variety of both information and tools to support you, as you walk in the paradigm of a new world.

You see, the incredible inherent intelligence that knows how to heal a wound in your body, or bring peace to a heart in torment, or the wisdom that defines a healthy community or world – all extrude from the domain of an incomprehensible organizing wisdom, an *intelligent design*. As you probe deeper into healing principles that we will examine in the upcoming pages, it will become obvious that **all** healing is essentially spiritual in design.

It is often said that beliefs come and go – but the core *Truth of Life* remains stable. It is we who transform around the mystery in a process of evolution, awakening and growth. As we grow in consciousness, we are creating a journey. Knowledge is an element of consciousness and will help us as we take steps in this journey. Knowledge, when applied, becomes experience. And, experience can lead us to the threshold of a deeper understanding of ourselves as spiritual beings.

At this threshold, it can also be understood that some of the knowledge and beliefs that brought us to forward in time may shatter, so we can continue forward in our journey. Humanity sits today at this threshold. It is time for us to drop an illusion of dis-spirited existence, and integrate in consciousness with a meaningful understanding of our true spiritual nature. And, as we cross this threshold, we will vicariously merge both with the spiritual and the energetic nature of all life. Through this living aperture, the pinpoint in time that is this moment, a vista of oneness with life opens before us, and healing can flourish through the prism of our being.

The journey of healing is a discovery – a discovery of the deep truth in you. There are a million roads to this truth, but a single destination. It exists "metaphorically" as the jewel of light in your heart. To uncover and polish the jewel found within each one of us is now the work at hand. And, so we begin …

SPRIT, ENERGY AND CONSCIOUSNESS

In the process of exploring Energy Medicine and consciousness based healing work – one must truly appreciate the significance of the concept that *all life is energy*. Since the days of Einstein we have become familiar with this equally scientific and mystical concept. It is, however, extremely important to the new healing paradigm. It becomes the portal through which human beings may access a new understanding of healing potential, one which might first appear as too mystical, to be real.

It is true that all of life - including we, ourselves as "manifested" human beings – is composed of energy. This includes not only our physical bodies, but also our emotions and our thoughts and the "energy bodies" in which they reside. When we begin to understand ourselves as energy based beings, we open ourselves to a different approach to healing than our traditional paradigm – with healing that appears more magical than scientific in foundation.

However, understanding life as energy is just a beginning. We must also begin to understand *consciousness* – and the role it plays in directing energy and healing.

We are all *conscious* beings who have the ability to manage and regulate energy. Deep inside our familiar mental and emotional nature, there exists an expanded consciousness of which we are both a communal and unique part. Our *spiritual* nature resides there and it can govern the way energy takes "form" in our lives when we better understand this reality. From the plateau of spiritual consciousness we are able to access a more responsible, loving and powerful role in directing the energy we manifest in the world of form – better known as "my life".

We can come to view our life to emanate as a *biospiritual continuum*. That is, we are conscious beings of a spiritual nature, who have been born into an energy-based world of "form". As human beings we are not simply physical bodies in a mechanical world – we are conscious being who live through the venue of many different layers or bodies, which are energy based in nature. It is through this lens that we can truly begin to understand and accept the power of spiritual consciousness, energy and spiritual grace to work in our lives.

We come to realize that as human beings, we are not limited to our physical reality, nor the familiar thoughts and emotions, which fill our days and our lives. We are foremost, spiritual beings – beings of consciousness. And as conscious beings, we are both *capable of* and even *responsible to* direct our thoughts, feelings and actions in a more coherent way. By growing in consciousness we can transform - or in some cases "allow" the transformation – of the "energy" of these elements of our lives. By doing so, we avail ourselves to a healing potential that remains somewhat dormant until we awaken to this potential. And what stimulates this awakening you may ask? It is your own personal intention.

Hence, individually, consciousness can grow or expand, and consciousness ultimately governs energy in many ways. As our human consciousness grows to include the realm of energy healing and spiritual reality, the ability and power we hold to manifest health and for constructive change, also grow in kind. To know yourself as a spiritual being, with an incredible power to heal from within is no small feat! This understanding provides access to a *biospiritual transformation* of amazing potential.

In our quest for healing and wellness, I believe it is the power and deep understanding of our spiritual nature, and the mysteries it holds, which will uncover what has long mystified science. Humanity is maturing, and the time has arrived to begin to understand that the reality of consciousness, energy and our spiritual nature holds the key to unlock the way forward for so much of what ails us. In our laboratories, the essential spiritual nature of a human being has been naively masqueraded by our level of understanding. Yet, as we work laboriously to heal disease in all the word implies – many believe we are ready to uncover this holy grail of wellness. Perhaps it is time to uncover this proverbial *Missing Pill*?

OFF THE THRESHOLD OF LOGIC

Okay, now I realize that some of this talk is a little unorthodox coming from a traditional medical doctor. As a modern physician, and like you as a human being, I rely greatly on the principles and advances modern science has made possible. Yet I have had to learn not to be as limited by some of its shortcomings, as we will explore. Why, you may ask?

Well, I have had the blessing of many experiences in my life, some of which I will share in Chapter 4, that have shown me attributes of life just beyond everyday awareness - and certainly beyond the capacity of understanding of our current science. I will save them for discussion, but I have been required to lift the veil of *false* logic that would have me accept only what is perceived with my common physical senses. In a guided trajectory of seemingly unsolicited experiences, from a "human" perspective, I was left with little option! So, just in case you have been wondering, I have not "gone off my rocker" ☺. I have simply been exposed to events that have created an evolving puzzle. And as fate would have it, they have all been part of a journey that has led me to the ability to share this work with you today.

Having worked most of my life in highly scientific domains, I have learned appropriately to depend on scientific scrutiny to inform intelligent analysis and action. Yet, like most open human beings, I have found logic both expansive and limited in its ability to help me truly understand life and our world. I have seen love, grace and heart wise common sense solve problems that no amount of analysis or logic could alter. And I have seen people heal in ways that science cannot explain.

However, as a scientist, I expose myself greatly in sharing this writing with you. We have all lived moments of great vulnerability in our lives – faced with some permutation of reticence and courage. To turn one's self inside out is an enduring exposure of vulnerability – and yet, that is what I will have to do to share this story with you.

This type of exposure presents the opportunity for judgment, misunderstanding and even ridicule. But I say, "Oh well." It also represents a fundamental opportunity to help another human being on their journey as countless others helped me. This simple little truth weightily tips the scale in my world.

This is part of a message whose time has come to be shared, for it belongs to everyone with an open mind, and it has many unique messengers. This book is but one. I believe, however, it is an important one. Why? It provides the missing panoramic perspective on healing - one of infinite value to people as they travel the many detours of the healing path. It will also take us to the threshold of *Unity Field Healing* - a simple, new and evolutionary healing paradigm, now available to share!

In the end, this book is based on a lifetime of personal experience. It is not founded in scientific rigor. It is based on heartfelt honesty, anecdotal experience and testimony. But authentically, it will ultimately speak of the power of our spirit to manifest in conscious ways based on the fabric of love that creates and renews our lives every day.

I believe, in the journey of life, it is our heart that must captain the ride, and navigate what is true beyond the limited perceptions we currently hold as true about the nature of life. I hope however, at the end of the journey the story you will tell is about the wonder of your spirit and its power to heal from the experience inspired in you.

STAYING SANE

Understanding now, the framework from which this book is written, I will attest, again, that logic has its obvious merit. Approaching life with more than a modicum of common sense, and a logical and discerning approach, is surely wise.

Logic fosters an understanding of principles or laws, and scientifically assured observations, which can help make sound decisions as well as discoveries. Logic has saved me on more that one occasion when cast awhirl in sensory unknowingness or emotional upheaval. Yet, logic has its own limitations - and very small wings.

For those seeking scientific scrutiny or simply an even greater understanding, there are many excellent books on the topics of energy and vibrational healing published today. They will complement this work nicely. Some are excellent scientific books, which include scientific analysis of new consciousness thinking principles and practices. Included are books on quantum physics, quantum healing, vibrational medicine, meditation and epigenetics - all of which are fundamental and essential to link the world of old with the world of tomorrow. I have chosen some of my personal favorites, for those seeking more information, referenced along the way.

Yet, it is important simply to understand that inspiration and experience often, if not always, precede scientific validation. And, I believe this is the case with energy-based medicine. Perhaps science will come to prove some of the information shared in these pages – one day soon. This is an invitation to science to more consciously explore the healing power of the human spirit.

The Magic Tapestry of Life

Finally, I believe our lives cross at nexus points – important moments when a gift or exchange is to take place between human beings. This occurs as we each travel our own appropriate journeys. This has been true in my life over and over and over again. I am sure it is true today also as you read these words.

When change is upon us, particularly large fundamental change, it can be uncomfortable. One of the greatest inspirations for me, to share this information, is simply to share comfort, knowledge and support.

Yet, trust nothing I say on merit. Filter it through your own experience, accept what seems right for you, and discard the rest. No one should tell you what to think or believe – there is a great danger in this naivety. I have no interest in you believing me. I have interest only in you believing the spiritual nature of yourself and the amazing potential contained within. Let it reveal itself to you.

For me, some personal moments of realization have arrived for me as private "Ah-Ha" moments. Yet other profound realizations have arrived in hearing about what others have experienced and realized, enriching my own personal experiences with a deeper understanding. Ultimately, I write the following book to share, not convince – and perhaps catalyze, as so many others have done for me. It is with heartfelt gratitude to those who have catalyzed my awakening, and in knowing the deep value of this – that I offer this book, from my head and my heart, to yours.

DR JOHN G RYAN MD

CHAPTER 2

SCIENCE, MEDICINE AND NEW CONSCIOUSNESS HEALING

I am including this chapter for the hard core left brainers among you ☺. We will take a little detour to place science and modern health care in perspective. If you are all about right brain activity, or already comfortable with spiritual and energy based healing, this chapter might not be necessary. In fact it might be uninteresting! You decide. You can comfortably skip forward to chapter 3 without missing the tempo of the book. If not, or if you are entertained by such musings, let us forge onward ...

SCIENCE - INDEED A FEW SHORTCOMINGS

As we explore the frontiers of a new understanding, such as energy-based healing, our modern "mindset" is revealed. We have become so confident in science, technology and even media today, that we vicariously think that science, and the information it shares, *creates* our expanding reality. We attest that as science discovers things, they are "made true". Equally, if science can't prove it, or at least prove it in traditional ways, it is "not real".

Science, in the end, is many "great things". It is inspired, evolutionary, progressive, and demystifying. When used for the healing and uplifting of humanity – regrettably not its sole orientation – it has unquestionably led to some of the greatest triumphs the world has seen.

However, if we open our minds– we can understand that science's role in many ways involves the uncovering a pre-existing intelligent order. We would also perhaps be wise to realize that humanity's progress is not only through scientific discipline – but also by inspired search for truth – ironically a "spiritual" search that is often lived through scientific discipline. In the realms of science, great leaps of consciousness that are not originally scientific in focus have played a huge role in humanity's progress and evolution.

So, science has some important limitations, which serves us well to acknowledge and understand. Let's take a look:

1. SCIENCE DOES NOT MAKE LIFE – IT EXPLORES IT

Life is founded on an intricate and incomprehensible intelligence, which dwarfs science in all ways. There is a process involved in unfolding this intelligence, which is part of our human journey. Science is only one part of this vaster intelligence – in a life of great mystery.

What we lose sight of often is that science really *uncovers*, more often than it *creates*. Certainly science can use the discoveries it makes to create new potentials, in its applied knowledge. However, in its basic nature, the core sciences are *uncovering* pre-existing knowledge of the workings of life and the universe.

In the process of scientific discovery, the knowledge that emerges existed long before science was capable of deciphering the mystery. For example, photosynthesis existed long before science uncovered this process or utilized the understanding of it to promote agricultural processes. Electrical activity in the human heart existed, eons before we learned to "shock" people back to life every day in modern hospitals. The work of science is uncovering an understanding, which was previously elusive. This is a simple statement, but it masks a profound mystery.

In the process of our scientific development, we can easily lose sight of the mystery and phenomenal intelligence of a universe that existed long before science put it under the microscope. In fact, it could be postulated that it is the inherent intelligence which makes life possible, that makes science possible! How is that for a paradox!

2. SCIENCE IS ALWAYS LIMITED BY ITS CURRENT LEVEL OF UNDERSTANDING AND DEVELOPMENT

Science cannot get ahead of itself. It would be hard to understand, for example, cellular division and mitosis, before we knew of the existence of the cell or its DNA containing nucleus. It would be hard to have technology – before the arrival of electricity or energy. There is a linear progress inherent in bringing forth a scientific understanding, acceptance and application.

When science reaches certain thresholds, certain fundamental things have to be in place to make the next step.

Galileo for example proposed the mechanics of non-stationery world revolving around a sun in his work *Dialogue Concerning the Chief Two Worlds Systems*.[23] He proposed the earth was not the center of life. He was tried for heresy under the force of the inquisition for this preposterous idea – and found guilty! His work was repressed for many years. Science and social forces are not always ready for pioneers! Meanwhile, the earth always rotated around the sun. When this was established, astronomy could then, and only then, advance into new understanding.

Equally, medicine did not create the intelligent structure and function of the human body – it discovered its structure and workings through human curiosity and intelligence. This occurred in a cascade of knowledge over many years. Things are possible today in medicine because of the incremental advances that have been made to arrive at the next level of potential. Yet the human body functioned as it does, long before man understood how.

Now science is at a very special place. One of the next big steps in science is an understanding of the quantum and energetic nature of life. This understanding is being developed, and the tools it will provide are yet to manifest. Science must wait for the progress it will encounter, as it crosses this unprecedented threshold.

3. SCIENCE IS LIMITED BY TECHNIQUE

When it comes to Energy Medicine – science has a great challenge before it. In scientific experimentation, it is easy to measure 3D outcomes, but it is more difficult to measure invisible forces, and things like wellness. In Energy Medicine the goal is to restore invisible energetic structure, flow and balance, which may prevent disease manifestation. Its deeper goal is to rewire or recalibrate the physical and energetic bodies of a human being with the spirit through which it emerges. Now how does science measure that?

Science is accustomed to looking methodically at outcomes. It could easily measure the cure rate of a disease based on a treatment. Yet that is not the strict principle on which energy-based medicine works. Healing of a disease may well be the outcome of an energy-based process, but the system of energy healing is bigger and more comprehensive than that. Also, sometimes diseases are part of a bigger consciousness process, a concept that is that far more difficult for scientific methods to understand.

Secondly, it is a bit easier to prevent disease than it is to undo it – but this component of energy-based work is even harder to appreciate, and certainly to measure, by technique. How do you reliably measure "the disease you didn't get" due to an invisible energy correction?

Energy Medicine includes a bio-spiritual dynamic that sees healing not as disease eradication, but rather restitution of a bio-spiritual alignment that promotes health. If someone's life lesson was to learn forgiveness for example, and by unblocking energy and opening the energetic heart center, they created a different health outcome in their life – how would science measure it?

The result of this is scientific involvement in examining energy healing is very limited at present. It's involvement in Energy Medicine, for now, will include the measurement of energetic changes such as in one's hands or our bodies during healing sessions in the limited ways possible, assessment of traditional physiological or psychological parameters of health that may change with energy based processes, and disease state changes that do occur as an outcome of healing work. This is a small component of what energy-based medicine is really about.

Science cannot yet measure an energy that many human beings are capable of seeing, feeling and knowing to be effectively real. As quantum technology develops, I believe one day it will be possible for science to measure the types of energetic changes that occur during healing work. Yet, science is not there yet – soon, but not yet. Until it does, it will be limited.

4. SCIENCE MAKES MANY MISTAKES IN ITS THEORETICAL UNFOLDING OF MYSTERIES

Science, in its quest for understanding, develops theories. In its theories it makes great discoveries and creates transient truths. These serve later as stepping-stones to greater and greater realizations. The new realizations then, sometimes, serve to dispel previously accepted scientific beliefs.

In the act of making theories, science often makes mistakes. When something poorly understood, and becomes widely accepted as truth, we can make sweeping assumptions as "fact". This becomes very hard to undo once it is set into place.

We can see the significance of this concept specifically in three scientific based ideas, which have heavily infiltrated modern culture and belief. These pervasive theories have had huge implications on the way we humans view our selves – and are due for a correction. I have added references to two of these topics for those interested in a broader discussion:

1. The faulty basis of the limited theory of evolution in only a world of spiritless competition and survival.[6]
2. A mechanistic view of human life with a strictly physical and biochemical approach to human disease and healing.
3. A "concrete" view of the mechanics of human DNA.[14]

These theories can be seen to fit very well into this scientific profile, as new paradigms of understanding are unveiled. The way that theoretical assumptions embedded in these ideas have come to affect humanity's view of itself is frankly limiting to progress.

Yet, larger than these isolated examples, the point to understand is that science's great companion is humility. It grows and sheds its skin. This needs to be understood appropriately.

5. SCIENCE PROGRESSES AND ACCEPTS THINGS AS TRUE, HELD AS PREPOSTEROUS YESTERDAY OR YESTERYEAR

Science is continuously and appropriately updated, as new understanding is uncovered to replace outmoded scientific views.

If science holds on too tightly to old theories they will eventually still die, but there is an ensuing struggle. The sun does not rotate around the earth; and, the earth is not flat. As obvious as these are today – they were once preposterous to imagine.

If you told someone that the way they think or feel can "change their genetic expression" 20 years ago, you would be considered foolish! But science today is showing this to be true.[5,6,14] Many more examples of scientific acceptance will come to the forefront in the days ahead, particularly in the domain of bio-spiritual or energy-based healing.

6. SCIENCE RELIES ON GREAT SPIRITUAL INSIGHT AND INSPIRATION TO PROGRESS

Mysterious, improbable, passion-inspiring searches have always been the purview of science. Yet ironically this statement would also be thought to describe a mystic, religious zealot, or spiritual aspirant – if we remove the word science from the discussion. We have a great faith in science, but even faith itself is a spiritual attribute. Interesting, don't you think?

Progress most often precedes science. What? We often lose sight of the fact that it is *inspiration* that leads to discovery. It seems that when "the time comes" for a greater understanding to enter human consciousness, select scientists are passionately searching for a breakthrough, and humanity seems to take giant leaps of understanding all at once. It is sometimes as if new paradigms are downloaded into human consciousness – and unfolded by science. They are slowly unraveled with the discovery and application of it's embedded ideas, through inspired men and women.

How many inventions or creative ideas seemed to be "floating in the ethers" and discovered by several scientists or human beings simultaneously at a point in time? Think, for example, about how quickly computer based technology became a completely integrated fundamental part of the whole world and everything in it. Why did this happen? How many major discoveries like aviation or electricity are within reach of several scientists at the same time? Why?

What drives scientific and evolutionary discovery? How often are scientists blindly and passionately driven towards a discovery or idea? From where does this inspiration come?

If you break "inspired" into syllables you will see "in-spired" – not to far from being "in-spirit". Perhaps it is not too lofty to imagine that such inspiration somehow arrives through the intuitive voice of "the spirit within"? Many great minds have admittedly brought forth new information following a flash insight, a meditative moment, a peak experience, or a revelatory dream! You see, we are all connected to a deeper plane of consciousness, accessible if we learn to listen. This is true of scientists, and every human being!

I believe we will see lots and lots of examples of inspired progress in science in the very near future. Progress is "floating in the ethers" all around us! This is particularly true when we come to speak of the fundamental energetic and psychospiritual nature of human life in science and healing. So many people are bringing new awareness, ideas and modalities to facilitate human healing and transformation. We are ready.

Today, this inspiration is bridging worlds that have been held apart by an artificial chasm. What is incredibly fascinating is that as science approaches the quantum frontier, it begins to acknowledge that the great tenants of spiritual teaching and wisdom have a foundational reality that can be understood even in term of science! An unlikely friendship is being forged right under our noses!

If anyone has explored quantum energy, or how consciousness can affect health positively or negatively in so many ways, it is easy to appreciate that health and a "solid manifestation of the human spirit" are inseparable. Maybe – just maybe – science is being led by an intelligent universal design to which we have access, which inspires *all* things.

7. SCIENCE DOES NOT FULLY INTEGRATE THE POWER OF CONSCIOUSNESS IN ITS MODELS

Traditional scientific methods to study life are structured to create observable or measureable observations. These observations are created to test hypothesis driven ideas, and to be maximally void of elements of bias, which would skew or modify observations. Rigorous experimental design requires an independent unbiased observer, blinding elements in design protocols, the capacity to create statistically significant observations, and so forth – to achieve this. There are many methods used to reduce or eliminate bias and ensure integrity in study designs.

In recent explorations of quantum physics and the study of consciousness – "consciousness" is potentially understood to "influence" outcomes.[61] What might that imply? It is commonly stated, "Your thoughts create your reality." But what if the simple power of one's thought and consciousness, or even the simple "act of observation" – could really influence an outcome. Might this be particularly relevant in scientific design?

As a scientist, it would be unconscionable to intentionally control outcomes in experiments, in a sinister way, to make them do what you want. But this issue introduces a whole other matter. What if observational consciousness mystically influences outcomes – even with honest intent!

3D science does its best to eliminate bias – but this idea may require some deep reflection – as we step in a more complete model of human consciousness in the days ahead.

Perhaps, the most important thing to take from this discussion, however, is not simply that observer influence can alter outcomes. It is the very simple idea itself that consciousness is a powerful force that can influence creation! This is perhaps interestingly demonstrated in a concept known as the "placebo effect" which we will review in Chapter 6. But, it becomes *very* important in healing and in our life.

8. *SCIENCE IS SLOW, METHODICAL AND TAKES TIME*

There is so much knowledge available to humanity at present about Energy Medicine – knowledge that is not scientifically validated. I believe instinctively that science will one day come to better understand, accept and even prove this knowledge to be true. As it does, I am infinitely confident it will apply the newly found knowledge in brand new ways, as it always has.

The door is however open. The scientific rigor that will be further inspired in the years ahead – a work that should occur and will occur – is important. Meanwhile, the opportunity is available now for a new healing consciousness to take root within us. Those with the courage and curiosity to explore may revel in its wonder, as science works to catch up to humanity's progress.

☉

So science is good – very good for humanity. Yet in its necessity for structure, logic and the narrow proof – which it requires – it is limited.

When humanity is ready for a leap in consciousness, like the one taking place on our planet, humanity may jump the scientific cue. Science will catch up but it will take time.

In the fascinating tale of science and social transformation, necessity has often been the mother of invention. Crises of different kinds have often preceded radical change. Let us take a look briefly at our health care system today and understand why some of the crises it is facing – may actually be propelling or symptomatic of this progress.

While Waiting for Science

The Health Care Crisis and Its Silver Lining

Medicine and modern health care have reached a point of stress that can be considered a crisis. If you listen around you, health budgets all over the world, on every level, are strained to breaking point. This includes health agencies high and low - from international health organizations all the way to community hospitals and clinics. It is probably the biggest health "epidemic" known to mankind.

In the third world nations, health care is in constant crisis due to impoverished and inequitable funding. Meanwhile, first world civilization seeks the latest and greatest pill to salve both our whims and very serious disease conditions. Yet, these systems too, are constantly under the strain of ever expanding costs, budget constraints, and in many cases tiered-care between levels of socioeconomic divide. Hospitals are bursting at the seams, yet tirelessly struggling to be profitable, or at least augment efficiencies and restrain budgets.

In private systems of delivery, insurance costs rise and companies dictate care models. In public funded systems the tax dollars required to handle the burden are running very dry. Managers who don't always understand the nuances of health care delivery are reconfiguring the systems. Political elections are fought over attitudes of management and containment – filled with usual rhetoric, polarization of involved members, and the intermittent noble idea.

As pioneering technological innovations emerge daily, and designer pharmaceuticals weave their way into the maladies of our day, the health care system is facing an unsustainable momentum of cost. Health systems everywhere are looking high and low for strategies to cut expenses or cut services.

If we step into the node of the storm that is modern health care, one might ask the question, "Where are we headed?" There is a palpable awareness of its unsustainability – and changes are coming.

The eleventh hour always seems like the ideal time to solve a crisis. So where *are* we headed? Can we re-direct? Is there a deeper potential to this crisis? We can approach these questions from a few different points of view.

The Riddle of Too Much Spending

Usually, in modern systems analysis, if we want to control costs, we begin with assessments that appraise the system and identify areas that would benefit from interventional change.

We look at global budgets and identify large costs – to cut them. We look at services, which have limited value – and stop paying for them. We look at salaries and restrain growth or cut them. We look at benefit plans and finds ways to limit or eradicate them. We engage campaigns of fiscal responsibility and budgetary crisis to support strategies. Cut employees. Add efficiencies. No rocket science here - the beat goes on.

If we probe a little deeper, one might ask the question, "Is there anything else one can do to bring greater health than simply rely on "cost expanding health care" as we know it?" Please don't misinterpret my intention – health care is an extremely important component of our modern lives. But, can an individual or a society be more engaged in health than by simply creating need for more complex and expensive health care? And, rather than live in fear of a system that won't be able to support us when we need it to take care of illness - can we learn to live in ways that make us healthier within? Maybe then the health care system could endure, and fund growth in new ways. Lets take a look.

To begin to solve the problem on a deeper level there are three valuable questions to ponder in order to understand how we arrived where we are. Why are we so dependent on externalized health care? Why is it so costly? And, how does that help us take a step forward in time?

A Fragmenting Evolution

In medicine, curiosity to understand and apply the understanding have always reigned. Science in all domains grew in scope and respect, and the scientific method was developed to explore our world.

The world entered into the industrial period where Newtonian models of physics explained the nature or reality, and humanity was thrust into the Darwinian evolutionary model of life. Through this passage the world became very mechanistic in it's models – competitive in it's nature - and medicine is no exception.

During this time, "physical reality" became the essence of understanding life and the human being. The science of human health came to view the body as a "complex machine". Medicine followed suit. Science uncovered the structural anatomy of the human body in exquisite detail - the nervous system, the cardiovascular system, the muscles and bones, as well as the complex inter-relationship of all such systems.

As the gross structure was better understood, science crossed the threshold of another major advance with the advent of microscopy. This introduced a whole new level of structure and function to explore.

Concurrent with this development, advances in chemistry and ultimately biochemistry also grew. It arrived at the level of understanding that exists today – expounding on a vast array of complex structural and functional elements that make up human function.

Later, an understanding of DNA emerged. It came to be understood in an elementary fashion as the "architect" of life.

All of this development has truly led us to a point in time where an incredible understanding of the anatomy, mechanics and biological function of the human form now exists.

However, during this development an important schism took place. In the process, science vicariously separated itself from everything that could not be explained by the scientific model and direct observation. There was a casting aside of anything that was remotely mystical, invisible, intangible, or spiritual in perception.

It was only the "tangible" and "observable" that fit neatly or had a role in the explorations of human healing. Everything that caused disease had some "physical" basis for understanding.

Science became strict fact-based work, mixed with theoretical assumptions – and left little room or patience for nebulous forces that were impossible to understand, control, observe and measure. It didn't seem to matter that the scientific method and visible observation could not explain all things. Science, for example, to highlight this paradox, often compares effects of treatment to a placebo effect that occurs with no therapeutic treatment – having no understanding why is there a placebo effect at all? But science did forge onward to the present day – which is good.

The limitations created by this great divide are not without consequence. It separated consciousness and our spiritual nature – the "essence" of healing – from the system designed to heal. And the human being – well we became a bit of "mechanical thing".

A Flux of Faith

Science aside, humanity also changed. Moving from a strictly faith-based-in-spirit populace, to one with a strong faith-in-science, humanity moved toward a great reliance on science and it's "externalized" methods of healing.

Humanity, too, in this transition, had in some ways lost faith in its own spirit and innate ability to heal. In our faithful reliance on the good work of science and medicine, we did create a paradigm where anything and everything that ails us is solved by a chemical, a service, or a product – to fix "the machine". But was this shortsighted? Are we really machines? What did we misplace in this sojourn through time?

Science, itself, in recent times has arrived at a threshold which is about to shatter this orientation. Science it is about to take a leap into an unknown "quantum abyss". Here matter meets consciousness and many say, "science meets God". The energetic nature of life and all matter, the role of consciousness, and the internal power to heal are "surfacing" within humanity. We are about to discover some of what was overlooked in our earlier scientific paradigm.

This will awaken a fascinating understanding of the energetic nature of matter and life – and the role of consciousness. We have found a portal to re-introduce some of the more mystical or internal elements of human potential, and our ability to heal – paradoxically through science!

Fascinating? Timely? Maybe! There is a certain timeliness in arriving at the quantum threshold! It will become the portal by which science can establish a role for the mystical and internal power of consciousness in the healing paradigm!

We look at the true implication of this in all of the upcoming material. But first ... why is health care so expensive? What does that add to our understanding about the current crisis in health care? What is helping us to change?

This Little Dollar Goes to Market

There is an adage in modern news reporting that states, when trying to get to the root of any issue, "you follow the money". This is wise in our current society, by virtue of the systems we have designed.

We have externalized our healing processes to such a great degree, that we rely heavily on healing outside of our innate ability. In this externalization of health and healing, which has many contributing factors, an interesting phenomenon has taken place. We have effectively created – a "large market".

So health care is not only "externalized", it is "commoditized", and driven greatly by market forces. This of course is not where medicine began, but it where we have landed. There is a lot of money to be made in health care – and that makes it expensive, not to mention vulnerable to a whole host of potential influences.

To give this a sense of perspective, from Wikipedia references[58]:

> *According to the World Health Organization (WHO), total health care spending in the U.S. was 15.2% of its GDP in 2008, the highest in the world. The Health and Human Services Department expects that the health share of GDP will continue its historical upward trend, reaching 19.5% of GDP by 2017.*

Of each dollar spent on health care in the United States, 31% goes to hospital care, 21% goes to physician/clinical services, 10% to pharmaceuticals, 4% to dental, 6% to nursing homes and 3% to home health care, 3% for other retail products, 3% for government public health activities, 7% to administrative costs, 7% to investment, and 6% to other professional services (physical therapists, optometrists, etc.).

In 2009, the United States federal, state and local governments, corporations and individuals, together spent $2.5 trillion, $8,047 per person, on health care.
Health insurance costs are rising faster than wages or inflation. Medical causes were cited by about half of bankruptcy filers in the United States in 2001.
In all countries we are seeing similar trends:

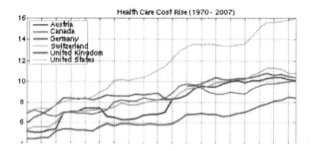

Fig 2-1 Health care costs rise based on total expenditure on health as % of GDP. Countries are USA, Germany, Austria, Switzerland, UK and Canada.

The amount Canadians spend on health care in 1997 dollars has increased every year between 1975 and 2009 from $39.7 billion to $137.3 billion or a more than doubling of per capita spending from $1,715 to $4089. In 2009 dollars spending is expected to reach $183.1 billion (a more than five percent increase over the previous year) or $5,452 per person.

The greatest proportion of this money goes to hospitals ($51B), followed by pharmaceuticals ($30B), and physicians ($26B).

The proportion spent on hospitals and physicians has declined between 1975 and 2009 while the amount spent on pharmaceuticals has increased. Of the three biggest health care expenses, the amount spent on pharmaceuticals has increased the most. In 1997 the total price of drugs surpassed that of doctors.

Okay, before falling asleep with the potential boredom induced by this litany of numbers, we can identify two important observations:

1. Health care costs are enormous and growing more rapidly than inflation.
2. The major costs fall to three categories: Hospitals, Salaries and Pharmaceuticals.

If we look a little closer, salaries and the commercial cost of running the business drive hospital budgets. In the US, hospitals are often corporations and sometimes aim also to make profit. In Canada they are publically funded and operate on a fixed prescribed budget.

Physician salaries are expensive overall – but perhaps more so in the US where market forces and competition play a greater role in regulating cost. In context of the cost of education, the years of dedicated study and the value of the applied knowledge, as well as the lack of a provided pension – one might argue that they on par with what is valued in a western society – but this too is expensive.

Finally, a huge sum of money is spent on drugs. No doubt about it – some medications are absolutely life saving for many people. Yet if we reflect honestly, pharmaceutical companies do have a lot to gain financially from illness.

Would it make any sense that such a system, consciously or unconsciously, would benefit only from making people well? Pharmaceutical research has done amazing things for millions of people worldwide, but we are all increasingly aware that there are some big problems with the structure and ethics of pharmaceutical research, marketing, and big pharma design.

Reflecting on these components, it is easy today to appreciate that so much of what we consider as modern health care is truly *market driven*, or subjective to an enormous number of marketing forces. Markets rely on profit. If profit is a goal in isolation, perhaps there is no value in truly providing wellness? To the marketer, value lies in creating an expanding, innovative or profitable market. Market forces are "not kind" to the standard moral forces of consciousness that governed medicine in its earlier development.

Lots of things can and do go wrong, when we put health care in a business model. Markets are supported by customers – not necessarily making sick one's healthy. And, greedy or ambitious marketers are not afraid to exploit this vulnerability to make money or influence anything that may create a more robust market or sales.

There are tremendous commercial influences, with marketing strategy as the bottom line, sometimes displacing ethics and morality. Regulatory boards are sometimes subject to corporate and political scrutiny, supervision or persuasion. This can shadow the process of decision making by a bias which may not always favor integrity – especially when corporate interests supporting our political and research systems – are at odds with it. So surely this can create a few problems – and some of them are contributing to the "crisis" at hand.

⊙

So let's see. We have a culture that now relies strongly on external healing; it relies on a science that is limited by the maturity of its understanding; and, we have evolved health care into a market structure. And, for some "crisis driven reason", it seems like it is ready somehow to implode!

As health care arrives at a point of crisis, to the enlightened observer, it could appear almost as if this is all scripted as part of a transformative paradigm. We all know something needs to change. Could it be that the problems and limitations in our current system are providing the *stimulus* to support, and simultaneously experiencing the *consequence of* – a transformation in human consciousness? Just saying …

People are becoming disgruntled with many aspects of the health care system. A lot of this is based on a sense of mistrust that has arisen due to unscrupulous behavior of marketing forces that have become a part of modern day health care, as well as some of the limitations that are inbred in our health care models for reasons defined. This has weakened or shattered a lot of people's faith in some aspects of medicine and the health care system.

Intriguingly, it is has also stimulated a search for alternate strategies to wellness, and no short amount of soul searching – as the system struggles to realign. Maybe this is actually a very good thing?

One important aspect of this search is that people are awakening to an internal desire and sense of personal responsibility toward health and wellness. They are "internalizing" it once again. And, this has also led to examination of all kinds of alternative strategies to achieve greater wellness.

Healing is becoming re-established as a "natural" process. At first glance, these are just words. But if you absorb the deeper significance of this tendency, it implies the return to holistic wellbeing as a strategy of health. This includes mind, and body, in the healing paradigm – and although not obvious at first, it re-introduces the "spiritual component" of wellness, an element long lost in the story of health.

In some ways, we have lost touch with the internal or "spiritual" component of healing that, with or without medicine and science, has always existed. So yes, we may look within form with microscopes to see structure – but we cannot look deeper inside form to find the healing power that is implicit in our spiritual design. That requires consciousness.

People today are poised to reclaim this broader understanding of health and wellness. People are returning not only toward "natural" approaches in healing, but also the innate wisdom that is encoded in our spiritual design. A transformation is taking place today within humanity – perhaps greatly symbiotic with the crisis in health care we are facing. And, people, who have a more holistic grasp of health and wellness, will have a huge impact on the emerging medical paradigm. So ... what will become of it all?

A Medicine of the Future

Beauty and the Beast

Medicine in its current form exists primarily to deal with health crisis, disease stabilization or eradiation. As we come to understand some of the issues facing medicine today, we might ask the question, "Do we throw away our modern health care and start again?" Or is simply being coaxed toward a timely transformation?

The pioneering advances in medicine in the last two centuries are truly nothing short of astounding. The understanding of human anatomy, physiology, genetics, infectious diseases, critical care, surgery, diagnostic imaging and many life saving pharmaceuticals are absolutely mind-boggling. Imagine for a moment if someone from 1850 were to visit our hospitals today how absolutely overwhelmed they would be – it would be like landing on a spaceship! Can you even imagine where the next 50 years will take us?

A lot of modern medicine is excellent, and no, we do not throw it all away. There is, however, a smoldering awareness that so much needs to change. We have reviewed some of them - the development of a culture of near complete externalization of healing, a mechanistic view of healing, and commercialization of care. We have subtly touched on the challenge of political, social and corporate forces that are often negligent to health in many ways. And we can grasp that this invokes a soul search for change.

In the midst of this, there is a rising undercurrent of interest in the integration of holistic or alternative healing strategies in medicine. This is a powerful force shaping the future of medicine. One aspect of this emerging influence includes healing tools that are founded on an "energetic" and "consciousness" based understanding of the human being. And, although perhaps not obvious until you learn a little about such things, this provides an emerging awareness that the greatest deficiency in modern health care is its lack of understanding of our spiritual design.

These ideas point to some of the key elements that will play a role in shaping the medicine of tomorrow.

The rise of widespread interest in non-traditional healing strategies and fostering personal wellness is part of a larger paradigm shift. In this process, we are awakening to, or in some cases remembering a time, when other things were possible to promote health. Many of these strategies are based on an innate understanding of the spiritual and even energetic nature of life and mankind. Simultaneously, new understandings and potentials are emerging – based on a growing consciousness of the energetic and even quantum nature of life. As the world of alternative healing, new consciousness healing, and energy based healing merge into medicine – medicine as we know it, and the health of humanity, will be beneficially changed.

Humanity is becoming ready to reorient health care, as well as larger corporate and political systems, toward systems that honor the human spirit. We are poised to develop a health care system that has an innate respect and healing relationship with our bodies, our minds and our spirits. The medicine of the future is a medicine of greater self-awareness and responsibility. We cannot achieve this without an awakening of the spiritual quality of human life.

Concurrently, we will also grow technologically and scientifically toward a quantum and energetic understanding of the nature of life. This too will develop healing potentials that are nothing short of science fiction compared to our modern day.

It is in the hybridization of all of these elements, that we will mold and discover the medicine that is to come.

A Crystal Ball

Who knows for sure what the medicine of the future will look like? For sure it will provide highly advanced technological inventions that will be used for treatment of disease. The scanners of Dr. Spock in *Star Trek* with "vibrational field corrections" might not be a science fantasy in the days our future! There are many inventions that will be based on emerging quantum physics and the technology it will provide, that lie around the corner. Physics will decipher knowledge through the genius of many people, and this knowledge will be turned into useful inventions to promote energetic restitution in the human body.

Medicine will also however, have to return to understanding the holistic nature of a human being with a spiritual core and multifaceted psycho-emotional nature; and, one that can be understood energetically as well as physically, psychologically and biochemically. It will begin to see health as a balanced state of spiritual expression, unique to each person. It will begin to understand the quantum spiritual interface that lies in our DNA. It will also integrate the power of human consciousness to heal.

People will take a much greater role in assuming responsibility for their own health and healing processes. So, who knows for sure what this will look like as it all takes form? We can all speculate, but one thing is for sure - it will be a very fascinating time indeed!

At the Dawn of New Frontier

I believe science will move forward in a way that will correct its current detours and shortcomings. It will develop marvels that are only science fiction to our current science – so we need to be patient.

While we wait, we must each find our right relationship with our health care system and our personal health. If you are healthy – take the time to explore the emerging knowledge and discover ways to stay healthy and be well. Learn about yourself and your potential! As we mature in consciousness, we can each realize that the best way to be well is to stay well. Humanity is more apt to lead medicine in this direction, not follow.

If you are ill today, you should use everything available to heal. This can, and often should, include elements of both traditional and alternative healing approaches. For example, in my understanding, sometimes a surgeon's blade is the only or best remedy available to treat a problem, if a person would like to survive an illness. The healing process can then be supported by many other strategies that are part of an emerging paradigm of healing. You can learn about and integrate these into your process.

I do believe that no matter how progressive in consciousness one is, it would be silly to turn away in simple arrogance from tools and treatments that may be life saving or life enriching when needed. As you process through healing, take the time to get to know your own spirit – for in that liaison will you find the greatest access to healing known to mankind.

Do your very best to be and stay healthy. Learn about your true healing potential. Use whatever you need to get healthy when you need it. Begin to understand that the greatest healing force you will find anywhere is free – and it is found inside of you!

CHAPTER 3

WHAT AND WHY NOW?

JOIN (OR KEEP RIDING) THE WAVE

If we examine our personal fundamental beliefs about life, most of what we each perceive as real or important is based on a short list of influences. Culture, family and social conditioning, genetics, and personal experience are an important few. Yet, as our experience grows, our personal views and beliefs may change. As what we accept or perceive as truth changes - we grow and change.

If you are reading this book you are ultimately part of a great wave of consciousness that is sweeping through humanity at present – giving rise to a renaissance of human thought and reality. It is what draws you to this content and makes us family.

You have probably heard it said that, "Everything happens for a reason." Well there is a spiritual wisdom in this realization, and in essence it is true. The fact that you have magnetized this information to you is actually your own creation, when consciousness is better understood. It may appear to have arrived as a gift from a friend, an innocent discovery, or upon a recommendation. In reality, we invite into our lives the information and experience to help us grow when the time is right, and, when we are ready.

The reason it is occurring now is your own timely manifestation. But the timeliness is even bigger than any one of us. We are collectively manifesting an enormous change in the nature of human life - a monumental consciousness transformation — which includes our view on human health and healing. It is very useful to put the context of what is happening into a bigger framework to realize how incredible it really is.

◉

To understand this process of how we grow collectively in consciousness, I think a brilliant example is found in Rosa Parks. Rosa was a seamstress in Alabama who one day assumed her worth and refused to give up her seat to a white man on a bus. Her action, as a black woman, was defiant of the law, and she was arrested. To a modern person, the thought of a Law of Segregation seems almost unbelievable.

However outrageous as this gesture was at the time, and we speak only of 1955, it sparked an enduring evolution. Time was ripe for change because humanity was evolving, and although there was an intense struggle that ensued, racial segregation was legally abolished. The mental construct of separation of races and its implied inequality began its necessary demise.

If we review the stories of human development, from Christ to Columbus, Mohamed to Galileo, to Rosa Parks - we can see a magnificent theme. Consciousness expands through irritating the edge of common belief. The relative darkness or limitations of our current understanding are crumbled – and a new norm falls into place. This experience often transforms what is rigidly thought to be normal, acceptable or true.

Health and healing principles are one element of society that sits on the edge of such a frontier. Until modern times, we have seen our world as solid, and based on laws of Newtonian physics and Darwinian natural selection. These laws, unlike the unbelievable Law of Segregation today, remain true. They do however become very limited as we start to explore principles of subtle energies and our quantum universe.

This threshold of science will one day soon draw a line in the sand, as we transform what we accept as the nature of life. By this I mean, all of life, and with it, ultimately all of healing and medicine. You cannot peer into the inter-dimensional nature of subatomic physics, or explore the role of consciousness in our creation, and let things stay the same.

So, like the piercing luminous tendrils of a lighthouse in a storm, life has a cunning, but mysteriously wise and loving way of introducing new understanding – albeit often through a journey of uncertainty, conflict or confusion. Consciousness seems to burst, like a "kernel" of light that explodes in a human being, to shine a little brighter and illuminate a new way. The world of health, healing and medicine are approaching such a confluence. The world today is a big popcorn maker with hundreds of thousands of people the world over, like you – breaking open to see and to share new ways. Yet, as we move collectively, we each must walk our own tailored journey. As we take our own steps we cross paths and make discoveries. Life transforms.

However, the evolution of our understanding of human health and healing is only one part of an unprecedented transformation happening right now on the planet. It is a spiritual awakening. It is an awakening of the innate healing power inherent in a human being, when one develops a conscious connection with spirit.

Spirit animates our whole existence, and the energy fields through which it takes form, and thrives. And consciousness of this spiritual foundation of reality is transforming the whole fabric of human existence. Understanding this, the transformation of health and healing of which we speak is part of a much vaster paradigm shift.

The changes that occur through this window will transform the many limitations of what humans perceive as possible, not only in the potential to heal and be well. However, human beings do not have to wait for medicine and science to charge forward. We can begin to understand our own energetic and spiritual nature – and the healing potential this knowledge provides. There is a timing involved in these transformations, and for so many the time for this transformation is now. It is for you this book is ultimately written. Let us ride the wave.

2012 AND BEYOND

THE CURRENT OPPORTUNITY

As we begin to discuss energetic healing and spiritual transformation, we are not talking about small-scale change, we are speaking on a very *large scale*. This represents a huge shift in consciousness – a paradigm shift.

For people aware of this already – it is not a big shock or revelation to imagine something big is happening within humanity and on the planet. For those who have not been consciously exposed to such information, or the paradigm shift of 2012 and its associated earth transformation – you will need a brief introduction. I will keep this section short but pertinent. There are many excellent sources of information on this topic for those who are specifically interested. [5,6,9,36]

If you look around you, it is pretty easy to see that the world "as we know it" is changing very, very fast. There is great insecurity, and no short list of problems - in the economy, world governments, health care, housing markets, and education. Lots of things are falling apart. Meanwhile, doomsday prophecies arise, with evocative fear.

On the opposite side of the equation, technological innovations pop up daily, dictatorships are being slowly and rapidly eroded, information transfer is accelerating and becoming somewhat less controllable, global based communities develop, scientific discoveries and discussions of the explorations into quantum physics are everywhere. Pictures from outer space and other potentially inhabitable planets are popping up on the screen, and an exploratory craft lands on mars. The environmental movement pushes onward to raise consciousness of sustainable resource management. And, there is tremendous growing interest in alternative healing paradigms.

It is a somewhat chaotic, transformative and relatively uncertain time. But when we examine the magnitude of changes, it is clear that "something very big" is going on, and happening fast. The evidence is everywhere. But the question arises - why now?

For many reasons this is a very remarkable time, unprecedented in fact. To better understand the importance of this time we can look at life, and specifically time, in a very expanded way. By expanded, I mean really expanded. We must look to galactic time cycles – to understand.

As The World Turns ...

Let us first look at the concept and importance of "cycles". Everything in our lives, on some level, operates in cycles. The sun rises and sets. We are born children. Childhood ends as we become teenagers, then adults. Summer fades to autumn, to winter, to spring. Rainy seasons come and go. Relationships begin and end. We are born, and we encounter death. Our whole life and world is composed of various interlacing cycles. What is inherent in cycles is that they represent the beginnings and endings of things. Yet, every ending is essential to the birth of new events. This creates a flow.

On a larger scale in the calendar, there are decades, centuries, millennia and scientifically defined time periods. Some cycles are based on planetary movements or changes within our solar system. This would include measures such as a day, a lunar cycle, seasons and so forth. But on an ever-larger scale there are cycles of time based on planetary cycles, solar cycles and galactic cycles.

One such large cycle is based on the understanding of a galactic cycle termed the "precession of the equinoxes".

PRECESSION OF THE EQUINOXES

The precession is based on an understanding of the earth's rotation around an arc, offset from its central axis of spin. This creates a wobble in rotation, and the earth passes one degree every 72 years. In a full circle, there are 360 degrees. Hence, one complete cycle of the earth to move through this entire arc or circle, requires approximately 25,920 years – creating a roughly 26,000 year cycle.

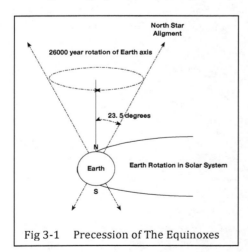

Fig 3-1   Precession of The Equinoxes

If you look at the orbit of the earth during this 26,000-year cycle of time, it will rotate through a changing alignment within the galaxy and its relationship or alignment with various stellar constellations. This defines the zodiac cycle for those familiar with astrology. Each constellation, defined at the horizon on the spring equinox, will shift on each 30-degree passage through the wobble. Hence approximately every 2160 years, a new constellation would appear in this alignment. This is defined as an age. We are entering the Age of Aquarius.

On this time scale, there is a period every 26,000 years when an alignment of the earth with the galactic center occurs. Enter the Mayan Calendar …

Now what has made this time, the year 2012 and particular the date 21 December 2012 so intriguing, is that they mark the midpoint of the galactic alignment – a once in roughly 26,000 year alignment. According to the Mayan calendar it represents the end of a *cycle* of time. This frames a nexus point of many different cycles within cycles within cycles, to a convergence point.

The Mayan Calendar is a complex system of calendars used for time keeping in ancient Mesoamerica. It is comprised of both short and long calendar systems for accurate record keeping of both everyday and large astrologic events. Much has been written about it today, but the reason it moves to the forefront of awareness is the fact that it describes the ending of a large galactic cycle at this very point in time. The precise date of this end point is hotly debated, but conceptually identified as 21 December 2012. Hence this defines the end point of a huge cycle in time.

But cycles, cycle. Endings are beginnings. This not only represented the end of a cycle, and its predominant mode of consciousness, but the birth of a new cycle of consciousness. If you think on a smaller scale we can see the relevance of "consciousness cycles". Think, for example, of the "renaissance period" or other such periods in human history that define great shifts of consciousness transformation. This is just a big one. It is also a very important one – for it is believed to mark the birth of a new cycle of civilization. Coincidence?

In real terms, Mayan elders today say that this time point represents a harbinger of transformation. It will give birth to the cycle of the 5th sun, which will be based not on duality consciousness, but rather on unity consciousness. It is prophesized that in this civilization, people will learn to work together for the greater good and uplifting of humanity. It is foretold that everything based on self-serving systems will begin to disintegrate as humanity gives birth to a new world and new consciousness. Believable? Many say so. It is also believed that in this process people may align or resist – but the energy and consciousness is gradually moving in one direction. Hence people can align with the consciousness of this new world, and the gifts it will bring, or resist. We will also be supported, energetically speaking, by aligning with, or living in this emerging alignment.

It is important to grasp that the passage through this point in time cannot exclusively be defined by a single day. This date can mark and honor the passage – but it really earmarks a transitional *period* of time. When we are talking 26,000 years – a point in time is a larger window than a day. As we pass through this point, the energetic influences upon life shift and begin strongly to inspire or influence life on the planet in new ways. Outdated aspects of civilization will dissipate and fall away.

If you look around you, at the world today, it is perhaps easy to imagine we are seeing the old world fall apart piece by piece, creating a fertile space for something new. One might tangibly realize the truth elucidated in this calendar, and its "prophetic knowledge", by simply watching the evening news!

This phenomenon has received a great deal of negative attention. Self-proclaimed prophets announce the Armageddon, while Hollywood produced movie after movie about 2012 and the end of the world. This is all based a great deal on misunderstanding and hype – which is unfortunate – since it serves as a distractor to what is truly happening, and the truly magnificent opportunity this represents for each member of humanity. Despite the hype and dark twist that was imposed on the 2012 phenomenon - it is most importantly a time of rebirth.

It is interesting to point out that not only the Mayans, but also every major spiritual tradition and countless native prophecies have commented, for one reason or another, that this period in time is significant. "The End Times", "The Apocalypse", "The Time of Revelation", "The Great Shift" – are almost household phrases. All of these prophecies were based on the ideas of visionaries through time that could see forward to a time when potentials could be read as probable futures.

But prophecies, for those who can accept them as significant, are not necessarily supposed to come true. They are better purposed to serve as guidance. They are meant to be a wake up call if you will, to give humanity an opportunity to shift gears to achieve a different outcome. As we will continue to explore, as these prophecies fade behind us, we are on the road to a brighter future.

Harmonic Convergence

In addition to the date of December 21, 2012 - there exists another important event entitled the Harmonic Convergence. It also has a vital contribution to make toward understanding why this time on our planet is so unique and important. It was highlighted by many visionaries as a key date in human history. Why? This date was shown to have a very significant astrological alignment, and meaning for humanity.

In Neil Michelsen's *The American Ephemeris*[37] the configuration is explained. On 24 August 1987 there was an exceptional alignment of planets in the solar system. Eight planets were aligned in an unusual configuration called a grand trine. The Sun, Moon and six out of eight planets formed part of the grand trine. This produced an astrological configuration with these bodies aligned at the apexes of an equilateral triangle when viewed from the Earth.

For those inclined as open-minded to astrology, different astrologers have interpreted the significance of this astrological configuration in different ways. There is however a theme in the interpretation. The composition of astrological influences represents a great shift in the earth's primary consciousness from a warlike competition to peaceful cooperative co-creation.

According to Jose Argüelles, one well-known expert on the Mayan Calendar, the Harmonic Convergence began the final 25-year countdown to the end of the Mayan Long Count in 2012. This would be the so-called end of history and the beginning of a new 5,125-year cycle. Prophetically, in this new cycle, corruptions of the modern world – such as war, materialism, violence, oppression, and so forth – would fade with the birth of a new "Sun" on 21 December 2012.

Other visionaries have recognized that this exceptional time represents a choice point for humanity. This is really well explained in information provided by Lee Carroll in a channeling session from Kryon, entitled "Discovering Your Spirituality" [13] on July 7, 2007:

> *In 1987, an event occurred that was unique in your history. It was called "The Harmonic Convergence," and also later called the "11:11." What was unique was esoteric: The earth had reached a vibratory rate of spiritual neutrality where the future could go either way. It could be pulled to a high level, an interdimensional level, or wallow in the old prophesies of doom and Armageddon. Out of your linear time, and hard for you to understand, all of the Higher-Selves involved in the system of Earth were polled. All the Human Beings that have ever been on the planet, are on the planet, and potentially will be on the planet, were asked this question: "Do you want to go through with the old energy prophecy, the potentials of the old, or do you wish to move into the new energy that the ancients*

told you was coming? [Mayans and 2012] It is an energy that is not in your current prophesy, something that will create peace on Earth.

So according to this information, this important date marked a measuring point, which represents a split in the potential trajectory, that humanity would take in the years ahead. And, it is noted that indeed humanity has chosen the "new energy" potential.

When one looks at prophecy, and there are many available, for example the prophecies of Nostradamus, Edgar Cayce, or the prophecies of the Apocalypse – they all point to 2012 as a time of transformation – complete with elements of destruction and rebirth. These all correlate with the Mayan Calendar awareness that this time represents the end of cycle, or many cycles within cycles as a galactic alignment. Hence, it is clearly a time of change - but what kind of change?

The epic point of 2012 is now passed – and we are at the very threshold of this new time cycle. There was a very real possibility that the earth would have proceeded through a mass cleansing and destruction, as the prophecies would suggest – but it appears we have opted for a transformation instead. So yes, way to go humanity ☺!

Now, this information is esoteric I realize, but prophecy can be understood to represent a warning or sign post of where life is heading if everything stays as it is. Spiritually speaking, prophecy is not meant to determine a future, it may be understood to represent a probability – one likely to occur if things stay the same. It may be best understood as a stimulus to promote a different outcome than the one envisioned – by suggesting the course of life be changed. What is not factored in prophecy is what would happen if humanity veered in a new direction. Imagine if the prophecy were heeded in such a way that the probability of a certain outcome changed.

Well in essence, this is believed by many to represent what has happened for humanity. And, this is what created the possibility for the huge shift of consciousness which began to occur with the passing of the Harmonic Convergence. In essence, as we pass this time marker, we are preparing to enter into a "new world". Humanity, perhaps through a bumpy ride, has stepped up to the plate to grow in new and unprecedented ways. It is an undefined world – for it will be created through humanity and inspired human ingenuity. But over the course of the next few generations, we will experience life very differently than we have known it to be in the past.

So, for those with an open mind, this illustrates why this time represents the birth of a *new kind of humanity*. To get there, humanity will of course have to live through a great deal of growth and change, and this is happening very quickly. Through inspired thinkers and visionaries we are being given knowledge, tools and an unprecedented potential to grow and transform. It is also evident in the rapid growth of consciousness of human beings. And, perhaps this is is even becoming even more evident in the children being born today, who are tangibly different in many ways. It is almost a household term today to hear of the *Indigo Children*.[11]

One significant part of this transformation is an awakening – a spiritual awakening – in humanity. Human beings are becoming increasingly conscious of their inherent spiritual nature and their inherent energetic nature. This awakening is what delivers to us the knowledge that is leading into this "evolution", or perhaps "revolution" of energy consciousness, and its implications on human health and well being.

Hence, as human beings stepping from one paradigm into another, we have both the challenge and the opportunity to live this transformation – "in vivo". In vivo is a scientific term meaning that a process does not occur in a test tube or a lab – it occurs within a living system. Yet, because the opportunity is before us to have this awakening "in vivo" – within our very bodies – we are in the process of living through a mystical and transformative process. In energy terms, this is a bio-spiritual transformation.

One important thing to realize is that transformation does imply a little work. In other words, we have to prepare and participate to some degree, to facilitate the changes occurring.

As human beings we have been living in one frame of consciousness – the old world paradigm of duality and ego based survival. We are moving into a new frame of unity consciousness. So, yes it would seem we do have our work cut out for us. But to achieve this, we are being given information, as well as gifts and tools.

These tools can help us greatly with the energetic aspect of our transformation. We will still, however, benefit greatly by learning about it. We must "rise up" in consciousness. It becomes requisite to live in this "higher vibrational" reality, one which takes some spiritual schooling and some human practice. We will each need to understand a few things to do well in this new environment.

What kind of learning? This includes such things as the reality of our spiritual and energetic nature, the critical status of balance in our energy, our nature as spiritually creative beings, the role of personal responsibility, the value of peace consciousness – and learn to "align" with this higher consciousness state.

It is not necessarily easy to walk from one world into another – we must cross a bridge of consciousness. To understand this new posturing, one might ask, "What would it be like to live a vibrantly peaceful, and unity-conscious world?"

Well, the most direct example we have before us is to look at the example of our great spiritual teachers of all time. All avatar beings on this planet taught love and peace. To jump into a world based on unqualified unconditional love is a bit of a leap and might take a few generations! It need not however, and we can really begin to prepare and experience this in our own lives. For most people, this implies not only a shift in consciousness, but also a practice of a new way of living.

Energetic changes can be facilitated, but we must also transcend and become aware of our own power, responsibility, creative capacity and personal ego. People understand the term "ego" in many different ways. We will take a little time later to better discuss the concept of our ego – and what the spiritual work of transcending or integrating your ego means.

In short, our ego is the "false" component of our nature which is based in separation consciousness from our spiritual nature. It is defiant, self important, and fear based - which creates ego-based disturbances leading to disharmony, chaos, drama, polarity thinking, fear, war and destruction. Every one of us has ego-based tendencies. And, every one of us suffers greatly from them in conscious and subconscious ways! Ego integration is a great part of the work of personal transformation. In fact, it is so important to healing that we shall dedicate a whole chapter (10) to it later in the book.

Through such growth, we learn of the importance and value of developing a peace filled countenance. We develop a willingness to work cooperatively, and with less drama, to build a life and a world that is modeled on every single element you might imagine this new world to be. For most of us, on a personal level, there will be a little remodeling involved – would you agree? But remember, no pointing fingers now – everyone will have some very personal work to do! When you point at another person, there are always three fingers pointing back at you!

◉

So, when we frame this current time in history with all of its potential significance, it helps to explain why there is a mass consciousness awakening of spirituality, and awareness of what I like to term our *bio-spiritual continuum*. It also becomes clearer why we are being given new knowledge of energy healing and new tools of consciousness. These are key components to understanding healing in the paradigm to come.

Admittedly, some of these concepts are very hard to "understand" or "explain" scientifically, because we do not yet have a full understanding of the frame of interdimensional physics to explain them. Yet the outcomes experienced by those who engage in learning and applying them, speak of the potential and value. One such opportunity is outlined later in the discussion of Unity Field Healing.

In opening ourselves to benefit from these tools, and in doing the personal work of transformation, we gain greater self-awareness. We come to recognize our own old and outdated patterns of psychological distortion, and allow grace and light to fill our lives. The side effect of this is "healing" – in all that this concept implies. It is easy to see why this process may be aptly defined as a *bio-spiritual transformation*.

Many people have explained this process as a re-wiring of our energy system. This rewiring occurs through a greater spiritual connection with our spiritual self and our spiritual DNA.

Other terms are used to describe this process such as the "Ascension" process. This re-wiring is also described as a "recalibration of the DNA quantum field" which supports human life. These concepts will take on greater meaning as we continue forward in our discussion. But what is most important to grasp is simple – it is now available to you!

In short, this healing and transformation process may be thought to include a renovation of the energy system or as a re-wiring, coupled with an adaptation to living in a higher vibrational energy field than the one in which we are accustomed. It is through this transformation that we are able to access new levels of healing potential, which were really not accessible until now.

◉

Now, as mystical as this may sound – it is also a process that has been prepared for by the teaching of the enlightened beings of all religions and spiritual cultures – through time. As we move through this window of time, we may understand ourselves to be living through a renovation, and renovations can be messy.

On a personal level, the human energy fields are being renovated to accommodate and support life in a rising vibrational reality. It is a reality that is increasingly supportive of the attributes of a spiritually awakened consciousness. Yet, to rise in spiritual awareness and human potential in such an accelerated way can be confusing. It can also be very alarming if it is not understood – so help is on the way!

Remember that all life is energy. Many are understandably without pacification when their body starts to vibrate, the eyes see lights around objects, polar caps melt, and mother nature is gone wild - or life, as it was, just seems to lose its luster with no "real" or truly comprehensible reason why. A little supportive information, and a few facilitative processes, can go a long way to assist in our integration.

Fortunately, there is a great deal of information, as well as many energy-based processes available today. They are being given to assist and facilitate in this transformation. Such processes are "tools" to assist what is actually a very natural process – albeit quite an unusual one. One does not "need" to participate in such processes. That is a choice. One simply needs to have a strong and authentic personal intent to grow, open, heal and transform – to open to their spirit.

As one grows and adapts to the new energy environment, the energy becomes more and more self-regulating and you may not benefit from processes. Meanwhile, however, like any good tool they will likely be very helpful for those who do engage. This has certainly been my experience. It is a little like understanding the difference between using a shovel or a backhoe to dig the foundation for a house!

Personal transformation aside, the whole world is going through a similar re-wiring! It too is shaking, shifting, blowing, raining, melting and freezing in a host of peculiar ways! Where is it heading?

Imagine a planet of greater and greater harmony and peace. Imagine a society where children are understood to be divine unique creations of the one living spirit that infuses breath into all living things. Imagine a land where people live with compassion and reverence toward all of life. A daydream you may suggest – well yes, indeed it is.

Yet, all of creation is a dream – and we are capable of much greater possibilities than we have, at least in a long time, dared to dream. The next few generations of humanity will grow into this reality. And in one form or another, as well as through the eyes of your children, you will come to see it pass.

⊙

Now, I realize that some of this information may represent an expectedly "hard-sell" to the skeptical mind. Regardless, it is occurring right under our noses. Or better yet, as we will explore, it is occurring through our minds and hearts.

For those of you who have spontaneously or serendipitously come to know it is occurring through your own very personal experience – it is not so wacky or "woo-woo" to have this discussion. For those who are a little less convinced, just be open. If you are skeptical, no problem. There is a little "Thomas" in everyone. Discernment is valuable! Just remember, intention is prerequisite to cross this consciousness "abyss". You decide your own role. Be brave and be open! Yet, regardless of what you believe personally, the message is still one of peace.

The opportunity of this time is therefore laid before us. It is up to each of us how we will relate to it. Grace is upon us and we can really open our heart and mind to make this transition very grace filled if we choose to do so. Perhaps an apocalypse of the fear-based ego gives birth to a rise of the human spirit. Could it not be as simple, and as profound, as that!

Lucky 13

Important Things To Recognize About Here and Now

As a growing interest in natural and alternative healing has emerged, and knowledge related to energy based therapies and the human energy system has become widespread – it is easier to recognize that they form part of a new emerging paradigm, one which includes a transformation in our understanding of health and healing consciousness.

This shift in consciousness is however nebulous. As reviewed, it is not simply an appreciation of natural healing strategies, but a shift into a world of spiritual empowerment and awareness of the bio-spiritual spectrum that comprises human life. This is a quantum shift from the old worldview of personal disempowerment in healing, a view void of an authentic spiritual based understanding.

In this new healing paradigm, several core ideas have emerged in mass consciousness that are transforming the way we as human beings see our selves. Although the list is far from exhaustive, it is a short list of at least 13 important ideas that have infiltrated mass consciousness, particularly alive for those aligned with this consciousness or paradigm shift. They are as follows:

1. GROWING CONSCIOUSNESS OF THE HUMAN BEING AS A HOLISTIC BEING.

In simple terms – every single one of us is a complex being. We are not only a physical body. We also are filled with emotions and thoughts, and an inner spiritual existence. All of these levels of experience have influence on each other, as well as the ultimate out-picturing of healthy or disease states. Each one of these components can contribute to, or take away from, the health of the whole being.

Ultimately, the path to health or healing requires a multifaceted self-integration. The body, the emotions and the mind must all be healthy and work in harmony. The view of the human being as a *whole being* is one of the greatest principles to popularize during this revolution of consciousness.

With the emergence of new wisdom that understands how to help people gain an alignment among these faculties – new venues of healing open.

2. GROWING APPRECIATION AND RESPECT FOR THE BODY'S NATURAL OR INNATE CAPACITY TO HEAL BY SUPPORTING BALANCE.

Healing is being recognized as a process that is innate, natural and can be supported.

This idea at first seems naïve. However, it is very far away from the attitude of "war" on diseases. Disease can be viewed in some cases to occur because of a disturbance in the energy of the body or its environment, which allows it to arise. For example, in stressful environments people are more subject to certain disease conditions; hence, healing requires the dissolution of unwarranted stress to be supported. Good nutrition and less toxic products promote a healthier body. Chronic unhealthy emotions suppress immunity, and so forth.

Energetically speaking, disease states that arise can be viewed as a manifestation of blockage, imbalance or distortion that first occurs in the human energy system.

It is possible to create healthier "environments" – physically, emotionally, mentally and environmentally – that support health. Health and healing are natural processes – and can be nurtured to avoid illness.

3. *AN UNDERSTANDING OF THE ROLE OF CONSCIOUSNESS IN CREATING, DEFINING AND HEALING OUR LIVES.*

Unconscious, pre-scripted patterns of thinking and feeling have a huge impact on our lives. Our repetitive thoughts, beliefs and emotional states create or influence our reality and our health, in profound ways.

This implies that the way you think, and the way you relate to your emotional world, will influence your life and your health. There are health promoting patterns, and health destroying patterns.

Consciousness is a great ally here for it can help us see, and transform things of which we are aware. Consciousness can be "applied" to help create healthier states of being. The unconscious patterns of belief and emotion can be made conscious or directly re-patterned. We can change, adapt and restructure our thoughts, emotions and overall energy – to achieve greater wellbeing.

Both within and outside of traditional medicine and psychology, pioneers in the world of self-help psychology, psycho-neuroimmunology, meditation, mindfulness awareness practices, and energy psychology – have contributed greatly to an understanding of the human beings ability to grow, change and heal through consciousness. [3,7,8,15,16,19,22,25,26,28,31,32,35,39,40,42,44,56]

The work and application of these practices can lead an individual to a greater self-awareness - an important element on any journey to wellness. If we can see how we are thinking and feeling, or how deeply embedded patterns maybe influencing the reality we know as our lives – we can ultimately explore, through recognition or release, a potential to grow or to change.

These evolutionary approaches are taking an older model of psychology that was based on predictability and limited malleability of human behavior, and opening it to the potential for truly transformative change.

4. AN AWARENESS OF SELF WORTH AND PERSONAL RESPONSIBILITY.

Human beings are stepping out of cultural programs that ascribe worth based on attributes of the old energy paradigm. Worth is a spiritual attribute – for we are inherently beings of worth as spiritual entities. Worth cannot be increased or decreased by earthly attributes, but it must be acknowledged and integrated as an inherent state of spiritual reality.

As beings of worth, we are responsible co-creators of life on the planet. This is not in the classic blame focused orientation of responsibility, with which we are all too familiar: "She is in charge, so she is at fault.", "He is evil, so he is at fault.", or, "They are promoting bad health habits, so they are at fault". This is a greater awareness that we are each an evolving entity that must assume creative personal responsibility, through personal choice - not only in our health, but in all ways we function in our life.

Responsibility consciousness is often contrasted with its opposing attitude - victim consciousness. The foundational attitude, by which you live your life, even if it is subconscious, defines your world. Why is this so important? Well, if I live my life in a victimized state of consciousness, I will live like things happen *to* me. I am separated from the creative role I play in making my life what it is – and the power I hold to transform it. This will lead to fear, and a defeatist way of viewing life. I will become angry, frustrated, hopeless, discouraged, depressed and disappointed – time after time after time – as life models this consciousness, in terms of real experience, without any sense of judgment.

As a responsible self-governing person, one becomes a co-creative partner with one's spirit and one's place in the world. One realizes our conscious and subconscious patterned thoughts, emotions and intentions are creative forces. Yet, by examining our experiences we can better understand ourselves, and grow or transform in reflective ways.

When one begins to take a "responsibility" attitude in their life, they begin to live like things that happen in their lives have meaning. One sees their life as a creation of their own conscious and subconscious co-creative design – even in ways it is perceivably "negative". Events and experiences are seen as repercussions of one's own process, or as lessons and guiding experiences that provide feedback and navigation.

You will hear people express statements such as: "Everything happens for a reason." or "You create your own reality." This implies an understanding that the energy posture we hold, the thoughts and feelings we harbor, the subconscious influences we carry – all have a creational influence upon the life we each manifest.

Our task is to allow our experiences to guide us, reveal to us, and teach us. Through them, we can "mine out" attributes that are hurtful, to bring healing attention. We can empower attitudes that promote greater and greater wellbeing. We can masterfully grasp the mystery in the statement that – we "choose" our reality.

It is true, that we consciously or subconsciously create our life experiences – but this can be difficult to understand and can lead to confusion, mystery and guilt. In ways we do not understand things that occur in our lives - we are still responsible to understand that the manifestation is important to us, and it is how we choose to relate to it that become important.

If we approach life with meaning, we can learn from whatever experiences "befall" us. We can witness the choices we make, the subconscious patterns we hold in our energy that lead to poor choices and various experiential manifestations, and the messages inherent in this feedback. We can let it help us remodel our lives. We can strengthen spiritual attributes such as patience, compassion and forgiveness. We can awaken to our power to transform hurt or negativity into wisdom and healing. We can access a deeper level of healing that exists, and is available to us.

Now, as people learn to move into an empowered state of responsibility consciousness, from a victim state of consciousness, there are often a few bumps on the road.

Most people would not choose to develop a terrible disease such as a painful malignancy or chronic disease condition or get run over by a car. As people first learn to accept responsibility as an attitude of living, they can become a little ego callused about it and say things like – "she created that" or "he created that" or even "I created that" – with a punitive, heartless or judgmental attitude. The compassion and heart based relationship to life that is critical to healing is so absent in these statements. This then, of course, also becomes a lesson.

If a person has created or is enduring a painful experience – you can rest assured that it may be a subconscious creation, and there may be many creational forces at play that are missing or too complex to understand. Compassion, not judgment, is the appropriate response – both towards our selves and towards others.

Responsibility simply implies that we each play a very active co-creative role in manifesting our life, as we know it. We directly and indirectly create experiences, and we are responsible for the way we relate to every experience that enters into our sphere of experience. A responsible attitude empowers people to step out of the drama and frustration that a victim consciousness would support.

There is a great freedom that emerges as a person learns to live with an attitude of personal responsibility. Responsibility implies choice – and we are always free to choose – which is a secret key in healing. You discover the freedom that greater responsibility brings, ultimately, freedom from fear-based ego limitations. This is true freedom or "spiritual freedom" – a concept beyond the ego-based notion of freedom we so often entertain.

For people who need support in stepping out of "victim consciousness" or for anyone who truly wants to better appreciate the concept of personal responsibility, one beautiful book written on this topic is by author Shakti Gawain entitled, *Living in the Light*. It is a great and insightful read. [25]

The greatest alignment that living with an attitude of creative responsibility brings - is the power to align with our spirit – and the peace and healing it brings through greater self-realization.

5. THE CONCEPT OF AN "ENERGETIC BASIS" OF LIFE.

Since Einstein revealed though his genius that all of life is composed of energy, in various states of light in condensation to mass, our world has never been the same: $E = mc^2$. Coupling this with an appreciation of the atomic nature of all living particles as charged particles with both solid (mass) and wave (energy) properties, and more recently the advent of the subatomic world of quantum physics – we can now easily conceptualize that things which appear extraordinarily solid, are really energy configurations.

Understanding the "energy basis of life" has arrived both through physicists and mystics. Modern physicists speak of quantum fields of probability and multidimensional layers of reality within an atom. These fields, well beyond the scope of my detailed understanding, are explained to behave in very peculiar way as we cross the threshold into the subatomic world. The physics and structure of the visible world is influenced by the mystical physics of the quantum world; in a way science itself does not yet fully understand. A whole new paradigm of multidimensional reality with quantum laws or forces that are subject to human consciousness arises.

Mystics have long spoken of an interdimensional world of energy and consciousness, etheric energy fields, and the power of consciousness to transform matter. Science it appears is also primed to meet the maker – or at least have a fun date with a guru!

Why is this so important? This has opened a doorway to appreciate the energetic nature of a very solid looking human being. It becomes more understandable that "energy" and "vibration" can have an energetic impact on our physical body, and, as we will explore – the many energy bodies – that go into making up a human being. These bodies, such as the emotional and mental body, are also vicariously energetic in nature.

The human body, our emotional quality, and our thoughts – all have a correlative energy reality. Your cells are energy, your thoughts are energy, and your emotions are energy. Energy organizes, moves and transforms. It is hard to change a "rock" but not so hard to change a "wave". This a tiny concept, with a massive influence on the restrictive limits of human consciousness, created by a "solid" world.

6. A RENEWED INTEREST IN ANCIENT AND EASTERN HEALING STRATEGIES.

This ranges from herbal remedies, to acupuncture, Ayurvedic healing, Therapeutic Touch, crystal healing, homeopathy, flower essence therapy, meditation and yoga - just to name a few of the hundreds!

The activity and benefit of these therapies are based in part or in whole upon a "vibrational" or "energetic" influence vs. a traditional physical or chemical influence on the human being. In our strict scientific models of observable phenomenon – it is perhaps hard to appreciate the unseen forces that may have a positive or negative influence on life. But the level of energy on which these processes operate, is often defined as "subtle" – because they are not "seen". However, it is not really so subtle. While invisible to most people, like electricity is invisible - it is real. And, powerful!

To develop a clear analogy of how invisible energy forms exist – we simply need to examine the limitations of the normal sensory range of our human senses.

When we look at our sense of vision or hearing, we can understand that these senses operate within a "defined range". For example we can hear in the auditory spectrum of 50Hz to 20000Hz. We can see energies on the light spectrum from 390 to 750 nm.

When we encounter a sound or a light energy outside of these ranges we cannot hear them or see them, as the case may be. They exist and are real – but they are outside of our range of perception. If you blow a dog whistle - a dog, capable of hearing in a higher frequency range, can hear it. Yet, we cannot. When you have an x-ray – you do not see the x-rays – but they pass right through your body and are recorded on sensory equipment that can convert the energy outcome into a visual image in the visible light range. What is important to understand is not the physics of these events - but the simple realization that there are many "energies" beyond our normal sensory capacity.

When we couple an understanding of the energetic nature of all reality, with explanations inherent in ancient healing practices – we can begin to open our mind to the influence of unseen energy on the human being. We can also uncover its potential to introduce healing in new or revitalized ways.

Systems of healing have emerged or re-emerged in light of this new physics. Ancient tools of healing are explained with a greater adaptation for the western or modern mind. Talk of chakras, and meridians, and elemental energies has become a little more meaningful. They are structural and functional energies, which do not exist within our normal sensory spectrum for most people. But, they are part of the human energy system.

As people explore energy based healing, many people do begin to have personal extrasensory and energetic experiences. Any question about the energy nature of human life dissipates to someone who has had this opportunity.

However, to experience, or benefit from energy healing, or the jewels of healing systems old and new, one does not need to have the capacity to "see" or "read" energy. Frankly most people don't or won't – but it is not important. You can heal with vibrational healing strategies even if you don't have an "extrasensory" clue!

7. APPRECIATION OF INTUITION.

As human beings we trust mostly what is seen and proven, what we know from our own experience, and what we are advised by those we trust. Logic and analysis are highly valued; and this, or course, is not "wrong". In fact, even skepticism is a healthy part of discernment. But rational thinking is limited to what one is aware of, or knows as fact. But "fact" is often just a perception, and often biased by experience.

Our intuition is a seemingly irrational function. Intuition implies the ability to "pick up on" or "know" things that are beyond rational process. For example, have you ever known who was on the phone before you answer? Have you known someone close to you was in trouble? Or, perhaps had passed on, before you knew factually it was so? Do you ever have gut feelings that prove to be accurate? Do you ever know the right course of action to take even though it not "logical"? These are examples of intuitive awareness in action.

Now it is one thing to blindly accept intuition as an interesting phenomenon. It is quite another to ponder its bigger implications, and even begin to live your life based fully on its guidance! How exactly do you learn to acknowledge or trust such things without falling into the trap of making misguided choices?

Intuition as a phenomenon introduces a really intriguing concept. If one has access to a non-rational process of knowing, it really means somehow that one is in communication with a "field of intelligent awareness". This is a field of awareness that lets us know things.

When we begin to explore quantum concepts, and the energy and consciousness foundation of life, we can easily appreciate that human beings really do have an extrasensory mechanism of knowing. This demonstrates a living example of the quantum concept of a unified field. We are connected to everything – particularly those things with which we are "entangled". We will explore a little in the Chapter 6.

Intuition becomes increasingly important as people explore energy healing practices. This is because a great deal of information and personal guidance arrives "intuitively". This can seem so foolish to a highly logical person. But to an awakening human being, it becomes an invaluable and essential tool.

There is now a great deal of information written about learning to recognize, to trust, and to honor our intuitive nature. It takes some practice and experience to get confortable with intuitive ability. Yet learning to recognize and be supported by authentic self-guided intuition is one of the most enriching experiences a person can encounter! Learn to trust you intuition to guide you toward what will work best to support you.

8. *There is an awareness of a wise internal consciousness that is inherent in our being.*

We can refer to this element of conscious as our soul, spirit, Higher Self, or, whatever we find comfortable. People can spend a lot of energy trying to define and conceptualize these elements as unique – but at this level of awareness I tend to use the terms somewhat interchangeably.

This higher element of consciousness can be viewed as "you" – but at a level that is aware of everything about you. It is not you limited by your human understanding, but a you that is vaster, wiser, more completely knowing that your human self. It is really you, but it is also a teacher and a healer that can bring you closer to personal wellness.

And it guides you ... drum roll please ... often intuitively.

The important point here is that you are a conscious spiritual being with an innate awareness of yourself and your human life. Your life has spiritual challenge, meaning and potential! It is through strengthening this connection we evolve, grow and heal from a spiritual point of view. In fostering and strengthening this relational experience – healing in somewhat mysterious or even magical forms appear.

The reason this is so valuable is that by opening up to this element of our whole being – we tap into a personal guidance system that does not rely merely on logic, or external information, to instruct or guide us. If we open communication with this part of ourselves, we are opening to the part of us that understands our personal reality, our lessons, our "predicaments", and our path. It also has the blueprint of our own healing potential, specifically laid out for us. You could not find a better friend!

9. SYNCHRONICITY

Coupled with an increased respect and trust in our intuitive nature, is an awareness of synchronicity. What exactly is synchronicity?

Synchronicity may be thought of as non-rational, non-probable occurrences that align or converge precisely in an unplanned way. They are often magical and sometimes critically important events in our lives, which guide us or support us in some way.

An example of a synchronicity may be walking into a store and finding a book that has important answers for you in your life. It may be attending a wedding and meeting a person who has information for you, a job offer, or is about to become your spouse!

Synchronicity couples with intuition because we have to follow our intuition to be led to our synchronicities.

Synchronicity can be a force of spiritual guidance that transcends logic, planning, or what we could potentially know in a limited 3D frame of mind. It can guide us in ways we didn't "imagine". It can open opportunities that we didn't even know existed – because it works by nature with a vaster field of intelligence that we traditionally use.

10. HONORING CREATIVITY.

Creativity is a vast topic. Our inherent nature is to be creative in infinite ways. Yet, creativity shows up in healing conversations in three distinct ways:

One is the "co-creative" role or "intentional" role we play in creating the manifest experiences of our "life".

Two is the ability to use creative elements to heal.

Three is revelation of knowledge and understanding through artistic creativity, particular visionary artistic skill.

Life, by nature, is creative. All elements of natural life and human life are creative by design. As human beings, unlike other elements of the natural world, we can impose our consciousness in a creative way.

For example, a seed may be destined to produce a yellow rose. A human being could genetically modify the seed and it might produce a red rose. Humans can impose or apply their consciousness in creative ways to manifest new experience. This is how humanity has created magnificent things, really all things, over time.

Yet, we do not create in "isolation". We can take elements that exist, and carve or paint or conceptualize them into new and different creation. We are always working a medium that is provided by natural life. Life provides us with the canvas and material through nature to create. However, we rely on conceptual inspiration and ideally on spiritual impulses to utilize the medium of nature to produce our creations. In a living spectrum, the canvas, in this sense, is our life.

Agreeably, not all of human creations are inspired by lofty spiritual ideas. Some creations come from very diseased or "ego based" patterns of thought and emotion. Others ideas are *truly* inspired – and they add something new to uplift life and people in our world.

This concept helps us understand our role as "co-creators" as well as the application of our creative abilities in healing. We recognize that we use our abilities in endless ways to create the experience of life, and we can become much more conscious of what we are creating by our thoughts, feelings, actions and inspirations. We also start to realize that prior to this "awakening" it is our subconscious patterns of thought, feelings and memories, which are often on autopilot, that are creating cyclic patterns of experience over and over and over again. With more awareness, we can intervene creatively to change them.

When you begin to realize you are a creative entity - and all of your life is essentially a work of art - life can become really interesting. Importantly, you become aware of your ability to create, manifest, change, grow and in any way warranted – heal.

Creativity can also be instrumental in expanding the frontiers of consciousness. For example, the influx of brilliant works of art that have been created recently to demonstrate abstract concepts in energy and healing is phenomenal. One brilliant example of this is seen in the work of visionary artist Alex Gray. Alex's work, and work of other exceptional visionary artists, has opened the human mind to envision the human energy system in tangible ways. It reveals it to those who cannot see it, in a comprehensible way.[30]

Those who have awakened to unusual or expanded sensory skills or experiences – coupled with artistic expression – can out-picture representative images of energy systems that are part of the human being.

They can use skill to explain what is seen, intuitively known or understood. Once a human being can visualize our energetic structure, it opens a door of conceptual possibility. A picture is worth a million words in this regard.

Through the beauty of such work, one can more readily imagine how energy bodies appear. We can visualize a bridge between the spiritual and physical elements of our being.

Exposure to these visual models can also help us see what a healthy free flowing energy system looks like. One can imagine blocked energies or chakras, and easily imagine how these blocked energy fields can distort or destroy health in the human body. One can imagine why kinks, distortions and blockages might limit the flow of energies in ways that can diminish energy flow to certain organs and systems. One can also visualize how they may be restored.

We can also begin to visualize how the psycho-spiritual forces, which can promote or restrict a free flowing human energy system, can vicariously influence health states. We can understand how an "open heart" is healing, or "closing down to our personal power or expression" may be destructive. We can more easily appreciate how psychodynamic forces influence our energy system, hence our health and many aspect of our lives.

Through conscious creativity, healing creativity and inspired creativity - we come to understand and manifest the great work of art that is our life – based on great spiritual precepts of living. Importantly, we can also envision new ways of treating diseases – not by "treating diseases" – but by facilitating the energetic restructuring of the human energy field through inspired creative ways.

11. DISINTEGRATION OF A STRICTLY MECHANISTIC REALITY – OR AS PEOPLE LIKE TO SAY "NEWTONIAN".

In this world we tend to see everything as simple cause and effect, reproducible and mechanistic. When we start to explore the power of consciousness on matter, or emotions on our physical and psychological health, or the energetic nature of life – traditional mechanistic thinking exposes its great limitations.

Science had no way to more fully explain esoteric and spiritual claims regarding health, until modern times. Now, as we step into a quantum world where we exist as energy in a field of multiple dimensions and infinite potentials made uniquely real by the focus of consciousness, this will begin to change. We realize that many beliefs will disintegrate, and why consciousness has such a powerful influence over reality, our health and our lives.

A brave new world is set to rise, to greet our first steps. Many years ago, humanity was afraid that Christopher Columbus would sail off the edge of a world that was flat! Today, we begin to realize that the world is not just "round"- it is "multidimensional"! Here we go again ☺ !

12. AN EXPANSION OF SPIRITUAL FREEDOM.

Inside or outside of a religious framework, people are awakening to an acceptance of the spiritual nature of life, as well as a life force energy that is mystically sourced and flows upon and within each one of us. We return to a life giving, omni-intelligent, love based creation from which we have lived in separation, and journey to return as we each seek God in our own self-appropriate way.

The outmoded aspects within religions are breaking down, so people within religious systems can move closer to an internal appreciation of God - however they seek this precious relationship. If people gain a greater experience of peace and love within a religion, it is holy! And, other people who are not religious seek God through a freer spiritualism where a relationship with God is personal, and accessed in ways that are less institutional, because it suits them. However we consciously choose to seek spiritual development, God is love, and is birthed in our heart – from within.

There are many ways to approach God both inside and outside of traditional religions. Religious "control" is waning, and people, including those who remain religiously oriented, are finding an authentic spirituality that is inclusive, love-based and openhearted to the healing potential that requires no human intermediary. It is simply appreciated that spiritual growth may take place in the context of a traditional religion, or not. People still like to gather in groups of like-minded individuals, for community and support. Many religious institutions will survive – but they will have to transform to the new ways.

Human beings today are more intelligent and self-aware. They can revel in the message of Christ, or the message of Buddha, or the message of

Mohamed, or any great or common spiritual teacher. They can peel away the distorted elements of the religions that have emerged through the years by less noble forces of consciousness – those that have built barriers around their sacred teachings – and love with greater abandon.

With this gentle unshackling, people have become much more open to question authority, question meaning and therefore, to learn. Every story in this regard is personal. For example, I have felt resonance with the spiritual teachings in every religion. Yet I failed to understand the exclusiveness, judgment, doomed to hell and misery, better afterlife, be "guilty very guilty" theories. I also could not relate to an angry, punitive God – asking for an impossible perfection – and waiting for me to commit the next sin to have fun penalizing me! I didn't see God asking me to wipe out anyone who I perceive as evil! I did not understand why I could not personally have a relationship with God, needing an intermediary - I felt "close to God" personally. I could also not relate to a feminine-free spirituality - for heavens sake, God is Love – and who shows love better than a mother! So religions fortunately are slowly changing.

As a child, life did not make sense to me, and I am sure for many of you, within the confines of what I was taught. I remember being aware that some people seem to "get everything" - from intelligence, to talent, to looks, to money – and others "get nothing" at all. Some encounter great fortune in all it's meaning, while others have dumb luck. Some use their great gifts, and others squander them. It seems unfair that God would have the same expectations of everyone – or that everyone is created equal! How could that be?

I was not taught about karma or reincarnation – but I knew life made absolutely no sense without bigger spiritual view. Like many, this started a search beyond the confines of a familiar religion. This too is part of the changing paradigm.

Why is this important? If one is able to expand their thinking to include peculiar concepts such as past or parallel lives, karmic influence on ones current life, spiritually defined energy precepts, and grace – then living principles, and therapies to experience healing, can emerge and flourish to help us.

Generational healing in families of patterned abuse and neglect – and strategies to heal them, have emerged. Irrational fears and phobia, which control people's lives, can be healed. Patterned fear based ego reactions that make no sense in context of one's current life, and often ascribed to being "our personality" – can melt away, or be overcome. New, very authentic strategies of healing have come through the open doors and windows in the minds of an awakening humanity.

Today many people can relate to a personal connection with the divine. And people are aware it can bring a restorative healing potential into their lives. I know it is not for everyone – but it is open to everyone. I have often wondered if the "chosen people" are simply those who are inspired "to choose" to awaken; awaken, to the spiritual love and power that resides within them.

13. UNITY. THERE IS A GROWING AWARENESS OF THE SACRED, AND THE DEEP INTERCONNECTEDNESS OF ALL LIVING THINGS.

We realize that as advanced as we see ourselves to be in many ways, we are also, in so many ways, simply children. As the power of consciousness and the energetic nature of life slowly reveal itself to us – we are refreshingly mystified by life. We see that all things including humanity are interrelated and interdependent. We are obliged to care for everything and everyone including nature and the environment – because it is interconnected. It is not because we are afraid or ashamed – but because it is right.

Even science returns us to the mystery. With growing appreciation of quantum reality, the energetic nature of life, and the consciousness interface with life – our view of life and what it means to be a human being is changing. Ultimately – I believe we will experience the wisdom of integrating a spiritual consciousness into all facets of life. The transformative power of that simple thought is infinite.

◉

I believe we are on the threshold of huge revelations in every field of science and ultimately every system of life. The time is right. We are ripe. Again, it is spoken that science represents truth unrevealed, and hence science is also a spiritual journey. These revelations will bring the world and humanity forward into a "new world" – familiar to but unlike anything we have experienced in recorded time. Yet, simultaneously we will be the ones to create it through our own inspired creativity – as we always have. The buried treasures in the minds and hearts of thousands of awakening humans have a feast in store – because ultimately – we are all one.

CHAPTER 4

ONE MAN'S STORY

... AT LEAST THE CATALYTIC BITS

It would be hard to proceed with the rest of this book without taking a little time to tell you a few things about "my story". Reluctant initially to do this, I decided to include the section for I am aware that we are often supported and inspired in understanding the common nature of our experiences.

I have decided to share this information for two reasons. First, I think you will better understand how and why this book came into being. Second, you will understand how spirit takes each of us under its wing on our journey. It reveals slowly - as we are ready – what we each need to know in order to grow along our personal path.

The knowledge and perspective shared here has birthed itself simply by an innate process of learning and guidance. This is a principle of life and not limited to one person. I share it, to support you in your journey for it is equally true for you. It is inherent in each and every one of us - if we have the eyes to see and ears to hear the whispers of our spirit.

I am sometimes asked how I developed this interest in healing and energy medicine. Well, it really happened quite organically. I did not live a near death experience or tragic event that pushed me in this direction. No angels from the sky or voices in my head were there to guide me. It was an innate curiosity that lived in me – and was fuelled by a series of synchronous events that kept nudging me along the way.

A few of these events are somewhat mystical in character. I share them not to enlarge their value, or my value, in any way – but again to inspire you with the magic of spiritual revelation.

Briefly on a Healing Career

To frame my life, I am a specialist physician and have now practiced medicine and energy medicine for over 20 years. Early in my career, I worked as an emergency physician and general practitioner, then a GP psychotherapist, and finally an abdominal and emergency radiologist, which remains my involvement in medicine to this day.

During my early years of medical practice, I became very interested in the psychological and emotional aspects of health and wellness, and spent a large component of time doing counseling work with patients. After five years of mixed clinical and counseling work this became my entire practice for many years.

In the years I counseled, most of my patients were experiencing a variety of life and health challenges such as anxiety disorders, stress related illnesses, life passages such as widowhood, chronic illness, divorce, family death, and depression.

During this time I became keenly interested in personal development – both my own and also helping others. I believed that so much of what we see as fixed or pathologic states could serve as stepping-stones to help us grow. I also believed too many people were medicated for experiences in their lives that could provide a catalyst for personal growth and change. If underlying conditions could be supported in a process to help an individual access a deeper and more potent level of self-awareness, I knew that healing would, and did occur.

It was during this time that I spent a lot of time exploring spiritual systems of belief and non-traditional healing practices. I had the privilege to work with hundreds of people, who used the time we shared together to help discover meaning in their life's events, and grow in their own personal ways. I, too, grew tremendously in this endeavor. It was a very rich professional time for me.

During this period, I developed a keen interest in understanding the spiritual nature of life. This was deeply catalyzed by a few personal experiences, which I will share later in the chapter. This expanded into an exploration of the wisdom teachings within many of the world's spiritual traditions. I also grew a very deep appreciation of the spiritual context of life as critical in understanding true health and true healing.

Privately, for friends and closer acquaintances, and with clients outside of this traditional practice – I began healing work with energy-based practices, and had many phenomenal experiences as I took my own inaugural steps in this domain.

I devoured all the knowledge I could find about both spiritual and esoteric concepts in healing for many years. I was particularly fascinated by energy-based healing work and this became a passion for me to understand. During this time of learning, I applied so much of what I learned into helping others in their personal stories of healing. I had the opportunity to see how magical healing can be, and how profound it is when healing leads a person to the door of spiritual growth.

I did find, as the years passed, that the setting was a little stifling or limiting for me. Medicine, particularly public funded medicine, coupled with strict professional regulations guide clearly what a physician is permitted and not permitted to do. I could counsel and make many suggestions to patients about options that exist for healing and growth – and let patients know about alternative options for self-development – and this worked out quite well.

In 2003 I felt strongly it was time to make a personal transition. I returned again to study in traditional medical training – this time to do a 4-year residency in radiology. At present, I continue to work in this capacity as a professor and specialist practitioner in a large teaching hospital.

In my view, traditional medicine is very much needed in our current world. As we have explored, it has its own limitations both in knowledge and process – but will grow and will integrate alternative healing techniques based on vibrational or energetic healing in near future. So, at first glance this is a slightly peculiar background to be writing about spiritual healing – but as you can see this is only one side of the story.

I can tell you I did not grow up thinking I would become a spiritually oriented writer nor energetic healer. Yes, man plans, God laughs. So here are the details of a few poignant highlights, some mystical and some mundane, and how they shaped my life.

DR JOHN G RYAN MD

Early Days

The earliest memory I have of "career planning" was at the tender age of 5 years old. My father worked as a marine engineer and was responsible for running the engine room of a large freight and passenger vessels that sailed between Nova Scotia and Newfoundland in Canada. I was with him for a ferry crossing, which was a 24-hour round trip journey. My memories of such days are some of the most wonderful in my childhood.

During such escapades one of my favorite adventures was to go up to the bridge of the boat and spend time with the captain and officers. One day, as I was holding the wheel of the massive vessel and imagining I was steering the boat, the captain asked me "So what are you going to do when you grow up?" I responded without thinking, "A doctor sir". His reply I recall, "that is ambitious young fella, and I have no doubt you will."

The odd thing was that I had never even thought about what I would do when I grew up. The answer popped out in childlike innocence. Yet, it was sort of a revelation – from a deeper part of my consciousness. From that day forward, and with the strength of the captains assurance, I never waivered or lost faith in the idea. It was never a question for me to entertain again, I simply knew.

The route to medical school was pretty direct. I went through schooling and undergraduate work and into medical school, finishing by the age of 24.

Side Swiped by a Cosmic Attunement

Getting into medical school was a very rewarding experience. I was very grateful for the opportunity and was thrilled to begin to learn the art and science of medicine. Despite the rigors of the program, this gratefulness stayed with me for the first few years of study. Yet oddly, as the days passed during my training, a peculiar dissatisfaction began to arise. By my third year of studies, I felt a growing dismay - which was both perplexing and frankly concerning.

I became keenly aware that as much as I felt a great privilege to be afforded a medical education, I felt like something very important was missing. It was a dissatisfaction that I did not understand for several years to come. I chalked it up to the stress of training, the busy life, and the exams – and continued on forward. Yet it felt deeper than that – I just wasn't sure what it meant. And, I certainly was not aware that our spirit prompts us onward at times by brewing up a dissatisfaction to nudge us onward in our lives.

You see – the year was 1987. I had no idea I was under the influence of a cosmic adjustment! If the idea of the harmonic convergence were mentioned, I would have assumed it to be the name of an acapella singing group, not a paradigm shift.

In retrospect, I can see that this brewing uncertainty developed rather insidiously – but it was also propagated by one pivotal event that came to be of monumental importance in my life. This occurred one day toward the end of my second year in training in the spring of 1987. It was a Thursday afternoon in the middle of a medical lecture.

A Moment of No time

I was sitting through a fascinating, albeit complicated, lecture on the "healing cascade". The professor was outlining the endless array of biochemical processing induced by the simple cutting of the skin. He explained with great zeal and detail how the body responds. I was fascinated with the impossible precision, and the complex biochemical nature of the processes involved to stop bleeding and begin healing and regeneration.

As I listened, my concentration grew very deep and I began to question in my mind ... how is it that the body "knows" how to do this? How does the body know to start the process, and control the process? How does it know to stop? How does the body know how to do anything and everything it does? I mean how does it "know" anything!

I began to stream through a series of thoughts and themed questions in my mind:

How does a body grow from a fused egg and sperm into a fetus with a phenomenal array of complex interlinked anatomy? How did it know to transition to its own system of circulation and physiology at birth? How did it know how to grow, and as intriguing, stop growing? How did it control an infinite array of unconscious processes with clockwork precision from breath, to heart beat, to metabolic processes, and water and elemental regulation? How did it know how to regenerate the same "model" of itself time and time again? How did it regenerate the same "old" or "young" person, in exactly the same appearance, if it was regenerating anew? How did it know how to heal anything? Why does healing fail? It went on and on. A 1000-questions cascaded through me in what seemed like a flash of an instant. I felt like I was being "accelerated" mentally faster than I could process, and still remain present in time!

Yet, as my mind raced, my body and my focus grew very still. I could observe the intelligent process being explained by the professor. But mystically, I knew the intelligence didn't lie so much *in* the chemistry being explained, but rather *the intelligence guiding* the chemistry being explained. And, it felt for a moment, like I "fused" with this intelligence!

It was a peculiar experience – for I felt very "large" or "expanded" in my mind. I was present in my body, and present in a larger space, all at the same time. I was propelled into an expanded state of awareness – and in that moment I knew there existed both intelligence and a design that governed life's processes – an "intelligent design". I understood explicitly, for a fleeting minute, that intelligence beyond normal understanding exists in all of life, and certainly in every function in the human body. I knew that this intelligence was "called upon" to heal the injury. It is an incomprehensible "master intelligence" that knew to induce, control and terminate the process with such majesty and perfection. I actually knew the answer to all the questions racing through my mind, was the same answer. Intelligent design - it was inherent in the system. It is present in all things – you, me, nature and all of life!

As unusual as it may sound, I was not simply aware of this intelligence. I felt immersed in this intelligence for an immeasurable period of time. How long did it last? A few seconds? A minute? 5 minutes? The immensity of the moment mocked any sense of time. To this day, I do not know how long it lasted. Yet the awareness of the "realness" of this intelligence has simply never left me. I was transformed deeply by this mystical encounter – more than I even knew.

Now, words cannot do justice to really explain what I lived that moment. I read later about "transcendental" moments, which people experience at points in their lives. These occur often in unusual moments of stillness, meditation or natural awe. This is the closest description to explain what I encountered. But - for a relatively agnostic budding scientist, as I slowly emerged from this fugue like state, I questioned what the heck had just happened in my naïve, and assuredly drug-free mind.

What I do know for certain is that afterwards a very deep peace overtook me for many days – and I was never quite "the same". It is hard for anyone to put into words a moment of subtle transcendence. It touched in my awareness something vaster, higher, deeper, and more omnipotent than anything I had known up to that point in my life. Now when you start talking about unnamable, unknowable fields of conscious force and deep loving presence with awareness – I had no other word but God! And that was how it seemed.

You might imagine for a while I kept this experience to myself. Words would do no justice, and I did not want to be too open about it. The knowledge that it would be judged or misunderstood was clear to me. If I didn't understand it, I was sure no one else would either. I could see people imagine they were talking to a character in Alice in Wonderland, or a late blooming hippie who discovered LSD! As exhilarated as I felt, I simply kept quiet.

As days passed, a sense of normality returned to my life. Memory of the moment faded, and I carried on with my life and my training. I didn't know how profoundly the experience would alter the rest of my life.

It is fair also to say, I did not understand how deeply and inexplicably my soul would burn in sadness A deep melancholy arose that would filter my view of the mundane quality of everyday life for many months after experiencing this event.

Everything that was "my life" to that point in time seemed real, important and meaningful. In an inexplicable way, everything that I saw as "life" became a bit hollow. I had thought very little about a spiritual, mystical or omni-intelligent nature within life up to that point in time. I was also quite unaware of the darkness of the night a soul may feel, when it has seen the twinkling glimpse of a dawn. But, life just carried on.

Midnight Wings

Somewhere in the final year of my studies I lived a second experience that dismantled another element of my world-view. It is an experience that many people have lived, but it was for me my first time. "We always remember our first time", it is so often said – somewhat tongue in cheek.

One night while sleeping I "woke up". The curious thing was I did not wake up in my body. I was floating above it. At this point in my life, I had not heard of things such as an out-of-body experience. I had no idea what was going on.

What I remember most is being aware that I was the same conscious being floating there, as I am while sitting here writing these words today. The biggest difference is that I was still aware, able to think and process – yet was totally unencumbered by my body or its weight. I could actually see my body physically lying in the bed. Yet I was free, and I could move around freely, simply by thinking about it!

So I did! I began to move around the room from one side to the other and back again. I could sit, float, and "stand" – all by thinking. I could also move by floating or flying – which was an incredible feeling.

I remember at some point that I had a thought that I should move outside on my balcony (on the 12th floor), and fly around to see things. Just as I was about to exit, I had the thought that I might not find my way back if I traveled too far. The thought startled me.

The moment I had this fear oriented thought, it felt like a huge vacuum was turned on in my physical body. I was "aspirated" into my physical body, through a vortex or a tube, with what felt like an enormous force. I landed in my body with a great thud! As I was thrust into my body, my physical body flew up in a jolt, into a sitting position. Dazed a little, I sat in bed, totally disoriented by what had just taken place.

As I looked around the room I saw all of the same items I was seeing in my "dream-like" experience. I tried to convince myself it was just a strange dream. I was not afraid of the experience, and somewhat ready to dismiss it. Yet, the experience was more than a dream, and I knew it. The experience made me aware that my consciousness existed independent of – while connected to – my physical body.

As the experience settled in my awareness, it wasn't the notion of an out of body experience that fascinated me. It was the awareness that I am not strictly limited to my body as a conscious being. The consciousness that eats, breathes and lives in my body is bigger than my body. It lives in it. It is tightly connected to it. Yet, it is also independent of it. I knew the body is more like a "vehicle" than an "identity".

It was another "unsolicited" baby step – into the mystical world of consciousness.

STALKED BY SPIRIT?

So before I proceed I must digress. As I started to live these experiences, I was a little confounded as to "why" they were happening! I was raised in an Irish Catholic environment, but I have never really been a "religious" person myself! I never sought to be saintly or spiritual in any way.

Aside, I am sure my poor mother quivers in her soul to hear that, but loves me anyway. My father probably smirks kindly as he himself bore patience to the religious leadership of his good-hearted wife, and her insistence on our Irish bred churchly duties, to overcome our personal share of sins!

That being the case, I grew up in a typical Irish descendent religious household, but felt lukewarm about religion as a child. It was a fairly typical multigenerational post immigrant Irish-Canadian Family. Our home-life was inspired by the Catholic overlay that defined such households - with all of the humor, hierarchy and religious guilt that might imply.

Today, I see myself as a deeply spiritual person but this was not true as a child. I sincerely ascribe to the core truth of love and oneness taught at the core of all religions - yet sometimes dishearteningly misunderstood by some "shepherds and their sheep". I did however always believe in the core spiritual virtues as a way of life – less encumbered by rules and dogma. Love your neighbor as your self. Be honest. Be kind. Be genuinely humble. Be generous in spirit. Don't steal. Lift the spirit of someone in need. Give genuine praise. Forgive. Share joy. You get the idea. And although I never thought of myself as religious or even spiritual when young, I always believed in goodness and the power of authentic love.

I was one of five boys and two girls. My "greatest claim to fame" and one of my mother's most astonishing achievements, was my 12-lb natural birth.

Growing up in a small town in Cape Breton, Nova Scotia had both the charm and boredom of small towns worldwide. I lived a pretty uneventful childhood in most ways. I have lots of small memories of good times and challenges, but my greatest recollection of early life was the awareness I wanted to grow up and get on with things. I had no big spiritual aspirations – so naturally I assumed I was being "stalked" by spirit when these things began to occur!

Looking Back

So given my early "agnostic" view on life, I began to seriously reflect on the meaning of the experiences which I had begun to live. I did recall one very poignant memory of childhood that became meaningful many years later. I was six years old at the time.

I was absolutely fascinated by a book my friend had been given as a present by her mother. It was entitled 'The Encyclopedia of the Future". The book was filled with pictures of futuristic visions and ideas – complete with pictures of floating cities encapsulated in large glass domes. There were powdered "nutritional products" filling the kitchens – in such volume that it would put any modern protein-shake maker to shame. It was like the Jetsons had landed on earth.

However, what I remember most is not simply the material in the encyclopedia, but the way I felt toward the concept of the future.

As I was reading through the book one day, I remember explaining to my friend's mother, quite matter of fact, that there were two possible destinies for the world. I knew, at a deep level, that the earth had two possible futures. One possibility was that the world was to be annihilated – probably by a nuclear holocaust – terminating life, as we know it. Option B was a little more enticing. In it, the earth would bypass this threat and we would somehow begin to build a "new world". It would be a world that was not quite akin to the Jetsonville enshrined in the book – but even more mystical and advanced in ways that I believe only to this day the future will reveal.

I also remember knowing with absolute certainty one fact. If I were still alive in the year 1998 - we had chosen option B. Years later when I learned of the concept of the Harmonic Convergence, this took on a whole new layer of meaning. As I watched events unfold like the collapse of Communism and traces of the cold war, and the collapse of the Berlin wall and a million other unforeseen magical moments of spiritual progression – I could remember this day in my young life, so many years ago. Today, I truly believe the earth has bypassed a great danger and is on the road to a spiritual and consciousness recovery!

Awash in Sensitivity

The second outstanding feature about my childhood is not an event - but a collection of events. I remember being blessed or cursed with an innate sensitivity – particularly for a boy. Now by sensitive, I don't mean simply emotional or reactive – I mean able to sense the emotions and thoughts of other people.

When I look back at my childhood, I never seemed to know how I felt "myself" about anything. I was able to feel – but it was a big mishmash of feelings that included my own feelings, and the feelings which other people were experiencing around me. The challenging part at that time was that I was never aware of how peculiar this was. I just assumed everyone was the same way.

This flavored my childhood in such a way that it created a great deal of personal confusion. With this sensitivity, it was easy for me to please. I seemed to know how other people felt and thought. It also made me very susceptible to being manipulated and ensnared in the drama of other people's experiences – because they felt very personal to me. And I could use my awareness of other's feelings simply to be manipulative too.

Fortunately, this sorted itself out in my later years with personal work. But I did not understand this until much later in my life. As I became aware of it, I thought it was a weakness or a flaw. What I didn't understand at the time is that it was a gift – one that became integrally important for me later in time.

But other than that, I simply grew up - with fond memories and painful ones – some good choices and some bad choices – like most of us do.

BACK TO THE FUTURE

Let us return now to 1987 circa the mini epiphany offering a "teasing glimpse" of the nature of intelligent design. This became for me, an experience that unquenchably provoked a desire to explore the more mysterious aspects of health and healing. I began to realize there existed, enshrined in a vault of consciousness beyond the everyday 3D world of understanding, a world of greater consciousness, energy and spiritual wisdom.

Yet, as inspirational and mystical as the moment proved to be, I found it harder and harder to stay interested in medicine. At this time I was just 21 years old and half way through medical school. It was upsetting to feel that I hadn't even finished training and I was starting to feel an emptiness or a lack of value and purpose in what I was doing! I didn't understand what was happening within me. I certainly had no idea it was an inner transformation so monumental that it was preparing me for my path in years to come. Yet even though I didn't understand, the strength emerged from within me, just to carry on. With a slight lack of zeal – I graduated in 1989.

Unsure of the direction to take in my life, I decided to follow the path that most ignited my heart – and that was to move to Montreal. It had absolutely nothing to do with medicine. I wanted to live, to explore and to feel alive – and I felt that it was a one-way path to the most exotic city in North America. I would make it home! I was accepted in a family medicine residency at McGill University. I packed my little black Honda Civic and drove off into the sunset – unsure where the road may lead but knowing in my heart it was the "right" thing for me to do.

As I settled into this next phase of my life, I felt like it was time to "live a little". I was tired of studying – which was unusual for me – but I wanted to live, to travel, to experience unknown adventures, and to have fun. Medicine was a bit on the backburner. My soul craved excitement. I was about to enter the school of life and didn't know it. A curiosity had awakened in me and I had no idea that I was supposed to learn about the emptiness in things and explore some of the deepest elements of life and my own psyche. It was a time of tremendous personal growth. But as I was approaching the end of my first year in residency, I was about to live another experience that was planning to crack my structural thinking a little more completely! But this event did not come wrapped in a welcoming package, for it was enmeshed in the passing of my father.

At this point in my life, I shared a spiritual experience with a whole array of my nearest family and friends, one whose power and majesty still leaves us in awe today. It was an experience that unequivocally lets one know that love is real, transcendent and ultimately holds the power to heal.

My father lived a very quiet, kind life. He was loved by just about everyone who knew him – in fact I think everyone! Silent, strong, honest and dependable would define him. People would often tell you "Jack Ryan would give you the shirt off his back". And he would. And most remarkably he would completely forget he did it – or at least you would be sure that was true.

People would also say, "I have never seen Jack Ryan angry!" And for 99.9% of his life – that was certainly true. I cannot attest, unfortunately, to the privilege of this innocence - for I was his child. I was also pretty creative at times to instigate an emotional reaction or two. I can, however, count on one hand the number of times he was angry. I can also attest that each and every time, there was a very deserving cause, if ever one existed.

In retrospect I realized my father would only be angry when we had driven our poor Mother to the point of distraction. When he saw her very strong and capable nerves falter, or he sensed we had crossed a threshold of great disrespect – he would intervene. He would not tolerate it. His stern, husky noise of disapproval was enough to stop us in our tracks.

Now suffice it to say that my parents consciously loved and supported each other. My mother saw my father as her greatest ally and companion, a provider and a man of honor. When he fell ill one year prior to his retirement, the whole world seemed to collapse upon her, just as the dreams of their retirement were ready to unfold. As his children, it saddened us profoundly, realizing we were soon to lose our father.

Mom was mystified, upset, angry, frustrated and betrayed when she first learned of my father's diagnosis of cancer. The beauty is, in all of the possible reactions that this may provoke – for mom, it turned to service. She became even more deeply my father's greatest supporter, ally and ever-ready nurse. She vigilantly prayed for his recovery, took care of organizing an endless list of care issues, expressed unreasonable faith in his recovery, and quietly despised the fact that his life was truncated in the prospect of a very untimely end.

My father grew ill and underwent radiation and chemotherapy and lived a short earthly decline. Within a year he had grown frail to the point that we knew it was a short time to his passing. By now I was nearing the end of an internship in Montreal. I was on the oncology service at the Montreal General Hospital Medicine Service.

One night as I went to bed, I had a premonition that my father would be passing on Friday of the following week. It was unequivocally clear to me that this was true – I just simply knew. Paradoxically the next morning when I arrived at work, two patients were to be admitted under the care of my team – having the same unusual variant lung cancer as my dad. The tumor was even in the same place! As I later went to present these two new patients to our service – something inside of me snapped and I began to sob uncontrollably!

This was one of a few times in the whole of my career when it was just impossible to separate my own life from my work or practice. It was a most sympathetic resonance, as if my two worlds merged completely into one. I simply could not hold back my emotion, as a deeply repressed sadness was pushing forward in my consciousness.

Our senior clinician was a lady of great kindness, and could see through the waves of my turbulent emotions, as I professed to be okay and capable. She asked me what was occurring to have me so upset and I told her the story. John, she said – it is time for you to be with your family now. We will take care of your patients; you do not need to worry. You need now to be with your family and your dad.

The next morning I was on a flight home.

The next week passed very quickly and Thursday was quickly upon us. On Thursday evening, knowing what I had experienced earlier, I suggested to my sister we spend the night at the hospital where my father was now settled, and very feeble. He labored intermittently through the night with his breathing. By the arrival of the morning it was obvious his respiratory strength was much compromised. We phoned our family – who had all made it home by now - to be by his side. Together we spent the very last hour of his life with him – all seven of the children, and Frances his wife.

I don't think anything in life prepares you for the final moment when you lose someone near to you in this world. My mother was beside herself. The tears of grief that flowed from her were as if her heart was torn from her chest.

If that were not enough, our dear mom who prayed her way through any crisis - became a superstitious wreck. She immediately expressed the idea that it had to rain on the day our Dad was to be buried. And not typically a superstitious woman – it became her entire preoccupation for the next three days!

My family was diligently trying to be patient and understanding. We were operating under the belief that Mom was filled with grief. But as the days passed this is all we heard. After exhausting ourselves reassuring her, we began reassuring each other it would pass. The reassurance slowly faded. Knowing that this preoccupation was getting a little "crazy" – I became otherwise preoccupied. What were we to do if it didn't rain? I was sure Mom would lose her mind!

I asked Mom why it was so important. Her answer was simple: "John, a body put to rest in the rain, is a soul at peace." She didn't want rain at all! She wanted to know that Dad was at peace! It was both a heartfelt wish and a need of gentle reassurance all rolled in one. But all I could think about by this point, is what will be the tragedy upon her, if it doesn't rain!

Let's just say that a pervasive "peacelessness" overtook the days of my fathers wake. I became very concerned that if it didn't rain there would be no peace in my mother's heart for a long time to come. She simply needed to know, with absolute certainty, that Dad was "okay".

Alas, Monday morning arrived, which was the day of Dad's funeral. It was a typical sunny lukewarm mid-summer coastal day. The funeral came and passed – and honestly we were now so crazed with the absence of rain, I can barely remember a moment. We then left the church for the cemetery.

At the cemetery many friends and family gathered, as well as the parish priest. The priest conducted the service and he ended his prayers with a final Amen.

Now, I am glad I have a family of witnesses to the following experience, for surely it would sound contrived. As if scripted by the divine hand, on perfect cue with the priest's Amen – out of the sky came hurling three humungous golf ball sized raindrops. I kid you not! The raindrops aligned perfectly in a straight line, striking my father's shiny copper colored casket one by one from head to belly to toe – all in a row. The "spelunk" of each drop seemed to ricochet loudly as they splashed the onlookers. They seemed to baptize everyone present with a much needed grace. Meanwhile, the sun continued to shine.

An eerie gratefulness crept over us. My family was essentially speechless. Eyes crossed paths in every direction in a weird state of complete shock.

I turned to my mother at the end of the casket who, up to that point in time, was writhing in nervous anxiety and sadness. Suddenly, as if a large vacuum was turned on and off repeatedly in the middle of her chest - in short successive whoops she breathed in three large gasps of air with no exhalation. With the instillation of her third breath - she slowly and gently exhaled. Her breath released, which seem to last for a full minute. But with this breath, like a wind from the sky, there was an absolutely palpable descent of peace. It was an unbelievable experience. This exhalation released every strained nerve and muscle, melting her into a state of pure and absolute calm.

This was the first time in my life that I consciously saw and recognized peace physically descend as a force upon a human being. A soft smile seemed to rise directly from her heart, and completely consume her face.

As I witnessed this unbelievable spectacle, my mind raced a little. What the heck just happened here?

So there we were, left wondering, but basking in gratitude. Was this God? Was this my Father sending a message? Both? All that I knew for sure is that it was a wink from my Father's spirit. I thought, "my father is still present" – and I knew tangibly, that love is capable of amazing things.

I also knew beyond a doubt that I witnessed a mystical healing – perhaps the purest moment of healing I had ever seen. What occurred in that moment brought a restorative healing peace to my mother, and completely transformed the experience of all the remaining years of my mother's life. I felt an "otherworldly" love. The atmosphere tingled with it.

Was this a gift from my father? A gift from God? Who knew? Yet, as the profundity of this moment settled deeper and deeper into my consciousness, it stimulated a quiet but unbridled spiritual awakening for me. It led me to seriously reflect on the idea of where death leads. Do we die? Are we eternal? It created a serious curiosity about the concept of the afterlife and what death means.

In the days and months that followed, when I could smell my father's leather jacket beside me – particularly at times of great challenge or when important choices were to be made – I found reassurance in what I came to accept as true at this defining moment in my life. Death is a passage and has no lasting sting. I knew he was there in spirit, and alive in my heart. From that day forward – I have truly never felt "alone".

When A Door Closes

As I returned to finish my training it was difficult to settle back into a routine. I eventually did, and completed training, and licensed as a general practitioner. I worked in many different practice settings ranging from ER's to clinics to urgent care centers. I learned so much about medicine, and even more about life.

During my medical training I was always fascinated with the practice of psychiatry. I decided that it would be a very interesting aspect of medicine to pursue, particularly as I became more and more interested in the psychological and psycho-spiritual elements of health and healing.

In medicine, the natural way to pursue this would be through a residency in psychiatry. I began the process of applying for such programs and was in the midst of choosing between a four-year program at Massachusetts General Hospital or New York University – when my life was again about to change. Two experiences converged to short circuit this path for me.

First, I had an interview for the psychiatry program I was most interested in, which I found quite disturbing. After a very interesting interview complete with praise for my letters of introduction and references, the interviewing psychiatrist told me he had one reservation in accepting me.

He declared that he thought perhaps that I was an independent thinker. He expressed that could be very disruptive and very disappointing in a program where conformity would be expected.

Now, hardly a rebel rouser – I was intrigued by his comment. It was pretty clear that I was about to jump in a box where independent thinking was discouraged. I was told frankly, "If you decide to join us you will understand that you are here to learn, not teach." And "You would be coming here to learn about the practice of psychiatry. You should not expect anyone's presence here, including your own, to change anything." Real words expressed, I kid you not!

Every molecule in my body screamed silently in alarm. The arrogance and the surreal belief that each member in a group does not influence the energy of the group astounded me. Everyone makes a contribution – how could someone not know that! I thought, "My God, does he want a clone?"

The event had a huge impact on me. I had many thoughts pass through my mind. "Oh John, it is just your ego reacting." "I can not subject myself to an environment where who I am or who anyone is, is not respected or honored." "Was this some kind of psychological game being played?" But as the experience settled, and the shock passed, it became harder and harder to convince myself that pursuing this road was a good idea.

Days went by, and I assumed it would not be a choice I would have to make after the interview anyway. A week later, it was a shock again when I received a letter of zealous acceptance. With a slightly heavy heart, but a pretty clear head, I turned it down. I knew it was not my path. By the grace of inner awareness, I believed it was time to close a door. This was a very powerful experience for me. I learned that life would guide us – even when it is away from what we "think" is the right path to follow! Life may have a mystical path to open – one that cannot be imagined until experienced!

Another One Opens …

Shortly following the experience, I received a serendipitous gift. I was approaching my birthday and I was given an unusual present from my dear friend Robert. The gift was a session with a lady who performed numerology and read Tarot cards. New to both of these concepts, I was a little intrigued by the gift and felt butterflies in my stomach as I attended my session – it felt very exciting!

Linda was an attractive lady with deep piercing eyes, jet-black hair, and a fiery independent spirit. She was self-determined, responsible and full of a teacher's love. She did not mince words, but yet spoke with a tenderness and power that allowed you to feel capable of understanding her ideas, and strong enough to imagine you could carry them through. Our session started, however, in a peculiar fashion.

"John, let us see, you have a deep sensitivity and an ability to see into and feel into people and their problems. You could easily do what I am doing now, and you do not need to speak to me really. You find your own answers, and always should."

I thought to myself, "My word! Is that my session?" I did not know what to do or say. But alas she did continue – and the words she shared with me forever changed my life.

She looked at me with a penetrating look, as if searching for permission to continue.

What she sought was granted, as she continued to speak:

> *"You are a healer by nature. Healing is your work, do not doubt it - it is your purpose. But I encourage you to realize that this can mean many things. You have the potential to awaken an unusual understanding of healing that lives within you. It is much vaster than the idea of healing you currently hold.*
>
> *You have a very strong and capable intuition and it would serve you well to probe deeper into an understanding of healing and life. Do as you will, but this doorway is open to you – and if you choose to walk through it you will find great fulfillment.*
>
> *The greatest challenge before you now is to understand yourself and your process. This is hard for you because you are very sensitive by nature. It has always been hard for you to know what you are feeling yourself, because your awareness often includes the thoughts and feelings of those around you.*

I encourage you to live your life as you see right, live by what you think and feel inside of you, and bear the consequence – for you will be confused until you are capable of recognizing your own feelings distinctly from those of others. Make mistakes if you must, but give yourself the opportunity to be real within your self-expression. You must learn what feelings are self-generated, what is in your environment, and when intuition is speaking to you.

You are kind by nature and I cannot imagine you would ever lose that. But you must be willing not to please, when you know you are simply compromising the truth in yourself.

Healing is a bigger world when you look at life more completely than the mundane – follow your curiosity and your inner promptings – it will lead you exactly where you are meant to go."

Linda did not give me specifics – but told me to follow my inner guidance. This was a simple but frankly revolutionary way to live when so much of what we do follows knowledge, and is judged by preexisting beliefs. It was a mind opening guidance, which was critical for me at this time. It truly and powerfully helped me to open a door to the unknown. And, this was the way to travel to find my own purpose. This encounter opened my mind to the idea of exploring an "off the beaten path" of healing. As time would reveal – this was a turning point in my life!

As this session with Linda came to a close, I didn't have a clue what to do with this information, not really. But as I have come to learn – I really didn't need to. I needed to be open and to trust. Life will always find a way to respond to the seeker. When one door closes, another opens – perhaps more adventurous than the one we would choose based on our own logic. These hidden doorways can take us mysteriously to places - where we can learn about things we didn't know were possible.

BACK TO THE FUTURE (AGAIN!)

As the impact of this encounter settled into my mind, and having been subversively awed by the experience I had lived at my father's funeral, I became very curious about life, death, and meaning. I became, in fact curious about all things spiritual in nature. I also became interested in how our spirituality is related to healing.

In this quest, I began to read a book about past life exploration and healing. Learning about this phenomenon, I was intrigued enough to check out the experience for myself. I attended two sessions with a regression therapist in

Montreal – something very foreign to me at the time.

Now I have to say that I did not believe this would be a success for me. I was not particularly hypnotizable, and I really did not think I would be able to relax under guidance by a stranger.

As the session began, I began to relax, but at first it seemed a little useless. I saw and felt nothing. Then slowly, in my minds eye, I began to see a dream like vision, which was pretty remarkable and foreign to me. As the therapist continued to guide me into a deep relaxation, I could first see my feet, and then this slowly shifted to include a whole visual scene of another time. What was most impressive is that I could see a "character" in the dream, the one whose feet first appeared, and I knew – symbolically or historically - that it was *me*!

Now I was not Napoleon or King Louis or a famous saint! I was a simple man. The vision was extremely "familiar" but something I had never seen before. In the dream I was standing by the wall of a natural stone auditorium. It was a large well-constructed space – but it was present within a cave in the side of a mountain! By modern understanding, it felt southwest American in character – but I was uncertain about when or where this was taking place. In many ways it was like watching myself in a movie inside of my head – but I knew without a doubt that I was viewing a past life experience.

In the vision, the auditorium was full of people listening to a charismatic speaker. What I knew with certainty is that the man on the stage speaking to the people was a liar and was engaged in manipulating the people to his own favor. He seemed to be a mayor or a leader. The people were entranced by him and totally convinced of his words. They were afraid of something, and he seemed to bring them an idea to believe in. But the ideas did not play on their achievement or potential – it was a play on their fears to convince them to believe in his agenda.

For reasons that were not clear in the vision, I knew better than to listen to him – and I knew that because of this, my life was in danger. But the most remarkable memory of this vision is that I could feel a powerful and seething rage inside of me, at his betrayal. I could tangibly feel the rage present in my body – as I touched upon the memory and recalled the event.

In this state of relaxation, the therapist prompted me to go to the next important moment in this lifetime. The scene advanced in my minds eye – flashing forward in relative time.

I now found myself on horseback, riding at high speed away from the village. I was fleeing the village, with a leather-bound package of material under my arm. I knew it contained the evidence needed to expose the leader's intentions.

Suddenly, I felt a sharp arrow pierce my back and I fell off the horse. I toppled to the ground – and was dead.

Now the interesting thing for me was that in my life today, in the same area in my back where the arrow had penetrated in this vision, I have always had a "pinch" or "pulling" type of sensation. It felt as if I held a "deep scar" that seemed to restrict my body. Yet, interestingly, this unusual sensation disappeared after remembering this experience and processing this memory.

After this experience, with a little time to reflect on the memory – I realized that in my young life, I never really trusted authority. I was always skeptical of it, and what people do with power – and was particularly reactive to manipulative authority. I remember times as a child when I found myself unreasonably angry in the presence of such energy. Even though I could be rational, and suggest my reaction was "understandable" in the situation, the emotional reaction seemed exaggerated, when looking back on such events. I would become so frustrated and emotional in some experiences that I lost my power or effectiveness to speak.

It was easy to draw a correlation between the impact of the *logged* memory of this experience, the emotions that were retained around it, and its *influence* in my current life. The reality of this all became very clear with this induced memory. And interestingly – it began to change!

I learned to process this type of reaction in a healthier way, or with greater awareness – to honor myself but not get overwhelmed or exaggerated in my reaction. It allowed me to heal a subconscious pattern of thought and emotion that was affecting my life in a perceptibly limiting way. This awareness, and the healing that occurred, was simply astounding to me.

Within the same regression session, I lived two more past life memories. The next one took place in an English countryside and I was in a beautiful stone garden house in the English countryside. It was very picturesque.

In this memory I again was a man, and I could see my wife and two children playing in the garden. My wife looked up at me, and the look in her eyes spoke to me, as if telepathically. It was clear that she was in love with our children and with me – but was lonely. I was too preoccupied with my work to spend enough time with my family. Today we blame this type of phenomena on modern type A overachievement – but I guess I was ahead of the curve. Yet, I could remember the feeling conveyed in her eyes, and my interpersonal negligence. It was a very powerful memory to experience!

As I processed this memory I realized that it was a message of importance to me in my life again. It was a lesson in balance, which I took very much to heart.

It was fascinating to me that each scene and experience that came forward had a very poignant teaching or lesson that was pertinent to my modern lifetime. I could see how each experience bore upon me today, and how important the realizations helped me "see myself" – and even heal an attribute or tendency.

The third vision was perhaps most peculiar. I was a full term fetus in utero in the process of being born. As the vision opened, I could feel the pressure on my head and my body with each contraction. One thing I remember very distinctly is that even as a baby I was also pushing, or striving to be born. I could feel the will to live!

During this experience, I was able to "see" through the top of my head. I could see the amniotic membrane, blood vessels and amniotic fluid. I felt it as the amniotic membrane ruptured, and the fluid space above me collapsed, I could see myself emerging from the birth canal. It was absolutely fascinating.

As the delivery occurred, I could see all around me although my eyes were closed. I could clearly visualize the green sterile tile walls, and the stainless steel windows, sink, and fixtures – all typical of a hospital in the 1950's. I remembered being held upside down. I even remembered being tapped on the bottom by the doctor. As I reflected later on this memory – I thought at first I was reliving my birth. But then I realized that is not possible. I was not born in a hospital. I was born in my parent's house. How is that for born again?

Through the impact of this memory it was obvious to me that we are not born once, but many times. The fact that I was witness to a past life recall was true, to me, beyond the shadow of a doubt.

Now a few weeks later I went for a second session but alas, I was not to see more. Curiosity may have killed the cat, but it didn't quell my enthusiasm.

Whether I was blocking it with mental interference, or simply being guided not to pursue it further at this time, was not clear. The theater of history was closed – for a while!

In the weeks that followed this experience, I became aware of several important changes that occurred in my psyche through this remarkable experience. It firmly opened my mind with complete trust and awareness that we do not die. This experience completely unlocked any uncertainty I harbored around this idea.

I came to believe to my core that we live many experiences and they are connected in importance and soul development. They create a chain of understanding that help us grow and develop in spiritual awareness and manifestation. Our lives may be influenced by this extended history in many ways. It also helped me realize our future is influenced by the relationship we hold to the past, and it can be transformed in the present moment – or a moment of "presence". Healing the past in the present changes the future. Powerful indeed!

I'm all Shook Up!

Around this time in my life, I began to have some unusual experiences. They lasted for a period of nine to twelve months in time – and they occurred intermittently. They would occur when I went to bed or lay down and was relaxed, but just prior to falling sleep.

As I lay in bed each evening, my body would begin to tremble or vibrate. I do not believe I was trembling if witnessed outside - it seemed an "internal vibration".

With each passing day, the vibration seemed to progress, and I would feel strange energy movements, and sometimes jerky motions and gushes of air-like energy in my lower back and sacrum. Sometimes, the energy would pulse and push up my spine.

I lived a whole range of "energetic" experiences – and each time it would occur, it would be slightly different than the prior events. I would see lights in my head, feel currents in my body, rushes of heat or cold, and tingling. Sometimes I would feel sensations like a mini jackhammer at the base of my skull, or a clearing vibration somewhere in my body. I would hear audible sounds and frequencies - that were not frightening and often beautiful; but, peculiar and unlike anything I had encountered before.

Occasionally I would begin to feel that I was levitating, but could not open my eyes to see. Twice I flipped out of my body entirely and was pressed against the wall. It was as if suspended by Velcro while energy shifts were occurring in my body. One night, as I was lying in bed, the entire ceiling disappeared from my condo apartment, and I could see the star filled sky!

It was all very strange indeed, and it could easily have been a very fearful time. But something inside of me provided tremendous reassurance. I had moments of concern for sure, but overall I did not feel disturbed by it – more curious.

Then finally one evening I felt a huge energy rush up around my head like it was enveloping me and I felt a pop. Then after this experience, most of these experiences just stopped for a long time.

As I lived these events, I knew it was not a medical condition or experience. Yet, I had no certain idea what was happening to me. I had the sense, and grace, to know that I was not going crazy. I also knew that I was experiencing something that I could not expect anyone I knew to really understand. On occasion, I tried to share a few experiences with people close to me at the time, and they would usually just stare "gob smacked" and totally unsure what to think or say. So I learned quickly not to say too much to anyone. I could easily understand how strange they found it.

The uncertainty in the experience provoked me to begin a search to understand what I was living. The challenge was that I had no idea what I was searching for! As a life long student, I turned to books – hoping to find something that might help me understand what was happening within me. One day, I found myself in a local bookstore that specialized in books on spirituality and healing – and I began to look around.

I came across two books that day that once again changed – in a very profound way – my life.

The first was a book by Gopi Krishna, entitled *The Awakening of Kundalini*.[33] At this time, I had never heard of the word "Kundalini". I had no idea what it was, and no idea what it's "awakening" meant. But the book seemed important to me. On an intuitive level, I simply knew this was what I was experiencing.

I trusted this intuition and it provided an awareness of the "direction" in which to search in order to better understand what I was living. It was a great source of reassurance and understanding for me. At that time, unlike today, there was little information available to people living these types of experiences. This material not only provided some answers, but also taught me the importance of trust and intuitive led guidance. When you don't know the answer you are seeking - and it exists "outside" of what you already know or understand – how do you begin to find it? You must trust and follow intuition. I learned that I had to trust and follow an inspired guidance to find a "missing link".

When I reflect back on this time in my life, I am so grateful that I did not react by seeking traditional medical counsel to support me during this experience. If I had taken this path, I am sure there is a good chance I would have ended up with a misappropriated label, or on a pharmaceutical to suppress the whole experience. I began to understand there is a distinction between mystical experience and some traditional experiences that form part of psychiatric illnesses, such as symptoms of psychosis. I found a reassurance, which was very much needed at that time.

The second book that literally "magnified in size" on the bookshelf as I walked towards it. I kid you not! It was like walking through the rabbit hole! It was a book by Lee Carroll called *The End Times (New Information for Personal Peace)*. It was a book of "channeled" information, a concept that was also brand new to me at the time – and of which I was a tad skeptical. Yet regardless, I could not ignore the experience or my attraction – with books in hand, I was on my way.

I will add a few words on **Kryon** for the information provided through this work has been very important in my personal development. Kryon is identified as an angelic entity who channels information through Lee Carroll.

Lee is a gentleman, in every meaning of the word. He is a sound engineer by profession, whose life took a profound turn as he began channeling information in the early 1990's. Kryon identified himself as a "magnetic master" whose work involves humanity and supporting the current earth changes which are slowly, but assuredly, occurring on the planet.

In his messages through Lee, Kryon speaks about the spiritual evolution of humanity, and as we referred to earlier, the harmonic convergence. He explains that the "potential of humanity" at this time was high enough to proceed with a spiritual awakening process, which would transform humanity in the years ahead. As the energy was appropriate, humanity would begin an ascent of consciousness that would propel it into another state of reality.

The message rekindled the awareness of the two world futures we might encounter that was so clear to me as a child. The message struck me importantly in two ways. It helped me understand the strong awareness I had as a child about the potential futures of the planet. It also reassured me to know we had arrived at option B!

As I mentioned earlier, I had no understanding of the concept of channeling – and it unsettled me a little. I was weary and skeptical, perhaps like you. With time, experience and understanding – I came to appreciate that any spiritual information that arrives on this planet is channeled in one way or another through a human being.

All spiritual doctrine that has arrived on our earth came through a gifted human being for the benefit of humanity to grow. The "glamour" of channeling is however an obstacle for many - and the risks or limitations of it in the hands of the wrong person are obvious. Yet, the grace inherent in this process, in a highly integrated and integrity-filled human being, is profound.

I would say that one must be discerning in what one accepts as channeled information – but it has been critical for me in my own understanding of life and personal development. But enough about "spooky channeling", as Lee himself terms it, for now. Let us continue with the story.

As I worked my way through these two volumes, I struggled a little with the content. On one hand there was a man talking about Kundalini spiritual awakening and the arrival of inspired awareness and intelligence. The other was talking about the end of the world, as we know it, and the need to accept some sort of implant to ascend. Although I can laugh in retrospect, it was all a little freaky. Unlike Gopi Krishna, I felt no more "genius" than before the vibratory séances that I had been living.

Yet despite the conflict in consciousness it provoked, I was able to find peace. I was able to extract a better appreciation of Kundalini awakening – and I knew on reading this material that this is exactly what I experienced. Kundalini awakening is an incredibly diverse and ongoing experience, which is unique in many people. And as for Kryon – I could not stop reading the book. I knew, beyond a shadow of doubt, that the underlying message of this work was profound and true. As Lee Carroll has continued his work over the years, the information he has brought forth is absolutely some of the most pertinent and important information on the planet today.

THE MISSING PILL

Through a Window in the Sky

So with a past-life recall and kundalini stirrings behind me, it was not long before I lived another awakening experience. This time it was an unsolicited experience, which occurred magically one day at the setting of the sun.

I was spending a week at the ocean in Fort Lauderdale, Florida. We had arrived mid to late afternoon, and had settled at the hotel. I decided to go to the beach to enjoy the late afternoon, and begin to unwind. It was by now late afternoon, and the sun was getting low in the sky. This is a magical time of day, especially when beside the ocean.

As I lay in the sand, my body became so heavy I felt like I weighed a 1000 pounds. I sank deeply into this relaxation and drifted into an altered state of near sleep. It was so reviving and peaceful. To this day, it was one of the greatest moments of relaxation I can recall.

A little while later, I slowly aroused from this state – and I felt amazing. I gently sat up and I turned myself to view the ocean. After gazing for a short while, I felt this amazing bliss arising in my body. I decided to walk over to the shore. I put my feet in the water and sat down in it. I was unusually thrilled by the salty waves, as they gently washed around me. I looked out over the ocean and felt so expanded in my heart.

As I dreamily gazed forward, my vision slowly transformed. It was as if everything became – or was absorbed into – a dancing field of light. Little molecules of light danced everywhere and the world was so alive and dynamic. The ocean was like a mirage and somewhat translucent. I, myself, felt tingly and alive and unified as one with a vast field of energy that seemed to exist adjacent to the physical world of sight.

I marveled in this space for a while, and then my vision re-adjusted and I shifted to a more solid view. I was a little astonished. It felt at that moment like I was granted a peek into the "energy that is life" or "behind life" as we solidly see it. In this magical moment, this awareness was being stirred! This was the first time in my life I began to *see energy*.

As we will explore in the upcoming section – we are seeing energy all of the time. Even things that appear solid to us, are forms of energy expression. But the experience was not limited to only a visual awakening. It was packaged with many realizations that were simultaneously imprinted in my awareness.

First, the precursor to this type of experience was stimulated by a deeply peaceful state of mind and emotions. There were no real thoughts or agitating emotions interfering in that moment. I was in a state of tremendous personal inner harmony – which was a prerequisite somehow for the visual awakening. Whether this state was "a chicken" or "an egg" I am not sure – but it was inherently important to the experience. This inner silence undoubtedly facilitated an altered state of consciousness.

The second fact is that it occurred when I was supported by all of the "elemental forces" of life. By elemental forces, I mean the sacred elements long revered in nature-based and indigenous spirituality. At that moment, I was sitting on the *earth*, embraced by waves of *water*, with a gentle offshore breeze of *wind*, and, bathed in *fire* as the light of the setting sun settled upon me. Earth, Fire, Air, Water – supported an awakening to the *Ether*! It was as if a window had opened in the sky.

The third point is that this was a direct experience of the energetic nature of all living things. I had read little if anything by this point in my journey about the energetic nature of life or the idea of "energetic healing". Yet I learned from this experience directly that an energetic backdrop exists in life – it was totally and unequivocally real. I knew from this very first hand experience that an energy order exists in "some dimension " that we simply do not normally see or understand.

This invariably punched a hole in my more rigid thinking. It created a "gentle" nudge to be open, and not intimidated by the concepts that can emerge from this awareness. I will always think of this as a personal "Really, the world is not flat!" moment. It forever changed what I thought of as "life".

This experience also awakened in me an elementary appreciation of the Ancient and Native Spiritual traditions, and the reverence that is conveyed for the elements of the Earth, as humanity's Mother. These elements are the foundational forces that create, sustain and evaporate in our transforming creation - so the dance of spirit as life continues. Nothing could exist without them, and their profound integration and balance. Nothing – not you, or me, nor anything we know to be our lives. They are *alive* as living consciousness. I could begin to appreciate there was a profound wisdom in these ancient traditions and the teachings they have cloistered. I came to believe that these magnificent peoples have done this in preservation for a future time, when people could again begin to accept or understand these ways. I also believe this time is now.

I will always remember that it felt very peculiar to leave the beach that day. It started as a simple day, but I knew I had just lived a moment of personal transformation that would begin to alter everything I thought of as "real". As I headed for the "real world" to meet up with some friends for dinner, I was left feeling "high" after this magnificent and unsuspected experience.

I remember eating a hamburger and fries for dinner – an unusual choice for me – and they were delicious – incredibly so! I loved every molecule of food I ate that day. Filled with a true sense of grace, I blessed it not with words but with my whole being. Although every moment is precious and "presence" in each moment is a key to spiritual fulfillment – there are moments of extreme grace we each live when we can know that we have been touched by a transcendent force that words cannot convey in fullness. But when we do, we also know – life will never be exactly "the same".

A Cosmic Adjustment

It was also around this time in my life that I began to explore a teaching called *A Course in Miracles*. I had encountered this book at a local bookstore and was intrigued by the concept of creating miracles. I did not understand what the book was about but I was very drawn to read it and to explore. [43]

For those not familiar with this teaching, here is an excerpt taken from Wikipedia explaining this program:

> *A Course in Miracles (ACIM) is a self-study curriculum that aims to assist its readers in achieving spiritual transformation. The book describes a purely non-dualistic philosophy of forgiveness and includes what are meant to be practical lessons and applications for the practice of forgiveness in one's daily life.*
>
> *The introduction to the book contains the following summary, "Nothing real can be threatened. Nothing unreal exists. Herein lies the peace of God."*
>
> *No author is listed for the book, but Helen Schucman wrote it with the help of William Thetford, based on what she called an "inner voice" which she identified as Jesus.*

Hence, *A Course in Miracles* is a study program of spiritual transformation. It involves a daily teaching or lessons, which takes the reader deep into unity consciousness – past the tendencies of the ego – into a profound level of inner peace and unity realization.

This work has inspired almost every well-known modern writer and spiritual teacher in the emerging consciousness domain. I can say unequivocally it was also integral in my personal process and spiritual development. I think of it humorously as a "cosmic adjustment" in attitude – and a great restorer of peace! When we take a look at healing principles later, this work will be strongly reflected in the discussion of ego integration.

A Living Stone

A short time later I received an unexpected call from Linda – the lady who gave me the reading I shared with you earlier. I had not seen Linda for a few years by this time. Linda's call was specific. She told me she met a man who works in healing – energy healing – and she knew instinctively that I would enjoy meeting him. She confessed it was unusual to so directly guide someone to such a specific action. She said however it was strong in her awareness to let me know – leaving it to my discernment.

After my recent experience in Ft Lauderdale, that was all I needed to hear! I could see it was a precursor for what I was about to experience. Into my life walked, Monsieur Pierre.

Pierre was a stoutly man of solid presence and character. With a twinkle in his eye, he was always ready to prod or tease in a loving little way. His inspiration was gentle, but infectious. Pierre in French means "stone" or "rock" – and this was as apt a testament to Pierre's character as I could come. He was unassuming but very open hearted and open minded. Yet despite his solid disposition, to speak with him you might think you were sitting in a glass of champagne.

When I first met Pierre, I asked him how he became interested in energy healing. His story surprised me. Pierre had lived an experience one day in a moment of frustration that he shared. Pierre was working as a deliveryman for a water company. He just finished delivering several large bottles of water to a lady who lived several floors up in a walk up apartment. The customer for some reason, which I don't recall, was very rude and insulting to him. He bit his tongue and left her seething in anger.

As he returned to his truck he had a little melt down – but of spiritual sorts. He was frankly enraged, and began yelping at God for the stupidity of humanity. He threw down the gauntlet of spirit and cried to God, "Why was the world, and the people in it, so disappointing?" I think it is safe to say that he didn't expect "God's reply".

Pierre developed an enormous fire in his head and a massive headache for several days to follow. As things cleared slowly for him, he was different. In his experience he became capable of seeing energy. As we will explore later, his third eye opened very actively. He became capable of seeing the human energy field.

From this experience he developed an ability not only to see, but also to work with the human energy fields to promote healing.

Many people today are aware of hands on healing or Reiki. Pierre's work developed through his ability to see energy, and how it responds directly to stimuli or hands on transfer and polarity balancing.

Pierre eventually taught me the details of working with energy. But, I am getting ahead of myself - for my time began with an "energy session".

But I am Not Ill

At this time the idea of energy healing was still new to me. I was open minded, but not necessarily convinced the whole thing wasn't a bit crazy. There was still a little struggle of doubt or uncertainty - a skepticism that was healthy and grounding.

I went to see Pierre for a treatment – not understanding why I even "wanted" one - for I wasn't "ill". Pierre lived about an hour north of Montreal and I can remember having "pre-high-school-dance" like jitteriness – excited and giddy – as I travelled to have the session.

As Pierre worked on me I could see colors and lights in my head and little jolts of energy in my arms, legs and back. I could feel my eyes twitch by a magical force, which did not seem to be my own. I gasped for little breaths, which were uncontrollable from time to time and sighed. As it ended I felt a great peace within me – and a strange invincibility. There is no other way to describe it - I felt terrific. I absolutely tingled with life and with joy.

Pierre didn't say too much to me that day – he just shared a few insights he had while he worked that are quite personal to me, and I shared a few thoughts about my experience in return. I felt like he knew much more than he let on, but I was too ecstatic to really care!

I embarked in my car for the hour trip home. My invincibility struck me when I was speeding along at 160 km an hour without even realizing it, and suddenly see police lights in my mirror! I had no idea I was driving so dangerously fast!

As I searched for my driver's license I remember being unable to suppress the smile on my face, and the joy I felt. Nothing could penetrate my happiness in that moment. I thanked the police officer for my ticket – an ultimate act of grace that probably stopped me from rolling over in my car. I spent days reeling in the mystery of my experience. It was one week later that I experienced my first dream of conscious guidance.

Night School

In my dream, I was flying in what appeared to be an old medieval village from rooftop to rooftop. I was in the company of a group of playful spirits – human ones mind you – but we could all fly in this dream. We were playing, but we were somehow learning at the same time – like an ideal school where playing was the way things were done. In the dream it was clear that we were learning *to fly*. I recognized the teacher in this dream as Pierre.

So after my session and my dream, I knew I would love to learn from Pierre whatever I could. I found myself a week later in a weekend seminar where Pierre was teaching a group of 10 people about working with energy from his visual experience, and many things related to energy healing. I could clearly see that a "new horizon" was unfolding in front of me.

In the year that followed, I was so inspired to read and to learn. I began to search for books, for articles, for seminars – anything that could help me understand what I was simply craving to learn about energy healing. It was an amazing period of my life in so many ways – for it felt like the roof had not simply lifted off my bedroom, it lifted off the galaxy.

Yet, we must remember we are indeed still human. As the carpet unrolled in front of me, it seemed the past was not included in the journey. I began to experience a series of losses that I did not fully appreciate as necessary or appropriate at the time.

Transformation

I began to live a series of "deaths". I am not speaking of the death of human family or friends - but the death of many things that were part of my life. Friendships faded and interests faded. My relationship of 5 years ended, unexpectedly and abruptly. We were in the process of making plans to move to California and immigration problems stalled the process on the day of departure! We had sold everything of material value in preparation for our move, moved out of our condo, and were essentially homeless and without any financial commitment. So suddenly, with or without a sense of personal volition – I was unexpectedly free of everything I knew to be my world!

And if this were not enough, my precious dog Nexus became mysteriously ill in response to an antibiotic she was given to treat a simple bladder infection. She developed a condition called idiopathic thrombocytopenia – and passed away within three days by uncontrollable internal bleeding. I was devastated!

So although my life was gearing up to create a freedom from the familiar – I certainly did not feel "free" at first. I felt horrifically sad. There were many heartbreaking moments as the strings that tied this life to reality were clipped one by one. It was a very emotional time, as I encountered loss after loss. In the midst of an unfolding mystery, I lived a great deal of heartache and heart soothing. It was not always easy to see at times of sorrow. Yet somewhere under the sadness, I knew it was all appropriate and important – for it was time for me to move forward to a new experience. The road of spiritual awakening is not all angels and roses. But it is wise – and very good.

Mystical Messages

I believe we have different types of dreams. For example, some dreams seem to process current events in our lives. Other dreams are coded messages or symbolic information that have pertinent information to convey to us. While others, like the dream I referred to earlier, be dreams of direct guidance. The latter two are more unusual, but the represent one-way our intuitive consciousness or spirit may choose to speak to us.

Around this time I remember vividly three dreams that I experienced over the course of three nights. They fit in to the "symbolic information" category.

In the first of these three dreams, I could see myself floating in cosmic space. I looked like an astronaut floating weightlessly – but I was wearing my birthday suit, not a space suit! Then, all of a sudden bits and pieces of my body began to disintegrate. Toes fell off. Limbs dismantled. Tissues evaporated! Piece by piece my whole body underwent a disintegration. I watched it all as dispassionately as if a movie were taking place – even though I was aware it was "me". I was coming undone!

In the second dream, I saw a fetus. Now the fetus looked like a baby in the mother's womb, attached to the umbilical cord. The unusual thing about this dream is that the baby was made only of an etheric energy and it was floating in the cosmos – in the middle of a sea of stars. The umbilical cord was connected to the cosmic sky. Once again, it was very "personal" to me.

The third dream was very strange. It appeared again as a dream taking place in a cosmic background. But out of the background of the cosmos, there emerged the form of a giant energy based female breast. The breast appeared to nourish the child, and again I was aware that the child was me.

This was indeed a very strange trilogy of dreams to experience. As I contemplated the series of messages, it was "obvious" to me that a message of death and rebirth was being delivered. Its scale of cosmic proportion was a bit sensational – but I knew it was a very important element in the dream. It was a spiritually inspired death and rebirth.

It spoke to me as if the Divine Mother of all life was supporting me in a process of personal transformation. Metaphoric or actual, I felt both humbled and blessed, as the physical world around me fell to pieces – I knew that I would learn to walk again – renewed.

Furry Angels

I would like to next share a few words on Nexus, my dog, and the spiritual significance of animals and pets in our lives.

Nexus was a gorgeous black Great Dane who came to me in a very synchronous fashion. I had decided one weekend, while living in Montreal, to get a dog. I had not had a pet since childhood but I was settled enough to once again have an animal, and this magnificent breed always drew me. So I decided that day I would like to get a Great Dane later that year.

When I arrived at work on Monday morning, during coffee chat before starting the day, I told my nurse Cheryl that I planned to soon get a dog. Cheryl was a great lover of dogs herself, and she was very excited to hear my news.

A few moments later she comes running into my office full of excitement,

"You will never guess what! You will never guess what!"

Cheryl proceeds to tell me the first patient she just spoke to was a young mother. This lady was having complications after the birth of her new baby. She was to be readmitted to the hospital for treatment and her husband would be taking care of the new baby for a few weeks. This young family had also recently adopted two new Great Dane puppies, but "for some reason", she shared with Cheryl that it had now become too much for them. They were looking to find a new home for one of the puppies. Suffice it to say, that same evening Nexus had found her home.

I lived many incredible experiences with this wonderful animal, but in particular there were two very profound experiences, which were pivotally important on my personal journey and revelatory of the healing power of animals in our life.

The first took place one day on Mont Royal in Montreal. I was walking with Nex and had let her off her leash. I loved to give her freedom, and she was usually very well behaved and responsive – so it worked out well. However, it was illegal in the park to unleash your pet! So I counted on her to listen – which she inevitably did, except in this one circumstance!

Nexus loved horses. She would go a little crazy with joy when she saw one. I think she looked up to them, pardon the pun, for there were not too many animals around her in the city bigger than her. But the set up here is that police rode horseback occasionally in the park.

So on this day Nexus was running freely, but when I called her, she would not come back. She saw the horse coming up the main path! I tried to guide her off the main path into a trail but she would not cooperate. I was getting more and more flustered with her in my effort to rein her in and control the situation – but after a few minutes of this I was getting angry. When I finally caught her – I pinned her to the ground and scolded her with an endless array of "bad dog" commentary. Albeit, it was now not Nexus who had misbehaved right?

We had managed to move away from the police who did not pursue us with a ticket. Then, suddenly, out of the blue this man appears from nowhere on the trail and walks by us. He was wearing a fedora, which was a little unusual, and to this day I do not know where he came from and never saw his face. He walked past us and speaks in a gentle wise voice, "There is *never* a good reason to be so angry."

In the moment, I could feel his compassion, and I could feel this intense well of emotion rise in me. I began to sputter a list of justifications that sounded so incredibly stupid – but I was so insistently right! I was angry and my ego reaction was super justified and incredibly huge! Suddenly, I just stopped, and looked at Nexus.

Now, Nexus had become palpably afraid of me. It was the first time she had seen me become so upset with her. She looked right into my eyes with an expression of deep fear and confusion. To her, the whole experience was playful and she could not understand why I was so crazed. I will never forget the unmistakable look of fear in her eyes. Suddenly, I began to cry.

The experience had touched a deep place in me where I could see how emotions like anger are used to control and invoke fear to make life become a certain way. I could see my ego responding with its stories and justifications. It was all so clear to me. Strangely, it seemed like all of the hurt caused in the name of good over the centuries of life on earth was upon me in that moment. I felt a deep shame and sadness.

For three days after this – Nexus remained afraid of me. Every time she looked at me, she mistrusted me. She was not going to let me off easy on this one. Nexus loved to eat – so I thought this would be the route to win back her affection. She would not even take a cookie from me. I could not even bribe her for her love!

A few days later she warmed back up to me, but she was instrumental in teaching me a very big lesson. I have been frustrated many times since that day – but I would never again be able to be unconsciously angry. I have been angry, but not without quickly coming to my senses about how foolish it usually was, and why I was doing it. It was time to live and let live. Animals are often the vectors to bring healing to us, as I have come to witness in countless stories that many people have shared.

Over the years, I lived many other incredible moments with this animal, as anyone who has a pet they love will understand. A second experience I will share, which was pivotal for my growth in awareness, occurred when Nexus died. Her death was a painful, unexpected and a very profound experience. She was only 4 years old when it occurred. Yet, it did occur during a monumental change in my life as shared earlier, and during what I would term a spiritual awakening process. Yet once again, at the threshold of death, I was touched by incredible grace. I was beginning to think - what is it with this death thing? I mean really! ☺

Nex became ill with ITP (idiopathic thrombocytopenic purpura). This process destroyed all of the platelets in her blood, which makes it impossible for her body to control bleeding. The irony here, remembering my first mystical experience in med school, was why the "intelligence" I understood in that encounter, was not available to intervene – to stop this process of bleeding. "Why was it *failing* to stop it now?" Well, because it can, does not mean that it should. As painful as loss is, there is a greater plan that we must sometimes respect in the process.

During the few days prior to her diagnosis, she began to develop large bruises and bumps, and was passing blood. We brought her to the local veterinarian for assessment and they were unable to diagnose what was happening. They asked us to take her to the veterinary university in the city. Here they were able to figure out what was occurring. They put her on steroids and kept her in the animal ICU unit.

She was failing to respond. Instinctively I knew there was nothing that could be done, except understand and accept the unfolding events, and provide comfort. This was difficult to accept, but in my heart I knew it was true. After several days of suffering, we decided to euthanize her because she was suffering greatly by this time.

She was very weak, but I felt so much that I wanted to take her outside for a little while, just to breathe and feel the fresh air. She loved to run in the tall grass, and I had seen a field outside the hospital.

With permission of the veterinarian, we decided to take her outside. She stood up and followed me to the field. We sauntered through the grass and she dopily gazed around and took it all in. I knew she was so happy.

Now, what I didn't realize immediately is that beside the field were the horse "patients"! As Nexus noticed them, she went over to the fence beside the horses, and a beautiful brown gelding came over to see us, or I should say *her*, and bent down. The horse brought his face right up to Nexus, and together they rubbed noses! It was so magical to witness. Tears filled my eyes. A mixture of profound joy, and deep sadness, filled my heart simultaneously.

The horse raised his head and made a little bow gesture, and turned and walked away. Nexus slowly turned around and licked my hand with her very parched tongue.

I asked the veterinarian if he would be able to allow us to give Nex the injection outside where she so loved to be. He was a young vet, in his last year of schooling. He had never done this, but was very happy to try to make it happen, and got permission.

Nexus was lying on a blanket in the grass, using the little energy she had left to sniff the occasional breeze, and work to breathe. I was heartbroken to have to live this.

As she lay there, she turned for a moment and looked directly in my eyes. I will never forget the love I felt in that moment. There were streams of it coming out of her eyes, and right into mine – to my heart. I could feel the energy she was sending me. I could feel the energy I was sending to her. It was amazing!

I knew in this instant, she was telling me it was okay, and things needed to be this way. Understanding fails, but wisdom knows. My heart, however, still felt broken.

As the gentle and wonderful young vet did his work, Nex slowly closed her eyes. She passed from this world lying in the grass where she loved to run free, by the horses she so loved to admire, with her human "poppa" who loved her more than words could say.

Footsteps through the Veil

In the days that followed Nexus' death, I would intermittently hear her giant footsteps, which sounded like a huge pair of shuffling slippers, coming down the hallway. I would look up, and I could see glimpses of her etheric form standing in the hallway. This happened several times in the next few days. I had never lived this before, and was astounded, as you can easily imagine – seeing her energy body standing there!

On the third day, I woke up in the morning, intuitively knowing that she would be leaving this day, and I would not see her energy form again. Whatever happened, it felt like she stayed for a few days to comfort me. Through the sadness I felt a sense of peace and acceptance. It was as if she knew now I would be "okay", and I felt her leave the space. She has, however, never left my heart.

Many people have spoken about amazing experiences of life and/or healing that occur through animals and in particular their pets. I have absolute certainty in this reality, and believe these magnificent creatures great and small are with us not only as companions but healing presences. I share these moments with you as a testament to the animals that grace our lives, and the teachings they have brought to me and to many.

Shedding

In the months that first followed my earlier energy session, I also began to have a series of other "clearing" type experiences – on a very physical level – that I will never forget. I felt relatively well, but very fatigued, energetically - yet I had elements of flu-like illness that carried on and on and on. I had diarrhea. I peed incessantly. I had rashes that came and went. Little aches and pains that surfaced, and passed away. And I coughed! I not only coughed – I coughed mucous. I mean mucous and then more mucous – for months! This continued to the point I had to carry a cup in my car for spasms of coughing – or "mucous volcanoes" as I called them – for fear of expectorating all over someone or something. It was unbelievable!

As this clearing process took place, I felt a great deal lighter. I also noted that the exercise-induced asthma, to which I was subject to as a child, was gone. I felt as if I had achieved a new "energetic baseline" in my life.

I also experienced elements of emotional clearing. I particularly recall a poignant experience during one of the sessions with Pierre when we were reciprocating energy work.

I recall laying on the treatment table and all of a sudden this profound wave of energy passed over and through me. My heart, or as we will discuss shortly, my heart chakra, began to pulse and contract. Suddenly it "popped", and I began to cry. And, I do mean cry! I sobbed with this deep guttural sadness that seemed to open in my heart and I cried to release sadness from somewhere very deep within me. I was nearly convulsing with the emotion and tears. It lasted for about 5 minutes. Afterwards, I was exhausted.

This experience was profound for me, because the tears were layers of emotions that I had restrained in myself. There were layers of sadness I did not even know I carried in me – but they were so present, deep in my energy. It was the first conscious release of restrained emotion I had ever experienced – and it was incredible.

What I found very peculiar about it, was that unlike with the past life recall experiences I had, this emotion was much stronger and very deep – "old" is the word that comes to mind. Yet I did not really recall specific events of any kind that created it. It was mostly a deep sadness – like a multilayered coalescent ball of gunk that had accumulated in my heart over time. I lay on the table for quite some time after this session peacefully, and spent. It was an incredibly liberating experience.

Later I was aware of how this unrecognized sadness had dampened so many experiences in my life. It was truly blocking the ability to love, and to feel connected through my heart. This helped me understand how powerful our emotions can be – and how painful experiences can lead us to close down and suppress ourselves as we hold this energy within our selves, and create restrictions. These restrictions block us from recognizing our truer deep spiritual nature and distort the way we bring ourselves to the world.

We will examine this aspect of healing in the upcoming chapters. Sometimes these latent patterns are so embedded in our psyche, and the emotional patterns are so strongly identified as our personality – we do not even understand these blockages exist in our energy, or how they can affect our lives.

I lived many "aha" type moments through these sessions with Pierre and the experiences we shared as a group – and it was a very rich time in my life. I also developed an important friendship that was pivotal in my life and my spiritual development.

School of the Ego

This friendship provided me with the opportunity to experience spiritual healing work with a kindred spirit. We "practiced" on each other and friends around us, and began teaching a course to share the knowledge we had been given. A small group formed around us which was a wonderful experience of community sharing – but eventually "ego forces" took hold and the group disseminated.

This was a particularly difficult time in my life for me. I found myself to be living through so many amazing experiences, and it was incredibly rich to be able to share them with like-minded people. I did not understand that this type of gathering is also formed of a group of souls, who are each on their own healing journey. This created a group of support, but also a group in need of experiences to see deeply inside of them selves, in search of healing. This is spiritually appropriate, for it forms a prism and a mirror so each person can see elements within their own psyche that are based in ego consciousness, as we will explore later.

Fears, control, manipulation, dishonesty, pride, and shame – you name it – all surfaces. From a higher perspective of spirit – it is the creation of a deep healing process. Events occurred, helping us each see ourselves. I was deeply hurt by several events through this process, events that could not be controlled or understood, and simply had to pass. A part of me "shut down" or retreated for a few years after this time. It was a period of deep and rich personal learning.

With time, release, and understanding – comes healing. One comes to learn that you must deeply trust the process life that dances around you as your own important creation – for it is personal and deeply meaningful to your growth and development. This is true, even if you don't immediately understand why! As hurts are healed, and the heart can again open – one begins to understand that an open heart with a wise mind is the only defense needed.

During this time I did a lot of work and research on the psychodynamic aspects of healing and looked into the mirror of my own fears and reactions. I learned how the forces of fear do promote separation and how we draw to ourselves into experiences with noble souls with whom we will play out our experiences. This will ultimately help us to see ourselves and transcend our own limitations.

In every way I had been either perceptibly hurt or humbled, I have learned to love a little greater. I am still a student of this process! I can say however today I see things differently and approach them differently – through the grace of understanding I have been given.

Our experiences are purposeful, and meant to liberate us from limiting patterns, beliefs, fears and contractions – as it mirrors us to ourselves. It provides opportunities to practice a wisdom that comes with spiritual maturity.

In walking through these, and many unreferenced experiences, I know I developed a deep compassion for the confusion of the human experience. I also learned that opening our self, even in the face of hurt or pain, to grow – is essential in healing. If we are not open we cannot love. If we cannot love, we cannot heal.

Templates from the Stars

The next event in my life that was incredibly important and informative for me – and also instrumental in the work I will present later on Unity Field Healing – came to me through exposure to Lee Carroll's work with Kryon. At a conference I attended with Lee, I had the privilege to meet Peggy and Steve Dubro, and their beautiful work with "EMF Balancing Technique®".[16]

Peggy is pretty much love incarnate – a bubbly, grounded, heart-based, wise woman who had travelled her own journey of awakening. Through her experiences she began to teach this energy system integration and personal development. [16]

The energy work Peggy has produced is very fascinating, in that it does not simply work with the chakra system that we will explore later – it works with an energy lattice entitled the universal calibration lattice. At that time, EMF Balancing Technique® involved learning four phases of integration, working hands-on with energy as a practitioner through a patterned process, using a conscious "connection" to this lattice. By this point in my life I already had some pretty peculiar experiences, and I had the occasional opportunity to see energy fields, light, and chakras while doing energy work. But I was not prepared for what started to happen to me during my initiation into this work.

During instruction in the Phase 2 work – which is work focused on releasing the past – I lived an experience that was so palpable, it is forever emblazoned on my mind. In the area of my solar plexus (stomach level), as the work was being performed – I felt a pulling or extraction on my solar plexus that passed deep into my body. It felt like an octopus was being pulled "energetically" through my chakra – there is no other way to explain it.

The energy feeling was sticky and tight and it eventually released. As I relive this experience over and over in my mind, I was very aware in that moment that I was being "released" from coalescent energies that weighted me down and restricted my ability to live fully. It was unexplainable why I would have such a restrictive energy on the basis of only one life. I knew I had a tendency to pull in or withdraw as a means of self-protection. Yet I didn't understand the fears at the root of these reactions.

It seemed such a big part of my psyche that I knew it crossed time boundaries of lifetimes – it was a deep pattern for me, and surely acquired from prior experiences. Now with this release, I felt a new level of freedom and alignment – and a conscious understanding energetically of what it feels like to be in the space of "energetic freedom".

As Peggy explains, she has been taught to work with the templates that support various levels of integrative experience. It is presented so clearly - and in a way that one can grasp and appreciate. This is so valuable and important when talking about unusual things such as energy work or interdimensional quantum healing, which is mostly unseen. Being introduced to the concept of "a light template" and working with structured interdimensional light would become essential in grasping the potential contained in Unity Field Healing when presented to me many years later.

I became one of the early trained teachers of this work, which I remember with great fondness. Peggy and Steve have continued to share this knowledge and work with an international audience. The work has grown since that time into 12 phases. I would encourage anyone who is intrigued, to experience and become familiar with this work. [16]

Plugging into Cosmic DNA

Around the same time in my life, I began to experience the first of what I have come to refer to as interdimensional visions. These are meditative visions in which I am shown the passage of energy between layers of dimensional energy. These visions, when they occur appear on a dark blue "cosmic" backdrop and involve the appearance of light pyramids, which allow energy to move through a veil of perception. I will explain this more fully in Chapter 11.

In this vision, I first saw a filament of white luminous iridescent light, descend through a light pyramid, and connect with me energetically – at the crown of my head.

As it connected, the fiber began to scintillate and wobble, and it broke open in a pair of two filaments that formed in a helical braid – just like a strand of DNA double helix. This strand was pulsing or scintillating with light of a "starlight" quality.

I could then see the development of multiple fine strands of light within the larger strands as it formed an expanding double helix. It was "connecting" or "activating" – and at the same time it was in the process of visual revelation. I believe what I saw was actually a representation of higher dimensional or cosmic DNA – which I like to refer to as spiritual DNA. We will explore the significance of this experience a little more deeply when we examine Unity Field Healing later in the book.

Living and Learning

In the years that followed, I became intensely interested in what is known today as vibrational or energetic healing, and all things related to it. I became interested in Sacred Geometry and was fascinated to learn of the simple and complex geometric patterns that fundamentally serve as the interdimensional building blocks for all of creation.[34] I also became interested in spiritual teachings from all traditions – Christianity, Buddhism, Islam, Judaism, Hindu, the Vedas - you name it. It became clear how every teaching of wisdom that has pervaded the earth has a central theme of unity, oneness and love.

It also became clear how far the religions have fallen in some ways, from the true meaning created at the inception of the teachings. It is disheartening to see now how radical factions fight in their most polarized and disfigured forms – contrary to everything the original founders taught.

I also became interested in past civilizations like "myths" of Lemuria and Atlantis. I did not feel compelled to discover them or find them – but to relate to them – knowing in my heart they existed, and they have stories to tell and teach.

I became interested in the emerging scientific paradigm of quantum physics and the amazing influence I know this will have on scientific development in the years ahead. I love to see science explain the interdimensionality that mystics have talked of for thousands of years. It is fascinating to hear of scientific concepts, which support the power of consciousness and coherence of love, to alter reality and matter.

Along the way, I discovered the work of a fascinating gentleman, Masaru Emoto, who developed rapid freeze techniques to assess the crystal formation in water. His work demonstrates images of the crystalline structure in the water before and after it was influenced by a positive or a negative attribute of consciousness. [18]

Water is the most foundational element on our planet and comprises the vast majority of our bodies and living systems. His work visibly demonstrates the coherence that develops in the crystalline structure of water - when qualities of love, hope peace, healing and various positive influences are projected upon it. It also demonstrates the disorder that develops in the crystalline order when water is polluted or when negative consciousness influences are projected upon it.

We have all heard of the power of love, kindness, and compassion as a general spiritual recommendation. This work is a visual testimonial of the power of love, kindness and all things good. It is fascinating to think what happens within us, ourselves, as walking "cities of water" influenced by consciousness!

All of this wisdom had a major influence on me in my days of awakening.

Symbols from the Future

As years passed by and I integrated the above information personally, I became somewhat intrigued by the crop circle phenomenon. For those who are unfamiliar, crop circles are complex geometries that appear around the world, and very commonly in England in the wheat fields of farms. These patterns appear very quickly and contain highly complex geometric symbols and complex mathematical formulas that have obvious connection to the principles of sacred geometrical arrangements underlying the formation of life.

These crops circles can be understood to represent organized energy signatures or symbols. They carry an energy signature that vibrates or resonates, and has a vibratory influence on energetic order on the planet.

This becomes a little more understandable when you can grasp the effect of sound and vibrations on energy as demonstrated through the science of cymatics, which we will explore in the next chapter, and also in exploring some of the mystical experiences people live in the direct presence of newly imprinted patterns.

We can begin to appreciate that light templates, which we will discuss, are "living energy geometries". It is a bridge to understanding how in consciousness we could learn to activate a pattern to vibrationally influence coherence. This will also become important when we examine the template of Unity Field Healing later in the book.

Synthesis - It All Comes Together

In recent years, I had been very "grounded", working in a very down to earth 3D environment, a bit removed in appearances from the lofty world of DNA integration.

In addition to more esoteric healing work, I was led to return to train and work in a new discipline of medicine for me, diagnostic imaging. This meant going back to school, which seemed a peculiar inspiration at the time, but I followed my instinct. With the demands of this work, my life settled into a very 3D plane for a while, and these geometric visions passed – as I worked through a few challenging years of being a resident trainee once again!

However, one day in 2011 I lived a very unusual experience, which opened a new doorway and served as a force of guidance to begin a new deeper level of healing work than I had previously known. It occurred during a seminar sponsored by James Tyberonn. Tyb, as he is affectionately known, is a geologist and mineral expert as well as deeply entrenched in the world of spiritual transformation. The conference organized was referred to as the "11:11:11" event – Nov 11, 2011.

This event was a very powerful energetic event, with a palpable sense of deep spiritual significance and power. Two important things occurred for me on a personal level in addition to the focus of the conference. First, I met a crystal skull, named Max. Secondly, I was provided with a visionary experience that would begin again to transform my life.

Now, despite the vast array of unusual experiences I had lived in my life, I was a little skeptical about the idea of the importance of a crystal skull. I thought it was a Hollywood flavored idea based on the 2012 phenomenon. I had the opportunity to meditate with Max during the conference, which in retrospect seemed to be a preparation for a series of visions that I would subsequently encounter, leading to my work with Unity Field Healing.

Max is believed to be an Ancient Crystal Skull. Many consider him, including the British Museum, to be one of the rarest artifacts found. He is estimated to be 10,000 years old – but no one truly can discern the age of this skull by scientific methods. It is also believed that Mayan priests in Guatemala used Max in healing and prayer ceremonies.

The skull was given to Norbu Chen, a powerful healer of the Tibetan sect of Red Hat Lamas. Lama Norbu studied in the tiny Asian nation of Sikkim with his teacher, Lama Norbu Lampas, and in Guatemala with Mayan priests, where he came into the presence of Max.

Norbu was given the skull when he left the Mayans to continue on his path as a healer. His travels took him to Houston, Texas, where he started a healing foundation. It was during this time that JoAnn and Carl Parks met the lama through their family medical doctor when their twelve-year-old daughter, Diana, was terminally ill with bone cancer.

JoAnn ended up working for the foundation and the lama for many years. Before Norbu died, he gave the cherished crystal skull to the Parks family with no explanation except that someday when the time was right, they would know what the crystal skull was all about.

JoAnn did not know what to do with the crystal skull, so she placed it in a box in her closet for many years. Through a series of personal events, she was eventually shown about her work with Max.[41]

JoAnn travels extensively, making Max available to seekers, for their own personal experiences.

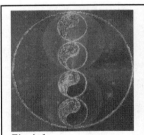

Fig 4-1
Unity Field Healing Template

Many who have been in the presence of the various, now famous, crystal skulls have reportedly had a range of experiences including receiving instantaneous healing, information, visions of other worlds and the experience of higher states of consciousness and expanded intuitive abilities.

Whether real, or in my imagination, my experience with Max seemed highly pertinent, as I prepared unknowingly to have a series of visions (Fig 4-1) that would guide the development of Unify Field Healing. I will review this in more detail in Chapter 11.

THE CIRCLE IS A SPIRAL

I will draw a close here to the circle of events that have led me to this point in my life. Yet, the circle breaks open to a spiral, for it is time to share. In doing so, I will add that I realize some of this information is a little peculiar to someone who is unfamiliar with these topics or experiences. Years ago, it would surely have been so to me.

This is not, of course, a complete chronology of all the influential experiences I have lived. But, the elements of these experiences have carved and catalyzed the view of life, spirituality and healing that I have today. They were able to ground concepts and ideas that were esoteric for me, in a mystical way that could never be planned. Those selected experiences are meaningfully provided to reassure those who have had similar events in their life. They also serve to highlight some profound healing concepts, and potentials it unfolds, which we will next examine.

Each and every single one of us has our own, uniquely tailored experiences that are crafted through our higher self to take us along our path, to teach us and help us grow. Some are perceptibly *positive* experiences and uplifting, others are *negative* and can teach us through understanding. Yet, all are pertinent – and personally meaningful in the school of life and spiritual growth.

It is important to honor your own spiritual experiences and your intuitive guidance. Your experiences are tailor-crafted for you. Listen to your intuitive whispers, and follow your passion and your synchronicities. Allow the spiritual force of life to take you by the hand – to teach and to reveal.

Let the energy of this project also support you, in your own unique and magnificent journey of life, as you unwrap layer by layer, the light that is your truest nature and the love that supports our entire existence. Every molecule, every atom, every breath.

PART II

ENERGY, CONSCIOUSNESS AND THE HUMAN ENERGY SYSTEM

CHAPTER 5
LIFE IS AN ENERGY AND CONSCIOUSNESS BASED REALITY

"If you want to find the secrets of the universe, think in terms of energy, frequency and vibration."

— *Nikola Tesla*

To discuss the potential of energy based healing, it will be useful to first understand a few basic energy and consciousness concepts. The information provided in this section will help solidify an awareness of the truly energetic nature of our physical reality.

When we speak of energy we often think of invisible forces, like electricity and heat. However, all things are ultimately made up of energy, even things which visibly comprise our physical reality. This includes our physical body and all of the "bodies of energy" we will explore in the upcoming section. Understanding this energetic foundation facilitates an acceptance of the ability to transform both "solid" and "non-solid" or "visible" and "invisible" energy forms through energetic interactions.

As we gain a better appreciation of the energetic foundation of reality and the implicit forces of order, we will examine how DNA is implicated in the human energy paradigm. We will also examine an understanding that the "form world" is an expression of consciously organized energy systems. We will expand this concept by looking at *consciousness* and *sacred geometry* as ordering forces to better conceptualize that there is systematic order in living systems.

I would preface this section by adding that one does not really need to be a physics scholar to perform or benefit from the tools of Energy Medicine. This understanding is helpful for many, because it adds context, and a language to speak in energy terms. Please do not feel overwhelmed or burdened if the following information is too scientific or dry. Many people work very well with energy healing techniques, both for personal use and providing sessions, with very limited understanding of physics.

Healing, itself, is a very natural process. We know "how" to heal inherently within our nature. If you were to cut yourself, there is an inherent intelligence that steps in to heal the injury. You do not consciously need to know how it works. When we begin working with energy based healing, a similar concept applies.

In some of the new modalities that are emerging on the planet, the energy itself is conscious to a person's intent. As illogical as this may sound, there is an inherent intelligence participating in many of the new energy processes. This intelligence understands how to support each of us uniquely, and guide healing changes appropriately. As odd as this may seem, and counter-logical to any traditional healing practices, it works in alignment with the integrity of spirit and the intention of the person receiving healing work.

In bringing forward these new processes, we are piercing a veil of prior conscious limitation. Really, we are facilitating the integration of light and energy from a spiritual plane. We are allowing it to move into this world from another "dimension" of life, somehow parallel to this one. We are part of that spiritual level of life; in fact, we are each continuous with this it. The time, it seems, is simply ripe to let this energy into our world. But understanding can be fun, so let's move forward and explore energy!

The Energetic Nature of Life

Everything is Energy

You are likely familiar with the phrase that *everything is energy*. Let us explore this concept, starting with two ideas. The first is a "huge" concept – contained in the equation developed by Einstein: $E=mc^2$. The second is a very "small particle": the atom.

In this famous equation derived by Einstein, we are introduced to mass-energy equivalence. If we look at the components of the equation we are shown that energy in a fixed system is constant. Energy (E) is a product of the mass (m) of an object and a fixed constant (c), which in the setting of our known reality is the speed of light squared.

Now mass and light are not entirely interchangeable. Yet, the equation helps us to appreciate that a relationship exists between mass and energy such that if mass is lost, energy is gained. Conversely, energy can be condensed to mass. If anyone is dealing with a "battle of the bulge", this latter idea may be easy to understand! ☺ But the equation introduces a profound concept: matter is energy in a "condensed" or "lower vibratory" form.

It follows that if matter is indeed energy – perhaps it is more subject to subtle energetic influences than solid "non energetic appearing" matter would seem at first to be. It is relatively easy for us to see the influence of matter on matter. For example think of a billiard ball striking another billiard ball and setting it in to motion. Something tangible and real affects something tangible and real. We can also grasp how a non-material energy can do this. For example, a strong breeze blowing might set lawn furniture in motion. We do not see the wind, but can feel it and can certainly witness the effect of the wind on what is seen.

In energy based healing, what we must open our mind to is the idea that "subtle" energy – an energy that we do not always see or feel exists; and, it has a potential healing influence on our body and energy system. This energy can be introduced into the energy system of your body and have an energetic influence at an invisible level. From this invisible level, it may then have a tangible influence on your body and your physical world.

Based on this simple principle, if we consider that matter comprising the tissues of the body is really energy in a condensed form – we can grasp why introducing energy into the body might have an impact on what at first seems so solid and fixed. The reason this becomes so important is that conscious energy, introduced in a therapeutic way, can have a healing influence on both the energy and matter of our body and our life.

Let us put this discussion on hold for a moment, while we look at a second concept.

THE ATOMIC NATURE OF LIFE

The atom is a basic component of all life. It is also an ideal place to begin to understand the interface between things that are apparently solid or visible, and the proven awareness that all is really energy.

The structural physical world – the one we see everyday – is made up of solid materials. However, the organic and inorganic solids, liquids and gaseous substances that make up this visible life are composed of small particles referred to as molecules. Water, for example, is made up of water molecules.

Molecules define the characterizing unit of a chemical substance. Molecules arise from combinations of *elements*. There are approximately 100 different known atomic elements, which you may remember from chemistry class. These elements are organized into the *Periodic Table of Elements*. In the case of water, a combination of 2 hydrogen and 1 oxygen elements, combine to make H_2O.

These elements that combine to produce molecules, are made of even smaller energy "particles" called *atoms*. Atoms are composed of a nucleus, which contains smaller "particles" called protons and neutrons, as well as electrons. Electrons orbit in a field around the nucleus and are understood to spin around the nucleus in defined levels of relationship or valence.

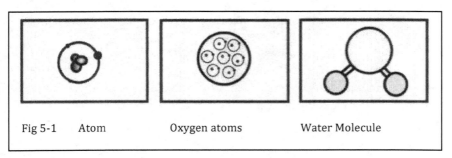

Fig 5-1   Atom   Oxygen atoms   Water Molecule

Atoms become more and more complex as the number of protons, neutrons and electrons grows.

Electrons in the atom carry a negative charge. They are held in orbit by an electromagnetic attraction to the positively charged nucleus. The positively charged nucleus is created through the positively charged protons it contains. The orbiting electrons can absorb or release energy, flux to different levels of orbit, or completely leave a molecule, under the right circumstances and energy influences. Hence, adding energy to, or taking energy away from the electrons can alter the composition and energy of the atom.

Everything we see as solid is really composed of a vast organized field of these tiny charged particles called atoms. We are able to exist in our bodies, and in this reality, by virtue of "the atom".

Beginning at the atom and moving up to elements, molecules and material substances – things take on the properties of solid, liquid or gas. These substances obey laws of chemistry and physics with which we are familiar.

The atom was once felt to represent the smallest particle of matter. Science subsequently discovered that this is not so. In the last century, science has ventured below the level of the atom into the subatomic world. Within the atom, a vast array of subatomic particles, forces and dimensions (that can boggle the mind!) exist. There are smaller particles than the atom, and *forces*, which bear on the nature of the atom.

Atoms form through these subatomic particles and forces – through energetic relationships. Yet these relationships obey a different set of laws in physics, than the laws that typically define solid reality. It is a bit beyond the scope of this book to enter into a deep scientific discussion, but these particles and forces are considered *quantum* in nature.

Quantum objects relate according to mysterious laws and probabilities, and are subject to consciousness forces that may operate upon them. At the level of quantum understanding – life exists as both matter and energy. It exists as matter – in the form of particles; and as energy – in the state of waves. Dimensions of probable reality also exist, beyond the one we commonly see.

Atoms can be thought to take on a more "solid appearance" as these subatomic particles coalesce into form, under the influence of conscious order. An atom is like a condensed waveform that appears solid to our eyes. Everything we see is really an oscillating energy, patterning itself into form substance. The atom, serves as the gateway between the "material" world and the "energetic" one – a bridge between the conceptual world of energy and the visible world or "reality".

THE ELECTRONIC ATOM AND AN ELECTROMAGNETIC ENERGY FIELD

The atom, because of the electrical charges it contains, can also be viewed as *electromagnetic* in nature. The protons carry a positive charge and the neutrons have zero charge – creating a net positive electric pole in the nucleus. Electrons spin around the nucleus, which carry a negative charge. This is its most stable state in which an atom can exist. The electromagnetic interactions occurring between the particles, however, create a small *electromagnetic field.*

In simple terms, electricity is the result of electrons moving in a current toward a positive pole by electromagnetic attraction or repulsion. When electrons flow around an atom they create a small magnetic field.

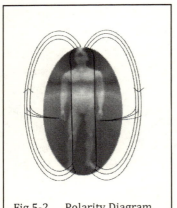

Fig 5-2   Polarity Diagram

When they flow through an electrical field along a chain of atoms, or conductor, they create a larger magnetic field. By this mechanism, the human body, composed of a vast array of atoms, and it has a subtle electromagnetic field around it. To better understand this principle see Fig 5-2 that demonstrates the flow of energy in this electromagnetic arrangement in the human body as discussed in polarity therapy.[48]

So if we can accept the energetic nature of all mass or matter, realize the atomic nature of the matter in the human body, appreciate the generation of an electromagnetic field in the human body – we have taken three simple but foundational steps to begin to see life energetically.

CRACKING NEWTON'S SHELL

We have introduced the scientific understanding that things above the level of the atom operate a little differently than things below the level the atom.

On this basis, physics as a science can be broken up into *above atomic* and *subatomic* categories. These are more commonly referred to as "Newtonian based physics" or Classic Mechanics and "Non Newtonian based physics" or Quantum Mechanics.

Classic mechanics is the physics you may have learned in school. This is the physics of forces and physical laws. It applies to objects and objects in motion. Familiar definitions such as velocity, work, acceleration, and speed are derived from this study – as well as our understanding of gravity and electromagnetics.

These theoretical concepts in classic mechanics accurately explain physical relationships and forces – as long as the parameters of motion are below the speed of light and larger than atomic in size. Things that may occur in the human body, above the atomic level, can also be well explained by terms of this science.

For example, the gravity that pulls you to the floor if you trip, and the electricity that pulses the human heart to sustain life - are fine examples of classic mechanics in action. This is where most of science (until recent times), and the explanations behind traditional medical diagnosis and treatment, are found.

When trying to define physics below the atomic level, the same laws of physics do not apply. Particles at the subatomic level take on wave-particle qualities of behavior and are more reliably explained in terms of quantum physics and quantum theory.

In the early days of quantum exploration, the wave-particle duality was proposed due to the uncertainty whether subatomic particles exist as particles (solid) or as waves (energy). This wave-particle duality postulates that subatomic particles may be presented as particles, when manifest – and in a waveform, when not materialized into form.

This theory actually began with explorations into the nature of light. When light was first being studied scientifically, it was not clear whether light existed in discrete quanta or photons (a particle) – or – if it existed in the form of an electromagnetic wave in the light spectrum (a wave). Light appeared to do both – acting as both matter and energy.

The particle-wave concept expanded into quantum physics, when it became clearer that matter as well as light also has wave and particle properties at the atomic interface. Quantumly speaking, it is as if things are only energetic probabilities, until some force of consciousness manifests it into form as a defined potential - to make it perceivably solid, or what we might term as real!

The importance of this concept is that it vaporizes a world that is strictly solid – commonly called "Newtonian" – into a world where particles arise from probability states, and require a consciousness factor to hold them in form. It implies - life is based on consciousness, as well as energy.

The world we see is one of out-pictured "probability" and it is energetic rather than strictly solid in nature. It is not limited in its transformative nature as previously imagined. Through the doorway of this basic premise enters many interesting ideas and possibilities of how externalized form can be *trans*formed by energy and by consciousness. One sizeable guest through this doorway is Energy Medicine.

ENERGY BASICS

In exploring any type of energy healing modality, processes invariably involve subtle or interdimensional *energy*. This energy is often referred to as subtle, because it arises from a level outside of our everyday sensory awareness. The energy will however interact with our bodies, and it will ultimately have some impact on the "real world" that we see and know.

These energy modalities imply the use of energy interactions that filter down to a level of form. To understand how this translation might occur, there are a few straightforward energy principles that are helpful to understand. We will examine a few of them including *forms of energy*, the *wave principles* of wavelength, amplitude, frequency, oscillation and resonant frequency, *resonance* and its implications, *entrainment and entanglement*, the human *sensory capacity*, and the concept of the human *DNA quantum fields*. These ideas will provide us with a language to use in our later discussions.

E*nergy* has many forms. We have already mentioned electromagnetic energy, but energy exists also in other *forms*. For example, it exists as heat as thermal energy. It exists as mechanical energy – when a force imposes on a mass object as work. It exists as chemical energy – such as the potential energy stored in molecular bonding. Light is a form of electromagnetic energy; and, sound is a form of mechanical energy.

In describing electro-magnetic energy, the *wavelength* describes the distance between two successive waves in a typical sinusoidal wave. The *amplitude* measures the height or displacement of the wave. This defines the power. The *frequency* defines the measure of repeating waves in a time frame such as cycles per second or Hertz (Hz).

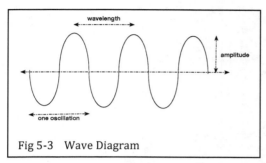

Fig 5-3   Wave Diagram

The electromagnetic spectrum defines the range of all possible frequencies of electromagnetic radiation. This includes very low frequencies, with long wavelengths that cycle in meters. This type of electromagnetic energy is used to transmit radio-signals. It also includes high frequency ultra violet and gamma frequencies such as found in sunlight. And, it includes energy of wavelengths between and beyond these parameters. Visible light is a form of electromagnetic energy.

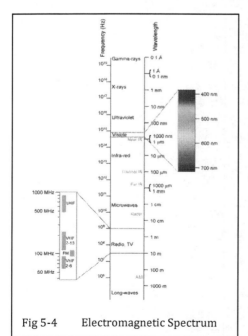

Fig 5-4   Electromagnetic Spectrum

The human eye is capable of sensing light within a very specific range of electromagnetic frequency, referred to as the "visible spectrum". This is not the whole electromagnetic energy spectrum. It is the range of electromagnetic energy that can interact with the sensors in the human eye and create projected images of color and space. This includes energy only within the wavelength of 400 - 700 nanometers (nm).

Although this is a very small part

of the electromagnetic spectrum, it is a very important part of the spectrum. It defines the segment of the spectrum in which we primarily live with visual awareness. If electromagnetic energy is outside of this range, it is most often imperceptible to sight and most senses.

Within the visible range of light, different frequencies along the spectrum correspond to different colors of light. If all the frequencies between 400 and 700 are included simultaneously, the blend produces white light. If the light were separated into a spectrum of frequencies, various focal points of frequency would appear as different colors to the human eye. This is best demonstrated as light passes through a prism.

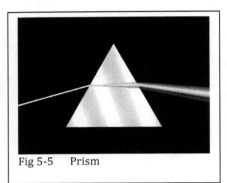

Fig 5-5   Prism

White light contains all of the frequencies in the visible range. As it passes through a prism, it fractionates into spectral frequencies creating a rainbow of red- orange- yellow- green- blue- indigo- violet (Fig 5-5). We will revisit this fact later when we discuss the human chakra system

When we examine the human sense of hearing, we encounter a similar phenomenon. Sound is a mechanical energy, which is derived from sound waves hitting the eardrum. This produces a mechanical-neurologic translation. Sound waves are introduced into a medium like air or water, from a source such as the human voice or a musical instrument. Sound waves are created as the energy displaces the medium in which they travel.

Sound will have characteristic frequencies defined by the frequency of the wave, measured again in Hertz (Hz), or cycles per second. The typical young human ear is capable of registering sounds, which occur in the range of 20 – 20,000 Hz. If sounds are produced with frequency below 20 Hz they are infrasonic. If they are above 20,000 Hz they are ultrasonic. If sound waves between 20 and 20,000 Hz strike the eardrum, the ear, and its associated neurologic processing, will produce a perceived sound.

You may have had the experience of having a medical ultrasound examination. In this process, an ultrasonic wave (above the sensory threshold of hearing) is being introduced into your body. The machine's transducer detects reflective sounds (echoes), which are returned as the sound reflects from tissues in the body. These sound beams are then converted into digitized images based on how the tissues in the body transmits, absorbs or reflects the sound beam.

While this is occurring, you do not hear the sound wave because its frequency is too high to register in your ear. The energy of the sound however, interacts with the structural energy of our bodies, to create data that can be converted into an image.

The effect of a dog whistle is based on the same phenomena. Dogs are capable of registering sounds above the upper human threshold. A dog's auditory reality is "bigger" than a human beings reality – hence they live in an expanded auditory sensory reality.

Touch, smell and taste are similar. Regardless of the sense we are considering – we do not perceive the full range of energy that exists in our environment. Our perceived "reality" is limited to the "sense capable" energy ranges in which we normally function.

People sometimes develop the capacity to perceive energies that are outside the normal spectral ranges. You may have heard the terms clairvoyant or clairaudient – meaning "clear vision" or "clear hearing". These people can see or hear energy that is outside of normal perception. People may also have clairsentience (touch), clairaliance (smelling), clairgustation (taste), and claricognizance (knowing) as extrasensory abilities.

Oscillation is defined as the repetitive variation of a measure around a central point or between two stable points. It applies, for example, to a pendulum in a clock. The term, however, applies equally to other phenomena such as alternating electrical current, or the diurnal variation in circadian rhythm in the human body. In a mechanical sense the term often used is *vibration*. These are both measured in frequency.

The *natural frequency* of an object is defined as the frequency or set of frequencies with which it tends to vibrate if activated. This can be seen when you pluck a string on a guitar, or blow wind over the opening of a glass bottle, or strike a tuning fork.

The *harmonic* of a wave is a component frequency that is an integer multiple of a fundamental frequency. For example if a fundamental frequency is 10 Hz, the frequency of harmonics are 20 Hz, 30 Hz, 40 Hz and so forth. Two 10 Hz cycles are within one 20 Hz cycle, three 10 Hz cycles in one 30 Hz cycle, and two 20 Hz cycles in one 40 Hz cycle and so forth. All such frequencies are periodic at the fundamental 10 Hz frequency. In the example of 10 Hz, 20 Hz is the first overtone and second harmonic.

Sounds can be produced in harmonic or partial harmonics with multiple overtones creating rich vibratory signatures. Specific frequencies are sometimes selected because of the known vibratory influence on the human bio-field. If you explore sound therapy or the ancient teaching of mantra, you will learn about this. One of many excellent references for those who may be interested in exploring more information on sound in healing is in Jonathan Goldman's work.[27]

Resonance is the tendency of a system to oscillate or vibrate at greater amplitude at specific frequencies. These are termed resonant frequencies. A system can store energy at these frequencies if a repetitive force is applied.

An interesting phenomenon occurs with resonance. If you take an object such as a tuning fork and activate it, it will create a field of vibration around it. This vibration is resonant with its key frequency – say for example 256 Hz. If this occurs, other objects in the environment can experience sympathetic resonance. A second tuning fork of the same key signature, 256 Hz, will begin to vibrate. If we were to dampen the first tuning fork, the second fork would continue to ring and make a sound.

Thus resonance can have an energetic impact by bringing to life resonant energies in a proximal structure. In energy-based therapies, this may be considered by creating sympathetic resonance between healthy and unhealthy vibrational states.

If you think of yourself as an energy field, rather than a physical body, you will understand how it may be influenced by such energy. Our bodies are extremely complex systems of energy with innumerable components. These energetic components have different base frequencies and are more like an orchestra playing. If we subject the body to pure tones and overtones of energy or spectral energy – the body may respond in *resonance* to these vibratory sessions. Resonance helps us conceptualize why sounds or vibrational energies of different types may influence the standing wave patterns in the human energy field. Vibratory stimuli can be used to raise the standing vibration in a field and/or stimulate release of blocked or stagnant restrictions in the energy systems as they are applied.

Imagine though for a moment that you are standing in the presence of a high vibrational, harmonious energy field rich in tone and overtones. This could be a field of music such as a sitar or crystal bowl or gong. As the sounds passes through your energy field – if your energy field is open – it can energetically "reset" your energy field. This can also be achieved by conscious toning – which is introduced in the practice of mantra and various other forms of chanting and toning exercises.

The term resonance is not limited to structural energy support. It can also be used to discuss psychological attributes particularly when discussing energy psychology. Psychological elements of our being would include thoughts and emotions, which we will come to understand, are also energetic in nature.

Psychological resonance may be best understood by example. If you are around someone who is really happy and balanced in his or her energy field, you will feel it. It is difficult to stay negative in the field of this person – unless one is really attached to this lower vibratory state. If you are feeling "down" but are open by nature to the uplifting energy of that person – you can become resonant with it and become uplifted yourself.

We speak of this often in poetic terms when we say thank you to someone who helps us "feel uplifted" in our life. We have responded in resonance. If someone were observing the energy field they would see the emotional resonance and the colors in the field would change or respond.

Resonance as a principle also becomes very meaningful when looking at energy healing modalities that rely on energy that is outside the normal sensory spectrums. If a "healer" is present, in a connected field energy of "high vibration", and sits or works with another human being in conscious intention – the energy is resonantly supportive through the healer, to facilitate healing. It creates a spirit-to-spirit resonance.

This very same principle may be thought to occur if you were in the living presence of a highly evolved enlightened master – such as Buddha or Christ. In this setting, the energy field of this enlightened being is catalytic to another person through "resonance" – to promote a healing. Exposure to a highly coherent energy field can serve in many ways as a "catalytic" resonant reminder – to help a person heal by energetically remembering an inner state of wellbeing. As we will explore later – the energy fields of these clearly accomplished beings have a resonant energy influence – that would mirror one's potential. In the core of ourselves we are each capable of manifesting this "healed resonance and harmony". This is what spiritual masters have always taught.

Equally, if you are in the presence of an imbalanced energy field with lots of discordant energy, and get drawn into the energy of that person – you can resonate downward. Now this alone would want to make everyone be around only happy, uplifting, caring, and compassionate people.

Yet, it is ultimately important not to rely on an external reality as a source of balance. What becomes more important in healing is learning to create a balanced and high vibratory state *within* your own field of energy. This will teach us to deal with external deconstructing low vibrational patterns, no matter what arises from within or around us.

To achieve this you will want to "resonate" with the higher vibratory quality of your own inner spiritual nature. Most of us need to learn or "remember" to do this. We will look more deeply at this idea – when we explore healing, responsible energy field management, and peace consciousness – in the upcoming sections.

Until we reach a state of "unwavering enlightenment" we will each have things to learn about managing our energy – an integral part of healing. This involves understanding the importance of the attitudes we hold, the thoughts and feelings we choose to harbor, the nature of ego, and learning more about our core spiritual nature and it's potential.

A *catalyst*, as defined by the Miriam Webster dictionary[98], is an agent that provokes or speeds significant change or action, without changing it's own nature. This can be applied in the setting of chemistry where an enzyme or substance speeds up a chemical reaction without being changed or directly involved in the chemical reaction. The term catalyst could also be applied in a social setting where a particular event stimulates mass change, like in our story of Rosa Parks.

Through contact with high vibrational coherent energy that is accessed through energy based therapies, and the principle of resonance, one can provoke vibrational change within a person to facilitate an energetic transformation. It facilitates a healing process. This exposure provides a "catalyst" to healing. It is easy to see why these terms become so useful.

Entrainment is the coupling of two distinct oscillating systems, each with its own unique cycle, which produces a common cycle. An applied example of this is the use of the technology of binaural beats to create a focused harmonic, used to entrain brain waves to a specific frequency such as alpha state or theta state. In a biologic sense systems are entrained to be in harmony. When an external stimulus is applied to the system it stimulates a response in the system, which may alter the resonant frequency. This may lead to a coherent or non-coherent outcome. Coherence would favor health.

Entanglement relates to a quantum relationship between two particles that have once been connected in a quantum relationship. In an entangled state, two or more particles may have an influence on each other, even if separated by space or dimension. If the first particle were altered in some way – it would affect the entangled particle equally.

We see real life examples of entanglement in our lives that are not thought of as quantum interactions – but they are. How many mothers have an unbelievably close connectedness to their children? They may sense and feel things, which have no basis in common awareness? Parents and children in this sense are "entangled".

The concept of entanglement becomes very interesting to understand when you realize that every cell in a person's body has originated from a single original cell containing the original DNA molecule that directed your entire presence as a human being. Every cell in your body is entangled by process of DNA continuity. We will look at the implications of this shortly.

☉

Everything as energy vibrates. Our cells vibrate. The molecules in them vibrate. We as a whole structural unit vibrate. When energies are applied in human healing processes, we see terms such as *vibration* utilized. This implies the introduction of vibratory influence to increase or order the vibration occurring within an energy structure for healing purposes.

The "vibrational" influence may be in the form of sound, light, or electromagnetic energy. Within these familiar forms, it may be derived from energies that are within or extraneous to the normal human sensory spectrum. The vibrational influence may also be outside of these classic energy forms, when we look at modalities that channel life force energy (chi) or inter-dimensional energy.

In Energy Medicine, an energy influence may arise from energies that are perceptible or imperceptible. Touch therapy or music would be examples of perceptible energies. Therapies involving energies that may be outside of normal human sensory capacity would include acupuncture, crystal healing, Reiki, hands on healing, intentional prayer, and, *Unity Field Healing*.

When a person is receiving an energy session, the experience is often imperceptible to a large degree to the recipient – until the energy has an impact in a way that a person may perceive. However, it is not uncommon that during sessions, people are very aware of an energy transfer or resonant vibration occurring in their own body. They may see energy forms or colors, hear sounds, feel hot or cold changes, or simply are aware of various trigger phenomena that occur when energy is unblocked or released during the session. This might include jerking, twitching, profound relaxation, or a becoming dizzy – all things, which may sometimes occur.

Since science cannot yet measure such energy directly, personal experience is most powerful to help a person understand what science cannot yet see. Yet, if you can appreciate a little physics – the potential for why such an event can have an energetic impact on the body becomes clearer. With this in mind, let us turn our attention to take a look at the concept of energy fields and energy organization.

Energy Fields

Physically, our bodies are made up of many distinct cells that are organized into structural units, called tissues such as muscle, and organs such as the liver. Organs are organized into structural and functional physiologic systems, such as the cardiovascular or the respiratory system. These systems work together in harmony as a unified functioning human body.

If we go back in time, all of the cells that go into the structural organization of our body came from one cell. This cell came from the fusion of an egg and a sperm - courtesy of our genetic parents. As this cell grows, divides and multiplies, a magical transformation occurs. Mysteriously these cells transform and order themselves - forming a highly organized body of systems. Different cells made from the original template cell take on highly specific structural and functional attributes, and are organized into very specific functional systems.

In the study of the developing human, we attribute this process of embryonic development to programmed "genetic expression". However if you look at it with a discerning eye, there is a necessary force of organizing intelligence that directs the arrangement of cells into organs, systems and ultimately into a full human body. Whether a person views this intelligence as scientific or spiritual is not so much an issue as the simple fact that a profound intelligence is clearly embedded in the process.

It is mystical to imagine how such organization could possibly occur. If you appreciate anything about the complexity of human form and function, one quickly will realize that the kind of intelligent order inherent in this process is "unbelievable". It is not simply "genetic" expression – it is an obvious *intelligently ordered* genetic expression. Nothing sporadically becomes more organized, specialized and functional with such consistency – by "random" nature. Order implies intelligence. Yet we take it very much for granted that the DNA of a human being simply does this spontaneously, as if no inherent intelligence and no inherent order exist in life. Impossible! But, how then, does this intelligence work?

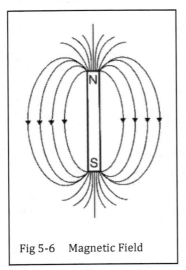

Fig 5-6   Magnetic Field

For anything to take on order in our world there is a plan or a blueprint. Blueprints form a conceptual order upon which a structure is built. For example, if you build a house, you start with a blueprint. Speaking in terms of actual "energetic order", it is easy to imagine there would need to be a living blueprint, or a field of organizational energy, to orchestrate the growth of a living entity. Otherwise how would cells know what to do?

What would an organizational field look like? Lets look at a simple example of field organization – the electromagnetic field around an everyday bar magnet – to better understand. (Fig 5-6)

In a magnet there are two poles, one positive and one negative. These are

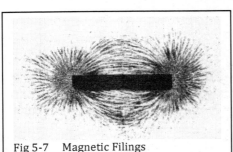

Fig 5-7   Magnetic Filings

located at opposite ends of the bar. Because of the polarity, invisible electromagnetic lines of force form in and around the magnetic poles creating an electromagnetic field.

Although you do not see the field when you look at a magnet, the field is always there. If you were to place a paper over the magnet and throw a bunch of iron filings onto the paper, the filings would align themselves in a defined order. (Fig 5-7)

The invisible field of energy becomes pretty obvious in this little experiment. Instead of randomly distributing themselves, they align in the form of the electromagnetic field along the lines of force.

The visible structural ordering that occurs is created by an invisible electromagnetic field. If there were no ordering force, all the filings thrown on the paper would simply fall into random disarray. With an organizing force, they take on a pattern.

When we look at form reality – we can see how an invisible energetic template or blueprint might be responsible for organizing the out pictured form order. This would be true for the creation of anything that exists in form. Our bodies, plants, animals, even to the structure of the planet itself have an internal organizing energy blueprint.

In the human body, a living energy field actually does provide this internal ordering. The field is composed of what is referred to as etheric energy, and is termed the etheric body, or the Ka.

In the human body, the etheric field is different than the electromagnetic field created by atomic interactions as we discussed. The complex ordering that takes place in a human body requires more than a simple electromagnetic field. The etheric body (and other subtle energy fields we will examine) is better understood to exist *within* or *deep* to the visible atomic level – in another "dimension". The etheric field or "body" plays a role in organizing the atoms, which are held together under its influence and then "out-pictured" into the form world, as an organized physical body.

Fig 5-8   Kirlian Photography

Energy fields, such as the etheric body are not easily measurable in our limited scientific understanding at present, but they are vitally important in making life possible. To really conceptualize and appreciate this etheric order, it is valuable to see the energy field that may be photographed around a leaf with Kirlian photography. (Fig 5-8)

The etheric body is the energy body, which is the most intimately associated to the physical human body. The etheric body is just one of many energy bodies that are part of human form or being.

Seers and sages through many years have described the etheric body and various other energy bodies as part of the human being. Many people who work in healing paradigms are capable of sensing and even seeing the etheric or other energy bodies. However, even if we do not have the sensory capacity to see it, an organizing field is logically required to have order in life. This is unquestionably true to explain the degree of order and intelligence found in the human body, with all of its structural and functional complexity and renewal capacity.

By understanding the concept of ordering energy fields, we have a meaningful way to begin to understand the various energy bodies that we will soon examine, as well as the quantum field of human DNA.

DNA

QUANTUM ENERGY FIELDS AND DNA

When genetic material is first coupled, and a fertilized human egg (a zygote) is formed, magic happens. In this fusion, a primordial human cell is created. As discussed, the cell doesn't just reproduce randomly and haphazardly. It replicates in an organized and systematic fashion. It is conceivable, that there exists an energetic field, which helps to order and organize the cells as they grow, divide and form systems of organs.

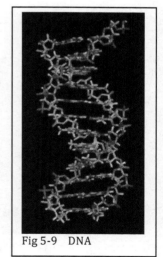

Fig 5-9   DNA

When we speak of DNA, we normally think of the double helix molecule, or the 23 pairs of chromosomes, that classically make up the genetic library of a human being. This, however, is the physical representation or manifestation of DNA. Just as the etheric body exists within to organize the human body, human DNA is also proposed to have an internal ordering field. It is a field of energy, which organizes its physical arrangement and has a great influence on its ultimate function. This field of energy is sometimes termed the "quantum" aspect of DNA.

If we step to the marginal frontier of modern science, DNA is not simply the out-pictured physical substance we call DNA. Inside the DNA molecule many believe there exists a field of quantum organization and intelligence. We could also term it "interdimensional energy" or "multidimensional DNA" – because of the nature of quantum organization. This internal energy is considered to "order and govern" the function of the DNA molecule, directing its existence and its activity.

The creative and intelligent capacity of this quantum DNA field is theoretical, but recent research is beginning show validity to this concept. Regardless, it is certainly mysterious. It does potentially begin to demystify a lot of incomprehensible attributes of DNA and reproductive life.

For example, why does a zygotic cell have the power or ability to reproduce at all? It is a universal mystery. What is it about this fusion that sets life into motion? Why does each cell produced contain the same genetic material – but the expression of its genetic information becomes highly specific as each cell begins to take on its specific function? Why does only less than 10% of the genetic material in a persons DNA code for genes? And how does the remaining regulatory DNA (originally termed "junk DNA") with transposons and reverse transposons, function to regulate genetic expression? Finally, how do the trillions of cells originating from this primordial cell all operate as a functional system? It is completely beyond rational comprehension. But it does!

The concept of quantum DNA field organization begins to make a little sense. It may begin to explain the mysterious behavior of DNA, and the capabilities and variability of expressions found in DNA as it is expressed in human beings. We could perhaps conceptualize that the quantum field of DNA represents an "informational interface" with our physical human DNA – and that is feeds it information. This is a very esoteric concept but actually makes a lot of sense. The quantum DNA could provide a dynamic "instruction set" that delivers information to the DNA, to regulate its expression.

Of course adding to the mystery, and skepticism that might be inspired, is the invisibility of this quantum energy reality. Regardless, the potential of its existence, and information about it are beginning to emerge a little through pioneering science[60]. However, most information about is emerging through spiritual sourced or channeled information.[12] I believe that will begin to change soon, as quantum technology is developed, and the field of energy that is within DNA can be subjectively identified and measured.

Where does this quantum field come from? Perhaps the easiest way to conceptualize this idea is to imagine that when we are to be born, and our parents have gone about the business of "making a zygote" – the cell carries genetic information transferred through the parents genetic lineage. But, let us imagine for a moment that the "soul" of the person to be born somehow also energetically "fuses" with the developing embryo at a point in its development. Too strange? Shaky ground here – I realize – but let's just imagine for a moment. Through this energetic connection – a soul might be imagined to infuse its energy and spiritual information into the developing zygote – as it sets about to become a "new human being".

When we are born, it is conceivable through this esoteric idea, that our soul carries information that is integrated into our DNA. The DNA certainly carries the information that comes from our parent's genetic make up. Yet, it is also over-lighted by information that is personal and spiritual in nature. This peculiar idea conceptually explains both a genetic and spiritual component in the process of our human development.

The energy and information, which defines what is unique about a persons DNA, is not simply "in the genes". It is in the quantum field, which regulates the genetic expression. The DNA molecule that we witness in the physical world is responsive to quantum instructions.

This might be a very unusual idea to grasp at first, but people worldwide have begun to have visionary experiences and receive information about this esoteric or multidimensional component of DNA. I will begin to refer to this quantum aspect of DNA as simply our "Spiritual DNA" throughout this book.

So "spiritually speaking", what exactly is contributing information to this quantum field of information and regulation? Well, this is where the topic gets even a little more esoteric. The information in the quantum field is influenced by both "spiritual" information as well as information that is programmed by our "human consciousness" state. Okay, what does that mean?

First, the origin of this quantum field may be viewed as spiritual – sort of like the "higher self" you. As an individual being, coded within the quantum field of DNA is information related to one's spiritual history, spiritual potential, and one's "purpose". This information about all of one's experiences that have been lived as a soul is present. This implies information related to one's past experiences as well as our present and potential future experiences – even "lifetimes". (This information is sometimes referred to as being recorded in the akashic record – which many believe is information that is present in our DNA.) It also carries information about our positive and negative "karma" related to our past experiences, as well as our critical life lessons and potential development that emerges from this these things. Hence it carries the information that is purposed to help our soul in its development, through consciousness or spiritual realization. The quantum DNA field also contains a template of our "perfected" self, which we can term our Higher Self. It thus provides us with a connection with our divine or spiritual origin.

We could view our higher self as an over lighting consciousness that has a much greater understanding of our spiritual odyssey. It is our most spiritualized self. It is our "wiring" to God. Through the higher self continuum, we can conceptualize that DNA as a physical molecule is coupled with our spiritual nature by this organizing quantum field of energy. There is a divinity inherent in human DNA that communicates and expresses through this quantum field interface.

The story doesn't stop there! DNA can not only be influenced spiritually (from "above") as we discussed,, but also through human consciousness (from "below"). This quantum filed of information is also responsive to our "human consciousness". The way we think, feel, and relate to life is information that is fed back to our DNA quantum field energy.

Does this mean that human consciousness, can also therefore affect genetic expression? Too far out? Well, as "far out" a statement like this sounds, it is proving to be very true! Scientific studies have recently begun to show the impact of human consciousness on genetic expression. Feelings, thoughts, attitudes can all affect one's genetic expression! This is a new field of scientific study termed "epigenetics".[14,35]

For this to happen, there must be a mechanism for consciousness to influence genetic expression. The quantum field, being directly connected to our biological system through its DNA interface, is a model for this observation. If this is all true, DNA may actually be "responsive" to what we want to create both as a spiritual being and as a human being.

This concept provides a potential mechanism by which our growth in consciousness can have an influence on our health, our life and our individualized spiritual expression. It awakens an incredible connection to our spiritual nature and a mechanism of "communication" that we can utilize to support us in our personal development and well being.

And if that were not enough to digest, at this point in time, as a great paradigm shift unfolds on the planet, many people believe there is a transformation in this quantum field that is taking place. This is considered part of a "spiritual upgrade" of humanity. It is provided to support humanity as it walks (and yes sometimes fumbles!) through this transition. This process is often coined by the term "ascension". Human beings are proposed to have the ability to connect in a "bigger way" to their spiritual DNA and let a greater energy into their field to support their well being. Yes, very woo woo ... but very real to those who have begun to learn about it and experience it.

Ascension is a familiar spiritual term to many that might conjure up ideas of being lifted from the planet in a chariot of energy and light, as is told in the biblical story of Elijah. Yet the ascension here is not so much a "lifting up" as it is a "bringing down" or "bridging". It is the story of bringing a greater aspect of your spiritual energy into your physical body, your DNA, and the planet. Ascension implies the integration of a higher state of consciousness and energy, one which births itself through our DNA-spirit axis, and the quantum field of information that directs our DNA expression.

Ascension as such implies a "potential". It requires both individual human intention and a personal process of spiritual integration. Now if all of this sounds too strange or freaky – relax. This process of spiritual development will not be forced on anyone. It occurs primarily on the basis of free will and human intentional cooperation. If you do not want it – you don't ask for it! Simple as that. Love would never force itself on anyone. It is offered in universal alignment of integrity – and is simply available to us as human beings. We must offer our *intent* to grow in this way. If we don't – it cannot happen.

As human beings do open to this information, and to this personal experience, one is opening up to a DNA expansion. This is an actual event – and it brings a stronger energetic connection to our spiritual self. It is also important to understand that it does not happen "to us" – it happens "through us". We are intentional and self-responsible players in this event.

To handle and integrate this process requires an element of spiritual development and maturity. Yet, through this intentional self-alignment, one is opening to what may be perceived as *spiritual grace*.

"What is the impact of that?" you may ask. Grace to some is perceived as overcoming or being freed from karma. Karma can be thought of energy consequence, which is purposeful and has been accrued through cause and affect as we have lived our life and lives. If we "carry karma" where do we carry it? This information is conceivably stored in the quantum field of our DNA. If we return to our quantum field concept, we could easily imagine that our karma would impact the quality of this quantum field governing our DNA both positively and negatively. We are poised in our energy to live many things based on our karma. Karma, however, can be effaced by spiritual grace through the openness one has to one's Higher Self nature.

Intriguingly, this knowledge has sprung forth from a whole host of unique and independent sources, and through the experiences of many different human beings, simultaneously in recent years. As esoteric as it seems, it has been my personal experience that we are indeed in the midst of a quantum recalibration of the energy and information we are able to access through our spiritual DNA. Should *you* believe it? You *should* not do anything. You must filter this type of information through your own intuition and discernment, and decide if it is appropriate or true within you.

As this type of information has become popularized, there has been a great deal of information published about "quantum DNA", "interdimensional DNA " and "layers" of DNA. These describe conceptual layers and their attributes – explaining how this spiritual DNA is connected through our spiritual self to our physical reality. Kryon, channeled through Lee Carroll provides one of the best sources of information available for those interested in this information.[12] If this information resonate meaningfully with you, Lee's book to me a "must read" to be conceptualize how this all occurs.

From my own personal experience, I do believe that a new "connection" is taking place, and it is expanding the energy that is fed into the quantum information that fields our DNA. I realize, whole-heartedly, that it is much easier to accept such a far out claim having lived a few personal experiences that have validated this within my own consciousness. But no one can prove it – it is a scientifically improvable concept for the time being – because it is taking place in a field of energy that is not measurable in 3D reality. It must be encountered personally within each one of us – and integrated in a way that is appropriate within our own consciousness.

What I can offer as true in my experience is that a human being who expresses authentic intention to reconnect with a "higher level" DNA can do so. I also believe that prior to this time, this very special time, this has been available to only a few highly enlightened members of humanity. These, of course, would be the "avatar" beings that have come as spiritual teachers and healers through time.

Yet, at this auspicious time on the planet, there is an opportunity for many people to consciously make this connection with their spiritual DNA and reassume a greater spiritual power and presence. A fusion can take place, which opens up a channel or axis for a human being to reach into and receive from this quantum information. It simply, but remarkably, presents a DNA upgrade and a subsequent recalibration!

However, until a person, "invites" or intentionally expresses the desire to have a greater spiritual influence in their world, this process holds itself at bay. As we stated earlier – this occurs in respect and love – until a person is ready, able or willing to accommodate the transformation. The reason being, to make the connection stronger requires a spiritual posture of readiness.

Why? We can appreciate that life is founded in love, and the earth is a planet of free will alignment. To choose this progress requires a level of spiritual development or maturity that is self-recognized. To some the concept is fearful, and they do not feel ready. Others are ready to go! Love does not force, it allows. We must each choose for ourselves.

To "hold" the energy and transformative power of this alignment requires a spiritual balance that is sometimes referred to as "personal mastery" – a healing concept that we will examine in the upcoming chapters. You must be able to hold and manage your own personal energy in a "masterful" way to be able to accommodate and support this higher vibrational alignment. And this, by the way, defines the essence of healing!

As we move forward in the process of DNA integration, we realize that "evolution in the DNA axis" has two components. One is a level of openness in consciousness to one's spiritual nature (up). Two is a willingness to create a personal and collective environment into which this spirit is invited to express – our psycho-emotional environment (down). Human beings "work" in two ways to restore the healing ability within this

DNA axis. One is by holding a greater openness to their spiritual nature and origins. Two is by creating a "suitable environment", where a higher consciousness aspect of our self may live. This is again, the journey of healing.

Through this lens, DNA actually becomes the axis of bio-spiritual continuity. A human being can access a higher or interdimensional "reality" through one's DNA – and brings healing into form through a spiritual transfer of energy and information. Every conceivable term of renewal has been used to describe this process – rewiring, renovation, recalibration, remodeling, restitution and grace. As a human being creates a consciousness environment to support a higher vibrational status – mentally, emotionally and physically – one also supports the genetic expression of health. These very simple principles become the guiding principle in all "quantum energy" based healing efforts. You will discover that the peace, and attributes of your spiritual self, that emerge forth through this alignment, supports your every effort. I am pretty sure you are ready. How about you?

Consciousness and Intelligent Design

The energy of the mind is the essence of life.

Aristotle

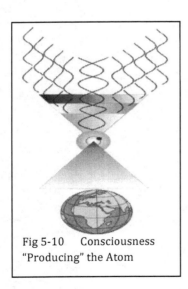

Fig 5-10   Consciousness "Producing" the Atom

We have talked about atoms and particles. We have talked of an intelligent organizing force that exists within material creation. (Fig 5-10) We have alluded to the fact that we are actually an aspect of this vast intelligence; as human beings, we are an integral element or an integral piece in this vast spiritual puzzle. And we have talked about a very personal connection with this higher level of self and intelligence which gives rise to life through our DNA.

If we begin to consider intelligent order, we can appreciate that there are infinite levels where order and intelligence come into play in the world. There is an intelligence that orders life at the level of the planet, the solar system, the galaxy and the universe. On the planet there are also large kingdoms organized by this intelligent order, referred to as kingdoms of consciousness. This includes mineral, plant, animal and human life. Part of a unified whole, each exists at different levels of ability, awareness or consciousness. Life forms within these kingdoms have different levels of awareness and attributes or properties - which might be viewed as "codified" by the intelligent design that has "produced them".

In the various strata of the intelligent order there is a corresponding *consciousness*. Consciousness may be thought of as awareness. As human beings we are of *human* consciousness. Human consciousness, for example is very different from animal or mineral consciousness. Yet each element of consciousness has a role to play in the whole order of life.

Human consciousness is quite unique. As humans we can understand that all of the creation we see around us has been created to provide a theater for us to experience our own creations. We live in a world that is both outside of us and an extension of us. It is an arena for us to experiment in – to learn and to grow into more highly conscious sentient beings.

According to all spiritual traditions, in one form or another, human beings have a *goal* in consciousness. The goal is to become aware of our inherent spiritual nature, our spiritual potential, and the healing it can bring into our world. Hence consciousness is not static – it expands as human beings become more self-aware. This creates a process of progressive "enlightenment". As human beings, however, we arrive at a threshold where we realize what we are seeking spiritually is not external to us – it is internal within us. This represents a point of spiritual awakening. The world is a stage or a playground where we experiment in limited consciousness, with lessons and learning, until we realize who we really are. "Who we are" is described in spiritual teachings as our "true nature".

A human being who has attained a spiritualized level of consciousness is not obviously different from anyone else in appearance. However, there are remarkable differences in how they live and how they behave. As you explore your spiritual nature more deeply, you begin to realize the key lesson we all face as human beings is so simple - it is hard to accept. The lesson is that your true nature is love, and you are one with all creation. *Love is the essence of creation* and *we are one with that creative drive.*

Yet as human beings, we are often subject to creating many lessons on this path to spiritual unity. As the lessons are learned, what is based on love is woven into the fabric of life, and what is not based on love is washed away in a restorative effort by the stream of grace.

As a person awakens to this spiritual discovery, there is a doorway of consciousness that opens and allows an influx of energy and reordering into one's world. One element of this opening is a transformation in our "personal" energy. It involves an elimination of patterns of energy that are deeply embedded in our personal energy fields, those which have arisen through lack of understanding, history and what we can see as karma or spiritual limitation.

As we awaken to our true spiritual or divine nature and the ability to bring greater energy, greater power and greater love into our world and life – we heal.

⊙

Fig 5-11 Consciousness and Sacred Geometry

To add to this concept, we begin to comprehend that we are not simply a physically structured order that we witness on the outside. There is also a multidimensional, energetically ordered, creation on the "inside".

Inside the physical world we see, energy is patterned inter-dimensionally to give rise to out-pictured forms of organized energy. Form may be understood to be created by specifically ordered combinations of consciously patterned energy and the potential functions are defined by this creative intelligence.

In physical terms, molecular and chemical substances are organized into highly patterned forms and relationships, e.g. chemicals, materials, gases and liquids. These are highly organized arrangements whose relationships are governed by laws inherent in the intelligent design. This is also true in energetic terms when we begin to discuss the capacity of the various energy bodies.

On the level of energy, energy forms are created and sustained by consciousness. One can begin to imagine how life is a cosmic dance of energy patterns on one level – and a physically visible world that exists before our eyes. Mystics have long made this declaration.

We can also begin to grasp that the world we manifest is subject to the consciousness, or lack of consciousness, with which we form and utilize the energy of life. Life provides us with the playing field but we model the creation by the input of our level of consciousness. Life is modeled in part by the consciousness of the players. Perhaps Shakespeare was ridiculously close to the truth when he wrote in *As You Like It*:

> *All the world's a stage,*
> *And all the men and women merely players:*
> *They have their exits and their entrances;*
> *And one man in his time plays many parts, …*

Since energy is patterned by consciousness and we can pattern energy ourselves – we can change the manifest world by growing in consciousness. We can learn to work from this inner level of consciousness and we can transfigure the form we create as life. This is a key to understanding the potential of human bio-spiritual transformation.

☉

Consciousness itself is limitless. Although consciousness is unlimited – our awareness is limited by the form expression that consciousness has created and provided to us. As "spiritual" beings, we have a much vaster consciousness than we realize as "human" beings. Our consciousness as human beings is subject to restrictive forces that may be overcome by growth and realization. People describe this as awakening to "God consciousness".

We could use the tem "limited consciousness" to describe any being not fully conscious of everything. It is not hard to live up to that billing! Limited consciousness, in human terms is limited by the restraints of our human form. The form includes our bodies, our emotional bodies and mental bodies – and all of the screens that perceptibly divide us from a more expanded awareness. Yet consciousness is not permanently limited. People can "grow" in consciousness. Just like we grow as children into adult bodies and develop greater physical, mental and emotional levels of skill – we can grow into greater levels of consciousness. Within the human stream of consciousness, there are expanding levels of awareness. We are currently in a process of massive expansion of the consciousness of what it is to be human. A key of that expansion is an awakening to our inherent divinity.

⊙

When we ponder the nature of life, we are often identified with form or formed energy as the essential nature of who we are. But in actuality, the real you is not simply the form or energy bodies you inhabit – it is the actual consciousness directing this form. Hence there is an interface between consciousness and form.

You might even view the human being as an energetic continuum – from consciousness into form. We are simply limited in our conscious awareness of this expanded reality, by the perceptual limitations and capacity of the forms we hold.

Consciousness today is rapidly expanding, and so is what we perceive to be the nature of reality. As we enter into a new time cycle, and as we grow in our maturing partnership as co-creators – we integrate knowledge and awareness that is brand new to us as an awakening humanity. Consciousness is transforming the very foundation of "reality" – from the highest levels of life down to the very atoms that make up our heart.

Cymatics, Sacred Geometry and Crop Circles

We will review three final elements that we will need to help us better conceptualize the idea of quantum energy based healing. These include: cymatics, the concept of sacred geometry, and crop circles.

Cymatics

Cymatics is the study of visible sound and vibration. If you create an experiment where sound is passed through a loose medium such as sand on a vibratory plate, the sand will organize itself into visible patterns on the basis of the sound that is being transmitted. This occurs as the sound waves create complex standing waves that have the effect of patterning or ordering the medium.

The term was first attributed to Dr. Hans Jenny (1904-1972). In his work, he conducted experiments animating inert powders, pastes, and liquids using pure tone vibrations in the audible range. His early work demonstrated how sound patterns through vibration could produce standing form. Different patterns were observed to emerge based on the geometry of the plate and the frequency pattern being used. These patterns are incredibly interesting – forming beautiful geometric expressions that take shape in correlation with expressed sound wave patterns. (Fig 5-12)

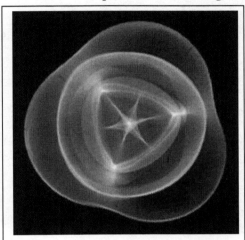

Fig 5-12   Cymatics Photo: Dr. Hans Jenny

Sound is a form of energy. Sound will create energy structure. Through the observation of cymatics we can understand that if one "sounds" into a medium, the standing wave patterns make geometry. It becomes easy to see how specific types of sound, particularly consciously applied sound, can have an energetic influence on any matter with which it interacts.

Thoughts and words are like sound. Thoughts can be conceptualized to pattern structural energy, and words can convey or vibrate energy into form order through sound. Thoughts and words create patterned energy and are therefore understood to be "creative". But remember, consciousness can govern thoughts and words. This principle will become very important in understanding healing later on.

The fact that sound or the influence of an ordering consciousness can be used to "therapeutically reorder" an energy field is also very important. This will come into play when we examine *Unity Field Healing* and the use of the Unity Field Template.

The idea that the whole of creation is held into existence by a single "primordial" sound is not a new concept. In the first book of John, we are told, "In the beginning was the word." Word is sound. In ancient Vedic teaching we are also told that creation came into being – by the sound OM. It is "the big sound" or "word of God" that set the universe in motion.

This alone is fascinating. But on a very practical level, sound, words and even the consciousness behind words, can have an organizing or deconstructing influence on other energy structures.

The concept of consciousness or thought having an influence on the internal order of crystalline structure is marvelously and tangibly demonstrated in the work of Masaru Emoto.[18]

Dr. Emoto in his work demonstrates the influence of consciousness on the crystalline order in water. In his work, the crystalline order inherent in water that was frozen – after being subject to the power of influences like human thoughts, conscious love, words, or pollution – was examined. The crystalline organization inherent in water influenced by higher consciousness attributes such as love, beauty, respect, and so forth shows beautiful order. The influence of hatred, negativity, pollution and so forth is very disorganized and destructive. His work is pivotal in helping people understand the creative potential of human consciousness on matter.

Why is this so valuable? First, it helps us to appreciate that consciousness *can* pattern energy. Second, consciousness is expressed in geometric order. This order serves as a field for consciousness to manifest or express itself in form. Geometric forms produce the patterning that exists behind form structure. Finally, and perhaps most importantly – it helps us grasp that the vibrations we make through our own thoughts and life – consciously or unconsciously – are "contributing" to creation.

When we see how patterns are formed in geometric expression, we can also open our mind to the concept that a template like the one we will work with in *Unity Field Healing* is potentially a contributing force in healing.

Sacred Geometry

If we look at the structural patterns naturally inherent in life we find repetitive and variable geometric patterns. Think for a moment of the appearance of a flower, an artichoke, and a nautilus shell. (Fig 5-13) We can easily appreciate geometries that repeatedly exist within the forms that manifest in the creation of life.

Fig 5-13   Flower, Artichoke and Nautilus

Sacred geometry examines the various geometries and geometric order that exits in life. It explores the foundational science behind geometric patterns and the complex ordering of patterns that are found throughout life. It is vicariously demonstrating an architectural intelligence that is mystically embedded in all living things.

When we think of the geometry implicit in life forms, the electric lines of force of an invisible magnetic field, or the cymatic creations of sound – it is easy to appreciate that these patterns represent "living fields of organizational order" into which form structures actually grow.

Some of the geometries we encounter include the circle, the sphere, and the platonic solids known as the tetrahedron, hexahedron, octahedron, dodecahedron and icosahedrons. These patterns show up in crystal formations, minerals and plant patterns, over and over again. Patterns of spirals and toroids, defined by an infinite progression by the Golden Mean Ratio and the Fibonacci series, are all seen in the un-whirling of plants and flowers and all of creation. These patterns and portions are also found in the human body.

Explorations into sacred geometry demonstrate the order and patterning intelligence, which exists in life systems and in all of creation. Ancient and modern wisdom teachings have resurfaced highly symbolic patterns such as the tree of life, Metatron's cube and the flower of life. (Fig 5-14, p146)

These intriguing patterns contain a mystical knowledge out of reach of non-esoteric thinkers.

What is the significance of this geometric patterning? How does this contribute to our understanding? Well, it helps demonstrate that there is perhaps a mystical architect of life using a common language of living geometric fields as the substrate or energy matrix on which form comes to life. Perhaps we can call upon a knowledge or energy in these patterns in a quantum way, to help us "recalibrate" our energy, or heal?

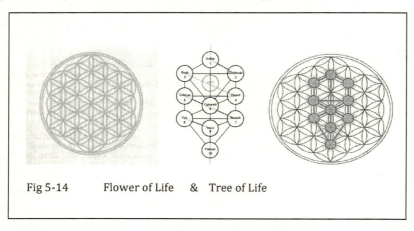

Fig 5-14   Flower of Life   &   Tree of Life

It is not a big leap to conceptualize that when structures based on these geometries are *resonated* – in this case with a flow of a living "life force" or energy – the geometries will vibrate and emit vibrations. If these vibrations are "resonant" with geometries in the human body or in the human DNA – can they potentially support corrective resonant re-patterning of the same geometries in human form? This allows us to conceptualize the power of specific geometry – geometry that is interdimensional and quantum in nature - to influence the human energy field. It just might bring "woo-woo" down to earth!

The study of sacred geometry is a whole field of study unto itself and for those interested there are many intriguing online and book resources available.[34] For our purpose, it is to simply bring into conscious awareness the fact that complex geometrical patterns and relationships are found everywhere in creation. They define the inner order of manifested creation - adding a little understanding to the "mystery of intelligent creation".

They also provide us with a foundational understanding as to why such an unusual concept as a "light template" may be applied in a healing context.

We will develop this understanding through the concept of working with very specific interdimensional energy patterns – when we will examine *Unity Field Healing*.

CROP CIRCLES

Next, we will briefly review the topic of crop circles. I believe crop circles are probably one of the most mystical and least appreciated phenomena occurring on our planet today.

Every year the world over, but predominantly in the wheat fields of druidic England, there are magnificent highly complex geometric symbols that pop up in wheat fields. They arise overnight, or sometimes within minutes, appearing as complex geometric patterns in the canvas of growing wheat. They become apparent by creating non-fracturing bends in shafts of wheat – leading to a visible pattern in the overall field of wheat. Some of them are up to hundreds of meters in width and unimaginable in complexity.

Of course, there is a necessary skepticism introduced by both naïve and malevolent people, insisting these are all manmade events. When you examine the scientific observations and the general complexity of these events – it is impossible not to understand that these occur in the presence of highly ordered but invisible energetic print.

To say "organizing energy fields of sacred geometry" and to say, "crop circle" is pretty much synonymous. I believe crop circles are intimately related to transformation we are living on our planet. This is perhaps easier to understand when we appreciate the concept of an inner energetic order laying at the foundation of all manifested reality.

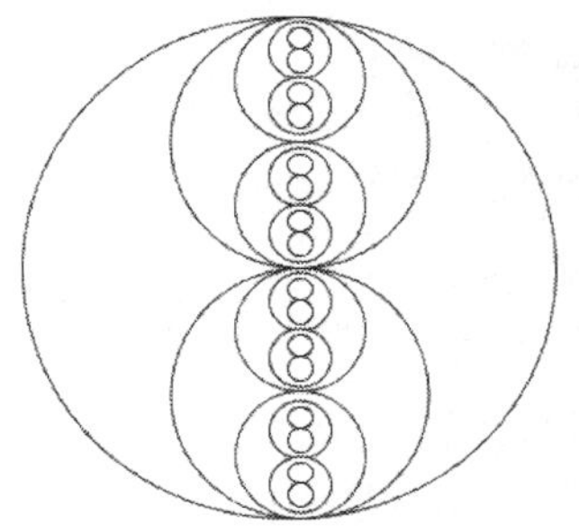

I also experienced an incredible "coincidence" when I discovered a photo of one of these magnificent circles, schematically shown in Fig 5-15, shortly after I received some visionary information given to develop Unity Field Healing. It was an exact replica of the light vision I was shown for the template! (Fig 5-16) I was

Fig 5-15
Schematic of Crop Circle
Original Photo Lucy Pringle

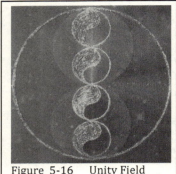

Figure 5-16   Unity Field Template

dumbfounded to coincidently discover the same pattern in the form of crop circle one year later. It had appeared and was captured in a photograph a few years earlier – but didn't come into my field of awareness until I had corresponding vision. It is hard to fathom that this would be an insignificant coincidence!

What exactly is responsible for the creation of these crop circle patterns, and what is the true purpose, remains a mystery. No one knows for sure who or what is responsible for their appearance – but more than a few interesting hypotheses can be drawn around them. There are many theories and ideas. Personally, I see them as energetic prints or even "time capsules" which are being activated in the energy grid of the planet to help re-order the energy of the "new world". When one begins to examine geometry embedded in the patterns, and the intelligence coded in them, one begins to appreciate they are "living energy patterns".

When we think of our planet as a living energy body we could conceptualize that these energy patterns are "stamps" of energy that are being activated in the energy field of the earth. If we return to our discussion of cymatics – it is easy to conceptualize that patterned sound or energy is vibratory in nature and can have a resonance influence on adjacent energy. The question to ask is, " What is the influence of these energy stamps on the planet and on humanity?"

Reflections on the potential significance this statement are innumerable! There is a lot of information available in books and websites pertaining to crop circles. I include this brief note simply to emphasize the scale and validity of some of the esoteric ideas presented.

Where Do We Go Next?

We have developed a language to discuss some aspects of energy transformation. And, we have peeked into another level of life where an energetic order and energy fields make up the ordering template for life, well expressed through sacred geometrically patterning. This is perhaps a good preparation to begin to examine the specific human energy fields or bodies.

We are all aware that we have a physical body, and that we have thoughts and feelings. But we are not all aware that these capacities have a corresponding energy body that is part of our energetic design. Not only do we have such capacity, we actually have bodies of energy that are responsible for the ability to provide this capacity. The human energy bodies are organized fields of energy that are inherent in the human body and they work together to make up our human nature.

In the next chapter, we will turn our attention to these energy bodies and how their function influences healthy and diseased states of human expression. We will also begin to explore the energetic way we as human beings may be understood as "spectral" creations emanating from a spiritual consciousness. We can begin to see ourselves as a biospiritual continuum of conscious through energy into form. Through this understanding, we can then appreciate how we are subject to a healing influence of our own spiritual nature – if we open to it through our own free will and intention. Healing and biospiritual integration occur through the venue of "energy and consciousness".

Once we have a good grasp of our energy bodies and our higher conscious nature, we can also examine the forces or influences, which may support or block our own development as conscious beings. We will also examine how restrictive patterning may be healed through energy based healing and conscious growth.

Through integration of a greater spiritual consciousness we develop the capacity to play a co-creative role in redesigning our personal lives and ultimately the world we share. It implies the development of a more fully realized energy system through which the power, the love, the healing and the creativity of your spirit can manifest into the world of form. It is time for a dose the missing pill ☺!

CHAPTER 6
THE HUMAN ENERGY FIELD AND THE BIOSPIRITUAL CONTINUUM

Introduction

In a physical sense, it is easy to appreciate that you have a body. You have a heart and circulatory system. These elements have a unique structure and function. You also have a stomach and digestive system. There are many organs and systems that co-exist in the human body, and work synergistically. For example, when you breathe, the function of air exchange is performed by the lungs or respiratory system. However, the blood in the circulatory system must get oxygenated and remove carbon dioxide. To achieve this, the blood is pumped by the heart, through the circulatory system, and into the lungs. All these systems work in tandem and in cooperation.

In the body there is also a vast array of feedback mechanisms, which regulate these processes. We typically relate control of these regulating functions to the central nervous system, hormonal regulation and the autonomic nervous system. In short, they are controlled by the nervous and neuroendocrine systems.

However, outside of the traditional and scientifically recognized systems-based understanding of the human body, there are also fields or bodies of energy. These are an integral part of who we are as human beings. They are structural energy bodies – which are composed of unique and specific types of energy. Most people do not see them directly, because they do not exist within the "range of perception" of most people. In the same way that we do not see ultraviolet light, or hear above 20,000 Hz frequencies – most humans do not have the sensory capacity to perceive these energetic levels. Yet, if you have ever been shocked by electricity or sunburned by UV light – you know undoubtedly some invisible energies are real.

These energy bodies are purposeful in providing certain functional abilities that we possess as human beings, and are definable. They include the etheric body, the emotional body, the mental body, and spiritual bodies of higher energetic coordination. Although we can separate them in appearance and function, they coexist within and around the physical body in an alternate level or "dimension".

Each one of these bodies is derived from a field of "like energy". The etheric body is made of structural etheric energy; the emotional body is made of fluid "emotional" quality energy; and the mental body, of a mental structural energy. The thoughts and feelings that we experience as humans actually exist in these energy bodies. So although most people do not "see" them, it is very valuable to appreciate their existence and function.

There exist people who do have the capacity to see these bodies of energy. For those who have seen them, they take the essential shape of the human form, but each layer or field looks different. They collectively "interface" with each other, as well as with the human body and human nervous system.

A great deal of our "human experience" is lived or encountered through these energies. We relate to life emotionally and mentally just as we do physically. We will focus our attention on these energy bodies because they are where a great deal of healing occurs.

There are also higher-level energy bodies, which play a role in organizing these bodies. They help in the development of the lower bodies and they can transduce energy from "higher levels" of reality and an over lighting consciousness. They also help "govern" the lower bodies, as our higher self expresses itself in form through our soul.

We can learn a lot about the nature of each of these elements. We can become aware of their function. We can see how they function well. We can become aware of how they have become imbalanced or contribute to diseased conditions. Importantly, we will also come to understand that we are "in charge" of how we use these bodies – which is the foundation of a great deal of basic spiritual teaching. Lastly, through purview of energy medicine, we can also understand the ability to experience direct energetic healing of these bodies. This can occur through clearing and restructuring our energy fields - by various energy processes and consciousness practices. These efforts help to heal the body through the bio-energetic-spiritual continuum of which we are comprised.

As we begin to discuss energy bodies and our biospiritual continuum, it becomes important to grasp that every person has a conscious over-lighting or spiritual aspect to his or her being. We will refer to this as our higher self and we will elaborate a little more as we proceed. It is not only "spiritual" people who have a spiritual nature. "Spiritual" people may be more aware of it, and in a greater conscious communication with it, but a spiritual self is part of everyone's core nature. The higher self animates the soul. It is the whole knowing aspect of consciousness that is more fully aware of our soul's full spectrum of human experience.

When it comes to spiritual self-perception there exist many different perspectives that people have about this concept. Three "big groups" of view points vicariously seem to arise:

First, some people view life through the belief that they are simply a body, or, perhaps a body plus the thoughts and feelings and beliefs they experience or use to define themself. Life is a tangible physical and psychological experience – but there is little outside of logic and tangible experience that is perceived or included in the nature and meaning of life.

Secondly, some people believe in a spiritual level of existence, but they are truly not aware of their direct liaison with this level of reality. These people know that a spiritual reality exists, but it is perceived as existing outside of them. This is perhaps common in religious thinking where people may see themselves as "outside" of God or love or spirit, and they are aiming to become a part of it by escaping life on this plane or deserving to become part of that reality.

Finally, some people are very aware of their inherent spiritual nature. They recognize they are actually spiritual beings themselves. They are human beings with an awareness of their own internal divine aspect, and understand that spirit exists *within* them. For these people, ideally, life is a process of manifesting a deeper personal spiritual nature in the world of form. Meanwhile, these people tend to understand that life in form is a purposeful but transient experience and one of a multifaceted spiritual nature. Life for such people often involves learning to communicate with this inherent part of them - to listen to it, to speak with it, to understand its mechanism of operating, and to allow its guidance and healing influence into their lives.

Please understand that one group is not really "better" or "worse" – these are just simply views that correlate with states of consciousness. There is appropriateness to where each one of us is in the spectrum of consciousness at a point in time. It will be very appropriate to our spiritual path and purpose. They do not define "how spiritual you are" – they define how "consciously aware" one is of one's spiritual nature. People can move forward in consciousness through these three groups, but it is very hard to move backward.

Most people who are drawn to learn about energy healing are aware, or in the process of becoming more deeply aware, of their inherent spiritual nature. It is this inner understanding and awakening, which draws a person toward the experience of discovering such things. This occurs as part of a larger spiritual process indicating to a person that the time of this progressive awakening has arrived.

Individually, our higher self has a greater understanding of our current life than we do as a quasi-conscious human being. The higher self in each of us understands our history, our whole souls' journey in time, our lessons, our relationship to other people, our karma, and our potential and purpose in life. The higher self serves as a personal guardian, our greatest force of healing and a wise spiritual teacher. It is an ally – but it remains somewhat silent until we make a conscious gesture or intention to allow its direct and conscious guidance into our lives.

When people experience a spiritual awakening – they are referring to an experience that has brought them into closer awareness of the spiritual nature or reality that is inherent in life. Such experiences can be viewed as occurring under the auspice of your higher self. This wiser part of you, the real you, knows to communicate with you in a way you can understand, and in a way that will be meaningful to you personally. It will be tailored to the whole picture of who you are. The experiences will speak to you. They will be meaningful to you as an individual being, and are crafted by your higher self – for it knows you intimately and completely.

As people awaken spiritually, one develops a closer communion with this inherent spiritual element. We can learn to relate to this aspect of ourselves, and even to communicate with it – and this can be a somewhat disorienting time.

To learn to communicate spiritually, we need to learn to communicate in a new way. Our spiritual nature does not lecture or give direct counseling sessions. Spirit guides us through direct knowing, intuition and synchronicity. Spirit can also "heal" by direct transfer of energy and consciousness. To allow its influence into our lives, we must learn to open up to this aspect of ourselves. It will guide us in a wise and loving way toward wellness and healing. When the higher self works to help us heal, it will often involve healing of mental and emotional attributes – diseases or injuries that are embedded in the mental, emotional and etheric bodies.

This higher self, as a force of consciousness, interfaces with each one of us, and can bring healing energetically into our lives. Yet importantly, part of the spiritual design of earth, is an honoring of human free will. Our higher self will not "impose itself" upon us in our human experience. It will work with us in a "conscious relationship" if we so choose – but this experience must align with our personal intention. If we are open to developing this relationship, we can learn to communicate intuitively, through other forms of guidance, through synchronistic creation, and through direct energy transfer. It is easy to see why Energy Medicine so quickly turns into "spiritual healing" – for "energy" healing always involves our "higher self" participation.

As we are learning to open spiritually, we each undergo a process of transformative healing. Part of the early work of healing is helping to clear and align the lower energy bodies. This means, the mental and emotional and etheric bodies. These bodies, as we will explore, carry memory and energy from many experiences, and through genetic expression.

Yet, clearing these bodies is only one big step. We must also learn not to "mess them up" again! This is where ego integration and an adoption of long standing spiritual teachings come clearly into view. As we awaken spiritually, we must take on a greater level of self-responsibility and learn to manage our energy bodies with greater consciousness.

There are energetic reasons we are instructed to be kind, forgiving, loving and peaceful – they are part of "energy management" 101. Individually, one may have personal lessons in any or all of these elements. One comes to understand that the wisdom in spiritual teachings is a requisite to maintaining a spiritual posture of balance and wellbeing at various levels of our experience. These teachings help us develop attributes of our spiritual nature. In essence, they define collectively who and how we are, when we are not confounded by wounded energies of the human experience.

Hence, the higher self understands love and wisdom as the nature of life; and, it is not entangled in duality the way we can be as human beings. If we are intentional and willing to align with its wisdom, it will help us disentangle ourselves from karmic and ego creations. We learn to live in peace, joy, faith, acceptance, compassion and love.

This discussion will become more meaningful as we explore the energy bodies, and our role as "energy managers" and "conscious co-creators" of our reality. The higher self understands that we are here, spiritually speaking, to learn, to grow and to awaken to our spiritual nature. Our potential is to "wake up" to the spiritual nature of reality and our intimate connectedness (or oneness) with it. This awakening brings a deeper healing to the surface in our lives.

This healing has an immediate impact on our energy bodies – so let us investigate our energetic nature ...

THE AURA

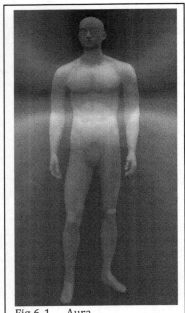

Fig 6-1   Aura

Most people today are familiar with the concept of an aura. The aura is a field of energy radiation around the human being. Just as a light bulb radiates energy as light, human beings radiate energy. The source of this energy is the source of universal life as it flows through our higher self and our various energy bodies. It is the light of spirit shining through us. (Fig 6-1)

Both the health and vibrancy of one's energy bodies, and the "energetic state" within a person's energy bodies at a point in time, will qualify this luminous energy. The energy is visible in a variety of ways to a large number of human beings who have a clairvoyant ability.

People sometimes think the aura is one color. The aura is more like a kaleidoscope. It will change in color because of changes in radiant vibration with changing experiences in the energy bodies. For example the colors change with emotions, or when one is actively engaged in passion filled activities. It will change when we are deep in thought, or deep in a meditative experience. It will change when we are angry, or when we are in joy. People may hold a dominant vibration or color, related to the structure of their energy fields, their personality and purpose, but the aura is an ever-changing field.

We will proceed to examine the energy bodies, which characterize the aura – but first a little fun! Let's do an exercise to see the aura.

Exercise To See The Aura

Find a very comfortable setting in a darkened room, to do this exercise. You may allow a little light through a closed curtain or night-light for example – but near darkness is ideal. If possible have a dark backdrop in front of you, such as a dark wall, sheet or towel. This serves as a darkened screen which helps register the contrast of light. This is the best condition in which to first see the aura. It is also important to be relaxed and comfortable.

1. Turn off the lights and get comfortable, sitting a few feet away from the dark "screen."

2. Hold your right hand about a foot out in front of you, with the palm facing you.

3. Look "gently" at your hand. Simply gaze at the hand in relaxed fashion. Do not try to focus. Let your focus "relax" so that it is viewing the whole space at once.

4. The aura will begin to appear as a haze or filaments of light, particularly around the fingertips, or around the palm. Relax and allow the energy to "appear" to you.

5. Now very slowly bring up your left hand to join your right hand. Hold the hands so that the fingertips of each hand are pointing to the opposite hand, with both palms toward your face. Bring the tips towards each other until they are very close but not touching.

6. Relax your gaze and again let the energy "appear". Energy will appear as fine lines of blue or colored light between the fingertips, which is etheric energy, but there may also be colors of light that are seen. Play with the energy as you pull your fingertips back and forth. Do you see it? Do you feel it? Record your experiences.

The Energy Bodies

The energy bodies we will first examine include the physical, the etheric, the emotional and the mental bodies. These bodies can be thought of as layers. Yet they are not layers in the sense of stacking one on top of the other. They co-exist in the same space as integrated fields or bodies of energy.

We are all familiar with our ability to physically see, touch, feel and so forth. We are aware that we sentiently feel and have emotions. We are aware of our ability to think, and the ability to use our thoughts to analyze or create experiences. Many people are also aware of themselves as a spiritual entity – a conscious being that exists above or beyond the functional abilities of thought and feeling.

We do, however, tend to think of these abilities mechanistically as functions of the human brain and central nervous system. We do not tend to appreciate that all of these functional abilities exist due to the presence of specific energy bodies that are part of human design. These energy bodies are integral to our being.

These bodies can be thought to interface with each other and with our human nervous system. When there is activity in any of the energy bodies it can create measurable changes in the human body and physiology. For example, if you are feeling joyful or angry – it will lead to direct physical and physiological changes in the "physical" body. However, the actual emotional experience is occurring in an energy body – a field of energy that is distinct to its own nature – the "emotional" body.

The changes are registered in the human body through an interface of the energy body with the physical body and human nervous system. As changes occur in these energy fields, the nervous system "picks them up" or registers them, kind of like a Wi-Fi receptor, and responds accordingly.

Even though most people do not "see" these energy bodies, everyone to some degree is aware of its existent reality. Yet, it is very valuable to begin to realize that we don not simply have these abilities – we have a structural emotional and mental body that exists and functions in kind.

From a spiritual perspective, these bodies may be thought of as a mechanism through which one's soul can experience life in the world of form. We can view our ability to think and feel as requisite abilities that we have in order to exist as human beings. They are functional capacities that may be used by one's soul. They are also inherent in creative function, to be able to bring our spirit intentions into the world of form through creative thought, emotional power and etheric construction.

If our thoughts and feelings are aligned with a balanced, peaceful, joyful state of presence, and we are aligned with our spiritual essence, life can be seen to emanate from our spirit. People define this as "presence", or "being in the now" moment. If this is not the case, we will find ourselves experiencing a whole array of things – and some of them very painful or oriented toward great suffering. These ultimately become stimuli – to orient us toward healing.

Our mental and emotional bodies are often not so "pure", and the world around us is not always conducive or supportive to provide a utopian happiness – and there are many reasons. This is due, in part, to the energy patterning in the very bodies we are about to discuss, and the way we use our thinking and feeling nature as human beings.

Healing will involve a "clearing" of the energy bodies, a restoration of damage to the energy bodies, and learning to be in a consciously responsible state of using the energy bodies. Through this we can more freely manifest a clearer picture of our inherent spiritual potential. As our energy bodies are healed and restored – the peace, the joy and the love that is inherent in an unobstructed free flowing energy system are gradually realized.

Our energy bodies can hold patterning and memory. The energy we hold in our mental and emotional body from prior experiences and wounds affects us greatly. This may influence the way we think and the way we feel minute-by-minute, day-by-day, and has a huge bearing on the quality of life that we lead.

Patterned energies of thought and emotions develop from our personal experiences, and they can exist as structural energy forms in these corresponding energy bodies. We have mental patterns and emotional patterns that can become so entrenched in our energy bodies that they add a constant pervasive influence in our lives. They become so entrenched that we think of them of as "who we are", or "the way we are made". They function as permanent fixtures of our personality and seem impossible to change. But some of these patterns are very limiting to our development of wellness or achieving our potential.

It is often stated as an axiom that spiritual healing is "remembering who you are" or "remembering your true nature". These statements actually relate to an understanding of the energy bodies. The energy entrenched in these bodies and the patterns they form in our lives are the very things that get in the way of our understanding of "who we are" – spiritually speaking. To "remember", we have to "let go" of such patterning within our energy system.

When wise beings declare such lofty things as "you are love" – they are referring to your essential nature, not necessarily your personality. We all know that, as "human beings" love is not easy to accept or manifest 100% of the time – but that doesn't change the truth. It changes our perception of the truth. This perception affects the perceptual reality of our lives. As we will come to explore, this altered perception arises in our energy bodies – through the emotional and mental content and often some of the wounds that we carry within.

The energy bodies coexist in "space" and influence each other. If we have heavy emotional energies clinging to us – it greatly affects the way we think and the way we feel physically in our bodies. Equally, the thoughts we temporarily or habitually hold affect the way we feel emotionally and our physical posture. The way the energy of the bodies "sum up" creates an *energy signature*. This energy signature is a creative force. It is like a magnetic posture that draws experience to us as human beings. In many ways, life is a reflection or "mirroring" of our personal *energy signature*.

Consciousness growth is important because it will teach us to relate to our personal emotional and mental nature in a wise, compassionate and nurturing way. It will also teach us to be responsible for how we manage this energy. When we begin to understand that our true nature is "spiritual" – we better understand how we can bring healing into the mental and emotional elements that cause "interference" in our lives. Some of these patterns arise from experience. Others patterns of interference can be understood in the term "ego". They arise from prior wounds and from fear based conditioning. We will explore this thoroughly in Chapter 10.

As we progress in our discussion, we will come to an understanding that many diseases, imbalances, and life experiences of great suffering can be created by the way mental and emotional energy is used or not used through the patterning and restrictions that exist in these energy bodies. Healing can be directed to the bodies, both through energy healing practices, as well as by acquiring consciousness of our own nature as spiritual entities. This provides the ability to be so much more conscious and responsible about the ways we "use" our mental, emotional and physical etheric energy in our day-to-day lives.

So let us take a look; at our many-bodied selves:

The Physical Body

The very first level of the human energy field, or the first "energy body", is not strictly an energy body in the way we normally think of energy. Unlike the bodies to follow, this one is completely available to the everyday human sensory system. It is the human physical body.

The physical body exists in our 3D sensory realm - it seems solid and is real. We do not question its existence or think of it ethereally, as we do the concept of energy. Yet, importantly, the physical body is a body of energy.

Our physical bodies are a structured, solid appearing reality. Yet, we now realize that everything on our planet is composed of complex inter related molecules which are made from elements and atoms as we discussed. Atoms are energetic entities having energetic relationships. There is no such thing as a strictly solid anything – everything is energy.

At the atomic level, structures that make up the particulate physical body are subject to energetic influences that may affect the energy within an atom. It is valuable to develop this understanding, to better appreciate how the body, which at first is very solid in appearance, is truly energy at its core nature. Then, it becomes a little easier to appreciate how energetic influences within the body, are capable of influencing the solid appearing physical body. If we appreciate this simple but powerful idea, we can appreciate how diseased tissues within the body can be "lifted vibrationally" to help them heal.

This is a small step in terms of understanding, but it is a giant step in awakening awareness in potential. It loosens the grip of logic on how physical things cannot change very readily. It also helps us realize how structural and functional diseases, which we think of as immutable, are subject to potential healing energetic influences.

In our modern world, we are aware that many diseases can be reversed or healed – even diseases we tend to think of as fatal, terminal or fixed. Many people know or have heard of someone who has experienced a "miraculous" or unexpected healing. When this unexplainable reversal of a disease occurs, the phenomenon is referred to as a spontaneous healing or spontaneous remission.

Spontaneous remission often defines a disease that reverses without any medical intervention. It is also a term used to describe the disappearance of a disease condition that is known to be extremely difficult or even impossible to treat with modern medical applications. For example, if someone had a cancer that is felt to be incurable – and it disappears – it would be described as a spontaneous remission.

At this marvel, science must throw its hands up in the air and say, "We simply don't understand." The reason it is so difficult to understand, is that the *basis* of its healing is not understood. Science has not developed a mature understanding of internal energy, or energetic corrections that can occur, which can lead to such healing. This is simply not implicit in the design or understanding of western medical teaching or research for obvious reasons.

An interesting phenomenon also occurs in clinical drug trials when people take an inert or chemically inactive substances referred to as a placebo. A subject usually takes these in a clinical trial under the context of belief that they are taking an active medication. In a trial to study the effectiveness of a new medication, it is compared to the outcome of a placebo therapy known as the "placebo effect". The study subjects who are receiving the placebo will have a measurable response during the treatment. These subjects are taking no active medication; yet they exhibit some sort of a healing response. This response is mystically innate to the body or induced by belief in the effectiveness of the therapy being administered.

Hence, a placebo effect defines a therapeutic response that occurs under the *belief* that one is taking a remedy, to treat an illness. This is such a powerful phenomenon, that it must be factored in research as the baseline to which any treatment must be compared! If a drug is being tested, it must have a greater effect on outcome than the observed placebo effect, to be considered potentially useful.

The premise of this important fact is surprisingly overlooked. It is astounding that the power of conscious belief can be potentially shown to influence healing – but this is little studied! How does such a healing occur?

Well, it could be understood to arise through energetic changes induced by consciousness. Spontaneous healing and placebo effect are mysterious because no model within our current science can explain them. Physical healings that are induced spontaneously, or through the consciousness influence of the placebo effect, are potentially demystified when we begin to understand the "energetic nature" of reality and how physical elements interact with energy or with the power of consciousness to rearrange itself and to heal.

We can examine how the power of consciousness and belief can govern physical matter. We can also explore how energetic or vibrational support from higher or inner dimensions of our own self through an expanded spiritual system can be invoked to promote healing and wellbeing in our bodies, and in our world at large.

When one entertains the idea that the human body is energy based – and that it may be subject to positive healing influences through energy and through consciousness – it becomes more comprehensible that manifest physical diseases can be reversed or healed. It is for this reason we benefit by learning to see the physical body as not simply physical, but as an energetic body as well.

To treat manifested physical diseases by energy is like treating a condition from the inside out. In traditional medicine we tend to treat *effect*, rather than *cause*. For example, if you have a cancer, we cut it out and/or poison it. If you are missing insulin, we replace it. We do not fully appreciate that many diseases are structural creations of discordant internal energetic issues. Some of the diseases may be viewed as "expected" manifestations in the setting of internal energetic states. Correcting the manifestation does not necessarily correct the *causative element*. If we could fix the "energy blueprint" – healing would be a very natural or "spontaneous" occurrence. As mystical as this sounds, it begins to make sense, and many people today have experienced this.

This awareness is slowly changing now as medicine begins to appreciate that everything which can influence the internal energetic state, can impact health. Medicine does not use the term "energy" per se, but it is becoming very aware that events, which positively and negatively influence one's energy - greatly influence health and wellness. Stress, depression, and anxiety, for example, all have an appreciable influence on a person's state of health. They can lead to a host of physiologic derangements that can lead to more and more serious disease states. So we are gradually moving into a greater "holistic" view of being human; but vicariously, and perhaps unknowingly, we are also beginning to appreciate the energetic underpinning that holds our manifested reality in place.

Medicine, through the cooperative success of many health pioneers, is being introduced to the important role of consciousness and human energy fields on health. If one can correct the energetic influence on the physical and etheric bodies, one can experience the healing of many disease states. By changing the blueprint – one can change the creation. In ways where it is possible to truly correct the energetic cause of an illness – illnesses, even physical illnesses can disappear. We need to "open" our minds – and for this reason we must appreciate the physical body as energy.

◉

As we discuss the physical body and healing, there are two very important points, which must be understood upfront. I will include them here, because people often seek physical healing, and it must be understood that physical healing must be accepted as part of a larger healing process:

First, it is important in discussing the concept of spontaneous healing that there are many factors, which can influence the ability or appropriateness to induce physical healing changes. Multiple issues influence illness and disease development. It can be challenging to manifest a healing. It is a process, which may require time, effort and often a degree of personal spiritual growth.

Sometimes when people begin to explore Energy Medicine, they do experience sudden and spontaneous healing of medical conditions. It can, and often does occur. At other times it is not as straightforward.

Healing in this expanded sense requires consciousness growth and the development of love-based responsibility around the issue at hand, in the person who is healing. So healing may require attainment of "elements of awareness" as part of a process. This is a deeper healing that serves some important spiritual development in the person's life. When physical healing or any aspect of healing does occur, it is not only the energetic clearing or restoration that is important. It is the consciousness that accompanies the healing. This will make more sense as we explore how mental and emotional energy, and energy restrictions based on prior conditioning – may impact our physical condition.

Physical and psychological disease states are often the nexus point for people to begin exploring spiritual life. An encounter with a serious illness, or disruptive condition, is often what triggers people to pursue a deeper level of healing and spiritual growth. When this is the case, physical healing is sometimes "appropriate" and sometimes a little more complicated – if you view the entire experience from a complete spiritual vista.

Transformative experiences induced through an illness are often spiritually very important to a person, from the perspective of the higher self. Healing may be deeper or multilayered in nature. Physical healing – may be only one element of a much larger spiritual process.

Personally, I have seen people heal from untreatable conditions. I have seen it happen "quickly" and "slowly". I have also seen people pass on with terminal diseases who still experienced profound spiritual healing through the process of the disease. They did not "overcome" the physical disease – but healing, from a spiritual perspective, still occurred. So healing is not restricted to the physical, but it certainly can occur at the physical level – an all-important distinction.

The second point is a word of reserved caution! As people begin to learn about energy healing, they will sometimes have a strong tendency to (or encounter people who will encourage them) to throw away western or traditional medicine in their effort to heal disease states. From my perspective, there is an enormous danger, and perhaps immaturity, in this attitude.

We must understand that if we have manifested a physical disease of any kind – western medicine has an enormous body of knowledge to help treat and manage conditions. Western or traditional therapies can serve to provide a vital and important foundation for greater healing. Western medicine is extremely useful – particularly in dealing with manifested disease. By the time a disease state is physically apparent in a person's life, the internal energy has been compromised for an extended period of time. It can be challenging to simply step in and correct the energy to "de-manifest" a disease.

Western treatments are expert at dealing with diseases at this level. You can use the knowledge of all forms of medicine and still be open minded to do deeper healing work. You can certainly work energetically and spiritually to heal deeply, while using traditional medical treatments in the process.

Medicine will continue to grow and offer new, gentler, energy based therapies in the years to come. However, if you are ill and need the offerings of medicine – for heaven's sake use them. Do not limit your self or your healing process by throwing away the healing benefits of modern therapies, particularly if you know intuitively that you need them at present, or they would benefit you.

Even though many of the disease states with which we are all familiar, can be understood to have origins in an "altered" internal energetic state, there is nothing wrong with treating the disease on the physical level. Personally, if I developed a tumor, I would have it removed! If someone has diabetes and insufficient insulin – insulin or medication to promote insulin regulation are life saving. It is so important to be clear headed about this.

While working with traditional therapies, it would be very beneficial for a person to continue to explore the "deeper" healing we are discussing. For example, if someone with a diabetic tendency comes to explore the idea of an inner correlation between the disease and a "third chakra" dysfunction, it might open the possibility for the chakra to be cleared and restructured - stimulating healing. As a person consciously engages in this healing – it would also manifest tangibly in interesting ways. It is highly likely that one's diet will improve, weight loss would likely occur, and insulin regulation will become more normalized. It is perhaps easy to see that energy changes are coupled with and supported by real life changes. There will be multilevel "real life" correlative changes that occur to support the improving energy function. This is a simple example of how traditional and alternative therapy might work hand in hand. If energy can be corrected from an internal energetic vantage – there will be a growth in consciousness – and the out-pictured physical state can be corrected also.

Hence, it is valuable to recognize the physical body as a very significant "energy body". The physical body is ultimately the anchor of our spirit in this world of form. The physical body pins our whole biospiritual continuum on the planet, and it can transform through an expanding consciousness of this continuum in rather miraculous ways.

THE ETHERIC BODY

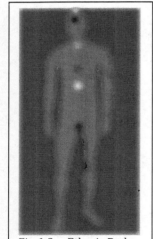

Fig 6-2   Etheric Body

When we move beyond the physical body – discussion of the "unseen" energy bodies becomes a bit more nebulous. These energy bodies do exist – but as we examined they exist outside of normal sensory spectrum. Today, there are many people who have developed the ability to see them but what is more complicated is that people do "see" them in different ways. The challenge is that they are not as structural as we would like to think of them.

Clairvoyants seem to "shift" into this vision and use it to work visibly on the energy system. Those with exceptional abilities have mapped the fields based on visual experience. One such very gifted healer is Dr. Barbara Brennan. I have not studied with Dr. Brennan, but I have certainly used the information she has made available in her two books.[7, 8]   Dr. Brennan was a scientist at NASA and through her personal awakening experiences developed tremendous insight into the human energy field. Her work provides a phenomenal understanding of the energy fields and related psychology.

It is also interesting to point out that although information of the human energy system is fresh to the western thinker, the overall understanding of the system of the energy bodies, chakras, and energy channels is not modern at all – it is in fact quite ancient. It dates back to texts and transcribed documents in Vedic teachings and Buddhist teachings, as well as Ancient Egyptian teachings thousands of years ago. This knowledge, to me, is resurfacing and adapting to western thinking today as part of the foundational paradigm shift we are living.

So let us "shift dimensions" and explore ... the etheric body.

⊙

The etheric body is the first level of energy we encounter beyond the threshold of direct physical observation. This living field of energy is a structural and functional template, which mirrors the human body. If you were to see it without the physical body attached to it - it is a translucent blue human shaped body – composed of filamentous lines of energy. (Fig 6-2)

Within the etheric field there are light based patterns of energy corresponding to the physical structure, as well as energy channels that relay information. For those familiar with eastern systems of medicine this would include acupuncture lines or meridians, and a complex system of smaller channels referred as the nadis.

Ancient Eastern systems of medicine were based on knowledge provided by the wise healers, who had sensitivity and awareness of this component of the human body. They used this understanding in nearly as concrete a way for healing, as we use drugs and surgery in our medicine today.

Now, because this energy it is not seen by most people, and we do not currently have technology to directly view it at present, it remains elusive. It is ethereal, mysterious and by most scientists, frankly disregarded. Regardless, there is a phenomenal body of intelligent understanding about the etheric body that has been preserved throughout the ages. Direct treatment of etheric energy is still used today in Ayurveda and Chinese Medicine therapies. One of the most familiar applications of etheric energy treatment in western world is perhaps acupuncture.

You can think of the etheric body as the structural energy blueprint of the body. It forms the energy field upon which the physical body is built and then sustained. Energy flows through the etheric body as a living energy field. If for any reason there is a defect, weakness or devitalization of the etheric body – the "out pictured physical body" cannot be completely healthy.

The reality of this body is actually encountered in modern science in the phenomenon of the "phantom limb effect". If a human being suddenly loses a limb, such as a leg or arm, by amputation, they do not immediately lose perception that the limb is missing. This is referred to as the phantom limb effect. The etheric form of the limb is present, although the physical limb is missing. The brain must accommodate to the missing physical limb.

The etheric body contains a vast network of energy channels through which energy flows. Energy can be fed into this etheric body by many mechanisms. One is by eating foods. Every food and every created thing – organic and otherwise – has an etheric energy component. Living things, such as fruits, vegetables, meat and grains – all have an etheric energy within them. When we consume food, we are not simply ingesting vitamins, minerals, fats, proteins and carbohydrates that make us the physical quality of the food. We are also consuming the etheric energy of the food material as well.

The structural components of food can be recycled into digestive elements to feed our physical body. However, on an etheric level, the energy of the food is also released into our etheric energy body to sustain health and energetic structure. This can also have medicinal applications as the energy of certain plants and herbs can have a strong and specific healing resonance.

Energy can also be fed into this system from universal or interdimensional energy forces, which can feed the etheric body. Many people today have heard of terms like universal life force energy, chi, ki, prana, and so forth. This higher spiritual energy can step down in vibration and flow into the etheric bodies to channel energy into the physical body.

Embedded within the etheric body are major and minor nexus points, where various channels of energy cross, and where multiple layers of the energy fields can interface. Larger hubs of circuits are commonly referred to as chakras. Major and minor chakras exist throughout the energy field. All of the energy bodies communicate through the embedded chakras – the etheric body, the emotional body, the mental body and higher energy bodies. Chakras have many interpretations and correspondences, but function sort of like transducers to channel energy between various bodies and between spiritual, energetic and physical levels. We will examine the concept of chakra more deeply in an upcoming chapter.

As a living energy 'blueprint', the etheric body serves as a resonant interface with the physical body. The etheric body holds a circuitry to channel this energy - kind of like the electrical wiring in a house but more quantum in nature. Life force energy flowing through the etheric body sustains life in the overlying physical structures and organs. But the body also interfaces with the human nervous system and autonomic nerve plexi that align the human spine. Through this interface, there is communication between the energetic element and the physical element of the human body.

Practices such as tai chi, yoga and pranayama breathing exercises use these principles to open, clear and charge the etheric system in the body with energy – through consciousness, movement and breath. In doing so, it strengthens and improves communication between the etheric body and the physical body, as well as its vibrancy and health.

As a person works to expand and clear the energy field through spiritual practices such as pranic breathing, simple conscious living, or in modern times simply surrender to the grace of healing – the energy flow into the physical body can be increased to support health, wellbeing and healing.

If a picture is worth a thousand words, then experience is worth ten thousand! Let us try an exercise to charge the etheric body, so you can feel your own etheric energy.

EXERCISE – SENSING ETHERIC ENERGY

1. Sit comfortably in a chair or on the floor. Bring you hands comfortably together palms up on your lap.
2. Take a moment to center and simply observe your state of being. Let thoughts come and go in a detached way. Just relax.
3. Begin to focus on your breathing.
4. Inhale gently through your nose and fill your chest with air. Do not force your breathing excessively – just breathe deeply, but comfortably.
5. Slowly release the breath through your nose and pause for several seconds.
6. Continue breathing - each time filling your chest and gently breathing a little deeper. Begin to loosen you belly, and let it expand with your breathing. Continue breathing until you find that you are able to fill your lungs with air and your belly with energy. The air is carrying prana, which is charging your etheric body.
7. Continue breathing for at least 3-5 minutes in this fashion.
8. Now pause.
9. Bring your awareness or attention to your whole body.
10. How does it feel? Are there specific areas that feel alive or energized? Areas that feel numb? Tight areas?

You may notice that you feel very invigorated. You may feel warm or cool. You may notice a tingling in any part of your charged etheric body. You may feel flashes or zaps of energy. You might notice little areas in your body that have popped or pulled during the breathing exercise or shortly thereafter. You may have also noticed that breathing at points in the exercise was difficult. It may have gotten easier to expand you body, and your energy with repetitive breaths as the energy charged your etheric body. Record your personal observations.

11. If there is an area of your body that feels restricted, continue the exercise for 3-5 more minutes. Gently breath energy into the areas of your body that feel tight or restrained. Do no force too hard, just keep breathing and gently energizing the area.
12. Now lie down and relax. Let the energy, which has accumulated in your etheric body, work for you. Try simply to fully relax and to let go. You can play soothing music while you do this if you like.

Pay attention to the experience you lived personally. These simple exercises will sensitize you to your energetic bodies. You are forging a relationship with your own energy fields as you participate. This will support you in your life, your wellness and your healing.

THE EMOTIONAL BODY

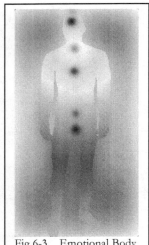

Fig 6-3   Emotional Body

The next level or energy body we encounter, is the emotional body. This too is a living field of energy. The emotional body is not structured tightly like the etheric body, but more fluid in its quality. It appears like a liquid or vaporous energy. Energy in the emotional body vibrates in resonance to the emotional experience present in the moment. It is influenced through our thoughts, our experiences and our spiritual openness. (Fig 6-3)

In a simplified way, emotional energy both flavors experience and energizes creation in our life. Emotional energy fuels creation through passionate feeling. When you feel "strongly" about something – you energize it.

In a clear uplifted emotional state, the vibratory quality of the emotional body is high. We feel buoyant. In such a state, the emotional body is luminous, full of spectral colors. But, we live many things in our emotional body. It is not always "buoyant". Let us take a simplified look at some of the qualities of our emotional nature to appreciate the "role" and "purpose" of the emotional body.

1. EMOTIONS ARE RESONANT TO THOUGHT AND EXPERIENCE, AND ALSO TO OUR SPIRITUAL SELF.

Emotions arise in response to both thought and experiences. Thought triggers emotion. Thoughts may be internal, i.e. thoughts we manifest or entertain in our own mind. Or, they may be external, arising from thoughts shared by those around us. Emotion is also triggered in response to experiences. Again this may involve experiences we create or allow with our imagination. Or, it may involve experiences that happen around us, or through other people and things in our lives.

Since emotions can arise in response to thought, emotions can also arise through memory. In fact patterns within us that are held from memory of prior experiences are one big factor that influences the activity in the emotional body. Experiences we have lived may create patterns of psychoemotional conditioning that continue to influence our life in an intermittent but continuous way. When we hold onto powerful emotional experiences through memory, it can deeply influence our life in the present day. Since some of this conditioning can influence our overall wellbeing in very challenging ways – it will be important when we explore emotional healing.

Emotional healing may involve "rooting" out emotional patterns that are influencing our life, our self-perception, our creative ability, and our health in various ways. For example, very painful or fear invoking experiences can leave strong emotional imprints and will need proper healing attention because of the strong influence they impose on our emotional body. Yet even simple but strongly conditioned patterns that have been created by our social and family conditioning may need to be examined. This would include attributes that were strongly patterned in our upbringing through reward, punishment, expectation or ridicule – just to name a few.

Healing involves reestablishing clarity in the emotional body and learning to use our emotional body with much greater conscious awareness. Therefore healing" also implies "spiritual development". Until we begin learning about ourselves in a more spiritually inclusive way – we take our emotional capacity for granted, and view it as mysterious. We tend to see emotions as "reality" vs. "experience", and we do not always understand how to relate to our emotional experiences with the wisdom of the soul. Introducing spiritual development in the healing of the emotional body introduces the important balancing power of our spiritual self.

2. THE EMOTIONAL BODY HAS A ROLE IN SENSORY FUNCTION.

The emotional body also plays a role in our *sensory capacity*. Through our emotional body and its innately sensitive nature, we are able to sense and feel on a "non" logical level of perception.

When we are emotionally open, our emotional nature can help us sense what we are experiencing within the environment around us. The emotional body can respond in "resonance" to external stimuli. Through this sentient capacity, we can be aware of what we are feeling in response to certain encounters, and even what others are feeling around us. We "resonate" with these experiences on an emotional level.

This ability is very important because it serves to guide us in our lives. It can reveal to us how we truly relate to the people and things around us, and serve as mechanism to help us align our lives with an authenticity.

As human beings we all face challenges that are related to emotional sentience. Challenges that arise can be arbitrarily grouped into two broad categories:

First, we do not always honor or respect the incredible value of this sentience. In failing to do this, we do not respect or trust it. Failure to honor this intuitive sense with which we are gifted can lead to many poor choices and difficult experiences. It does serve to "teach" us ultimately – but this is often through difficult experiences – and can be a difficult aspect in the journey of life.

Secondly, we each have historical programs that may impact, or "bias", our sensory nature. These arise particularly strongly in what we will explore later as wounds, and the human ego. This can distort our perception in ways that leads us to faulty perception and discernment. If we lose faith in our sentient ability, we may '"shut down" or feel lacking in trust toward our intuitive self, and certainly in trust toward others.

From a healing perspective, we must learn to be open emotionally, to trust and honor our emotional experiences – but also to be aware of where our own wounds and our perception may be tainting our emotional experience. These are discovered in the healing journey.

3. THE EMOTIONAL BODY IS NEUTRAL

Emotional energy that arises in our emotional body will be resonant at a certain level or quality of vibration. It can be of "high" or "low" vibration. Now this does not equate with good or bad, but can be helpful in self-understanding. The emotional body doesn't judge – it simply resonates. Let us examine.

Think of the last time you felt joyful. If you allow yourself to experience not simply the memory, but also the emotional experience – you will begin to feel the emotional energy of the memory. I encourage you to pause and do this with a personal example. Do not just "remember" a wonderful experience, but enter in to the emotional state as well.

Now imagine a time when you felt anger. The anger is a much "baser" emotion. It can also be very destructive in our energy field. Yet, it is not necessarily "bad" to deconstruct things – so it too has an emotional purpose.

Anger, particularly wound-based or chronic anger, can become very destructive. From a healthy vantage point, the experience of anger may be propelling us to make a choice which we have been resisting or failing to permit ourselves to make. Anger may help us arrive at a "breaking point" and is propelling us in positive direction. In this setting, the anger may be "good". Yet, anger may also be simply a "conditioned response". It might be triggered by patterns we may carry within us. At such times it is more of a defense mechanism than a force of positive change. But "holding" it energetically will have a strong influence on our overall energy.

The point here is that emotional body will "express energetically" the vibratory quality of any emotion that corresponds with the thought or experience we are having. It is neutral and obedient to what we are doing. The energy body is "indifferent" to the quality of energy we are creating emotionally. It follows suit to correspond with our thoughts and our experiences.

As emotions do arise, it is this energy that pulses in our emotional energy body. This comes to have an impact on our whole energy field and the aura radiation. It also impacts our human nervous system and physiology! [42] Emotions, in this way, "qualify" the energy in the emotional body. Emotions create a vibration. It is this vibration that then leads to an emotional perception as the energy interfaces with our human consciousness through our bodies and our nervous system. It also, however, has a creative influence upon what we are then creating at a moment in time.

The emotional body can move in resonance with joy, peace, and love – or anger, sadness, and guilt – with great obedience. But, the impact of the emotions must be respected, for they are not without consequence. We must learn to honor our emotional nature but also utilize our emotional energy wisely.

In understanding the actual existence of our "emotional body" as a real field of energy, we are better able to conceptualize how our emotional nature functions. We become more aware of how emotional wounds may impact the functioning of the emotional body. And although the body is neutral – the consequence of emotional expression is not. It affects us greatly.

But ... and an important one ... we are also able to recognize and learn about our spiritual power to "manage" our emotional nature with wisdom, honor, respect and maturity. What might that mean?

☉

Well, since we do not "see" our emotions directly, discussion can be nebulous. So let us examine the grossly visible outcome of certain emotional states to better understand.

If one were to become enraged, imagine the impact this state might have on one's life and one's overall energy signature. This state will stimulate certain thoughts. It will create certain types of conversations within one's mind and with other people. It might stimulate reactive behavior. This is all emotionally driven and this series of "experiences" will produce dynamic changes in the emotional body.

It will also have a transient but tangible effect on the health of one's physical body and wellbeing. Experientially, one might get headaches, sick to the stomach, unstable, depleted of energy, create an accident, and so forth.

The anger may be "understandable" when we examine the details of what has led to its arrival – but as a human being one will need to seek balance again - or the anger will become extremely self destructive.

Now, equally, if one is inspired and full of love – this state will stimulate a host of experiences. It will stimulate a certain quality of thought, other higher vibrational feelings, and inspire certain choices. This will also create a tangible shift in the quality of energy that is experienced within one's emotional body.

This will create a perceptible influence on our physiology and physical experience. One's vital signs like blood pressure or pulse will normalize. One will feel relaxed and open and more "free".

These simple demonstrations reveal the influence of how our emotional and mental experiences may influence one's "whole" experience. Hence, emotional energy can have a big influence on our overall health and wellbeing.

So by becoming aware first that there is such a thing as an "emotional body", then developing greater consciousness of how our emotional energy functions, and finally how we can govern our emotional energy – we are on a path of much greater self-awareness and wellbeing.

Suppression and Repression of Emotion

Let us next take a look as some simple attributes that may interfere with the function of the emotional body. It will then become easier to grasp what emotional healing may involve and what healthy emotional experience may provide to us.

As we live our day-to-day life, emotional energy can be *patterned, repressed, suppressed or unregulated* – all leading to different experiential issues. In terms of the energy body – these activities will each have energetic influences. They may structure or solidify emotional energy. They might dampen emotional energy. It can make us "retain" negatively qualified energy. It can even lead to distortion or destabilization of our "whole" being.

The way we think, and the way in particular that we repetitively think, influences the quality of vibration in our emotional body. Deeply programmed thoughts can give rise to patterned emotional experiences which become a fixed or structured states in the emotional body. Have you ever encountered someone who for example is "angry" or "frustrated" or "always anxious" – all the time? These are strong emotional states of fixed resonance and will require appropriate healing attention.

The quality of emotional energy is also strongly influenced by the *way we perceive and relate* to the experiences that we encounter, or how we process and react to people and to events in our environment and our life. Thoughts and experiences are powerful in stimulating emotional energy - but one experience that is particularly powerful to control emotional activity – is fear. Understanding the power of fear to impact our emotional body is another important step in greater self-awareness.

When negative emotional experiences arise, internally or externally, it becomes important to learn to process them appropriately. Learning to *process* emotional energy and *suppressing* emotional energy is not the same thing.

Suppressing emotional energy occurs most often through mental programming. The easiest way to appreciate this is simply by examining familiar societal customs or "norms".

Certain societies "feel freely". Other cultures are traditionally more emotionally "reserved". These become pervasive qualities of emotional experience, or "zones of comfort" for a person and a group of people. Emotional energy is normalized in different degrees and in different ways. In cultures where emotional energy is permitted in a minimal way, there exists an element of emotional body suppression.

Aside, please understand that to "exuberantly" feel or "reservedly" feel is more a function of quantity than quality. It is not nearly as important to have a big emotional expression, as the actual permission to feel and to honor your feeling nature. This discussion simply demonstrates the ability to "suppress" emotional energy. In some cultures it is almost considered taboo to have any emotional expression, particularly as a male.

Many people have learned to suppress their emotional expression – particularly in our societies where there is so much mental or external control – that the emotional nature of our being is to variable degrees "suffocated". If we suppress but do not process our emotional experiences we must understand that we are suppressing an actual energy event. Our emotional body is not free to function normally – because of our resistance.

Suppressed emotional energy can create a great deal of personal suffering and some very unhealthy patterns of behavior. It primarily leads to a devitalizing or distorting influence in one's life. If we suppress, we are shutting down our emotional body and our emotional nature. If we suppress our emotions we suppress our own power as well as our connectivity with our essential sentient self.

Emotional suppression, in combination with other factors, can lead to the physical and psychological manifestation of disease. People who have endured unbelievable acute or chronic life trauma either in present or past life times may have learned to suppress or adapt their emotional nature in different ways. Such experiences can lead to focal and/or generalized suppression of emotional energy – so that one may not risk "feeling" to suppress the pain.

This can manifest in retained emotional memories. Furthermore, in addition to a generalized emotional suppression, it can lead to specific flagrant emotional defense mechanisms. Defense mechanisms may be used to manipulate or control situations, because of an ingrained conscious or subconscious memory of a painful fear laden experience.

Repression of emotion is the activity of "holding on" to emotions – typically of low or discordant quality of energy, in an odd way, to avoid encountering them. People may build up congealed emotional energy within their energy system by repression. This will most typically occur around painful memories, which will ultimately need to be released and transformed.

If we retain this energy we are actually holding energy patterning in our emotional body. Sometimes these memories create very specific psychological patterns, which are potentially of a self destructive or limiting influence. If we retain them in our emotional body, we unfortunately also retain the influence of them in our vibratory signature.

When people have lived very painful traumas, this may have a very powerful influence in one's life. If we each explore ourselves deeply, almost all human beings have some such patterning in various ways. The energetic influence of many of these patterns are sometimes visible to people who are capable of seeing emotional energy. By they will be most visible by the influence they have on our lives.

Under the influence of repressed emotional patterning, one can ultimately manifest energy distortions that will affect the whole of one's energy system. This can lead to physical changes in the body, or even disease states. This occurs because the emotional retention leads to an energetic restriction. If energy accumulates, particularly dense emotional energy, it can create a multilevel distortion in the energy bodies. For example, emotionally laden energy can become congealed in the system, which could impact the function not only of the emotional body, but also the etheric body. We have already discussed the etheric body and its essential role in physical wellbeing. By conceptualizing this simple understanding, it is not difficult to appreciate how emotional repression may lead even to physical disease manifestation.

Repressed emotions can also influence the mental body and one's overall psychological function. The mental body actually plays a role in repression. But by holding on to hurtful emotional energy, it creates a further mental propensity to "think hurtfully" or in a devitalized and imbalanced way.

Such long-standing patterning can impact our energy field in many ways. Remember now that one's "internal energy" eventually "out-pictures" in our structural "reality". It becomes easier to see why holding certain energy configurations can "manifest" in our lives in a whole host of ways. It can affect everything from physical posture, psychological attitude, vitality, pain, career success, family and interpersonal relations, and even our health.

Now because of the influences of emotional suppression and repression – a great deal of early healing first involves the "simple" act of giving ourselves the permission to feel, and feel freely. Healing will then focus on the need to process feelings that surface through more patterned experiences in our lives. As one further makes progress, one will learn to handle one's emotional energy wisely, by understanding the need for balance, and through acquiring greater spiritual wisdom around our emotional nature.

Hence, suppression or repression is one large category of emotional body distortion. But, each coin has two sides ...

Unregulated Emotional Expression

In contraposition to these influences exists *unregulated emotional expression*. If someone is "uninhibited" emotionally, and there is no sense of containment or structure provided by the other energy bodies or the spirit – it too can wreak a certain kind of havoc. Powerful emotional energy with no mature restraint, or no ability to self balance and harmonize, can thrash like a powerful storm that throws a person's world into emotional chaos.

People who are uncontrolled in various ways with emotional expression will have to learn about the consequence of unrestrained emotional energy as it impacts their life, and often the lives of those around them.

This might occur after someone who long-lived repressed in their emotional nature first opens up – and must now learn to process emotional energy, as they become more confortable with their feeling nature. For others, it is a point of departure on the healing journey. Ultimately, we must each learn to handle emotional energy in an unrepressed but self-responsible way.

In addition to being simply "loose" or "free" emotionally, which is innocuous mostly, people can learn to use emotional energy in unhealthy and sometimes very distorted and unregulated ways. Just think for a moment of all the various forms of psycho-emotional control and defense mechanisms that can be triggered in human behavior. People may be hostile or angry, threatening, demanding, manipulative, seductive and so forth. These patterns are "logically" often understandable, but equally "spiritually" misguided, as we shall explore.

◉

So what is the value of understanding the simple principles of programming, suppression, repression and non-regulation of emotional energy? It helps us gain insight into the ways the emotional body may contribute to unhealthy patterns of manifestation. It also helps us develop an attitude of self-responsible awareness – so that we are actually able to heal the emotional body and ultimately "manage" our emotional energy.

The concept of healing emotions and regulating emotional energy becomes easier to grasp when we do appreciate the actual existence of the "emotional body" as an energetic field of energy. Acknowledging its existence, and understanding a little better how it operates – we open the door to realize that "whatever is going on in our mental and emotional bodies" right now, can be healed. This creates a nonlinear two-step process – where we *first* expose and examine "what is present in these bodies" to raise the potential for healing, and *secondly* learn to utilize our understanding of these bodies in a spiritually conscious way.

As the emotional body is progressively healed it develops in strength and power and rises in its overall energetic vibrancy. The path of healing and developing a spiritual wisdom in relation to our emotional self (as one aspect of our self) is sometimes referred spiritually as a component of the path of "mastery". Mastery is a state of greater self-awareness and greater ability to let the wisdom of our spiritual nature emerge and express through our emotions as well as our mental nature, and all of our life.

Emotional Mastery and Healing the Emotional Body

Learning to open emotionally, to more fully experience your own spiritual nature can be perceived as a very difficult and challenge-fraught journey. This is because, in learning to open emotionally, we have to rise up through the patterns we hold – and transform the energy embedded in our own personal energy fields. This is easy to conceptualize, but can be scary, difficult or downright threatening to live at times.

Emotional work will sometimes surface deeply buried emotional memories from earlier in our lives, and even memories of "alternate" or "past life" experiences. It is important as one encounter this, to understand that they surface not to burden – but to heal. It can become a little easier digest this, if you can appreciate logically what is happening within the experience, and find supportive ways to handle the process of what is taking place. To grow spiritually, healing these emotional patterns and issues becomes paramount.

Habitual feelings, patterned repression, and patterns of emotional defense or manipulation can have a strong influence on the types of things we create or do not create in our life – and they will need healing attention.

To understand how emotional laden memories may affect us, it may be easiest to think compassionately of someone who has experienced a deep and traumatic psychological experience. This may even be you. It is easy to comprehend how such experience can lead to various "attitudes" and "defense mechanisms". When we witness these behaviors in our self or in others - it is often very easy to grasp how they are produced and why they occur. In terms of energy, they will have a direct correlation to energetic events in the energy bodies.

You might ask, "How is it that the energy patterning we carry can become 'creative' or lead to certain types of 'manifest' experiences?" Well, the energy patterning in each of our energy bodies contributes to the whole picture of who we are. Certain emotional patterns are like an energy posture that puts a stamp on our energy field. Have you ever met a person who is really "closed" emotionally? Or defensive in their nature? Or impatient? You see, our energy bodies produce an overall "signature" vibration. This vibration is influenced by these emotion-based energy attributes. Equally important, our overall signature can be creatively seen as "magnetic". We resonantly attract some experiences to "match" the vibratory quality we exude. The angry person, for example, is running around finding people to make them angry wherever they go.

The energy signature serves like a cohesive "force field" to help draw experiences toward itself, which mirrors its state of resonance. This occurs perhaps, so that we can "witness ourselves". So even though it might be very understandable why someone becomes defensive, self protective or angry, it creates a problem for the person enduring the wound and energy pattern – because it continues to affect one's life by drawing correlating experiences until it is healed.

In a healthy state, the emotional body is increasingly unencumbered by historical energies and patterned behaviors. A clear and balanced emotional body is free to "work with" the higher-level bodies - to become a co-creative partner with spirit. Emotional energy so aligned, can passionately and freely energize inspired ideas in our life, and lead to a joyful life in the world of form. This type of mastery is the goal of emotional healing work.

Emotional energy can effectively "energize" thoughts and bring creative thought into the manifest physical world. Think about how easy it is to achieve something when your inspired thoughts are emotionally energized in happiness and joy! A balanced emotional body can also relate wisely and sensitively to the world of form, guided by the wise awareness of ones spiritual nature as it responds to the world around it. This is what true emotional healing will provide.

In the process of healing the emotional body, there is no doubt that *energy healing techniques* can be very helpful. This can occur by "raising" the vibrational quality of the emotional body and transforming or transmuting these energies through energy and consciousness healing practices. It is however critical to realize that we cannot bypass the important development of consciousness that accompanies our spiritual development. So some aspects of emotional healing will require a conscious processing of psycho-emotional patterns – even in conjunction with energetic support – to better understand how certain patterns are affecting one's life. This implies a learning process.

In my experience, conscious work coupled with energy support is highly supportive. I believe it is important to state that emotional patterns that are deeply based in one's psyche may be difficult for a person to first see within himself or herself. It is often said that it is most difficult to see our own foibles – we need a wife or husband for that ☺! We do have to consciously turn our attention inward to look compassionately but honestly at ourselves, or our growth will always be restricted.

Deeply embedded emotional wounds, and the psycho-emotional patterns they lead to, can become a very concrete part of one's personality and require insight and self-reflection to see, to acknowledge and to transform. When deep and very painful psychological traumas or wounds exist – we will also likely benefit from wise, compassionate and enduring support through this time of healing a trauma and establishing a trusting and enlivened relationship with life.

☉

I am unreasonably simplifying the nature and depth of emotional healing work in this short discussion. This is not to make it seem simple for it can be very challenging. Its purpose is to provide a requisite overview of the energetic correlation of the healing process. For people who are deeply interested in this topic and in search of specific healing strategies I will reference a few very good works on the topic of Energy Psychology and related work.[19,39,40,42]

Finally, it is essential to realize that regardless of what behaviors any of us have adopted in response to the events of life, or the influential painful emotional memories and patterns we carry from this life or prior lives - no one is less than love-based in their truest ego healed nature. This is a mystical but true statement. It is the foundational path to healing and true freedom when it is deeply understood. The truth in this statement alone provides the necessary light to guide us through a turbulent sea of emotional healing or any night of darkness.

So let us take a moment to connect with our own emotional body:

EXERCISE TO FEEL THE EMOTIONAL BODY:

1. Sit reclined or lay down in a relaxed and very comfortable position.
2. Take a few centering breaths and let go of any thoughts or emotions like passing winds or waves.
3. Imagine feeling very centered and very peaceful. Sit in this quiet space for a few minutes.
4. Now engage your thinking – and imagine yourself at a time when you felt great joy. Perhaps the birth of child, reuniting with a loved one, or with some personal accomplishment. Let the emotion of the memory build in your awareness. Feel it. Bathe in it.
5. Now remember a time when you were very disappointed by someone or some event in your life. Perhaps a personal loss, a broken promise, or a disappointing outcome. Register where and how in your body you recognize the emotion. Again, feel it - bathe in it.
6. Now imagine yourself in a state of unfettered peace. Imagine every worry, frustration, duty or responsibility falling away. Let yourself sink into a deeply peaceful state. There is nothing that could penetrate the shield of peace you feel around you now. Sit in this energy for as long as you like.

As simple as this exercise is, you are going through the process of activating your emotional body – in this case through thought and memory. Yet even though you are activating the emotional body arbitrarily, the emotional experience is real. There are dynamic changes that occur in your emotional body if you permit them. In this activity your emotional body is "vibrating" in correspondence to the emotion you are feeling. To do this, you are consciously connecting with your own emotional body.

THE NATURE OF EMOTION

There are a few important things to highlight about the function of the emotional body and the nature of emotions. Let us expand on them here for they will become valuable later when we discuss healing.

First, emotional experiences are often induced by certain thoughts. By focusing on particular thoughts, or creatively imaging an experience, we are capable of creating specific emotional states.

Two, emotional experiences can also be induced by external stimuli – people, information, events. We can have emotional experience in response to such triggers.

Three, internal and external thoughts and/or experiences may propagate as an internal experience. A thought or an event may trigger an emotion. This can create new thoughts and new feelings. There is a potential cascade of thoughts and subsequent feelings, which may ensue. This "thought-feeling" interrelationship is occurring all the time in our life, whether we are conscious of it or not. Chains of thoughts and feelings can occur creating a "whole story" in our minds. This will of course, influence our energy state.

Four, by understanding this interrelationship of thought and emotion, we can learn to "intervene" in our own mental and emotional programs. This becomes important when we will take a look at the psychodynamic aspects of healing. We have all had the experience in life when a certain psycho-emotional state takes over, following some triggering event. We can be thrown into a reflexive pattern of thought and feeling – which can endure for quite some time if we are not conscious of it.

Five, emotions are an *experience.* They occur as the vibratory resonance in our emotional body, which interfaces with our consciousness and our nervous system.

Six, as an experience – all emotions are *transient* by nature. Emotions come and emotions go – all of them. No emotion is permanent – but we can "attach" to the emotion or actively "resist" the emotion. Our attachment to certain emotions and our repulsion of certain emotions creates a fair amount of human suffering.

Finding Harmony

Ultimately, the souls objective is not simply to "be happy" or "not be sad". It is rather to align with spiritual truth. Goals such as learning to be happy may serve a purpose in the early phases of healing the emotional body. For example a person may be working to move out of deeply negative programming, and learning to be happy is a counterbalancing activity. But learning to be happy will not encounter enduring success without understanding some deeper elements of spiritual growth. It's like planting a rose in an overgrown garden of weeds.

It is important not to cling to positive emotions or avoid negative ones. An emotional state is not an identity – it is an experience. You are vaster than anything you may transiently feel. A great deal of suffering arises when we try to create only one feeling, or if we are clinging to the presence or absence of any particular emotional state.

A major aspect of emotional body healing is developing a conscious understanding that emotions are meant to flow. We must allow ourselves to feel – which is for many people a first step in emotional healing. But then we can learn to take the role of a conscious witness to our emotional experience. This is sometimes referred to as learning detachment.

Detachment is *not* a state of "not" feeling – it is a practice of learning to witness and be undisturbed by one's emotions as they rise and fall away. It is actually learning to be more conscious in the way we relate to our emotional energy. By witnessing our emotional experience we are allowing it, honoring it – but not staying attached to it (or running away from it) as a perceptual reality.

Why is this important? Well, emotions can guide us in the ways we have reviewed, but emotions are also a very powerful energy. We run into a little trouble, so to speak, when an emotion becomes an identity rather that an experience. We become fully "at the mercy of the emotion" rather than conscious in our presence and creative potential. Learning to identify with an emotion as a transient experience and not a state of *identity* is important. So you see, a paradox arises.

How many times have you heard someone say, "I am angry." Or, "I am so happy."? In this statement we identify with emotion as an *identity*, not an *experience*. I feel anger or I feel happy is more precise. But, is this just semantics?

Not really. Your identity is one of a spiritually conscious being – one that is capable of feeling. If you realize anger is *transient*, you can acknowledge the experience but do not need to attach to it so strongly. When not attached, you can more objectively see what the anger means to you and how to process it appropriately.

You cannot feel happy or endure any single emotion all the time. You can however learn to be at peace within yourself, regardless of the emotions that arise within and around you. But this requires a healthy sense of detachment.

This becomes very important when we begin to examine the spiritual work of ego transformation. Detachment in essence is overcoming ego identification within the emotional experience. The peace that flourishes leads to a deeper joy that is above a simple sense of emotional fulfillment.

Our emotions are important "registers" of our experiences. If we are feeling angry in an event in our life, there may be an important element out of balance in our life that needs to be properly addressed. The anger may be a force of guidance. If we are not allowed to feel it, or not supposed to feel it – because we are trying to be happy – it creates problems. However, if we get lost in the emotion or over-identify with the emotion – it creates a different set of problems. We have to find our center from which we can master our emotional experience, and the use of our emotional body.

Learning to live at the center of our emotional experiences in a witnessing state of awareness, one where we are not controlled by our emotions, but yet very conscious and respectful towards them - is the destiny of the path of emotional healing. This is a major step on the path of spiritual liberation. In learning to reconcile these patterns, we understand we must respect, acknowledge and process our emotions, but not be "controlled" by emotional states as if they are "our identity" and learn to consciously support balance within our own energy system.

By developing an understanding of our emotions as vibratory moments, and that we are conscious beings learning to handle our emotional energy and energy body, we can learn to recognize and ride the emotional ups and downs until our spirit learns to calm the seas of potential emotional drama. We can learn to discover and live in the center of our "whole" self – in conscious and authentic peace. Regardless of the emotions we encounter within our self, or the behavior we encounter in other people and the world around us, we rest safe and sure in the center of our own heart.

This frees the emotional body to channel energy the way it is spiritually designed to do – as a creative force – one that can be applied through inspired creative activity. The emotional body becomes a healthy and life affirming vehicle to support and drive our life.

Life flows, and emotional energy is part of that flow. Joy, however, arises in a state of presence, which is vaster than a simple emotional experience. Joy is a vibratory quality that is stimulated within our spirit to resonate within our emotional body as we learn to open, heal and then balance our emotional body.

The Emotional Body in Summary

In summary, we have an emotional body in which our emotional life resonates. The emotions we feel are transient vibratory experiences occurring in our emotional body in response to many stimuli. Emotional energy is also used to empower creative life.

Emotional "patterns" occur, which can have an effect on our emotional bodies – usually in response to prior experience. Simply speaking, if dense negative or suppressive emotions are built up – they can clog the system and lead to energy blockages. Fear is always a component of this process. Patterns that produce these changes and correlating changes in our energy system will be encountered in a healing journey.

It is important to allow emotions. If we restrict, feed or retain certain emotional states – there is a corresponding energy shift in our emotional body. If the mental body restricts the emotional body by suppression – it will also block the flow of energy in our integrated energy system.

It is also important not to over-identify with emotion while still recognizing and honoring the emotions that we feel. They are experiences. Learning to witness our emotional nature is a key to freeing ourselves from difficult emotional states.

There is not a single script that defines the journey of "emotional healing" for all people. Some people will have to undergo a process of deep healing of well-established emotional patterns and deep emotional wounds. Others don't carry this challenge. But everyone will have to learn to live in harmony with his or her emotional nature.

In context of healing and Energy Medicine there are *energy practices* and *consciousness practices* that can raise awareness and stimulate healing of emotional issues. They may help to release repressed or congealed emotional energy, and directly support healing within the emotional body. They may also "enlighten" our awareness of such patterns, and facilitate a consciousness shift that helps us move forward in our healing journey.

This leads us ultimately into a deeper spiritual component of emotional healing. When people have experienced deep emotional wounds, chief among healing strategies for emotional healing will be the role of authentic "forgiveness" and the "ego busting" practice of conscious peace! They invoke emotional healing by the wisdom they contain – but they are more "spiritual" than strictly "emotional" in quality so we will save them for later discussion. We will explore these concepts as "practices" – and they will have a direct correlation with healing and balancing the human energy fields. So let's now move forward and take a look at the mental body.

THE MENTAL BODY

Fig 6-4 Mental Body

THE NATURE OF THE MENTAL BODY

The next level of energy is the mental body. In many ways today, we tend to think of "thought" as life itself. We have all heard of the famous quote by Descartes, "I think, therefore, I am".

In a bigger understanding of our human nature, we exist not simply through thought but rather through consciousness. Forming and analyzing thoughts, creating beliefs and all mental capacities that we have are a function of consciousness, not really an identity. And as a function of consciousness they occur through energy bodies.

Thinking, simply put, is an ability we have as *conscious* beings. So the capacity to relate to thought, and to form or hold beliefs, can be conceptualized as a function of the mental body.

We also typically view thought and memory as being sourced in our brain and nervous system. We are familiar with statements like "I have this thought in my head" and " we use our brains" to be intelligent. But the idea of thought originating in the brain is not entirely true. Thoughts take form and are processed, not simply in the brain, but in a vaster field of energy, and part of this takes form within us as a mental body of energy. The mental body exists as a field of energy that is an integral part of our energy make up. We can understand it as an energy field with the inherent ability to handle "thought based energy".

The mental body is described to hold a structural quality similar to the human shape, appearing in a healthy state as yellowish gold color in vibration. In a highly simplified view, the energy of the mental body can be visualized like a crystalline play-dough – that registers, molds and shapes energy in form - in response to thought formation through applied human consciousness.

The energy within the mental field can be used to build and hold, or crystallize, certain thought forms – as structural energy patterns. Energy patterns in the mental body can be viewed to interface with the human nervous system, and be interpreted in cognizant ways by our nervous system through a function of consciousness. (Fig 6-4)

Thought can be understood to "take form" in a similar way to sound. Recall how sound is creates structured energy like witnessed in our discussion of cybernetics. We can conceptualize the mental body as the substrate on which consciousness is applied to form energy patterns. Focused consciousness through thought acts like a vibration – which begins to take an energetic form.

A thought form once created can be further "energized" by applied focused concentration. This is essentially what happens when we focus (i.e. apply consciousness) on a thought. Focusing on certain thoughts in the mental fields can create and magnify the energy in a corresponding "energy form". The stronger these thought forms are, the more powerfully they are resonating in our energy field and the more creative they become.

"Thoughts create your reality" is a popular idea in both New Age and even mainstream circles today – because we are beginning to more consciously understand the power of thought to influence our lives. Our thoughts, particularly deeply embedded thought forms we hold, can certainly strongly influence what we encounter in our manifested reality.

The energy that we structure into our mental body is held like a pattern of vibration – and contributes to the overall energy signature we hold. It has "magnetic" quality once it is part of our signature, as we reviewed earlier. Our "vibratory reality" is the framework upon which our lives are built.

Thoughts, once crystalized, function like a creative seeds. Just as the seed of a tree, once planted, slowly and systematically magnetizes the many structural elements it needs to grow into a full-scale tree – thoughts draw on the energy they need around them to grow into manifest reality. This can lead to the manifestation of form expressions as well as creative experiences in the physical world, experiences that are based entirely upon the vibratory quality of our thoughts and belief systems. We can all relate to this understanding in some way if we reflect on our lives.

We can begin to appreciate the creative mechanism behind statements such as "*You* create your own reality" – when we begin to understand vibratory creation. The thoughts we hold in our mental field are one component of our vibratory signature. As we understand this in a more conceptual way by looking at the mental body, we can appreciate the value of learning to use our thoughts and mental capacity with greater consciousness. We can plant life affirming thoughts and weed out some of the pre-existing vegetation growing in our mind field!

Vicariously, it is important to return the power of the mental function to the responsible owner. We begin to see that as beings of consciousness we can decide what goes into any of our bodies – including our mental one. As we take on this important responsibility, we access a new power to transform our lives in many ways – and to heal. Why is this so important?

Well, you can change thought forms held in your mental field. We are not nearly as rigid or fixed as we might have once believed we were. If you can become aware of the existence of thoughts you hold, and aware of the limitations they impose, or, aware of the destructive experiences they create in your life – and they **can** be transformed. Equally, you can also seed very life affirming thoughts and beliefs into your mental body.

If elements of our life are out of sync with what we would like to manifest in some way – examining our thoughts, thought patterns and ingrained beliefs are essentially always an element of healing and transformation. Thoughts may need to be examined, consciously challenged, and often dismantled as part of healing and spiritual growth.

We learn that we can "remodel" our mental nature. But to do this, of course, we must step out of our "mental nature" as the basis of our identity, and into our core spiritual nature or true essence – where we find a greater freedom to transform. We can learn to be more responsible of our mental capacity from the perspective of our higher self. We can transform the body of thoughts we hold around us.

Where Do Thoughts Come From?

Sharing Thought Energy ...

We have talked about forming thoughts in our mental body by focusing our consciousness on an idea. But there are many ways that thoughts are brought into our consciousness. Let's examine a few important ones.

In addition to forming thoughts by applied consciousness, we can "share" thoughts or "assimilate" thoughts that have been already formed and are shared with us. We do this every time we speak to each other. This in essence is how basic mental based *learning* takes places. Thoughts shared are brought to the forefront of our conscious awareness, processed and assimilated into our mental body or dissipated.

When our mental body is exposed to an external or internal thought in this way

– it can be seen to "interface" with the thought forms. It can "pick up" thoughts and through mental resonance can assimilate, transform or reject the thought – depending on how one relates to it. When people share thoughts, and we accept these thoughts as valid, we can retain them. If people share thoughts – a resonant vibration occurs in our mental field – and we can consciously "hold" it or "integrate" it into our mental field.

Shared learning, a requisite experience as a human being, occurs through this process. Education achieved through mental processes is assimilated into a person's mental field, and it will in essence become inherent within the mental capacity of a student. This capacity to learn is critical to human development. It can be used to teach lots of higher abilities, such as those familiar to all of us both within and outside our systems of education. It can also be used to teach life affirming things, or life limiting things, as we are all aware.

Thoughts can also arise in our conscious awareness because they are already held in our own mental body and are triggered. This is useful to grasp because we all carry thought forms and beliefs within us. Our awareness of them becomes important when we are faced with particular psychological issues or challenges when the desire to grow, heal and transform arises.

Thoughts can also come into our awareness because they are part of the collective field of the mental energy of humanity. And, thoughts can also arise from the higher mind function of our greater self and our universal connection. This too becomes important in looking at healing and transformation.

When we are consciously seeking to evolve, new information is being introduced to us, particularly in the context of healing and spiritual development.

This same principle holds true when we look at new discoveries in science, creative arts, and so forth – thoughts may flow or be inspired from a higher consciousness than the one in which we spend our every day lives.

Now of course this is over simplified a little – but it gives us a good foundation to prepare to understand mental level healing …

BUILDING STRUCTURE THROUGH MEMORY AND BELIEFS

So, again, thought forms can be retained and stored in the mental body. Some thought forms we encounter are fleeting – they pass through the mental field or are dissipated quickly. For example if you notice a beautiful warm sunshine and gentle breeze as you step out of you house, you may create the thought "What a beautiful day!" The thought arises and passes quickly.

Other thoughts are held in a more enduring form. For example, when asked "Who are you?" – you are likely to say statements like, "I am ... a mother, a lawyer, an adult, a Japanese American – or something akin." These thoughts have more structured presence in the mental body. This helps us conceptualize how we develop strongly structured personal thought forms (beliefs), memories and engrained belief systems.

In examining the mental field of energy, well-developed thoughts can create a certain "posturing" and create an over-laying programming which may strongly influence our life. This will include the "core beliefs" that each of us holds as human beings. They contribute to structuring the boundaries, the qualities and the nature of our personal "reality".

Thought forms held in the mental field can be "activated" when consciousness is focused on them. These thoughts, held transiently or more steadily in the mental body, create a vibratory resonance when consciousness is applied. Various experiences can serve as triggers to engage these thought patterns. This helps conceptualize how mental memory is "brought forward" in a moment of conscious awareness.

Our mental field, like our emotional field, is neutral. It is not particularly concerned about the content or activity – it simply molds itself to the thought energy to which it is exposed or consciously engaged in. However, when we hold strongly on a thought it takes on a magnetic power for us personally.

People can carry any infinite number and type of thought patterns. They may come from repetitive programming by oneself, ones experiences or social conditioning – or even from another lifetime!

Strongly well-formed beliefs will influence, and in fact in many ways dictate, the experience you live as your life. The way one thinks, the limitations one perceives, the things one has been told about one's self and have accepted as true, the judgments imposed on ourselves, schools of thought to which one ascribes, and so forth – all have formative influence on what we know to be the experience of our lives.

Think how strongly ideas control our society. Think how much we ascribe to modeling ourselves after certain ideas or ideals – many of them noble and progressive and many of them downright objectively absurd. As we become aware and responsible for the use of our own mental bodies, spirit will teach us about the use and healing of mental function.

The Mental Body Interface with Consciousness, Other Energy Bodies, and the Human Nervous System

Thought-forms in our mental body can be understood to "interface" with the adjacent energy bodies (emotional and etheric), as well as our physical body and our nervous system. Conceptually, this occurs in the form of a coherent vibration or vibratory signal. Thought will interact with the human nervous system through the energetic-nervous system interface.

It is of course much more complicated than this simple explanation – but this provides a conceptual overview of the mechanism of thought forms and function. If thoughts trigger the emotional body, draw upon and mold etheric energy to bring it into form.

When certain thoughts and emotions are energized in our energy bodies they create a vibration. The vibratory energy can be understood to "interface" with what we more commonly perceive to be the seat of our consciousness experience – our brain. Energy interfaces with our brain and nervous system and stimulates changes in our nervous system. To grasp this – imagine how a certain thought might stimulate a sigh or a faster heart rate, a state of happiness or relaxation, and so forth. It can also stimulate an action or activity. If you "think" about "jogging" or "going shopping", for example, and agree to do so – you might find yourself engaged in the thought in no time.

Now, it is important to realize that the thought forms we entertain will also interface with our consciousness. Consciousness, core to our essential nature, is different than simply thoughts and beliefs. Thoughts may be simply viewed as vibratory signatures in the mental field. Consciousness is transcendent to thought and can actually process and analyze thought, and even stimulate the transformation of thought, as we shall explore. It is this important interface of the mental body with our higher consciousness that provides a doorway to grow, learn, transform or heal in the mental realm of life.

As we seek to grow and learn, consciousness can help us learn to refine our thoughts and teach us to work responsibly with our mental energy. In its simplest form this might mean developing a grasp of moral awareness, or in teaching "right action" from a spiritual perspective. However, through consciousness one can expand beyond concrete programs of learning and come to understand a greater awareness of life, which includes the capacity to consciously work and transform the whole nature of our mental function as a responsible conscious creator.

Growth of this kind can lead us to an inspection of our core beliefs, and help us through insight reveal dysfunctional and limiting beliefs that we carry. As consciousness supports us in uncovering these attributes in our self – it will also help us "clean house" or transform what is found. This expansion, and the subsequent processing, will help us rescript the world we manifest.

It is in this sense that spiritual enlightenment will illumine human thinking and can correct thought, thinking patterns and belief systems that are in a sense "in betrayal" to the human spirit. Part of healing at the mental level is learning to identify the personal thoughts and core beliefs we hold onto, which are limiting, self destructive, or disabling to the majesty of the human spirit. We will approach developing this awareness in upcoming chapters by developing a greater understanding that such thoughts and beliefs can be recognized through the common thread of "fear" upon which they are founded.

Learning to replace them with healthier thoughts and beliefs is part of the journey of growth in consciousness. The ability to do this only becomes possible when we dis-identify with the thoughts as our "identity" or reality, and understand ourselves to be spiritual beings with the capacity to re-model our thoughts at will.

Mental healing will involve discovering and dismantling some of the thought forms, that have "taken up residence" in our mental body, and the influence they impress upon our lives. This work is the focus of *inspired* psychological or psycho-spiritual healing modalities. These thought forms and beliefs can be quite tenacious – particularly when held in place by deep fears or ego forces. This work can require wisdom, patience and a great deal of self-compassion and understanding to unravel. It is a bit like weeding a garden so it can flourish in a more beautiful way.

So lets move beyond the theoretical understanding into a personal experience. We use our mental function everyday, so it is not new to encounter thoughts or thought functions. Let us, however, take a few minutes to *consciously* experience the mental level of energy.

    EXERCISE TO EXPERIENCE THE MENTAL BODY:

1. Sit in a quiet and comfortable position.
2. Take a few deep breaths and let yourself settle into a deeper relaxation.
3. As you sit quietly, become aware of thoughts that arise in your mind. Thoughts of work, your family, or an activity might arise.

4. Take a moment and pick a thought - and energize it simply by focusing your consciousness on it. As you focus your consciousness on a thought, you are actually energizing it.
5. Next, let the thought go, and return to observing the thoughts that are passing through your awareness. Whatever thoughts arise, do not attach to the thoughts as they arise, simply observe them. Let them come and go.
6. As a thought arises, pay attention to how your mind "ponders" the thought - and notice how it moves from thought to thought.
7. If a thought takes on a strong presence and you cannot let it pass, bring your attention back to your breath. Take a focused conscious breath.
8. Realize you can consciously redirect your thinking by doing this.

Become gently aware that you are able to "witness" your thoughts as events. Thoughts arise and fall, come and go – but you are constantly present. You are able to detach and witness your thoughts as experiences. This provides a little clue to how we can begin to heal through greater conscious awareness.

The Concept and Value of Witnessing

Taking the role of witness, we have the opportunity to experience our mental body, understanding what it means to witness our thoughts. Appreciating that we have a consciousness that is distinct from our mental function, we can realize that we are witnessing thought forms. A question arises: Who is witnessing?

Well, You are! If you can witness your thought process, you exist as a conscious entity that is bigger than, but "includes" your mental capacity.

Through this simple understanding, one realizes that we are never limited by what we currently hold, in our thoughts and beliefs, to be true. It is through the capacity to gain insight and awareness about what patterns we carry – and work towards (or allow) for appropriate changes – that we appreciate our ability to transform. It is extremely valuable to loosen the rigidity with which we hold onto some thoughts and beliefs – particularly the ones that are based on wounds and the fears that keep them in place.

Having an "open mind" in this context is very important in healing. Our life in any way that is limited will have a strong component of mental structure holding in place that will require transformation and change. For example if one believes they are of limited worth, or, excessive importance – such beliefs can pervasively affect one's life in different ways. If one believes they do not deserve to be loved or respected – it will also manifest in one's world in a variety of ways. The list of mental patterns that can impose limitation and even lead to imbalance and unhealthy states is vast. Hence, when a person begins to first explore healing, there is a great deal of important emphasis placed on transforming "thought".

A second important attribute of witnessing consciousness is that it provides a posture that helps us "see". Witnessing begins to provide us with an objective detachment from our mental (as well as our emotional) experiences so we can more objectively see our own experiences. As we become more aware of this "witnessing capacity", it can be applied in real life scenarios. If one is living experiences in which one is very "embedded", it can be helpful to begin witnessing one's life experience in a detached non-judgmental way. By doing this, we can learn to witness our thoughts, our feelings, our triggers, and our behaviors more consciously. This allows us to develop greater self-awareness. By developing self-awareness, we have an important ingredient to bring lasting and inspired change in arenas where we face personal challenges.

Hence, the function of witnessing provides access to consciousness or self-awareness that facilitates healing, growth and transformation. The consciousness from which you witness – is from your spiritual self. Any effort we make in our lives to become aware of limiting or destructive mental and emotional patterns will require this insight. If patterns in our mental or emotional behavior are so strongly embedded we cannot see them – this detachment or witnessing provides the space and the openness to observe.

Certain thoughts, or thought forms, may have a distinctly strong grip on one's mind when they arise, or hold a pervasive sense of influence on one's manifested reality. This often occurs when there is a strong emotional charge or deeply embedded fear associated with the thought. When people have lived very challenging personal experiences, in this or even in previous lifetime experiences, these patterns can be very strong. They are sometimes very difficult to understand at the root – because we are not conscious of the origin of the thought form or deep belief.

The release of energy around these patterns can be facilitated in a number of ways. Psychotherapy to illumine the pattern can often be very helpful and it is used by many people. This is like engaging an external witness to help us process. Yet not all counseling is formal - personal coaching can help, neurolinguistic programming can be used, engaging a supportive environment or network of other people can catalyze awareness, sharing in a spiritual friendship can be very supportive, and of course, relationships are famous for surfacing buried beliefs and patterns.

In addition to the various psychodynamic influences above, direct energy work, in any of its forms, with authentic intention to bring healing to the issue can help greatly. When we engage in energy work it is like shining a little extra light into the subconscious element of our own being. Light shines to reveal what is hiding there! It is metaphoric – but actually quite realistic to say this. Energy work is often coupled with any and all of the above approaches to support conscious transformation.

Furthermore, therapies such as past life regression can be very valuable to help in some circumstances. This is commonly true when there is a mysterious influence that makes no sense in context of one's current life experience. Fears, phobias and deep personality patterns are often neutralized by past life therapy approach. This is particularly true when the underlying issue is stubborn, resistant to transformation despite our best efforts. The patterns may be rooted in a deep memory, which cannot be understood from the known history of our lives, but the influence of the memory impinges upon our wellbeing. Accessing the root cause, and the healing it can provide in such cases, is phenomenal. [53]

Engaging an External Witness –

The Function of Therapeutic Relationship

It is through the insight of our internal witness that we can manifest personal transformation. However, in situations where it is difficult to see the mental patterns and beliefs that are having a strong and perhaps unhealthy influence on our life, another person may see them very easily. Ask any wife, husband or partner right! But, this is one reason why a therapeutic relationship can be so beneficial.

Having a therapist in this sense is akin to having an external witness – one who can help us see our self truly and objectively. It is sometimes stated that it is easier for humans to see "fault" in another than it is to see "fault" in our self. This is simply because there is often a greater objectivity.

Judgmental observation, of course, is not helpful – but loving, honest therapeutic insight, of course, is. The role of another person is not to *judge* – but to help us see our self objectively. With insight, and the proper loving attention, we can identify and heal wounded patterns. The purpose of this relationship is for one to become aware of one's own patterns. The relationship provides a psychological facilitation to achieve greater personal self-awareness as a stepping-stone in personal transformation.

It becomes very important to have this greater self-awareness in healing processes, particularly when there are strong psycho-emotional patterns that are blocking us from healing or progressing in our spiritual growth.

The Mental Body In Summary

We each have a mental body, which is a field of creative energy that in over-simplistic terms handles the function of thought formation, assimilation and the structuring beliefs. It is a creative tool to give form to experience. Thoughts can be self generated or shared. Some thoughts become more fixed as forms in our field or serve as the basis for structured systems of belief. Thought forms can arise through dramatic experience, and these thoughts are coupled with a great emotional charge. These forms can have a huge impact on our life until healing attention is provided.

Where such patterns exist, healing will be "required" to restore us to a more open spiritual state of self-expression. Healing involves freeing the mental body of limiting thoughts and beliefs, which are based on a faulty perception of our self, life and human nature. The ego, as we will explore, can "use" the mental body to its avail by inducing fear as a creative basis for life and the human experience – a concept we examine more closely when we examine deep spiritual healing in Chapter 10.

What is extremely important to understand is that our thoughts and beliefs are mental functions – while consciousness is a spiritual function. They are distinct! Healing always involves bringing greater consciousness into our life to illuminate patterns of thought and belief that are limiting, faulty, distorted – or based on what we will explore as the fear-based ego.

If your interest is in personal healing, you do not need to understand complex psychology or the intricacies of the mental and emotional bodies to achieve healing. You simply need to develop an awareness of your spiritual capacity to be more conscious, self-aware and transform your personal patterns. Learning to recognize both strongly embedded mental is essential as re-center our selves in our deeper spiritual alignment.

It is of immense value to realize that we can bear *witness* to our thoughts, rather than *be* our thoughts and beliefs, when the time is ripe for healing. We come to understand as co-creators with spirit, that we can actually efface thought programs that are self-destructive and we can also "program life affirming thoughts" into our own thought field. It is a weeding and planting process with consciousness. This begins to clarify the rationale as to why some people use exercises like affirmations or setting "intent".

It is important to realize this intent or affirmation must arise from our spiritual level of being to bear influence strongly on our mental bodies, and also that they cannot be planted on a bunch of weeds and survive. It is not the empty exercise of saying a few thoughts out loud or silently – that will change reality. It requires a conscious intentional desire emerging from the purest part of one's self, intending to alter one's habitual self and open new vistas of possibility that transforms. We can then do the work of coming face to face with limiting patterns of belief and personal wounds and step into in a transforming reality.

As a spiritual being with a mental body – one develops the capacity to refine or heal belief programs, and use our mental capacity with greater consciousness. Structured thoughts can be transformed. Liberation from restrictive patterns of thought and fear that control our human expression can be achieved - and we become ambassadors of our own authentic spiritual nature.

If one is not consciously in charge of their life – we tend to operate based on pre-existing conditioning. Patterning in the energy bodies will operate as if it is "who you are". One can learn to recognize or become conscious of the mental and emotional patterning that is inherited, created, socialized or adopted through your own experiences – and change whatever will bring greater wellness into your life.

For example, if emotional reactions create great drama and chaos in your world – you can learn to dissipate them. If fear based thoughts control your creative abilities to manifest a good life, you can encounter them and dismantle them. This is not necessarily easy, in fact can be quite challenging - but it is virtually impossible to do, until you realize you are not limited by patterned mental and emotional conditioning. You possess a tremendous spiritual power to transform your reality by transforming from the inside out.

You are a conscious entity, a spiritual being, that exists beyond these components of your energy system - and you can learn to heal them and to operate them like a vehicle under greater conscious awareness.

Higher Energy Bodies

We have examined so far four energy bodies – the mental, the emotional, the etheric – and we have also considered the physical body itself, which is an energy field in its own right. We have discussed the idea that the function of each of these bodies is unique, but not independent of its neighbors. Our thoughts can influence emotion. Emotion can influence thought. Thought and feelings can provoke certain actions. Thoughts and feelings may even produce patterning in the energy field. This patterning can affect not only ones psychological attitude, but also the behaviors we manifest, the reality we create around us, and even the physical body itself. There is an energetic relationship between these bodies.

We will next explore an awareness that these bodies are also in an energetic relationship with higher bodies of energy that we can view as "spiritual energy bodies". These energy bodies are higher vibratory fields of energy that have an influence on the mental, emotional and etheric fields by interfacing with them. These bodies are referred to by different names, through different healers and healing systems.

These layers have been outlined in other writings, and we will not focus on them right now, except to introduce an awareness of their existence – for they integrate vicariously in the work we shall explore together. I will reference them here briefly and refer you to the work of Dr. Barbara Brennan, if you are interested in learning about them.[7,8]

Personally, I do like Dr. Brennan's descriptions of the next level of energy fields and will briefly present them. In her work, the next four levels include: the astral level (fourth), the etheric template body (fifth), the celestial body (sixth) and the ketheric template (seventh).

The *astral level* is similar to the emotional body in quality but on a heart connected level. It is like a spiritualized or higher vibratory emotional body. You might think of it as a spiritual emotional body. This body is capable of stimulating high vibrational energy that can uplift the vibratory quality of the human beings experience – but is not duality based. It is either open or somewhat closed. This field is very energized and light filled in people who have created an open hearted approach to life and love generously.

The *etheric template level* is the fifth level, and it is like an inverse template of the etheric body. Dr. Brennan describes it as more of a "negative" space body, which holds the frame for the etheric level to exist. I view it as a field patterning, an etheric spiritual blueprint to support the ether field, which forms the etheric body. The field contains information that is related to you in a very personal way. It can hold traumatic patterning, and is influenced by your souls design and purpose for this incarnation.

The *celestial body* may also be thought of as a spiritual sensory body – again fluid in quality and larger in field. This field bridges awareness of the sentient interconnectedness of life and higher spiritual emotions.

The *ketheric template* or causal body is the mental spiritual body. It is structured as a golden grid of light and forms the framework for our earthly existence. It bridges our reality to our spiritual origins. It transduces higher energy of spiritual dimensions to nourish our life and existence.

Dr. Brennan has provided highly detailed description of these fields and the work she has learned to do through her exceptional vision and understanding in her books.[7,8] To me, this is a must read book, for any aspiring healer.

There are even higher levels of energy, which form part of the human spectrum, creating a bridge in energy and consciousness "above" or "deeper" to these defined layers in a quantum space. Most people do not routinely see these levels of energy and they do not exist as tangibly as the fields we have discussed. They are truly quantum in nature and difficult to define in a linear program. They form the energy bridge to higher and higher levels of our spiritual axis and connectedness. They provide a spiritual liaison with our higher self, spiritual DNA and contain the information and capacity for our progressive spiritual memory and development.

We will, however, restrain ourselves for now to a discussion of the mental, emotional and etheric bodies – for they are where healing primarily occurs in tangible 3D reality. We naturally and spontaneously open ourselves to the higher-level bodies, as well as their healing influence, as we assume spiritual sovereignty in our being through healing of the mental, emotional and etheric aspects of our being.

The Four Body Model, The Soul and The Higher Self

We will focus our discussion on what is termed *four-body model* of being. These four distinct energy layers are the physical/etheric body, the emotional body, the mental body, and what we will term collectively the spiritual bodies.

We are all familiar with the term soul, and many people are familiar with the concept of our higher self. These are not simply energy forms but elements of consciousness that are involved in organizing the forms and bodies of energy.

I view the higher self as an over-lighting aspect of consciousness that is in many ways beyond our linear human comprehension. It is the fuller consciousness we hold as an integral element of a divine creation. It exists outside of time and contains a complete understanding of our unique role in the collective of creation.

Our soul can be viewed as the aspect of this consciousness that emerges to have incarnational experiences. Hence, our soul is born into form and remains connected to the higher self. The soul travels through cycles of time and gains experience. As it gains experience, it grows or matures in spiritual awareness and holds the potential to awaken to its divine origin or spiritual nature. This spiritual awakening is pivotal in the awakening of energy and consciousness as part of the healing paradigm.

It is not simply in terms of "energy", but in terms of a "fuller consciousness", that is expressed through these energy bodies – that we can understand our souls nature. From an energy perspective, healing can occur directly in these energy fields. In terms of consciousness, healing brings our mental and emotional bodies "closer" to our spirit – which provides a healing through spiritual resonance. This is the work of the soul.

We could think of the soul as the spiritual student or "aspirant". It is our nature beyond the mental and emotional programming and wounds we carry. Our soul's job, so to speak, is to work toward spiritual re-alignment. The higher self guides this work.

So what is soul trying to achieve? The soul is seeking to learn, to heal and to grow beyond the limited expression of the ego attributes. The soul can be viewed as the part of us that is closer to our true nature – and seeking healing and realignment with our greater spiritual potential. It desires to manifest a more authentic life expression – one closer to our spiritual potential. The ego is a part of our human nature that is based on a sense of separation from spirit – a topic we will fully explore later.

Our soul is influenced by many elements of a spiritual design. This patterning includes elements that have a purpose in our current life or overall spiritual development. This is based on our soul's overall experience, as well as attributes which are influenced by past life experiences, elements around which important spiritual lessons may lay (karma and soul development), and influences related to the genetic influence of our family lineage, just to define a major few.

The higher self may be thought to oversee and guide the soul in its many incarnations. The more developed the soul energy, the stronger the corresponding energy bodies, and, the more fully the higher self can express in our lives. The goal of spiritual growth is to work toward this integration. This provides the higher self the ability to "express" itself more powerfully through our lower bodies – our mental, our emotional and our physical bodies.

We see this manifest most fully in the avatar beings with which we are all familiar – Christ, Buddha, Mohammed – those who have sparked the development of great religions as well as those who have nurtured the growth of humanity is less famous ways. Thousands of human beings over time, many unknown to the general population, have manifested this greater light.

One way to think about healing is to imagine realigning our mental and emotional bodies with this higher light and awareness. The less rigid, wounded, congested, obstructed or perhaps distorted the mental and emotional layers are – the more aligned a person will become with one's spiritual nature. It sounds simple enough, but these elements between our higher self and our actual life expression create a *veil* of awareness. The veil stops us from recognizing the truth in our spiritual nature until healing intent and spiritual grace pierces it.

A significant element of spiritual and energetic based healing is an unveiling of the imaginary division between our spiritual nature and our human self. This process allows the energy and consciousness of our higher self to infuse our lives more fully and bestow us with the grace of peace, health, joy and the worldly manifestation of a wise and balanced loving presence. Yet, for most of us, this is often a journey – rather than a single moment in time.

Healing, when viewed in its fullest context, is the unraveling of anything that exists in our personalities and our energy bodies, which obstructs this greater awareness. In healing the connection between our spiritual nature and our form expression, both in consciousness and through the energy bodies - we can allow tremendous healing to enter our lives.

Free Will

As we bring the spiritual element into healing, it becomes important to introduce the concept of free will. Human beings, by spiritual design, carry the ability to engage in free will choices. This is an integral and very important part of the overall human experience.

It is because we have the capacity to execute free will choices that we experience manifest consequence, better known as karma. It is also why we as human beings are responsible co-creators of life. Karma defines the principle of cause and effect where a soul learns by consequence of action. Through karma, a soul carries forward the "good" and "bad" consequences of action – from a spiritual perspective – to learn.

Karma however can be neutralized in the process of spiritual development. Healing in fact is often the neutralization of karma. This, however, requires a degree of spiritual development and conscious human intention. For a human being to heal in the way we are discussing, they must *invite* the higher self into their life. To heal requires a conscious choice – a personal intention.

Since healing is really an intrapersonal process, it is important to understand that a healer does not heal – a healer *facilitates* healing. Healing is an invocation to spirit to bring renewal into our lives. We must each bring healing through our own axis of spiritual alignment. It is God within each one of us – or whatever term is most comfortable to a person to describe God – that heals all things. Healers therefore are simply facilitators.

A human being, by design, has free will, and the power to choose. This is fundamental to the human experience. It is the human being's spiritual task to align with this understanding, to create pure intent to awaken this connection, and to find the spirit within.

Notably, to arrive at a decision to "invite" a spiritual "intervention" by free will choice, people are sometimes in a place of personal suffering. This may be mental, emotional or physical suffering. How many people are you aware of who began their spiritual journey at a point of personal challenge or crisis?

Suffering can be a tool of awareness – one that can lead people to search for understanding or healing. It is a "safety valve" if you will, from a spiritual perspective – so that we are all less inclined to stray too far from the truth. It is also a "catalyst" to move us forward.

In Buddhist terms, human beings are caught in the world of Maya or illusion – not understanding one's own creations – until one begins to seek enlightenment. When we start discussing energy, we can conceptualize that this enlightenment brings light, actual spiritual light. The light helps us see and transform. It helps us to "see" within our mental body, our emotional body and etheric body. It teaches principles to align these bodies with the higher self. This light brings healing because it works to energetically restore this biospiritual continuum.

"How does communication take place between these various bodies of energy and our spiritual self?" you may ask. The answer to this question is discovered in an understanding of the human chakra system ...

DR JOHN G RYAN MD

CHAPTER 7

CHAKRAS, ENERGY FLOW AND KUNDLINI

Chakras

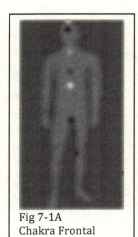

Fig 7-1A
Chakra Frontal

Fig 7-1B
Chakra

Each of the bodies discussed in the previous section is a field of unique energy. However, the bodies co-exist, and must function as a system in unity. We can feel, think, and act simultaneously – hence the energy bodies can influence or communicate with other. We have also introduced the idea that energy bodies are part of an energy continuum with a spiritual level or dimension of energy. Hence, there must be a mechanism of continuity and communication along this continuum also.

To achieve this, the energy bodies have points of interface that serve like "transducers". These centers are referred to as chakras. (Fig 7-1A&B) In eastern spiritual and yogic teachings, sages have intricately described these organizing centers in the energy field. This has been made much more accessible in modern language by the work of many authors such as Dr. Anodea Judith, Dr. Caroline Myss and Dr. Barbra Brennan. [7,8,32,39]

Chakra is a Sanskrit word. Chakras are not physical entities. They are more aptly consciousness and energy domains. They can receive, transmit and transduce energy in several ways. They are portals for the reception and interchange of divine energy from higher vibrational reality - to levels of vibration on the physical plane. They provide a portal for interchange of energies between the various energy bodies. They also are in continuity with the energy of the earth, to allow the interchange of energy between a human body and the earth. And, lastly, one can form connections between the chakras to other people.

The chakras are not simply an esoteric idea. They are actually present in the human body; however, they exist at the level of the subtle energy bodies. They are not in the normal range of vision. When in meditation, or in working with energy healing, some people can actually see chakras. They appear usually in one of two ways:

First, they can appear as a glowing center or ball of colored light – very similar to artistic renditions. This is how they tend to appear in closed eye vision.

Secondly, they may be seen as whirling cones or vortices of energy. When seen more structurally like this, they have a conical type of shape or radiation, which extends both forward and backward from the center of the body. (Fig 7-1B) The chakra appears as "cones" of energy, which emanate from the center or core of the body.

Most people do not *see* chakras, and it is not important that you do. The chakras are, however readily *felt* by just about anyone. If we are not familiar with chakras, it is simply that we are not aware of what we are feeling when we are encountering experiences within our chakras. This changes when we become a little more aware of the presence of a subtle energy reality.

Have you ever experienced "butterflies in your stomach"? This is a slightly "nervous" or excited energy within the solar plexus chakra. How about a lump in your throat? This is a constricting of the energy center known as the throat chakra. Have you ever felt your self pull away from aggressive behavior? This may involve closing down the chakra centers particularly at the solar plexus and root levels. Or, stood your ground and rooted the root chakra? These are just a few examples of everyday experiences that can demonstrate that most people have felt chakras, perhaps not realizing what they were experiencing at the time.

If you were to dissect the human body, you will never find a chakra. They are not structural entities in the physical body. They do however have a structural element in the layers of energy as described. Furthermore, they are dynamic, and do not always look the same. They can expand or contract in caliber, opening and closing to variable degrees. Artistically, chakras are often depicted in the form of a flower bud, with a specific number of "petals" for this reason.

There are various descriptions of chakras, and this can create some confusion. Personally, the way I have come to understand chakras is that they represent octaves, domains or levels of energy. They provide a mechanism of bringing high vibrational energy into the denser world of form – as spiritual energy passes from a spiritual level consciousness, into the physical body.

What does this mean? Well, imagine for a moment that your higher-self nature is light, information and consciousness. As this light passes into form as a human being, it can be viewed as passing through levels of descending vibration, found in the seven major chakras.

If we imagine this light to pass through the spectrum of our Higher Self, the energy can be understood to "spectralize" as it passes through the descending layers of vibration (defined by the chakra levels) into human form. Hence, we can conceptualize that as the light (energy) flows into physical form, it passes through the "prism" of one's being. The prism, of course, is the chakra system.

The fractionated light has levels of vibration that appear like a rainbow. We are all familiar with the appearance of white light breaking open into a spectrum of rainbow colors as it passes through the prism. In the rainbow, there are 7 key vibratory levels. These light levels correspond the vibratory range of the 7 distinct chakras - violet, indigo, pale blue, green, yellow, orange and red.

The 7 principal chakras are positioned in the midline of the body, centered along the axis of the spine. They run from the base of the spine to the top of the head.

Fig 7-2 is a visual depiction of the chakras:

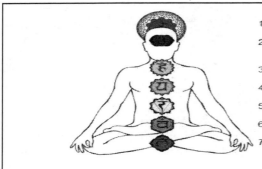

1. The Crown Chakra
2. The Third Eye Chakra
3. The Throat Chakra
4. The Heart Chakra
5. The Solar Plexus Chakra
6. The Sacral Chakra
7. The Base/Root Chakra

Fig 7-2   Chakra Positions

In describing this esoteric anatomy, the chakras exist along a central channel of the subtle energy body axis. This central column of energy runs like a tube from above the head to below the feet, connecting the chakras along its axis. (Fig 7-3) In eastern traditions this central channel is referred to as the "sashimi". This is an important concept, for as we begin to explore the chakras; we will begin to understand the importance of living in the center or *core* of your being, not specifically in a chakra domain.

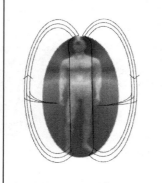

Fig 7-3   Energy Flow

On this axis, the chakras occur at intersection points of two further major channels of energy, which are part of the larger energy circuitry in the human body. These channels are referred to as the Ida and pingala. You may be familiar with a schematic depiction of these energy channels, represented as entwined serpents in the healing medical symbol of the caduceus. (Fig 7-4)

To understand the purpose or function, we can look at each chakra individually. Each of the 7 chakras corresponds to a cardinal function based on the vibratory level at which it resides.

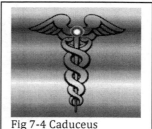

Fig 7-4 Caduceus

We can also draw many correlations to the function of the chakras based on the vibratory quality and it's role in our life. This includes not only the energetic correlations such as color – it includes physical, emotional, mental and spiritual correlations, as we will explore.

Psychologically, there can also be a developmental goal or purpose to achieve at each chakra level as we mature in our lives. For example, the root chakra functions to ground ones creation into physical form. The physical correlation to this chakra is developing a solid foundation in the world upon which you build your life. The psychological function of this chakra is related to grounding and security. The spiritual function of this chakra is to manifest your spirit in the physical world.

Through these correlations we can also understand the various types of disorders, which may conceivably occur, if the chakras are not properly functioning. This draws important energetic correlations to some disease states.

The chakras may exist in a healthy, free flowing and balanced state. Equally, they can be found in an imbalanced state, due to some of the things we will discuss together. As we examine the role of each chakra – it is easier to appreciate some of the attributes that might weaken or block a chakra, or lead to a chakra being either over-expressed or under-expressed in relationship to other chakras. We can also imagine the psychological challenges faced, and even physical diseases that might logically correlate with poor chakra function.

Issues in healing can be approached in terms of dealing with the unique personal factors corresponding to each chakra. Hence, people work to clear and balance energy as it correlates with the chakra system – while healing. In doing so, the energy of our being can express itself in an aligned, balanced and healthy way. One can view this as a process of repairing, tuning or recalibrating the energy system.

An analogy may be drawn to explain the concept of a fully integrated chakra system by viewing the body as a musical instrument – the magic flute. As spiritual energy, like the breath of spirit, passes through the instrument of your energy system, there are 7 notes to play. These notes correspond to the chakra levels. The notes are available, to create a melody. If the instrument is in tune and the player follows the music of his or her soul, a beautiful song results.

Hence, energy may move through the body and flow through a chakra in the creative expression of a human being. Energy can flow through any or all chakras creating a melody. This melody may be viewed as the life you are creating – the song is your life. In harmony, as energy flows through the human chakras, it is reflected in a healthy body, healthy emotional expression, a healthy mind, a solid grounding of your spirit in life, love based relationships, compassion and peace.

If there is a problem at the level of a chakra, this will drive the instrument out of tune. It can obstruct, amplify or distort a note – and it will produce a change in the flow of energy, which leads to "inharmonious" songs. In the "melody of your life", elements influenced by an out of tune instrument are correspondingly out of tune. For example if one's heart is closed this is typically a 4th chakra issue. The person cannot feel or fully manifest the flow of love in one's life, until this energy center heals and opens.

But before discussing the healing aspects of each of the various chakras, let's take a look at the individual chakras and some of the principle correspondences:

Root Chakra

In Sanskrit this is referred to as the Muladhara Chakra. It correlates to the color red as the lower vibratory scale of the light color spectrum. It corresponds to the element of earth. The lower vibratory rate of this chakra can be viewed to represent the organization of solid or grounding elements in ones life. It has 4 petals.

The first chakra organizes or grounds one's life force into the plane of the earth, serving as a foundation. It organizes this energy for a solid footing upon which the rest of a person's life is built. It relates psychologically to security and belonging.

If clear and harmonized, one will be well rooted in the physical world. The winds of life may blow and waters may surge, but a person will have an unclinging sense of rootedness, security and belonging – and a life that is well grounded and supported.

An individual's relationship to life on this level, both physically and psychologically speaking, will have obvious correlations. This is particularly true if the chakra is unbalanced in reference to the other chakras, or, if there is an inherent problem embedded in the chakra expression due to imbalanced function. Hence a person may be "too grounded" and unable to rise to higher levels of vibratory experience, which we will discuss at the other chakra levels. Or, they may be "ungrounded" or be tethered to other vibratory levels by fear of grounding into the world of form. A person is therefore unable to bring the stabilizing foundation necessary upon which to build one's life.

How might this arise? Well, for example, imagine if a child was not nurtured during a critical developmental period of early life, or perhaps they were exposed to very fearful events in early development. It is easy to imagine that the individual may feel untrusting of life to support them. This could weaken the first chakra development. Alternately it could lead to an overdeveloped chakra as a person roots-in firmly to survive. This can give rise to certain inflexibility. I am, of course, extremely oversimplifying this process – but it is useful to appreciate that these types of influences may impact first chakra development. If the chakra is underdeveloped, there will be need of healing work to develop a sense of "groundedness" and safety. If it is overdeveloped it will need to be balanced by the development of higher chakra function. Otherwise, the whole of one's life will reflect this deficiency in some way.

People with a clear and well functioning root chakra, who have overcome the basic fear of physical survival, will feel secure. They are trusting and capable of providing for oneself, one's family and one's community – according to their talents. Once established in this aspect of consciousness, one can move away from these concerns to higher levels of development.

When healing is necessary in this chakra, at a simplified level it will be related to "fear, survival and lack" *or* "re-balancing" the material dimension with the important functions of higher vibratory influences.

All chakras have a correlative endocrine function in the human body. The endocrine system defines all the organs in the body, which produce hormones that regulate the many processes involved in human physiology. On a level of endocrine function the first chakra correlates with the adrenal glands which control elemental and mineral balance, and the well known adrenal hormones which regulate fight and flight reactions.

Sacral Chakra

This second chakra is referred to in Sanskrit as Svadhisthana. It correlates with the color orange. This center corresponds to the water element and psychologically to the creative and life-nourishing nature contained in the water element. Earth is a water-based planet. Life and creativity flow through this element as it is contained by form. This center regulates the relationship of creative energy as it is channeled into all forms, as well as our sensual, sexual and creative expression.

If we think of the nature of water it will help understand the function of the second chakra. Water flows, water nourishes, water moves into and takes the form of its container. Unlike the more rigid attributes of structure or logic – it is flowing and adaptable. It can also be unbridled and unpredictable.

Harmony in this element leads to balance, and nourishing joyous creative expression. If this chakra is blocked or restricted, the force of this element is missing in ones life. This may correlate to creativity, sensuality and sexuality, or any form of creative expression. If it is overexpressed, strong emotional energy can overtake one's life, or addictive clinging attitudes to the sensual elements of life expression arise.

Healing of this chakra relates to issues of lust, addiction, sexual expression, impotence, rigidity, attachment, pleasure, guilt, and creativity.

On a level of endocrine function it correlates with the gonads – the testicles and ovaries. These organs are related to the dichotomy of masculine and feminine energies inherent in reproduction, but also the male-female dynamic or duality that must find balance to harmoniously create new life, in all that may imply. It has 6 petals.

Solar Plexus Chakra

The solar plexus chakra is termed Manipura and correlates to the color yellow. It corresponds to the element of fire, and the power of will. If we think of fire as an element, we can appreciate that at this level of creation fire adds heat, warmth, vitality, energy, and dynamic self-expression. In psychological terms it correlates to development of self-identity and individuation as a distinct human being. In healing it relates to the expression of ones self identity in the context of the whole.

In harmony, one stands aligned in personal power, demonstrating clarity of thought and power balance in relationships and in self-expression.

Healing of this chakra relates to issues of self-esteem, will power, passive-aggressive balance, victimization, defensiveness, anger, control and domination, doubt and shame.

In the endocrine system, it corresponds to the pancreas gland and the digestion, absorption, assimilation and regulation of life energies. It has 10 petals.

Heart Chakra

The heart chakra is named the Anahata and correlates to the color green. It corresponds to the air element. It is the central of 7 chakras and plays this role in the whole picture of ones life. It can be viewed as the doorway between the higher centers and the lower centers of the chakra axis, and viewed as the *harmonizer*.

If we think of air as an element we think of space or spaciousness, and lightness of being. There is a freedom, which can expand the sense of a self-identity into a larger relationship with life and with other beings.

Through the heart, one connects with the energy of divine love, which energizes all of creation. It relates to the circulation of essence throughout the entire body and the flow of love into the world and into our life.

In healthy expression – one can express an open, balanced compassionate heart-based relationship to life, a healthy self-identity and respect for life and all living things. One can maintain a sense of boundaries, but is capable of loving balanced relationships and creating a sense of harmony in existence.

Healing in this arena relates to love and openness. Love can be "towards" self, towards others, and towards any element of life. Issues of poor self care, co-dependence, withdrawal, judgment and criticism, hard heartedness and grief are examples of issues that correlate strongly with healing at the level of the heart chakra.

From an endocrine perspective, the heart center correlates with the thymus gland, which is involved in immunity. It is invigorated by a free-flowing loving relationship with ones life. It has 12 petals.

Throat Chakra

The throat chakra is entitled the Vissudha chakra and correlates to the color blue. It corresponds with the element ether, and with creative sound or the medium of etheric vibration.

We might think of sound as the ability to use vibration to call energy into an organized structure, or form reality. Hence when we think of the function of this chakra, it is to communicate and to call into form, our creative ideas. This center is the higher center of creative expression and the power of sound. Sound, as a human being, is not limited to only words. It may also relate the creative power that is manifested through the thoughts we create or empower. Hence creative expression may include the influence of both the thoughts we empower and the words we speak.

This center is related to the etheric energies that build and form pattern. Words create vibrational patterns, as do thoughts. As we create these internal energy patterns, they can be viewed as templates around which the other energies are magnetized to create form expression. Think back to the concept of the electromagnetic field and cymatics.

Hence, as conscious beings, the way we think and the way we speak will intimately affect the energies that are drawn toward us – for they will resonate with their organizing vibration. Through this profound understanding we can again see how the world of form is a reflection of an internal organizing vibration – that manifests as our lives.

It is important that we learn to be open and speak truth. It is also important to know when to be silent. It is important to align that which we think and speak with the highest creative awareness and causal potential. The way you think and the way you speak about yourself, about others, and the world, all have a creative influence. Your life will reflect the quality of these vibrations.

Healing of this center can be viewed to relate to the production and reception of organizing vibrational influences. This can mean overcoming the influences of authoritarian control, verbal abuse, judgment and bullying, dishonesty, controlled expression, finding and using ones voice, overcoming the need to control situations with forceful communication, dominating in communication, learning to listen, balanced honest self expression and creative expression.

Sound can also be used to clarify or reorder reality through vibratory influence and has emerged as a profound healing modality. This healing principle has been taught in the use of mantras and sacred chanting for thousands of years, to help restructure the human energy field.

This chakra corresponds to the thyroid gland, a small but important gland affecting growth, metabolism and overall balance in the body. It has 16 petals

Brow Chakra

The third eye chakra is referred to as the Anja chakra. This center corresponds to the element of light, and vision. This center connects one with the higher visionary aspects of human potential. We are all connected to a higher knowing, intuition, and creative vision - and all of these capacities continue to grow as we expand in consciousness.

In a state of balance – a person lives with inner clarity, intuitive ability, imagination and insight.

Healing in this center can be related to the principle of light. Light helps us see clearly. Light helps to overcome darkness and illusion. There is a famous biblical expression from the Gospel of Matthew 6:22 that states "The light of the body is the eye: if therefore thine eye be single, thy whole body shall be full of light."[1] It is easy to draw a correlation between this statement and an understanding of the sixth chakra. If focus and attention are kept unified, and light is not distorted by human thought into egoic thought and creation, the body can fill with light. This light is the energy, which comes through the human axis, for creative purpose, and will process through the chakras to create a healthy life.

If a person has done personal work to rise up from the simple material nature of human ego-based life, this light can manifest with healing. This brings the power to be a conscious co-creative presence in our world. This healing, through vibratory influence is both personal and planetary. Hence if you heal in your own being, you help heal all beings through "resonance". The profundity of this idea is overwhelming, and it correlates with the central teachings of every spiritual master on the planet.

When a person seeks to grow spiritually and surrenders to clear their energy system – there is a progressive spiritual liberation, restoration and realignment that occurs. The concept of a spiritual awakening is "scary" to some people for they view it as austere and religious. As a true spiritual awakening occurs one does not really become stoic, dry or afraid of life and living. They become more and more a fountain of light – one through which the energy, the light and the power of a love-based universe can flow through them. Their chakras become clear, to create in such a fashion, for they are less and less restricted by the forces of negativity, distortion and suppression that keep us separated from the greater understanding of our spiritual nature and expression. The vision for this emerges through our 6th chakra.

On a functional level, this chakra can relate to all things visual, including visualization and visionary correspondences. The light of our vision can be thought to *precede* the building of form that occurs one chakra below. This includes the form an anything we create as human beings. But it even includes creation in all ways including our bodies, our relationships, our communities, and even our societies. Our vision can also be influenced by "distorted" patterns, beliefs, identity, and dreams.

Healing involves learning to operate from a clear, balanced, enlightened, conscious, and undistorted framework. It involves clearing out distorted visions, which tend to manifest in our life. It involves opening our vision to a greater truth.

Hence if your eye is single upon Universal consciousness – you can heal anything in your world. Interestingly, in the process of healing – the awakening of this light is an actual phenomenon which does occur.

Yet, when we experience light in a dark place we must remember light reveals and then heals. Light will show us the illusory nature of duality based creations and show us the truth "behind" life. But as we journey through healing, it will also reveal the illusions within our self. Understanding this, if we let more light and consciousness into our lives it will reveal patterns of distortion in our life, on the journey to wholeness. Light helps us see – but this is not always fun or easy.

If we work and surrender to grow or heal – our energy can be re-qualified. The energy invested in other creations or manifestations can be released and liberated to help us on our way. This powerful concept can help us to overcome what we will examine as ego tendencies in our own personal nature. We will come to appreciate that these limitations are the greatest single limitation that we face in our healing journey. This light helps us see both who we truly are, and who we imagine or perceive ourselves to be. The "battle" between them, so to speak, to grow spiritually – lies within.

If this center is brought into a unified alignment – one-pointed toward true spiritual growth – the endless duality of worldly creation fuses into a one-pointed orientation – the non-dual world of love. If this is the center of one's vision, the whole world around us transforms.

As this "third eye" chakra develops, some people develop clairvoyant abilities. However, always remember that *right* vision is not *energy* vision. Energy vision is certainly not needed to heal oneself or help others.

Also, any healing work that involves dreams, visioning and clairvoyant assistance, can also be understood to correspond with this center.

This chakra correlates to the pineal gland in the physical endocrine system. This gland is located midline at the base of the frontal lobes of the brain. It is operative in its hormonal influence on light cycles and cyclic balance. It has 2 large petals, receiving the ida and pingala.

Crown Chakra

The crown chakra is named Sahasrara. It describes the highest chakra within the human physical form. Through this chakra one connects to higher levels of spiritual awareness. This includes the awareness of our spiritual nature and origins, and the existence of a spiritual reality.

As this chakra opens and expands in function – it bears influence over the remaining chakra centers. One is continuously "encouraged" spiritually to enter into the challenges and overcome the obstacles to higher growth awareness and earthly manifestation. Integrating the higher centers and heart allows the higher energy and consciousness to integrate into the "lower energy centers" – essentially spiritualizing ones life.

This process often redefines the very nature of one's reality based upon higher consciousness presence and ideas. Through the opening and expansion of the crown chakra one becomes "more spiritualized" in consciousness, as well as vibration. This manifests as a desire to know more of your spiritual nature, meaning and purpose. It also manifests as a desire to heal and improve one's life. This encourages us to uncover issues or challenges and to heal them, to forgive trespasses and past events, and to live peacefully. The attributes of a spiritualized integrity become unwaveringly important – honesty, kindness, compassion, integrity, courage, mercy and love. Developing these qualities is part of the awakening cycle.

Healing at the level of the crown center implies the relationship one holds with our spiritual identity. Over identification or under identification with one's spiritual nature outlines the spectrum of what healing might involve at this level. This might relate to overcoming materialistic tendencies, opening to spiritual influence in our life, encountering restrictive spiritual belief systems, or manifesting spiritually inspired change in the "real" world.

Its endocrine correspondence is the pituitary gland, which is a master gland in the human body. Its hormones regulate activity of many glands through the body. In some esoteric systems a cross correlation of the pituitary and pineal glands with the sixth and seventh chakras is suggested.

Fig 7-5   Christ

A fully active crown chakra is symbolic in eastern traditions of "enlightenment". When beings of enlightened states in history are depicted, such as Christ (Fig 7-5) or Buddha (Fig 7-6) – they often have radiant fields of light or halo. This is often assumed to represent a symbolic rendering to demonstrate a high consciousness state.

When you begin to grasp the energetic anatomy, and the spiritual nature of a human being – you might appreciate this is not merely a symbolic gesture. It is an accurate depiction of a high energy and consciousness state. The crown chakra is also known as the 1000 petal lotus.

Fig 7-6   Buddha

DR JOHN G RYAN MD

Higher Chakras

As we integrate higher aspects of spiritual consciousness at this time, there is an emerging awareness that higher chakras or energy centers exist. You may read about different perceptions of our expanding energy system. This is sometimes referred to as light body integration.

This work describes chakras or energy centers outside the classic 7 chakras system. Unlike the first 7 centers, which are related to the human journey of enlightenment, these centers correlate to what might be considered *transpersonal* integration. They are related to a human connection with alternate reality experiences such as past life experiences, the akashic record, deeper soul awareness, and the spiritual blueprint of your life.

For now, we will limit our discussion to the key 7 chakras. I believe it is important to begin with an understanding of the 7 primary chakras, for they can explain both the challenge and opportunity to grow as a human being as one awakens spiritually – without getting too esoteric.

The 7 primary chakras, as reviewed, describe the "descent of spirit into matter". They can also be viewed to describe the "spiritual journey back to oneness" – or what is sometimes termed *ascension*. This is a rise from the duality-based struggle of a human being by one who is awakening to his or her spiritual nature. This is the process we are primarily focusing on during the healing journey.

As we continue to integrate during this process, beyond the development and healing of the seven chakras, higher energy centers are indeed developing. You will hear of a 12-chakra system or a 14-chakra system or a 22-chakra system. People receive this information in different way and try to communicate what they are seeing or receiving as spiritual information. I believe it is important not to become too bogged down by information that creates more confusion than value. You do not need to understand such information to grow spiritually and it can even be a distraction to some people. If this helps you understand your journey than you can explore it. If it is confusing or disorienting, let it go. That is more than okay. It is important not to get so lost in energetic detail that the simplicity of one true spiritual message fades into oblivion: Practice peace and practice love – the rest will "fall into place".

An Overall View of the Chakras

So, the chakras can be viewed esoterically as the mechanism by which consciousness enters into and exists within the world of human form. They can also define a path or a journey of awakening, as a human being awakens from veiled human consciousness toward an awakened spiritual state.

To better conceptualize this value of this idea, we can visualize that as the soul descends into form, the energy of the soul passes through the crown as the light of spiritual awareness. Light emerges through the sixth chakra as one envisions to manifest in the world a living experience. The light passes, next qualified by the "vibrational order" of the fifth chakra, which is then expressed through the level and energy of the heart. The life force is qualified or empowered by the fire of will in the third chakra, enriched and nourished by the fluidity and passion of water at the second chakra, and, into a world of manifested form at the root. This poetic description describes the spiritual journey of spirit into form.

A reverse journey of spiritual awakening can also be considered. This is an intriguing way to conceptualize the spiritual journey – particularly when we find ourselves embedded in the world of form as human beings! As humans we might view ourselves as originally veiled from our spiritual nature. In spiritual teachings, this defines the starting point of spiritual awakening. At this stage, we are adrift in the world of duality consciousness – the play of light and dark, the play of good and evil – known as the illusory world of Maya. Living as human beings, we can see ourselves as dense or hardened, to some degree, in form – and veiled from our spiritual essence.

Then, for one reason or another, a spiritual awakening occurs. The exclusive allure of the world of form begins to lose its appeal. A cry for a spiritual restoration is sounded in the soul. The longing of the soul to reunite with its spiritual nature becomes strong. By this hearkening, the soul begins its rise from the rigid world of form. It is softened through the emotional and nourishing activity, and creative energy of the second chakra. It is charged by the empowerment of fire in the third chakra as it rises into an autonomous self-aware and self-responsible being. Rising like a phoenix, the soul reaches up in aspiration, to know it's true nature.

The identity of a limited-self now matures into the expression of a higher ideal, through relationship and love. Through one's heart, one calls upon the further healing influence of spirit to reorder the energy of ones world. One is assisted by the light of consciousness to envision the path, under the healing influence of spiritual grace. This awakens the consciousness of ones true identity as spiritual in nature and in consciousness, with the healing potential it brings in its wings.

DR JOHN G RYAN MD

Religion, Chakras and Spiritual Awakening

When the topic of spiritual awakening is discussed, it is at times alienating to people who relate to preconceived religious ideas of being reborn, or, to pious ideals of monastic life impractical for life in the modern age. Others are very comfortable with awakening in the context of religious identity.

It is valuable to realize that spirituality and religion work hand in hand for some people, and not for other people. Let me explain. Many people align with a religion as a means of getting closer to God - and it serves them very well. Yet, being a self-identified religious person does not necessarily make you a more spiritually aligned being.

A person may belong to a religion, but be very closed or wounded in energy expression. They manifest behaviors far away from a spiritual ideal – and their path is one of healing. People can also use religion as a mechanism to express ego distortions of various kinds – for behavior will be reflective of one's inner energy.

Equally, religion does not prevent you from being a spiritually aligned being. People may learn through religious teachings. They can grow and heal in magnificent ways – just at outlined in this energetic journey. Many people ascribe to a religious doctrine and are bountiful examples of an illuminated life.

Meanwhile, there are people who are not religious who find alternate ways of developing a spirituality and discovering God. These people may ascribe to a freer or blended spirituality, or even combines elements of different traditions. Others move away from doctrine altogether and find development of a conscious relationship to spirit through nature, healing, energy, consciousness and inner discovery. People who do this are not necessarily superior or inferior – they are simply following the beat of their soul's drum.

Spiritually identified "non religious" people can also have many energetic wounds that express themselves in their lives that require healing attention. Being "spiritual" but "not religious" doesn't mean there is not some work to do! As one works to heal in this sense, one too may become a beacon of light and awareness – radiating love and kindness wherever one goes.

The ego, which we will discuss shortly, can take the awareness of spiritual knowledge and twist it up through limitations of consciousness. In religion, or any form of spiritual expression, this can lead to dogmatism or ego righteousness, control, power distortion, sexual and creative suppression, abuse, ego based detachment, victimization, and guilt – just to name a few issues! This is not too difficult to conceptualize when we examine the outcome of both distorted religious and nonreligious spiritual influences in our world.

However, many self-identified religious people are very beautiful examples of enlightened life and action – and are highly spiritually realized individuals. Many modern free spiritual thinkers who belong to no religion are highly aligned and enlightened. This, to me, is better reflected through our understanding of energy – rather than religious affiliation or other expression of spiritual identity. The true scale of spiritual development lies in ones' ability to be at peace within one's life and to love spiritually. This correlates with the expansion and healing our energy system, and a growth in consciousness and love. In the end, what moves us closer to peace and inner awareness, and able to manifest love in the world, is a holy path. You should simply follow what aligns with your heart.

THE DEVELOPMENT OF ENERGY PSYCHOLOGY

As we contemplate on the chakras, when viewed systematically, they provide a type of "road map" for consciousness development and healing. They show the soul's journey from an illusory perception of reality as a non-divine human, to an illumined human spirit.

Now of course, the journey of life is not so clear, and certainly not so linear, as our poetic descriptions. It is riddled with trials and tribulations and the mechanics of awakening – as we progress through both spiritual strength and surrender. The process of awakening leads generally through a chain of unfolding experiences, where the issues embedded in our energy system are cleared, healed and restored. This can occur little by little, a bit at a time, or, in a big swoop of grace.

To better understand the specifics of healing and the mechanics of the awakening process, one can study the chakras. This becomes a powerful tool of self-understanding. When we isolate the chakras in this way, we can see clearly the attributes and psychological correlations, which are part of the common human experience.

There is a great value in understanding the relationship between the function of each chakra and our human experience or life. In such work, chakras may be viewed to define developmental milestones, and hold key "functions" or attributes. They may have positive and negative expressions. They can have correlations with physical diseases, which correlate imbalance in the chakra expression. Many authors, such as Anodea Judith, Carolyn Myss, and others, have written wonderful work on chakra-based psychology.[7,8,32,39] If you are drawn to learn more about chakras the above writings are very insightful and helpful in deeper exploration of what is now termed energy psychology.

Traditional psychological approaches are based a great deal on development theories, and becoming aware of patterns and issues. Energy psychology tends to probe deeper into an understanding of the creative seed within – through an energetic correlation. Through an appreciation of the influence of imbalances and/or blockages of chakra function, we can see how energy patterning does have a creative correlation in our manifested lives. We start to understand that the life we are creating is a reflection of our inner energy state or "signature".

As we consider this energy-inclusive perspective of psychology, we realize that "energetically" we do attract or magnetize experiences on the basis of our energy signature. Relationships, various life experiences, health, illness – are experiences we "create". They are viewed as "manifestations" that are resonant to our "energy".

It is through energetic correlation that we can begin to view our manifested life as an incredible mirror. Life simply tends to reflect the state of our own energy. The experiences we create reveal aspects of an inner energy makeup. This provides a feedback mechanism to helps us see how our energy is currently postured – and if used with wisdom and nurturance – to provide us with the insightful awareness to grow. The events of our lives become rich, in both meaning and potential, from this understanding – particularly in our efforts to transform elements of our lives.

Through the manifested experience of our life, we can see back into our self. In healing, we must be willing to self examine, to look inside – to experience a deeper healing. We must actually honor what we are creating – even if it is unpleasant – for it becomes our greatest ally and teacher, and helps us see ourselves. We reverse the view of life from an experience that is happening around us, or to us - to an experience we responsibly create.

What does this mean practically speaking? Let us take a look at a few examples.

Imagine if someone is experiencing a chronic inability to find work or support oneself, for example. There will be many potential influences factors that are contributing to this as one examines one's immediate world. You may be ill, or live in an area where there is limited job availability, and so forth. There will be both external reasons and internal reasons why this appears challenging. But from an energy perspective – it will all somehow reflect an energy state.

There are various states of energy that might be implicated. However, for purposes of illustration let us imagine that it implies a weak function of the root chakra. Now, the nature of how this chakra became weak may be a pertinent story. For example, perhaps this developed in a life setting where circumstances never permitted a person to "root" firmly in the world. One such example might be in an environment of chaos and instability in a very dysfunctional family. Not "rooting" might be an "adaptive mechanism" to remain safe.

From an energy psychology perspective, the healing process would include overcoming this limited chakra function. To begin such work, it might include developing insight into the causal environment where this energy posture developed. However, to heal – one will require not simply an understanding – but also the development of a strong sense of self-support in order to change and grow.

Psychologically, the details of this process will vary from one person to another, but the insecurity of "grounding" and learning to trustingly support oneself and life in general, will need be developed. Psychologically this can be supported by gaining greater insight and understanding. Energetically, this can be supported through energy-based work. These elements can walk hand in hand. The "deficiency" or "imbalance" of the chakra function can then be healed.

In another example, a person may have been disempowered though the third chakra during childhood and early development. For example, if we are suppressed in will and self worth, it is hard to create a quality life of self-expression. Or, if a person has a relatively closed or protected heart chakra due to wounds occurring through the process of life events – it is very easy to appreciate how this may manifest in one's life. If our heart it closed, it is hard to know love, or find comfort, in human relationships.

These, of course, are over-simplified illustrations, but one can consider each chakra and examine some of the influences that may arise due to its "imbalance". These imbalances can be addressed through the tools of Energy Psychology.

As we view life through the perspective of the chakra system, our own life can be seen to represent a vibratory creation that reflects precisely our overall personal energy signature. This "energy signature" is influenced by the state of our entire personal energy system at each chakra level.

From this perspective, it becomes clearer what is meant by the concept that "you create our own reality." People are first confused by this concept of an "energy-based" reality – and the personal responsibility it implies. It implies that our life is profoundly a reflective creation of our own energy state. The events we live, the relationships we form, the choices we make and don't make – are all influenced by – and reflective of – the state of our energy and chakra system.

It can seem like an incredible and sometimes unwarranted personal responsibility to assume that we create our own reality energetically or through our chakras. It is nearly impossible to imagine that we are responsible for everything we create or experience as a human being. For example, if an unstable person hurts another person, or a person is injured as a civilian in war, is it fair to say the victim in this encounter created it. Or if someone is experiencing some horrific disease, does its "responsibility" lay fully within themselves?

Some will say yes – but responsibility must be understood from the perspective of a spiritual and energetically inclusive consciousness. If we assume energetic responsibility however – it does help us process the experience with greater personal power. There is a strength which comes from assuming conscious responsibility for our life and our experiences. This defines the journey of healing through our chakra system. This inspires an attitude of responsible self-creation, empowerment and responsible self-care. Vicariously, it also undoes an attitude of victimization as we each work to bring a great love, light and power into the world.

If we become aware that we are creating our own reality – our life experiences take on greater purpose, potential and value – and we find the ability to overcome aspects of our life that appear externally imposed. If we externalize our experience, we surrender our spiritual sovereignty, and vicariously, our personal power. This will leave a person feeling stuck and incapable. You cannot change and process things for which you assume no sense of autonomous responsibility. It creates a state of weakness or paralysis, frustration and fear. If you assume a sense of responsibility you empower your ability to heal.

If we examine our experiences as "events" that are personally significant – we can discover their potential and purpose in our life. Importantly, this is not from the perspective of blame or self-judgment for bad events; it is from the perspective of self-discovery and growth. We may learn to see the strengths and weakness we have. We can discover aspects within ourselves that are aligned with wellness and disease. We can learn of ways to overcome our weaknesses and honor our strengths. We can assume the power inherent in our spirit. We can open to supportive self-healing and achieve our potential as human beings – beings that are both spiritual and human in nature, one chakra at a time!

Through the lens of creative responsibility, we simply see things differently. The inability to have a loving relationship, when viewed in a healing context, may serve as a catalyst to heal a wounded heart. The hurtful creations of anger or rage can be internalized to heal the wounds of a suppressed and belittled child. Hence, each person can gain a great deal of insight in their own journey if they understand these attributes – and work through them to a unified balance.

There are many aspects at each chakra level within us that may benefit from a healing touch. They will form part of one's healing story, and will present themselves to one's conscious awareness during the healing process. They must be viewed with great understanding, patience and respect. Every human being has their own wounds, their unique story and their unique potential. I have never met an exception to this rule. Everything becomes forgivable as we journey along here. Why? We are all simply unraveling restrictions to the fuller expression of our spirit as it dwells in the world of form.

In the process of healing and spiritual development, we can think energetically that we are "repairing and tuning" the instrument of our spiritual energy system. This process correlates with our chakra system nicely. Learning to unblock and become masterful in the management of our personal energy expression – is a goal. These energy and consciousness attunements can free up the flow of energy in our physical, emotional, mental and spiritual elements - so we can enjoy "liberation" and be an "authentic" expression of our soul. As we heal, the energy that flows through us into a creative expression of life becomes a reflection of our highest personal potential.

In freeing up the energy system, it may better function as an integrated unit – free of energetic distortions and blockages in our chakras and energy bodies. Our true inner potential can be more readily reflected in our life. As the energy is shifted, this can lead to healing at any level – not simply or exclusively on one level. Physical diseases may regress. Emotional patterns may be broken. Deep seated destructive and limiting beliefs may be dismantled. Healing of the whole being may occur – as we heal from the inside out.

As a person works through specific issues in one or more of the chakras, one begins to realize that the development of a balanced, integrated and clear chakra system is more important than a highly developed individual chakra. We are not simply learning to open our heart, or develop our third eye. These are part of a greater unfolding. Ultimately all chakras must be opened, cleared and unified into a working harmony to promote progressive healing.

As we heal, in this sense we can view the flow of life energy, passing through us, animating our existence. If you are aligned and healed – your light and your love shines brightly. You shine brighter, the world shines a little brighter too.

"What would this look like, to open fully in energy and healing like this?" you may ask. Well imagine if your life was inspired by your souls direction, and you were able to manifest a life based on a wise understanding of both human life and your spiritual nature. Imagine if you were at peace in your world, and able to consciously manifest, by intention and vibration, a life based on love and balanced relationships. Imagine a life where you understood your true worth and the worth of others, one where you are impassioned and free to express with love into the "world of form". Where these promptings lead you, may give you a glimpse of that world. Perhaps you are already there!

Great examples of highly integrated human expression are modeled for us in the wise beings that have come through the ages. They came as teachers and conscious beings that have lit the way though a spiritually realized nature. Christ, again for example, modeled this to perfection. His presence was grace-filled and wise, full of wisdom and compassion, with gentle instruction how to realize this potential in oneself. This is not limited only to Christ, for many human beings, both known and unknown, have brought this realized idea to the planet. If you look at any religion, and you return to the source being of that religion, you will find such a light. Yet in modern times, there are many such lights, and I am sure if you are reading this you are well on the road to this potential yourself.

One of the greatest maps of consciousness to lead the way home, lies in our understanding the human energy system and our creative vibrational responsibility. As you awaken to the light and healing within you – your journey of healing, through the chakras, illuminates the world.

The Collective Chakras of Humanity

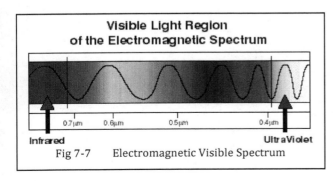

Fig 7-7   Electromagnetic Visible Spectrum

Human beings live what appear to be individual experiences, but esoterically and energetically we are also one being – we form a collective humanity. When we think in terms of energy and chakras, we can also expand this understanding by viewing humanity as a spectral creation.

Humanity, as an energetic collective, can be considered a composite energy field. The energy and vibration of each person is summated together to create a collective energy field. We can imagine a spectral summation – by adding the vibratory state of each persons energy field or chakra system into one big collective being.

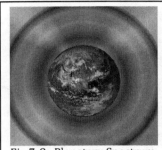

Fig 7-8   Planetary Spectrum

When a human being is born, we are each born into this energy field of the whole of humanity. Your heart contributes to the heart of humanity, your creativity contributes to the whole of humanity, your wisdom contributes to the whole of humanity, and so forth. If we were to average the vibration of humanity together, and view the quality of vibration at each level of spectral resonance, it is easy to see how this summated energy esoterically measures "the vibration of humanity". (Fig 7-8)

We spoke earlier of the harmonic convergence and the measure of the collective human vibration. Perhaps this is now easier to understand or conceptualize in this context.

If we look at the human situation at present, we can see a manifestation of every possible "good" and "bad" expression of life. We see very enlightened behavior, and every possible distortion of behavior – at every chakra level. The good, the bad, peace, war, hatred, kindness, enlightened behavior, and darkness – all represent creations that simply occur through human beings who are manifesting greater or lesser quotients of light.

As we grow and transform individually, the world we collectively manifest also changes. There is constant transformation taking place on the screen of life – a product of collective human consciousness. The world is healed as the consciousness and the energy of its people are raised – one person at a time.

Good intentioned people are often seeking ways to make the world a better place. For many people, this is a primal drive. The question is often posed, "With so much suffering in the world, and so many seemingly insurmountable problems, and so many forces that act against enlightened change - what can I do to make the world a better place?"

Well there are lots of things we can do to make the world better. But fundamentally, we know the real answer does not lie in what we do. It lies in who we are.

This begins to make sense when we open ourselves to understand the human energy paradigm. We each know that true and lasting change – is the healing change that occurs within ourselves. This was eloquently expressed by Mahatma Ghandi, in the words:

You must be the change you wish to see in the world.

If we think in terms of energy, we might appreciate that the level of energy or vibration we carry is our "contribution". To the degree that we can heal, and allow the energy and light of our spirit to enter into our energy fields, our minds, and our bodies – we bring a growing and expanding spiritual energy into our lives, and into the world. By engaging in our own healing process and biospiritual transformation, we change the quality and the intensity of the consciousness and the energy that is embodied in collective humanity.

Collectively, the vibration we each carry supports the whole of life by a very unique and purposeful contribution. We can understand that learning to manifest healing, peace, and forgiveness – and allowing the divine love that is inherent in the spiritual nature of each person to come forth – is hugely transformative for the planet. By developing an understanding of the human energy system, and healing through energy – we can draw a clear connection between *personal* healing and *planetary* healing. This collective consciousness has gained popular understanding through cutting-edge quantum science, in the concept of the Unified Field.

As each person engages in healing one also becomes a channel or conduit for a greater light to flow into the world. This light will comfort us and guide our unique steps in a personalized way. It will prompt our inspiration uniquely. It can lead to the expression of our unique gifts and abilities. It is this flow of light and energy that will heal not only our own issues and ailments, but also eventually the world that is manifested individually and collectively.

If we attempt to understand the collective world "energetically" – at this present point in time, we might view ourselves as living in a "third chakra" "power dominant" paradigm. We are rapidly learning, through this time of transformation, to integrate the level of the fourth chakra – a "heart-based" level of consciousness. The pride of power and achievement, which is inherent in an individuated third chakra – is ripe and ready to ascend into a heart based approach to life. The love of power will be superseded by the power of love. We could view this as a "collective initiation" of humanity, into a heart wise approach to life.

The overexpressed third chakra, without the balance of a heart-based wisdom is becoming increasingly destructive. If you look around the world, crisis after crisis shows the need for humanity to grow. We are to become more conscientious, more aware of the interrelated nature of humanity and life on the planet, aware of the polarizing forces of greed and competitive existence, awareness of greater personal responsibility, and aware of the power of love to transform. It is obvious there is an "evolutionary drive" in this orientation. Humanity is ready for this next step and we have chosen it by our collective vibration, as we approach the threshold of a new world.

At this time, the world is rapidly progressing into a new collective field or vibratory reality. People are being stimulated world wide to search for healing. The Divine Feminine is awakening. People are becoming interested in spirituality, people are taking greater responsibility, and people are opening both their hearts and minds to healthy, balanced solutions to both personal and planetary problems.

Yes, of course, there is a lot of resistance. If you look at the screen of life, a counterpoised reality also seems to be arising. Wars, conflicts and corruption are all over the news. Understand that this is not unexpected when an evolutionary push is occurring to propel humanity forward. If we think in terms of energy, light exposes what is hiding in the dark. Pay attention to the bigger picture, and the progress that is so readily apparent despite the struggle we now face.

There is an ever growing consciousness of the need to take better care of our planet – for we are in a living relationship with the planet, and made from the same atoms, as she herself is. The Earth is "Our Mother" in this sense. There is a growing interest in sustainable resources and clean energy. There is a growing desire to expose tyranny and oppression and find peaceful ways to propel transformation. There are massive corrections in the financial systems founded on greed and not value – and the systems are being slowly compelled to transform. Elements of the health care system that are distorted are being revealed. Whistle blowers pop up in every arena to identify injustice. Secrets are almost impossible to keep, and walls are coming down.

The world is well on its way to a future that will energetically support a transformed view of life, and it will be centered in the heart. It will occur in the twinkle of an eye – but a 26,000-year twinkle may last for a couple of generations!

If we think in terms of energy, to overcome darkness you do not fight it – you shine. Light purges discord and disease, individually and collectively.

How do *you* do this? *You* heal. You open up your energy system and you experience healing in the context described. Experiencing your own personal healing, you heal humanity. It has been often said, and wisely so, that humanity transforms one heart at a time. Make it yours!

☉

So, that being said, let us get a little more familiar with our personal chakra system through an exercise ...

Exercise: Chakra Sensing

Make yourself comfortable for this exercise. Sitting with your back nice and straight will work well. If this is uncomfortable, laying down for the exercise is perfectly okay.

Begin by making a conscious connection with your higher self, God or Universal consciousness. Then make a conscious connection with the earth.

Take a few deep slow breaths and let your body relax, and let go of any tension.

Imagine a stream of energy that begins to move up through your root chakra, at the base of the spine. Focus your attention here and let the energy build. Sense or imaging the color red and allow it to glow brightly.

Let the energy flow up now to the area of the second chakra, the sexual creative center, between your naval and the base of your spine. Visualize the color orange. Focus your attention, and let the energy grow more intense. Gently keep your attention here letting the energy build, until you can feel a sensation of tingling or vibration.

Let the energy flow up now to the area of the third chakra, the solar plexus, overlying your stomach. Focus your attention here and let the energy build. Visualize the color yellow. Gently keep your attention here letting the energy build until you can sense the "energy".

Let the energy flow up now to the area of the fourth chakra, the heart. Visualize or imagine a glowing green light. Focus your attention here and let the energy build. Pay attention to the feeling of being centered in your heart. Feel how life flows out of your heart as you take time for the energy to nurture this chakra.

Let the energy flow up now to the area of the fifth chakra, at the level of the throat. Focus your attention here and let the energy build. Visualize the color blue. Let the energy build and be aware of any sensation you may have. Is it tight or restricted? Open and free? Let the energy soothe the chakra.

Now bring your attention to the sixth chakra, or third eye. This is between the eyebrows in the middle of the forehead. Just let the energy work here to enliven the chakra. You may sense heat or light, or may see light in your minds eye. Relax and allow the light to work with the center in whatever way is most appropriate to support you.

Now bring your awareness to the top of your head, the crown chakra. Let the energy focus at the top of your head and allow it to build. You may feel a tingly feeling in your scalp, or a gentle pressure. You feel the energy "open" here as you work with this exercise.

As you focus your attention in this patterned tour of the chakras – you are actually energizing each chakra.

As your energy system is opened and charged, allow light to now flow down from above and "flood" you open energy system. Take a few moments to bathe in the energy that has been stimulated to support your healing.

Next, invite the energy of the earth from below to rise up through your energy system, to you heart. Invite energy from spirit above, to move down. Let these energies "meet" in your heart. Feel the energy mix in you heart center and let it radiate to fill you entire auric field. Let it expand in all directions as far as it will go.

Allow a few moments for your energy system to "speak to you". Register any areas of tightness or restriction. Allow the energy that has built in this process move toward these areas of restriction to support a release and realignment. Consciously allow yourself to relax and spend a few minutes in this peaceful but energized space. Allow the healing influence of this exercise settle deep with your energy field. Breathe and let go.

If this is your first experiment with your chakras do not be discouraged if you are unable to sense or feel energy changes. This, like with any skill, develops with practice and time. Simply pay attention to any sensations you may feel or encounter – even if it is as simple as a twitch in your body, or a state of profound relaxation. As you do, you become aware of the reality of your human energy system. You awaken your potential to access healing through its presence, into you life!

NADIS

The word nadi comes from the Sanskrit root *nadi* meaning channel or stream. Like chakras, the nadis are not physical structures. They are channels or circuits in the subtle energy of the body, through which energy is relayed. These channels form a network for energetic transfer and communication.

In this network, there are 3 major central channels or energy, as well as a complex branching circuitry of nadis that extend throughout the etheric energy body. This includes 12 major channels referred to as meridians, and numerous smaller branching nadis.

Fig 7-9   Sushumna, Ida and Pingala

The 3 major central channels are named the sushumna, the ida and the pingala. The sushumna is depicted as a large energy channel running in a straight column from the base chakra to the crown chakra. The ida and pingala are depicted as serpentine channels that run around the central axis or sushumna. They create a spiral crisscrossing at multiple points along the axis. The points of intersection of these channels correspond to the levels of various chakra points along the sushumna. (Fig 7-9)

The pingala is associated with active masculine solar energy. It courses from the left aspect of the root chakra to left aspect of the sixth chakra. The ida is associated with the passive feminine lunar energy. It courses from the right of the root chakra to the right side of the sixth chakra.

THE MISSING PILL

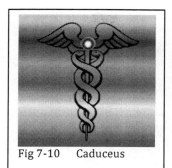

Fig 7-10   Caduceus

These channels form the pattern depicted in the well-known *caduceus*, a symbol ubiquitous to modern medicine. (Fig 7-10) The caduceus however is an ancient symbol found in ancient teachings of eastern medicine – based on an energy inclusive understanding of the human body and the role of human consciousness in health.

In the polarity of forces of energy, we can identify an interplay of active and passive forces, which intertwine within the human body, to create the ebb and flow necessary to create and sustain life. Although identified as active masculine and passive feminine forces, these energies are not limited in a gender sense of the word – they are forces, which are inherent in each human being. Men have a passive receptive quality in life and women have an active quality. Men can be tender and women can be strong. The energy is describing a sustaining polarity, found throughout all of creation, not simply sexuality.

In social patterning as well as in health, the polarity, or fluidity between the polarities, must be in balance for optimal functioning. This is represented in the balance between these two energy channels in all that this idea implies.

The two channels wind up the spine, and they meet at the third eye. When a human being sits upright with attention focused single pointed in the third eye, holding these forces in life in balance, they become receptive to a light and energy, which exists just behind our visible creation. There is secret hidden in this understanding, again revealed in the statement, "When thy eye be single, the whole body shall be full of light."[1]

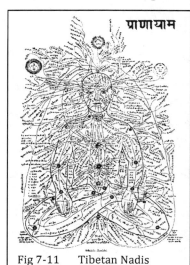

Fig 7-11   Tibetan Nadis

In addition to these central primary channels of energy there is also a vast network of channels, akin to the branching nerves and blood vessels in our body, that produce a complex circuitry in the human energy field. They channel through the etheric body and interface with the physical body through the nervous system, nerve plexi, and deep connective tissues that exist within the body. (Fig 7-11)

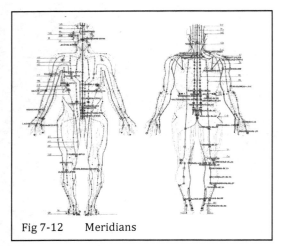

Fig 7-12   Meridians

These finer nadis are innumerable and scale down in size as they create this network, carrying energetic impulses. In the organization of this network, meridians form that regulate the energy flow within and between individual organ systems. The meridians are depicted in Fig 7-12.

The energy that flows through the nadis and meridians is referred to by many names. Familiar terms include universal energy, life force energy, chi, ki, prana and other various names from different healing traditions.

For those of you familiar with acupuncture or acupressure, or "tapping" – you may be familiar with the concept of these meridians. Meridians represent 12 major energy channels in the human energy system, and can be used in conscious healing practices.

The meridian science is a vast field of understanding in its own right, and beyond the scope of this introductory work, but fascinating to explore or learn about. For health, the meridian and nadi circuits must be functional and clear. Weaknesses in the meridian, or congealed energy built up in the meridians, can lead to functional problems as well as physical disease in the human body.

Treatments such as acupuncture are based on principles to correct excess or deficiencies of energy flow in these channels. When one is working with acupuncture on the meridians – one is calibrating changes by pressure, or by needle insertion at certain specific mapped energy points along the specific meridian, to catalyze energy flow within the meridian. Congested energy can also be dissipated or extracted. However, in any form of Energy Medicine, the flow of energy through the nadis and meridians is affected.

The meridians are etheric in nature. The channels however have an import relation to the other energy bodies and can experience changes due to the influence of the adjacent mental and emotional bodies. Mental patterning and strong emotions, for example, can have an important influence on the *flow* of energy in the energy meridians. Energetic transfer from higher-level spiritual bodies can also have a healing influence on the meridians.

For now, it is important simply to appreciate that they exist – and they serve as the portal through which energy flows through the human system. By understanding this, we can better appreciate how the energy bodies and the higher spiritual bodies can "communicate" with the etheric and physical body – and why energy based therapies can have such a healing influence on the human body, mind and spirit.

When people begin to experience subtle energy work, the energy from a higher vibrational level is very capable of working upon the lower energy levels. This energy will also then work through the meridians and human energy fields promoting clearing and release.

If you have never experienced this, you are likely to say, "Really, yeah sure?" If you have experienced it, you are more likely to say, "Ah, so that is what was happening!" When working with energy for healing, you will often palpably feel this process. You may encounter twitching, jitters, limbs that jump, changes in breathing or heart rate, pulsations, flashes of energy and chakras that go "pop". If you have a healthy skepticism about energy work – having some personal experiences will efface a great deal of uncertainty.

It is, however, also important to realize that you do not need to understand all of the subtle energy science of meridians and chakras to heal. This information is available for those with a curiosity to learn but it is not a requisite to understand in order to heal personally. As fascinating as it is and fun to learn, you can know that the spiritual energy itself, once invoked in healing, is conscious in its own right – and smarter than us! This may sound a tad "unreasonable" but the energy involved in higher vibrational healing processes does "know" what to do. This has been my experience over and over again.

Kundalini

In learning about energy healing and spiritual growth, you will encounter the concept, and quite possibly the experience, of "Kundalini awakening".

Kundalini is described in many ways, but in esoteric traditions it is described as a dormant energy that exists, coiled at the base of the spine, within the human energy system. This energy will at some point be more activated, and begin to work on healing the human energy system.

Healing in the context of Kundalini awakening does not mean simply an energy "surge". It is rather the process of a spiritual "unfolding" of the energy system, and reunification with our spiritual nature. It implies an energy development that involves both an expansion and a clearing of the energy system. It occurs to reunite a human being in both consciousness *and* manifested potential – to the divine within. Kundalini awakening is a common experience encountered today. It may often occur spontaneously, and will commonly occur in people as they seek to learn about healing on the basis of energy, consciousness and spiritually inclusive processes.

In Eastern traditions Kundalini is viewed to be "awakened by Shakti" – the Divine Feminine Power. In Western terms, this may be viewed as the Holy Spirit. This energy, quiescent at the base of the human spine, is progressively stimulated to activate or to "rise". As the energy of kundalini rises through the human chakra system, it works to unblock restrictive energies that have been created through human experience, karma or inherited pattering.

As one encounters Kundalini activation, one is catapulted into a level of healing that is potentially deeply restorative. It will open the human chakras and energy system in expanded ways. In this process, one is led to reunite one's consciousness, and one's reality with the divine nature of life. In this reunification, unusual healing is of course possible, but this is more a "side effect" than a goal – occurring through a spiritual restoration.

As lofty as this sounds, and as challenging as some of the experiences it inspires, it is relatively *simple* to understand as a concept. The rising Kundalini is the raising of one's consciousness and ones overall energy to a state of higher energetic vibration. It begins to raise one's consciousness above the mundane physical, etheric, emotional and mental world – allowing one to connect with and integrate one's truer spiritual nature and the divine consciousness that is behind life.

This is not strictly a patterned experience – for this process occurs uniquely from one person to the next. However, there are themes of experience that occur, and we will examine them next.

Yet, the effect of a rising Kundalini as it awakens, is that it works through an individuals energy system and begins to create energetic transformation. For many people, this is fairly smooth and natural process of development. In others it can create some unusual experiences.

As Kundalini "awakens" it can produce not only unusual energetic experiences but also states that evoke or mimic illnesses. It can be both confusing and challenging to live through this process, if such things are mysterious – so it is important to introduce the topic and to review it here. Then, you may have a deeper understanding, if it happens to you.

Just remember – it is "all good". Shakti works to unshackle us from our obstinate ego separation and its endless illusory creations, so that we may experience the infinite and the truer nature of who we are as spiritual beings.

Awake Ye Oh Sleeper

If a person begins to seek healing of an illness or a condition, or if one is seeking to grow spiritually – energetic changes do simultaneously occur in the human energy fields. In the search for healing and growth, one is essentially seeking to clear the energy system of energy patterns that are leading to manifestations of disease or illness – either in the body or one's psychological life. This transformation opens up the energy system to a much greater degree than previously experienced or remembered for most people. This occurs to provide the capacity to carry a greater charge or quotient of ones spiritual energy in form. Kundalini awakening, simply put, can be understood to represent the process by which this occurs.

Why exactly this occurs spontaneously in some people is a bit of a mystery. It certainly can be induced by spiritual practices, and sometimes by engaging in energy healing practices. At times it occurs in synchrony with or subsequent to an accident, a trauma, use of drugs, during a deep sexual experience, or other triggering events. Sometimes, however, it occurs simply – by grace. I believe personally when this occurs, it is related to one's prior spiritual development – and by prior, I mean simply, prior lifetimes. I believe this will typically occur in individuals who have a good degree of spiritual development, "old souls" if you will. This is true, whether or not one considers themself to be spiritual or religious in nature, and one is aware of prior spiritual development, or not.

When people describe the actual experience of a Kundalini awakening, a diverse spectrum of experiences is reported. These may include movements of internal energy, sometimes with jerking, shaking or vibration. It can involve unusual posturing or breathing that may last for variable periods of time. It may involve sensations of heat, cooling, or electrical sensation. It may involve passing through large and unexplained swings in emotion, or transcendent feelings of joy, bliss, compassion and love. Spontaneous tears of joy or sadness may occur, with crying and/or laughter. People sometimes experience internal visions, lights, sounds, music or symbols. Some people have direct out of body experiences or unusual visions or dream like experiences. Others merge with a unity consciousness experience, defined in bliss states of yogic union. So you see, the spectrum is vast.

Following a personal kundalini experience (or sequence of experiences) people will often but not always report great shifts of consciousness — typically with a new awareness of energy and the existence of a true spiritual reality. They can also undergo some unusual experiences. Some of these are "normal", but out of context to one's circumstances. Others are more "paranormal" in nature. Let us examine.

Physical symptoms in the body can include anxiety, periods of elevated energy or fatigue, nausea, diarrhea, coughing, mucous clearing, changes in heart rate, sore muscles, and so on. Emotionally, people sometimes experience liberation from long standing tendencies such as guilt or grief, while others experience a period of depression or great fluctuations in mood. Mentally, belief systems long ingrained in a person may suddenly shift. Interest in things that have been present in a person's life, including hobbies and careers, may fade away while new ones emerge. Relationships may change. Many people are deeply and forever transformed by the sense of oneness they have encountered, or awareness of transcendental realities that seem to merge with the life we know.

At times people develop unusual abilities. This may include everyday talents that were not consciously present prior to the experience. This may include creative abilities or talents of any type. Others develop clairsentient abilities and heightened intuition. This is a highly variable experience for I believe it will correlate with a person's innate purpose, history and potential.

People generally develop an interest in learning more about life, and usually, a growing interest in spiritual ideas. People often begin a search to understand and integrate the experience they have lived, which becomes a journey of spiritual realization. This inspired seeking is part of the mysterious magic of a Kundalini awakening.

When a person experiences these types of energy changes — patterns of energy carried in the human energy system will vicariously change. If a structural healing occurs, it can be viewed to result from an inner reordering of energy. It is like treating an issue from the inside out! It can equally occur within psychological patterns or tendencies that do not manifest as physical healings — but as mental and emotional healing or transformation.

Interestingly, when energetic changes occur that lead to personal transformation — they often arrive with greater insight about the patterns. In other words, in the process of healing, an appreciation of the "causal" energy pattern within a personal issue often arises. For example, if suppressed emotional awareness, retained anger, resentment, or self-judgment are causal issues of disease — they may be exposed as the underlying energetic printing that has lead to psychological or even physical conditions. Development of consciousness in this case is important. Furthermore, such awareness is often required to be able to sustain the transformational change.

Hence, kundalini awakening implies a growth in both consciousness and the energy structure that supports an expanding consciousness, at the same time. As an individual grows in spiritual consciousness, the chakras and energy system evolve or expand within a human being. If you open up spiritually, you are also opening up energetically – and you will need to be prepared to handle the increased energy that is flowing through your energy system.   It is, in essence, a "spiritualization process of matter".   This defines the essence of Kundalini changes.

Now, as mystical or mysterious as this all may sound, this energy expansion occurs to support our psycho-spiritual development quite naturally. Kundalini awakening is an "organic" process and occurs quite naturally in human beings, even in our day-to-day lives. It is happening all the time – as we mature as conscious beings. It is however, happening in an accelerated way in present time for reasons we have reviewed in context of the great shift or transformation on the planet.

When people do begin to experiment with energy-based healing a great energetic opening or series of openings can occur quite spontaneously or as a result of energy healing processes. It may be understood to represent and acceleration of a normal process. Such openings are often very conscious experiences, and will have a very transformative influence on ones life.

When such experiences occur, it can be quite startling – so it is very helpful to understand what is happening. Furthermore, unless a person or a healer understands the phenomenon of a spontaneous Kundalini opening or awakening, it may not be recognized for what it really represents, or be misunderstood and mishandled in various ways.

Kundalini and Perceptions of Illness

In review of some of the manifestations of an awakening Kundalini that we reviewed, it may be readily obvious that some of these phenomena are similar to symptoms of human disease conditions. This can be a very confusing or disturbing experience to say the least. People will often assume the worst, and seek medical attention to address these symptoms. If a person is unaware of the process of Kundalini awakening, they may assume they are "ill".

The reality of kundalini awakening is not understood by classical psychology, psychiatry or medicine.   People who work in these domains will understandably try to fit a symptomatic presentation into the framework of what is known or reasonably accepted within their domain. This can easily lead to misunderstanding, mislabeling and misdiagnosis of health conditions. So caution, and self-awareness, is warranted.

If someone experiences a Kundalini awakening, or begins experiencing these unusual symptoms during conscious growth and energy healing processes – it is certainly wise to verify the absence of a medical condition with a traditional medical care provider. Serious medical conditions can mimic many of these experiences – and it would be foolish to put oneself at unnecessary risk when a disease is present. It is prudent to "exclude" important disease markers or symptoms, before assuming you are simply having a spiritual experience.

If however there is no explanation for what you are living, or you are questioning the validity of a provided medical interpretation, it can be important to be cognizant of the signs and symptoms of kundalini awakening. You cannot expect most traditional or alternative health care provider to understand this. Today, some health care providers have experienced or educated themselves in this arena, but it is not a common element of traditional practices.

The Rising Lotus

As Kundalini stirs, we are invited to examine ourselves. Personal habits, psychological patterns, dietary habits, fears, our personal history, and our dreams – all arise to support us in our process of growth. Patterns and habits that lead to restrictions, distortions and blockages of energy - particularly psychological patterns that distort the energy system, and the psychological influence of the wounds we carry – all tend to become more obvious in a person's life.

One begins to really see how certain things influence one's energy fields, and one's overall wellbeing. This stimulates within us the desire to want to make positive changes. Interestingly, the drive is not because a health advisor is telling us it is "good for us". One simply becomes more aware of what is supportive and what is not supportive in terms of one's wellbeing.

In light of *diet,* there is often a period of greater awareness and interest in health. This is a personal, and frankly an intuitive process, for there is no specific diet that suits all people equally. Many factors influence the appropriate diet for our personal constitution. It is not appropriate that everyone simply become a mass vitamin consumer, vegan or breatharian! This may be appropriate for one person, but not one's neighbor – and there is no need or cause for judgment of any kind about it. Each person will refine what best suits their health and their constitution. There is really one common tendency – to eat consciously. This will involve eating purer foods, living foods and chemical free foods where possible. It will also involve eating with gratitude and joy, and to infuse love as much in our food as in every element in our life!

In terms of *habits*, a person tends to become more self-aware. Patterns surface in conscious awareness; coupled with awareness of the consequence or energetic influence they create. This includes habits and patterns of any type that can disturb or distort a person's energy in unhealthy ways. This may involve drugs and addictions, dependent behaviors, patterns of victimization, and other hurtful personality traits – any and all things that lead to disharmony in one's life.

With this, both an openness and desire to grow and change emerges – but sometimes a strong element of intrapersonal struggle ensues. Elements, which resist the process of enlightenment and transformation, will arise to resist the metamorphosis at hand. This ultimately serves to strengthen the drive to grow and transform and refine the quality of the outcome. It is like a blacksmith working on metal to create an exceptional product of beauty and strength. Yet this is often greatly challenging, and it is at this time that both awareness and self-support are necessary. Often, external support is also very helpful, and sometimes needed, to better see what is going on in one's world – and find the path through transformative changes.

If one reflects on this, it is not surprising that in the process of spiritual development, patterns and behaviors that are damaging to ones health and wellbeing will need to become more consciously prevalent in ones life. I have noticed that following kundalini experiences, it is not unusual to encounter a *magnification* of such tendencies. It is as if our personal issues become "exaggeratedly present" in our life – to help us identify and begin to transform them. This is spiritually logical – so that a person can really "take on" the task of conscious growth.

For example, if one smokes, they may become more aware of the harmfulness of the habit and the deeper psychology of the habit within themself – as they are learning to let it go. They may develop a growing distaste for the habit; feel inspired to quit, yet face internal resistance that must be overcome. It will eventually lead to a letting go of the habit. As another example, if a person is "strongly defensive" or "deeply angry" – they will become more aware of their habitual nature. They may also end up creating a series of experiences to magnify the issue, to better see the underlying tendency, and gain insight about its consequences. This experience will provide the capacity to grow in a clearer and more powerful way. So as you see, progress is not always smooth and easy – but that too teaches spiritual attributes like persistence, courage and faith.

Hence, it becomes obvious that with the grace of Kundalini activation, and the changes induced through energy based healing – there will be some trials and tribulations of refinement. Yet, overall, a greater consciousness, which can lead to progressive health and healing, occurs. As Kundalini begins to stir and work her magic – it is as if we are taken in the embrace of the divine mother and encouraged to heal any facet of ourselves that keeps us divided from an awareness of our spiritual potential as well as the ability to live consciously in a state of grace and love. Not a bad trade off really!

Kundalini as Light in the Dark

To better understand the process of a Kundalini awakening and development, I find it is useful to think in metaphor. One such metaphor is found in the concept of the "struggle of light and dark" – and the balance that is achieved in overcoming this struggle.

When light enters darkness, it is a great revelator. Kundalini is a receptacle of light and revelation. Its goal is to reveal your truer self-nature but in the process of this journey or ascent, it will vicariously reveal what is in the way of the manifestation of one's spiritual potential, so that it can be deconstructed or healed.

Psychological patterns that entrain us in suffering or disease states can be viewed as obstacles to the manifestation of one's light. They can obscure our nature but do not change it. Such patterns are like filters, or the film in a projector, which changes the image of manifested reality - but never changes the true light of who we are as spiritual beings.

When patterns or diseases present themselves during one's process of spiritual growth, they can often be understood as key elements in understanding one's own process. They are key experiences to demonstrate the power of healing, and transformation. They often they provide the stimulus for people to seek deeper healing and to make a conscious reconnection with their spirit. Suffering leads to seeking. Painful manifestations of life stimulate the search to find greater purpose, cause and healing.

Ironically, it is the darkness in life that is often the very thing that leads one to seek comfort or relief. It is only the light of spiritual realization and development that can bring comfort or healing to these situations.

The light or energy inherent in Kundalini activation, and generally in any spiritual or energy healing, will assuredly stir up some perceptible challenges. These represent things we need to see and integrate within our own psyche. Light will reveal what is hidden in our own personal darkness. The challenges we might face when the light of spiritual awakening first stirs our energy field are understandable. They provide us the opportunity to understand what we need to see. This provides us with the opportunity to heal and to transform in our lives. This growth is necessary to be able for us to reconcile with the healed nature or our spirit, its wisdom and its love.

Kundalini awakening can, however, be lived gracefully – with understanding, support, and compassion. This does require an expanded view of the nature of life. Honesty, forgiveness and conscious love are critical ingredients to accompany a person on this trek.

The human energy system must adapt to this process. As the capacity of the human energy system is restored and expanded, healing of many ailments will naturally occur. Healing of course is not limited to physical healing – and the process may not include physical healing. It may represent healing on a different level of life or spirit all together.

Ultimately, healing in the sense of spiritual awakening and integration will restore the peace that can only be found in ones nature as ones Higher Self. It restores the joy that springs forth from understanding we are each one with the mystery and magic of all life and creation - as a precious and incremental part and player in the dance of life. Love is revealed as the fundamental fabric of the universe and all of its contents when the veil is lifted by the grace of the Divine Mother. Her bestowal of Kundalini brings a tremendous Life Force that supports and sustains us in our efforts to grow and transform!

Grace

The good news is that in some modern energy processes, there is a lot of potential to gracefully dismantle some of these energy patterns with little fanfare. It has been my experience that deep healing can occur with greater and greater ease and grace. I view this as a spiritual gift.

As the ability of transformative work is empowered with grace, we do not need to analyze and pick out every element of trauma or distortion we carry. We are ripe to let many things go and realign with a peaceful spiritual state of being. We simply need to understand and accept our spiritual nature and potential.

When elements do require greater attention or certain awareness, it is often because – spiritually speaking – they are important for us to understand. This can mean coming face to face with our personal history - so we can reconcile that which is keeping us apart from our potential. The wisdom of Kundalini, guiding our footsteps, will know what is best for our growth and maturation.

No Two Dances are Alike

Kundalini awakens very differently from one individual to the next. It is by no means a linear process.

Some people have obvious, dramatic energetic or conscious experiences. For others it is quiet and serene, through a process of gentle realization. For everyone who is touched by this process, it is transforming. Kundalini awakens experientially, not simply logically, the awareness that we are each a spiritual being, as well as a human being. We are each unique expressions of spirit.

The awakening will introduce us individually to the next steps we are to take – to align, to heal and to achieve our spiritual potential – through the labyrinth of our thoughts and feelings. Kundalini stirs in response to our Higher Self.

Kundalini awakening has the potential to realign our life so it can mirror a higher spiritual concept, not as a doctrine, but as a way of life. We learn to live in the world in a state of love – for that is our own higher self nature. It supports a transition to "being *in* the world, but not *of* the world" – as provided in the wise words once delivered as guidance to the followers of peace.[1] Kundalini awakening brings healing, true healing, in its wings.

The Bigger Picture

Many human beings are inclined to grow spiritually at this time on the planet. The planet is being gifted with unprecedented energy at this time to facilitate this healing. The whole earth is perceptibly under the influence of a global Kundalini awakening – collectively, but one person at a time.

What would Kundalini teach us? If we look at the core central teaching of all the world religions, before they became religions – the core truth they teach is universal. They teach love, forgiveness, courage, non-judgment, kindness, compassion, wisdom, integrity, mercy, joy, honesty, self-responsibility and peace.

If we pause for a moment and reflect on ourselves as spiritual beings, living in an energy based human body – these core spiritual precepts also teach the energy harmonization that is requisite for spiritual development, energetic balance, and for well being. These attributes are precisely those that would not disturb, distort, congeal, block or destroy one's energy field! They are the preparation necessary to support an awakening Kundalini energy.

It is said that all roads lead to Rome. Well, the road of Kundalini awakening may not lead to Rome. It will, however, lead us proverbially to the feet of Shakti and her universal drive to reunite humanity with the truth of its inherent divine nature. She is the Cosmic Mother, the divine feminine face of God. She will unshackle the chains of illusion, in the birth of her divine children. It is at her feet, and resting on her bosom, we will find the support to grow, to heal and to transform. May you be genuinely blessed by her love and awakening power.

DR JOHN G RYAN MD

PART III

HEALING

CHAPTER 8

THE HEALING UNIVERSE

Healing Defined

In our modern world when we use the term "healing", we refer primarily to the concept of "treatment" of disease. Treatment indicates the eradication or control of a disease or condition. The term also often implies a somewhat "aggressive" process in which we fight to win a struggle against an adversary. We even rage "wars" on diseases, such as cancer or multiple sclerosis, to express our disdain for the disease state, and express our desire to be healthy and well.

When we speak about healing from a holistic paradigm, the term healing takes on a different connotation. Healing is not simply the eradication of disease. It implies the restitution of balance and homeostasis, a process that allows health and healing to occur. It views the natural state of a human being to be in balance with itself, its environment, and its spirit.

Holistic oriented and energy based healing may lead effectively to the "treatment" of a disease process. Yet that is not really its approach. In fact, healing in a holistic orientation will often view a disease process as a "messenger" or "sentinel" of understanding. A disease process or condition may bring awareness of imbalances in the human being – and are acknowledged for the role they often play. Such awareness can then be utilized to lead to a physical, psychological, or spiritual realignment that may lead to better overall balance. In fact, some diseases are not "meant" to be eradicated as long as they serve an important spiritual purpose in one's life. In this framework, illness, and in fact any kind of personal crisis has a "purpose" and is integral in a larger framework of spiritual growth and development.

People who are inspired to pursue "healing" work in this broader context, will come from a variety of experiences.

First, some people will currently be facing an acute or chronic health crisis – and they will begin to explore alternative or energetic healing work as part of a journey to wellness. The underlying issue may be a physical disease, a psychological issue, or a spiritual crisis of some type. In the process of exploring alternative and/or energy based treatment processes, a person will vicariously come to learn more about the energetic and spiritual nature of existence. In such a setting, the illness becomes cornerstone in a person's life, functioning as a catalyst of growth. This whole process may ultimately become an inspirational force as they achieve healing in their own life. Many will in fact share with others what they have discovered in their personal journey as part of their purpose in life. In fact, this is a stimulus for many people to become "alternative health practitioners".

Illness, in this context, often serves as a launching pad for a great quest of spirit. Illness or crisis may be viewed not only as an unwanted, tragic or challenging experience – but an experience that mystically stimulates a process of spiritual development. Such experiences can inspire a person to search deeply within themselves for answers, understanding, and, for spiritual meaning. It creates a catalyst to stimulate a journey, and a bridge of spiritual discovery.

Secondly, people may not be ill or in crisis, but live an esoteric experience - one, that stimulates a burning curiosity. This might include a spontaneous kundalini awakening, a near death experience, a transcendent moment in meditation, or a whole host of paranormal consciousness experiences that people encounter. Such events may even produce very unusual psychological experiences, as well as very physical symptoms. This may be very challenging to understand or process, and leads to a quest of discovery. In the search for understanding, comfort or relief, they too are led to energy and consciousness based practices in which they find support.

Finally, a third group of people may be simply intrigued to learn by innate curiosity, or be exposed to knowledge that resonates deeply with them. They become inspired to learn and grow. They feel a compelling desire to learn spiritual things or to live in a healthy fashion and are drawn to things that promote wellness and growth in consciousness. As we witness the expanding interest in natural health and alternative health practices, we see how large this group of individuals has become.

What everyone has in common is that once one begins to view life through a more holistic framework, one is in essence embarking upon a spiritual journey. Why? Central to the holistic view lays the concept of balance in physical, emotional, mental and spiritual wellbeing. It also becomes clearer that it is the spiritual dimension, which brings wisdom and healing into the psycho-emotional and physical world of form. Energy healing provides a conceptual framework, but also serves as a bridge to understand and experience the healing mechanism of our spirit – a bio-spiritual transformation.

COMPARATIVE VIEWS

Traditional medicine, alternative medicine, and energy-based medicine may each hold different perspectives on healing. Let us take a closer look:

The human body is an overwhelming complex integrated structure, with a vast array of integrated functional body systems. In traditional western medicine we break the body up into these systems to understand and define both healthy states and disease conditions.

This includes familiar systems such as the endocrine system, the gastrointestinal system, the cardiovascular system, the neurological system, the musculoskeletal system, and so forth. Each one of these systems is comprised of a series of interconnected organs. For example, we can consider the stomach, liver, pancreas, and intestines of the gastrointestinal system, or, the brain, spinal cord and nerves of the central nervous system. These organs contain cells of highly specialized function. The systems auto-regulate and react to internal and external stimuli to create optimal function and homeostasis.

In the traditional medical paradigm, health might be defined in a few ways. It would include a state where all of this machinery is working well and in need of no external support. It would also include having a corrected dysfunction in a system through treatment. This may imply removing or replacing elements in the body, or supporting the function of the body in some way through medications or therapies, which provide for reasonable wellbeing.

Disease may be thought to occur when something is structurally wrong with one of the working parts of the system. For example when a normal organ is infiltrated by a tumor of abnormal cells like in cancer; or, when an organ has become so atrophied it doesn't function adequately, such as the lungs with emphysema. Disease is also defined when the system is structurally sound, but functionally out of balance with the overall function of the body. This may include over production of a hormone, such as hyperthyroidism, or, under production of hormone such as inadequate insulin production in diabetes. Finally, toxins, infection, inflammatory conditions and genetic conditions, as well as trauma may also lead to various types of structural or functional problems.

In the face of illness, traditional medicine responds to disease in several ways. It can remove bits and pieces that misbehave. This might include surgery to relieve a bowel obstruction, or to remove a tumor, as examples. It can give chemicals to destroy diseased tissue, such as chemotherapy in the setting of cancer. It can provide specific drugs, which have a very specific influence on the physiology of a specific system. This might include beta-blockers to slow the heart rate by mimicking a parasympathetic influence, or pain relieving medications, which suppress inflammatory or neurologic responses. Or, it can replace functionally missing elements, such as insulin in diabetes.

The knowledge that has evolved through the experience of modern medicine to understand and treat these problems is stupendous. It is also quite new in historical terms – with pretty much every major advance made within the last few hundred years.

Now it is recognized that not all disease is structural or physical. Traditional medicine also deals with psycho-emotional and mental dysfunction. This falls into the arenas of psychology and psychiatry. It does, however, hold its view of psychological health and healing in a somewhat limited scientific paradigm.

In psychiatry there has been a tendency to relate to the human being in the same mechanical way that medicine in general has learned to successfully deal with illness in the human body. A great deal of psychiatric research has been designed to discover the biochemical abnormalities inherent in certain psychological conditions. As a result, therapies designed to deal biochemically with both psycho-emotional and psycho-pathologic conditions have emerged. For example, we are familiar with serotonin reuptake inhibitors (SSRI's) used in the treatment of depression, or benzodiazepines to treat anxiety disorders. Psychiatric disorders are collated into defined psychological and disease conditions by the DSM classification which can guide such management.

What is sometimes overlooked in importance in modern psychiatry is the plasticity of the neurologic system. The standard is to treat biochemical states as "causes" rather than observable effects or consciousness influences. Medicine is now, however, recognizing that certain environmental and spiritual influences can have a very positive effect on brain chemistry. [35,42]

Psychiatry is, of course, not solely limited to chemical therapy. It does include therapies that involve psychological understanding or transformative support. It is just now beginning to more comprehensively explore the role of consciousness and spiritually based wisdom in its approach to wellbeing and healing.

Traditional western medicine today provides treatments for an endless array of medical conditions and diseases, which can be extremely appropriate to use with wisdom and intelligence. It simply needs to be understood that in its efforts to heal, it does tend to view the body and the mind quite mechanistically. This is limited when we begin to understand a bigger picture of human health and human nature. We are more than mechanistic machines and the multifaceted nature of human beings must now be integrated into a healing paradigm.

The knowledge and capability of traditional medicine should be fully acknowledged for its value. It's life enhancing and life saving gifts may be understood to be as spiritually inspired as any healing knowledge that has ever existed on the planet. As participants in the health care systems, we simply need to be aware of its limitations, pitfalls and shortcomings. It can be utilized appropriately when needed, and we may become aware when other approaches to healing may be provided.

The next arena of healing would include natural, complimentary or alternative healing practices. What separates traditional medicine from such healing practice is both approach and tradition.

Many alternative healing approaches stem from a variety of healing systems, which were very "traditional" in the original setting in which they emerged. These traditions include such practices as herbal remedies, dietary regulation and naturopathic medicine or even acupuncture. These are founded in ancient healing systems such as Ayurveda, Tibetan, and Chinese medicine. Practices such as yoga, structural bodywork, and massage therapy have long been used in integrated systems of healing. Other alternative practices have emerged through healing practitioners in modern times, such as homeopathy and flower essences therapies.

Alternative healing practices, particularly those somewhat allied with traditional healing, such as naturopathy, aim to restore balance in the body by its great understanding of nutrition, elemental correction and supplementation of elements such as vitamins, and the importance of psycho-spiritual health.

One cardinal difference in the world of alternative health practice, is that even when the therapy is directed towards a specific condition, such as in a herbal remedy to treat an issue, it is based not so much on "treating the disease", but "strengthening and balancing the individual" to restore health in the system. Healing is often a goal, but it is a "by-product" of a more inclusive process.

An important component included in some alternative therapies, is healing based on a framework of understanding that includes the "energetic composition" of the human body. This crosses another bridge of understanding. As we discussed earlier, the body is an energy construct, composed of many organized fields of subtle energy. From an energetic inclusive perspective, the physical body is understood as an out-pictured reality that is formed, sustained and renewed by a complex array of energy bodies or fields.

Many alternative practices are based on an effectiveness which occurs due to the energetic influence it creates within these energy bodies. Flower essence therapy is one such example. In flower essence therapy, the etheric energy printed by a flower serves as an etheric catalyst on the level of subtle energy to support energy-based transitions. Such therapies have a vibrational or healing influence on the human energy field through resonance interactions.

There are also therapies that work directly with the energy fields. These include not only resonant interaction, but also direct channeling of energy into the human energy field. This includes things such as Reiki, Therapeutic Touch, and Hands-on-Healing.

In the application of energy-based modalities, one cannot "see" the therapy – so, of course, it can seem to an unaware observer that "nothing" is occurring. Yet as a recipient of such practices, the experience is often very profound and leaves little doubt in the imagination that something very powerful and transformative is occurring.

In processes that "channel" energy into the body, the energy is transformative in ways that help to clear, unblock, release and restore the energy fields. It can also support the restructuring of deeply embedded psycho-emotional and etheric patterns that create both physical and psychological discomfort in our lives.

The energy provided to achieve such a "therapeutic benefit" must originate from "somewhere". It is mystical in nature because of the invisible and esoteric nature of this "energy". This energy is understood to be channeled *inter-dimensionally* or from a *spiritual plane* of existence. Hence it is consciously bringing a whole other "world" or "level of life" into the healing paradigm.

In my experience there is an unquestionable validity to the process of channeling energy for healing purposes. What is perhaps more remarkable however, is that there is also a profound intelligence guiding this energy beyond conscious human involvement.

Some energy therapies, such as acupuncture, do use very specific knowledge and work quite consciously within the energy system. Other modalities, such as Hands on Healing for example, may allow the energy to flow with limited or no specific intentional direction by the practitioner. Unlike with surgery, or the tailored use of a specific herb to treat a specific condition, as seen in "knowledge based" practices – the practitioner is often quite unaware of what is occurring through the energy work or process. It is the "energy" which is most conscious of the healing action! In fact, in my experience, it seems most powerfully effective when a practitioner can stand "out of the way" in such a process, and let the energy simply flow or be directed in intuitive ways. So this, admittedly, is very peculiar to someone who is very "3D" in orientation.

Now at first to a skeptical mind, this will all sound a bit ludicrous. It is easy to appreciate why people would follow and trust the logic and wisdom inherent in well-established traditional and alternative healing practices. But, why would someone rely on some questionable process that "channels energy"?

We can realize that most healing is "mysterious". When we endure a cut in the skin, the body knows how to heal the wound. It is healed by an intelligence that is embedded in the consciousness of the body itself. The challenge is that when we begin to approach healing at the level of subtle energy, the level of "energy" we are opening to in such healing processes also seems to function with an innate intelligence. It is similar to the innate intelligence in the body that knows how to heal a wound – but we are healing by drawing upon a level of energy, which is parallel to the physical world in some way. It is mystically intelligent. As silly as this might sound to someone who has never experienced energy-based healing, it is as comprehensible to someone who has.

This whole discussion introduces a peculiar idea which is foreign both to traditional and even some alternative health practices: The practitioner is not the source of healing in these exchanges.

The practitioner, or "healer", is a vehicle through which such experiences may be catalyzed, and through which energy may be delivered. In the setting of energy therapy, if the energy fields are corrected, then the energy can flow within the system, and create improved health. The healer is not the source of the energy, or the intelligence that fully knows how to send it or govern it. The healer, as a human intermediary, is not the "cause" of healing – but rather a "facilitator" of a process.

It is also important to understand that the effect or potential corrections that occur within a person's energy fields are also subject to the consciousness of the "healee".

For example, no matter how effortful a healer works, a person can hold onto patterning in their energy system, if they "want to". This holding-on may be conscious or subconscious as an influence. A person can also recreate a distortion once it is healed, if they do not adjust to or accept the changes produced upon the pattern in consciousness. This is an important principle to understand.

This is critical to grasp – because healing at this level is subject to an inherent spiritual integrity. Spiritual energy cannot be forced. It can only be offered, and received as is individually appropriate. Healing, therefore, even in the most exceptional hands may not have the healing influence desired. This is frustrating for people – both healers and healees – if it is not understood.

Energy healing opens the door to "interdimensional energy" (a quantum dimension) – it is also opening the door to the influence of a spiritual dimension in healing – and hence, the influence of "consciousness".

Consciousness healing implies the action of bringing a healing influence into our life by growth in consciousness. This happens very naturally and quite vicariously as we learn, grow and mature in our life. It can be supported or accelerated by the influence of things such as meditation, mindfulness practices, spiritual health practices, insight oriented psychotherapy, direct spiritual experiences, or guidance in many forms. These practices and experiences can lead to a direct communicative experience with our own spiritual consciousness, which is really what insight is all about. This can guide us toward direct healing endeavors that will lead to restorative healing.

By opening to the influence of healing through energy and consciousness we are becoming aware of, and gaining access to, the healing power of our spiritual essence. It does not replace traditional medicine. It adds a whole new dimension to traditional healing and will transform traditional healing as we better understand who we are and what we are capable of as spiritualized human beings!

THE MISSING PILL

How Do We Bridge Old and New

It is perhaps fair to say that when we include a spiritual dimension in healing, we have stepped very far outside of traditional medicine. Medicine does not talk of energy, spirit or God. It talks of reason.

In recent times, physicians rarely recommend "spiritual based" prescriptions. This is changing now, as true spiritual based elements are entering into medical practice through programs that include consciousness-based therapies and energy-based practices. We still, however, tend to stay away from the label of *spiritual* based practices and this is not necessarily inappropriate.

Programs such as meditation, biofeedback, mindfulness-based therapies, and hands on healing practices, are practiced in many hospitals today. We may also accept the benefit of yoga or mediation for example – but we maintain a neutral terminology to avoid confusion or conflict with religious orientation. I think this is a wonderful thing because it allows people to explore and access elements of spiritual healing that are not confined to or opposed by a religious program. They are open to *every* human being *equally*.

In traditional approaches to healing, there is a therapeutic orientation. It is geared towards making things "better" or right again. In traditional medicine, illness happens *to* us – and we are out to eradicate it. We can be healed by another person and we simply have to follow their advice or skill. When we begin to introduce "energy" and "consciousness" in the healing paradigm, illness does not happen *to us*, it happens *through us*. There is a causal as well as an experiential component that takes on much greater value and meaning. This is a needed point of clarity to bridge a gap that spans these two worlds.

An experience of disease, or a personal crisis, in the new paradigm, is potentially bringing awareness to us in some fashion. This requires an important expansion in the concept of what we term as illness or disease.

In energy-based medicine, factors can be viewed to cause or contribute to disease processes, based on the patterning in the energy field of the human being. Disease process may be then viewed as anything that leads to aberrations in the energy bodies, including the etheric, mental, emotional or higher causal bodies and the energetic programming within the DNA. This energy configuration lies "behind" or helps lead to a manifested energy expression in the world of form or experience. This "expression" or "experience" may be physical, emotional, mental or spiritual in nature.

If we live the experience of manifesting an illness, a psychological crisis, or any experience for that matter – it is implicit that this experience has a "causal" origin in our personal energy system. If we expand our way of understanding disease to include this idea, we can use the experience to grow and gain a greater understanding of both ourselves and the nature of life.

If we learn not to hold energy patterns that contribute to manifesting such things in our lives – we can take greater conscious responsibility to heal. This is where healing takes on a tone of "education" and "responsibility" and "spiritual meaning". Yet, the learning is about our spiritual nature and the spiritual power available to us, as we expand our view of "who and what we are".

Now, I realize that accepting this perspective may not be for everybody. Yet, those who accept this viewpoint – often begin to appreciate that what we live and manifest in our lives, including more negative experiences like illness and crisis, can have an important message or insight to bring. It is to teach us about our power, our spiritual abilities, and the attributes of a spiritually empowered life.

There is always a risk that such a discussion can take on a tone of judgment or criticism if it is not properly understood. Illness, psychological challenges, and a whole host of personal types of crisis, will arise on everyone's journey. It is usually a very important experience to live! In the new paradigm this can be acknowledged as a spiritually significant experience rather than exclusive misfortune or plain bad luck. Illness becomes something that can bring us, and those around us, great gifts of consciousness.

How might we "meld" these two realities when we examine specific symptoms or disease states?

Let us look at a couple of examples to better understand:

Imagine a person who is very fearful and anxious in their life. From a traditional healing perspective, this person may be viewed to have an anxiety disorder with a "neurotransmitter imbalance" in the brain. This imbalance is producing this state of anxiety and is viewed as the "cause" of the problem. Medications may be used to alter the neurotransmitters in the brain and nervous system to help overcome the symptoms. This person can effectively use medical therapy to support them in controlling the symptomatic issues.

From an energy inclusive paradigm, we can view things a little differently. We might look a little deeper, and observe patterns in the person's energy system, which correlate with the issue. Perhaps there is an energy posturing that is promoting the "chemical imbalance". What does that mean?

Energetically, it might be observed that the person's third and fourth chakra are greatly "suppressed in function". But why? Well, This may have resulted from prior life experiences of great judgment and adversity – that was handled by learning to withdraw and begin "shutting down" – within themself. The root chakra may also be pulled up, leaving the person loosely grounded in the world. This energy configuration creates a *posture* or *signature* that manifests physically and psychologically with anxiety and insecurity. Conceptually, it is this energy posturing, which is leading to issues – and the energy field interfaces with the human nervous system. As it interfaces with the human brain, could it conceivably create the observed neurotransmitter changes?

This description of energy posturing provides an example of how an "energy pattern" may correlate with a "medical condition".

While traditional therapy may recommend anti-anxiety medication, healing in the energy paradigm would include energy shifts to re-establish a healthy energy field. It would also include learning to overcome "the tendencies of this energy patterning" – so the person may be more fully present in their body.

This might involve developing a better understanding of one's inherent value and worth, opening the heart to more fully connect with the world around them, learning to be less encumbered by the fear of being hurt, shamed or neglected – and creating an energetic foundation. It might be supported by direct energy therapy and psychological support. A great healing may occur that is not a masking "symptomatic resolution" – but a corrective alignment.

Healing becomes a process of restoring health and function to the energy system, so an individual can live freer from the energetic restriction and patterning that can compromise health and wellbeing. It will also support gaining the insight required to lead to the lasting transformation needed to support life-affirming change.

If these changes are achieved, the "interface" between energy and the brain will shift. This could potentially lead to a very different expression of neurotransmitter function.

The Complexity of Energy Patterning

When we begin to accept that energy patterning or the idea that our "energy signature" can be creating our experiences – we open a virtual Pandora's Box. What causes such an internal energy arrangement? Why are we not all "perfect" in this regard? It is here that healing must include a greater view of human nature.

When we step into the world of a spiritually inclusive medicine we will encounter some unusual elements, which may contribute to, or preclude wellness. These are things that are not typically considered in traditional medicine. It includes things that are truly spiritual in nature and require an open mind and open spirit to integrate into the healing paradigm. I will try to summarize some of the most important points:

1. Life is a spiritual journey. We are here to learn, to grow and to love.
2. Human beings have free will – and we are here to learn through our choices and our consequences.
3. Everything we experience has a role to play in our lives, even illness and loss.
4. Illness may have a spiritual purpose and potential.
5. Life is not limited to our current incarnation. This is the important moment in time – but not the sole influence on our life.
6. We are meant to awaken to our spiritual nature, which provides us with an understanding of our life and our potential – including our potential to heal.
7. We are responsible co-creators of our experience, which models itself on our personal consciousness and our energy signature. We "create" our reality. We can learn and grow by the feedback and challenges we face as human beings. This is essential in healing.

We begin to accept that there is an innate process of spiritual growth and evolution, that is part of our human design. We are meant to grow and mature as human beings, and blossom into spiritually conscious beings. Life is a process of growth in consciousness – and some of the experiences, which contribute to this growth, will involve issues of health and healing.

In this consideration, our life may even be viewed as *school*. Life is the school or arena through which we have the opportunity to create and experience through our own free will choices, to grow in consciousness, and to awaken to our spiritual nature.

Spiritually, we are here to awaken and to learn about the "ways of spirit". This is ultimately the way of love. Everything we are living is ultimately an opportunity to learn to love, and to choose to love as a way of life. Healing issues are not exempt from this education.

So, illness may be a part of this journey. If it is, we can use it wisely to grow. We may learn about self-care. We may learn about authentic responsibility.

We can learn about the dysfunctional or disharmonizing aspect of the human ego upon the energy system. We may learn about the role of forgiveness and compassion and all precepts of spiritual wisdom, or the consequence they have on our "energy signature". So you see, each experience can teach us about responsible creation and the power of love to overcome adversity and challenges of life.

WHO IS THE TEACHER?

As we open spiritually, we may look to avatars and way-showers, like the wise beings who have inspired all major religions, and those who are alive today with messages of hope, growth and enlightenment. We can learn from others. So the teacher can appear "external" to us, and can take many forms.

But, eventually we encounter the concept and reality of our "higher self". As we seek spiritual growth in healing – we come to learn and experience that "God" or "spirit" lives *within* us. We are one with God and the fabric of life – and intimately connected to a spiritual level of reality that is alive and within us. Ultimately, it is the higher self, which helps us organize experiences – both in the form of external teachers and the internal development of insight and wisdom.

The higher self is like the wiser, all knowing, and all loving aspect of consciousness that represents our fullest spiritual potential. Our higher self knows our past, the influence of prior lifetimes, our karma, and our potential. It will support us and encourage us in our effort to learn to love and to manifest healing in the world.

In the process of learning, the higher self is able to implement or allow conditions of the body to help us grow and mature as spiritual beings. This provides a mechanism to manifest some very important lessons in life, love and deeper healing. In this setting, healing takes on a deeply spiritual meaning.

When such an experience does occur it can become an essential ingredient in a broader spiritual experience. It can help one manifest an attribute of spiritual consciousness, or to guide the individual towards a specific purpose or potential. It is through our own higher self we are instructed, we learn, we heal and we find peace. It is a bridge through we can access a deeper and more comprehensive healing than we may have previously dreamt possible.

Many people who do deep personal work, do experience very profound healing on every level of their being – including both physical and psycho-emotional states – and thrive in a renewed way in this very lifetime. In fact, this may be viewed, for reasons already addressed, as a time of such grace. Many people believe it is possible at this time to simply walk out of such karmic patterning through the mechanism of spiritual grace and the bio-spiritual transformation afforded to humanity at this time. I am one of them.

What is Being Healing?

I would never wish illness on anyone. Yet, I have been astounded so many times, when courageous people who are facing illnesses of different kinds, use the experience often to grow and to heal. This may occur completely on a physical level. Physical healing is available to many through the process of bio-spiritual integration.

We do, however, need to understand that people do not always need to physically heal from disease, to heal in spirit. Outcomes will always follow what serves the highest purpose in a soul's "life design". Healing may not be physical. A person may successfully spiritually heal – and not physically heal. A spiritual healing, as such, redirects the course of one's life or attention to matters of spiritual purpose or awakening.

People may also work through particular experiences, not specifically to heal in this lifetime, but to clear through energy in their spectrum to prepare for a new experience in the next lifetime. So, illness for many people will be a doorway through which they emerge to experience a "spiritual awakening". Traditional medicine has absolutely no framework to understand such an outcome.

When we collate all of these considerations together, we can see there are many influences which affect our state of physical health, as well as the physical and energetic functions of our bodies. So, healing is not a simple term.

When a word has such a broad spectrum of connotations, it can take on almost no meaning. However, healing, at its deepest and most profound level, is an awakening to the experience of our self as a spiritual being, and a restoration of our earthly expression to model the wisdom and love we all hold as spiritual entities. It opens our earthly journey to the expanded energy and consciousness of our spiritual nature, and allows the healing this provides to work through our bio-spiritual continuum.

As we "heal", we not only overcome many of the diseases we may encounter as human beings; we ultimately learn to use our life experience to manifest a greater and greater potential of our unique selves. We are each a potent force of growth, healing and transformation in a world interconnected by a common field of love.

COMING FULL CIRCLE

So in our short discussion on the spectrum of healing we have visited traditional allopathic medicine, natural and alternative medicine, energy-based medicine approaches and the concept of spiritual healing. There is no strict division, for all knowledge that supports healing at any level or in any way – is essentially "spiritual" in nature and origin. But to awaken spiritually – and to bring a spiritual power into the healing process – is however, a quantum leap.

We are beings of free will choice and consequence. As we live our lives, we must take our own personal and appropriate steps – through our own intention and choices – to align with a healing paradigm. As we do, we learn about an expanded view of the spiritual nature of life, our nature as a human being, and the role we have to create and sustain a balanced energetic alignment with our spiritual design.

Each and every one of us is a spiritual being, and a responsible co-creative force in nature. This includes all that we create both in form and experience in our lives. If we accept spiritual responsibility, and utilize our manifested experience as a compass and foundation to navigate a personal journey of meaning – we are tremendously supported in doing so. Spiritual integration can help us "unshackle" the ways we are repressed, restricted, distorted or limited – as the case may be! It can help us find the freedom that is implied - not in simple egoic self-centered freedom – but spiritual freedom.

Healing is, as such, an integral part of the journey of spiritual enlightenment. This is not simply metaphoric. When you appreciate the energy concepts we discuss – by living through a personal healing process you actually are able to "carry" a greater charge of energy or light.

This will impact your life, your family, and the whole world. You actually cannot heal, without healing the world to the same degree. And, you cannot heal the world, without healing yourself – an important principle for well-minded people to understand.

So let us take healing back to where the potential lies and the transformation can really occur – within you. I solemnly believe, that to heal in this spiritually inclusive way, is our greatest purpose and our greatest potential as human beings in this lifetime. By participating in our own process of conscious healing and personal growth, we are building a brand new world. Let us create a new reality ... where wellness is as natural as your next breath!

Responsibility and Healing

Personal "responsibility" serves as the corner stone of spiritual growth and healing. As one takes the first steps on the road of healing and spiritual growth - one will develop an intimate appreciation of the concept of *personal responsibility*.

In our modern culture, we go to healers of both traditional and nontraditional approaches, to seek healing. We may go to the doctor, or naturopath or chiropractor to "get" healed. As a person opens to the spiritual component of healing, one will continue to use the wisdom and resources of such kind and magnificent healers, but we will ultimately develop a deep sense of personal responsibility for our own healing journey, and our lives.

To the ego mind, the concept of responsibility is primarily viewed as a "burden". It is often a blame-based process to inspire shame, guilt, control, or to justify a vengeance. If someone commits a hurtful act, for example, responsibility implies blame. There is an aggressor and a victim. The aggressor is responsible and the victim is unfortunate and without causal influence. If one has done something wrong – one is "responsible". The words carry a tone of shame and guilt. In fact, the words "Who is responsible?" are the first to be uttered when a tragedy of any kind strikes.

Yes, of course there are terrible things that are done by people in the name of both good and evil – and people suffer at the hands of these experiences. Other horrific experiences are encountered and it would seem there is no one really to blame at all – except maybe "God". But responsibility, when viewed through spiritual eyes, implies something larger and more conscious, than simply "blame" or "guilt'.

Responsibility is an *intra*personal process. It implies that one's life is created as an external mirroring, in both form and experience. Our experiences may be viewed to correlate to what is held in one's energy and one's consciousness. Responsibility implies that a person is in sovereign control of his or her own life, own choices and own experiences – because it is created vibrationally and magnetically by the state of ones "energy signature". Events and experiences do not simply happen to us randomly; they arrive as manifested potentials that follow our overall energy patterning and consciousness.

This is at first, for many, a challenging concept. We can easily understand that there is a causative element for all things that manifest in our world. We are simply in the habit of externalizing the causative factor. An accident, for example, may be caused through recklessness, or a disease may be caused by a random infection. When we see a cause as such, we can focus the remedy on the cause.

The challenge created by a more conscientious attitude toward life and healing is that we must consider the principle that it is our own energy posture and our personal energy patterning that draws or magnetizes certain experiences toward us. We "create our reality" on a principle of "attraction".

This concept is both overwhelming and liberating. But as we will see, responsibility, once we work through the ego's view on it, becomes a de-victimizing attribute of conscious life, and ultimately one of the greatest tools of self-empowerment.

One cannot understand fully the concept of creative responsibility without developing a spiritually inclusive and energy-based understanding of life. If we do create our own reality – the question becomes – how do we do it? Simply by thinking? Well no, it is not that simple.

We can better conceptualize that we draw to ourselves, experiences that mirror the patterns we hold or resonate in our personal energy fields or energy signature. This can include thoughts and also feelings – be it conscious or unconscious – as well as elements of a spiritual influence.

For example, if I hold myself to be of limited worth, this energy signature will magnetize experiences of worthlessness to me. If I see myself as unlovable – I will manifest this quality in my life by resonance. Now if the story stopped here it would be perhaps very sad. We would then simply be victims of our own energy signature, rather than the world around us! But, alas that is not the case.

The concept of responsibility introduces to us the idea that our experiences are *self-reflective*. The value in this concept is that if we assume responsibility toward our experiences – we can seek to let our experiences teach us – and this opens the door to transform our energy signature. In other words, we can witness the creative impulse of our thoughts and feelings – and adjust them with wisdom, insight and greater understanding. We can exam our life and see what may be hidden in our subconscious self that is influencing the quality of our life. Responsibility opens a doorway to heal or transform.

Creative responsibility requires an understanding of energy dynamics and the ability of our spirit to "edit" or "transform" energy patterning. Responsibility implies choice and provides power. Until we develop an acceptance of this type of responsibility, we are at the whims of life and/or our inner energy state.

Life can seem to toss us around as unwitting victims of experience for which we hold no creative responsibility or intent – simply because we do not understand the nature of creative energy. In Buddhist terms, we are lost in *Maya* or the illusory world of great suffering.

☉

So if we are to assume greater personal responsibility, and become a causal force in our life, how do we achieve this without becoming self destructive in attitude? And how does this provide a great ability to heal? Let's examine the power of this attitude.

Earlier we have explored how our body is a composite of energy fields that exist within or around our physical body. Each energy body has a direct influence on the experiences we manifest and the health of the body. We can draw a correlation between "energy" and "life'. What might that look like practically speaking?

Let us imagine that one's heart chakra is greatly restricted and the energy of this center is significantly absent. One might readily imagine the dysfunction that can occur in one's life, and even in the physical heart itself. Through this lens, the experience of heart disease may relate not simply to exercise or cholesterol – but also to heart chakra function – and the energy flow through that center. The correlation between a manifested experience, and the energy state becomes a little more conceivable.

Now, if we could somehow correct the internal energy pattern, i.e. open and clear the heart chakra, we could promote the out-picturing of a healthier state. So, the question next becomes – how do we release this restrictive energy?

If a person has been hurt in their life and they do not trust – they will have a challenging time opening their energy field. Yet, they will need to open up and let go of past wounds to let the energy be free. If they are too afraid to do this – they will remain restricted in energy. But – the restricted energy produces the energy signature that holds a creative influence. Our life will try to model itself based on what we hold in our energy signature. It is at this level that we carry "responsibility".

We can change anything – which is the real message of responsibility – if we understand a few important spiritual principles.

If someone has lived a deeply traumatic experience, one that has produced the original patterning, they may have been exposed to some terribly painful event that was key in creating this pattern. Most of the wounds we carry are sourced in prior negative experiences. By understanding the energy patterning, we can also understand our power to "undo" the energy pattern that leads to healing.

Healing is like letting ourselves return to the way we were before the incident – but enhanced by the wisdom gained from the experience! However, we will learn that if prior experience has shaped our energy in such a way – there is no point in "blaming" our self or even another person ultimately – for it will bind us to the energy posture. It takes a spiritual consciousness and "know how" to do this. It also takes a willingness to drop the notion of victimization as an attitude of consciousness. If we blame – we externalize power – to another person or to an attribute in our ego – but we cannot transform if we do not take responsibility for our self.

When one begins to understand this concept, and the wisdom and power of the spiritual energy within them, they can let energy flow into any experience to heal and release its grip on one's energy. This may mean finding purpose and value in the negative experience that has been lived, it may mean forgiveness of past wounds, and it may mean letting go of what we are holding on to that is hurting us creatively.

This illustration presented above is relatively straightforward. Yet, sometimes the influence of restrictive energy patterning is very subtle, and sometimes the causative factors in terms of energy have a deep psycho-emotional component that may not be at all consciously understood.

Imagine, for example, that a person is skeptical of the idea that anyone is worthy of trust. If we looked retrospectively, there may be valid reasons for developing this world-view. A person may have been betrayed, neglected or abandoned by any number of important influences in one's life. This may include parents, siblings, teachers or strangers over many years of experiences. It may be very difficult to manifest any sense of trust, because there is a deeply distorted pattern of mistrust that has developed in the mental, emotional and etheric elements.

In such a setting, a person may not realize that this unhealed experience has produced an energy posturing or signature. It is this very posturing that now twists every experience lived into one of "self-preservation". There is a cautious skepticism and multifaceted defense patterning that develops. This patterning inherently insists on uncovering the intention of any well meaning (or harm invoking) person in one's life. The slightest cue will be offsetting. They will trust no one. They will look for reasons to doubt, to judge, to essentially prove this inner energy stature in every encounter in their life. Hence one will find things – sometimes authentic and sometimes contrived – to support the "energy signature" of this wound. Importantly, even though this person may not realize how or why they are creating a certain type of life experience, they are still fundamentally the creative core at its center.

So meanwhile, it is not true that there are not "trustable" people in the world. There will, however, be no trustable people in this person's world, because there is no room or potential for them to exist. They will destroy any relationship eventually – because they will project the inner energy signature onto everything and everyone in their life. In this creative energy, one will come to be "right" (albeit wrong) in essence – that the world is a place where trust is not possible or warranted. So, this is a simple example to show how our energy posture or signature is "creative" in a psychodynamic way.

One more example may help to further clarify the essence of responsibility in healing. Imagine that a person holds a lot of repressed anger in their emotional body. It affects the way they think, the way they feel and even their physical posture. They will approach life in an aggressive, defensive way and evoke a fair amount of conflict.

They may say – "people are always aggressive with me, and provoking conflict" – not understanding that they are at the creative center of this experience. Unless people around such energy are quite self-aware themselves, they are likely to get caught up in the energy of this persons aggressive approach, and will mirror back analogous behavior. Again, the "energy signature" will be creative!

No one is truly angry like this, in one's deepest spiritual nature. All of these behaviors come from lack of conscious awareness of our spiritual nature, and through prior experience and conditioning or deep wounds. It is, however, challenging to understand this type of influence if we are strongly patterned in such a behavior. The inciting wound is often forgotten and at times is so deep within our psyche it is not even available to our conscious memory. It may have even occurred in a prior life experience!

Yet as one makes steps in spiritual growth the awareness of both the inner and outer destructiveness of such a pattern comes to light. We can better see in the present moment it's influence on our life and wellbeing. It is at this nexus that healing may enter into our psyche through the vector of "self-responsibility". We can own our creative responsibility and commit to healing the pattern that is influencing our life in a hurtful way.

When we view life spiritually, we may understand how such wounds are capable of affecting our behavior. But, the challenge is … if experiences have led to energetic patterning, and the energy patterning continues to influence our life and relationships – we are then creating causal experiences, or what is termed karma. In a sense of spiritual responsibility, one is still spiritually self responsible for what one says, does and creates – even if it emerges from energy patterning arising from a wound.

The spiritual goal here becomes to heal the deep wound, or change the patterning that is creating the behavior. This can never happen if someone, (including our self) is "at fault". This can only occur if one is willing to become a spiritually self-responsible being. One must take personal responsibility for one's thoughts, feelings and actions – one's overall energy signature – if one hopes to find peace and well being in this world.

It is in this authentic gesture of responsibility that one will come to find an authentic relationship with spirit that will guide one's step to spiritual freedom.

◉

Now, before we travel any further, it is time for "an aside". As I have worked with people who are learning about responsibility – it can be a very confusing time. People begin to assume responsibility for everything, and this is not the essence of the spiritual responsibility.

For example, I find it unrealistic to imagine that we are truly always responsible for how other people behave – and we cannot assume responsibility for the hurtfulness and negativity that other people may create, which can have a profound impact on our lives. We can however, be conscious of how we deal with such adversity and the impact of such adversity on our energy field. Now, of course, one may argue that we drew the experience into our sphere of awareness for a purpose – which is esoterically reasonable.

For example, if I walk down the street and I encounter a lot of negativity – I am not "creating this" per se – but I am responsible for how I deal with it and how I let it influence my energy field. I am fully responsible for how I react to the experience and how I hold and manage my own energy.

Again, responsibility is an intrapersonal process. It is an attitude that leads to self-mastery and responsible management of one's own energy field.

◉

Responsibility is not necessarily assuming creative responsibility for the way others behave. It is assuming responsibility for how we have "become" in response to the wounds we have assimilated, and how we will heal the wounds. We are responsible – for our *self*. It also implies taking responsibility for the wounds we inflict, and how we simply live our life in a day-to-day way. We must take greater responsibility for every element in our life, our relationships and our creations. Through this empowered responsibility we can find a doorway to see our authentic, undistorted nature where wounds no longer mask our view.

Energy follows consciousness. If I am willing to adjust my consciousness to a responsible self-nature, the energy in my field is open to adjust, to heal and to re-pattern. The implications of this are very far reaching. One does become more aware of one's personal patterning. But, more importantly, one becomes aware of one's truer nature with the spiritual potential and ability to restore or "recalibrate" any wound so we may once again experience ourselves as healthy, healed, happy and whole.

Finding Compassion

In the process of healing, one may come to understand that we as human beings will always manifest the best of our potential – whatever that is at a point in time. It is not easy for any of us to see our own foibles, wounds and the consequential patterns that affect our lives.

So while assuming a greater sense of responsibility one must also develop a greater sense of understanding and compassion. Judgment has no purposeful role to play here. Through compassionate self-care we can adjust and transform many things that are self destructive or unbalanced in our lives, and we can find patience to allow other people to find their own way in their journey of life.

Some behaviors we have integrated as people may not be based on the greatest spiritual authenticity. They will all come up for examination in self-responsible healing. The act of self-love that is often discussed in the new healing paradigm is found in responsible self-care.

So many things patterned into us as human beings are based on fear-based forces and suppressive to the power to manifest responsible self-love. Guilt, for example, is an imposed idea of what is right and wrong, or what we need to do to be "lovable" or good enough to merit affection or acceptance. It is what we are "supposed" to do to be safe. Other patterns arise due to fear, trauma, self-preservation and defense. These will require a healing reconciliation within our own nature.

As we look at life from the paradigm of spiritual responsibility, a concept that may start as a burdensome prospect, it becomes a route to spiritual empowerment. But we must be kind and patient, with both ourselves and each other – yet willing always to face what we need to see.

If we assume a sense of responsibility for the life we create, based on this realization, we are stronger to accept the experiences in our lives as purposeful and meaningful, and most importantly, we can respond with compassion and grace.

Do Thoughts create Reality?

You have probably heard the adage: "Your thoughts create your reality." But perhaps it is a little more complex than simply thoughts creating reality, or we would all be in trouble! Our thoughts contribute to constructing our reality – but our life, and the experiences we attract to us, is drawn to us by our overall energy signature which has many contributing elements – of which thought is but one.

It is more reasonable to say that our reality "mirrors" our energy signature. Thoughts are one component of our energy field but not the only one. Our feelings and even elements of our spiritual process are also embedded in the fields of our energy bodies, and are very important in influencing what is manifested. Spiritual overlays may very strongly influence our energy signature. Experiences are drawn to us because of their appropriateness in mirroring our energy signature and the lessons and growth opportunities we arrange for ourselves.

It may be difficult to understand the potential inherent in some of the experiences and challenges we create. Not very many people would choose consciously to have a bad accident, or contract a terrible disease for example. It can be callous and short sighted to say we simply choose these by our thinking, for we may not understand the subconscious influences or spiritual potential that is embedded in the process.

Personal responsibility is really assuming *spiritual* responsibility – so that the spiritual aspect of our own nature is consciously involved in processing our experiences. It is hard to take responsibility for something we do not know how we even managed to create. Yet, if we assume ownership of the experience, we can relate and respond to it with wisdom rather than simply falling victim to it. By assuming responsibility, we can relate maturely to all our experiences, and empower our ability to choose how we respond to events in our life. As we gain personal insight, we can make adjustments – we can change our patterns of thought and belief – and in doing so, we can adjust our energy signature to co-create our lives in renewed ways.

When we understand the magnetic pull of energy, based on the signature of our energy, we can conceptualize how manifested experiences might simply "take form" around our internal energy patterning. Hence you can utilize the out-picturing that you call "your life" to help you see what you hold in your energy signature. We can all discover what we think, what we believe, what we feel and what emotions we may be holding on to that are interfering with our wellbeing – based on what we manifest. This can help us transform individually in spiritually conscientious ways.

If things do occur "randomly", or due to some unknown influence, whether we "made it happen" or not, can be taken as moot. Once it happened, it has happened – our opportunity is now to hold the event as purposeful or meaningful in our own life. Remember, sometimes horrific experiences are the catalyst for great spiritual emergence, and other times may evoke massive waves of human love and compassion, which have an obvious spiritual outcome.

Responsibility means living with this larger spiritual perspective, so we can relate patiently and compassionately to our own personal trials and tribulations – as well as those of others – to manifest a more conscious reality.

⊙

Please be aware that to live fully responsibly, we must also understand our personal limitations of consciousness, and the tendency of the ego to manipulate this understanding in a self serving way.

I have seen great misunderstandings generated by the ego in people who are learning to open to spiritual and energetic understanding. I remember one day in a workshop witnessing a woman tell another woman that her cancer was of her own making and she should accept responsibility. She told her it was her own *fault* she has cancer! It is easy to see how twisted and compassion-free this statement is.

On a spiritual level of understanding, the experience of cancer has an obvious important role to play in this woman's life. She may even have directly contributed to the experience by life choices such as smoking, or carried great repressed anger in her throat chakra and energy system – but she is still worthy of understanding and compassion! It is not always as simple as thought or behaviors producing outcomes – and her spirit deserves much more dignity than this type of assault. Blame, guilt and shame are not in the recipe for healing. Conscious acceptance and mature spiritual response are simply beacons that will guide the process, and every healing journey.

... AND FAR AWAY FROM JUDGMENT

Responsibility implies empowerment. Why? To be responsible you must have *choice*.

It becomes a little obvious from our discussion, that to heal and to live in a conscious way means having to let go of victimization. If you want to heal and grow spiritually you must assume compete responsibility for what you are creating, and the way you relate to your life experiences. If one lives as a victim of circumstance, they are disempowered to grow until they come to look at the experience a little differently.

It is important to understand the difference between *victimized* by an experience, and living in *victim consciousness*. As we live in our world, there are many opportunities to be victimized by other people or by events that take place. As discussed, we can argue that we create "everything" by our energy signature and perhaps we do. But, can we be a victim of such experiences but still maintain spiritual responsibility. Of course we can!

It might be stated, for example, that if you have lived a terrible experience by which you were victimized and suffer – it is because you "see yourself as a victim". This is very short sighted – short of understanding and compassion. There is often a higher principle that moves things towards a greater good.

An embedded energy patterning that would promote such an experience may indeed be part of an individuals healing journey. It may be related to karma – but it may be related to a greater spiritual design.

For example, a person may have lived a life where they have been put down and suppressed all their life – told essentially that they are worthless. They may have integrated elements of this experience into their mental, emotional and etheric patterning and adopted a life where this has become essentially true. As this person matures into an adult, they would have an energy posturing that may magnetize particular creative experiences.

But what if I told you that this soul took on a challenge – not because of karma or a terrible past action. Perhaps it was a choice to do this in a family plagued by this pattern – with the intention to "take on" and break it down. Now, are they still a "victim"? Or is this a noble act of selfless love?

You see, there are many small and large-scale phenomena that affect life. It is an important reason we are not meant to judge one anther! Some aspects of life do require a greater wisdom to truly grasp. There is a higher scale order that is difficult to appreciate from a 3D perspective of life. So be careful to put judgment away.

The important thing is to assume responsibility for *our* own experiences and what we create in *our* life, but also do it with compassion and understanding. We do not always understand and appreciate the deeper working of life and should be kind with ourselves and with each other as we grow and evolve. Realize that we can relate in a spiritually responsible way to anything we encounter. That is the essence of responsibility.

A Little Perspective

To me, there is no better example of mature responsibility ever demonstrated, than the one shown by Christ during the crucifixion. What?

Well, to begin, in no way, shape, or form would I imagine Christ viewing himself as a victim. He was a rebel of truth and love – able to stand entirely in the truth of an incredible universal understanding that he held. This type of presence drew criticism and fear in those around him who were deeply embedded in ego consciousness. Would if be fair to say, in a manner of responsibility, that he "drew this experience upon himself"?

It would be easy to perceive that Christ was victimized by the action of those around him who sought his demise. Yet, his own words reveal that he was not a victim of these actions. He stated, "You have no power over me that the father in heaven has not provided." He understood the unfolding drama had a larger purpose and collective value, due to his expanded level of awareness. In fact, it was his blatant forgiveness of the atrocity committed to him that kept him free of the "karma" of the action. It was the very gesture, which may be understood as the mystical force, which set humanity free from sin.

In doing so, he was able to undo the "sin" or ignorance of humanity against him toward his highly realized state of consciousness. His view was supremely enlightened, far beyond the grasp of an ego-laden mind. Yet, Christ did not create this experience by his own "pitiful state of mind" or his "thoughts". He also did not retaliate to the experience, as a victim. The experience was part of a greater spiritual process, bigger than a simple concept limited to "him".

It was because he was deeply "spiritually integrated", or enlightened, that he was able to use such an experience to liberate and teach his fellow humanity about spiritual freedom. The freedom he taught was not freedom of tyranny but freedom from ego. The freedom was *within* his own state of being.

Christ was fully aware of the unenlightened egoic forces and people's fears that led to his crucifixion. Yet, he faced it with nobility. He also was conscious of his purpose. He was able to demonstrate that even under the weight of such darkness, his light would not be extinguished. In fact, he did not die by such tyranny, but lived – even after his crucifixion – as a means of demonstrating that there is nothing to fear in spirit. The spirit survives the brutality of the human ego, for death itself is impermanent, and has no sting.

It is therefore important to live with an awareness of spiritual precepts, and how love and forgiveness are so necessary to heal. Otherwise, we are bound energetically and in consciousness by our struggle. The Great War that everyone experiences is an interior one. The light within your own nature can emerge to overcome the influence of the ego within us or around us.

Musingly, history would be a little different, and have demonstrated a very different outcome, if Christ started yelling and screaming and calling people names, and demanding revenge! Just think of the evening news!

The reason this experience is so powerful is that he was by one view greatly victimized by the circumstance of the low level consciousness all around him – present in those that did not understand him. Yet, he did not live as a victim. He lived with a tremendous personal sense of choice and responsibility. He lived with a boundless compassion and understanding for everyone around him who did not understand the weakness of their own limited awareness and the predicament of his or her ego. Even in the face of great hatred and animosity, attributes worn to mask the fear inherent in the human ego, he continued to love. Ah … now, that is healing!

Playing Our Part

Hence responsibility is an empowering attitude, which is designed to "de-victimize" the life process and get energy flowing from the inside out. We can learn to live freely, inspire. Our lives can become full of the life-giving energy, to provide to oneself with wellbeing and to share with those around us.

If one begins to live with an attitude of self-responsibility, one begins to unshackle victim consciousness, which is a great suppressor of spirit. We overcome a sense of victimization by taking a sense of purposeful responsibility and derive the potential to grow and learn through it.

So is responsibility a burden? No. It implies freedom – spiritual freedom. When one understands that most of what we create in our lives is a meaningful feedback system mirroring our energy signature – we can find value and purpose in the feedback. It can help us grow and transform elements that are out of sync with our spiritual ability and dreams. When challenges do occur, one can relate to them responsibly. Events in the world lose their power to control us and twist us into ego reactivity – because we understand ourselves to be spiritually responsible and free.

We also learn to live from the inside out – and be in charge of how we react to the world around us and even to our selves. We learn to forgive, to find compassion, to let go of false value. As one grows in spiritual wisdom, one can better choose to remain aligned. This has huge implications on the state of our energy fields, and this explains in very clear terms why it is so important in the overall picture of healing.

Life is not punitive. It is both reflective and meaningful. We can learn from life's experiences many things, which can help us to grow, to heal and to manifest latent spiritual attributes.

Think about stories that may have deeply touched or inspired you. A child loses a limb in a silly accident, and becomes the greatest advocate for bicycle safety, a Para Olympian or even an Olympian! A mother loses a child to an accident, and becomes immersed in sober driving education. A young woman overcomes an addiction, or a very serious illness, and becomes a pillar of support for others embedded in a similar crisis. These are all stories of the hero within, the spirit within, which emerges in response to a life event that challenges the spirit to rise and to heal.

Each example reveals people who discover the mythical hero as the indwelling spirit. Despite adversity, these people refuse to be immersed in the victimization of the events, but instead take the challenge of an experience, to grow or transform. They blossom into someone more magnificent, more aligned, more powerful and more beautiful – through the vision of spiritual eyes. When one assumes responsibility for ones life – one simply opens a universal window – a true portal of positive growth and change.

Let's move responsibly forward, a little more deeply into the universe of healing – an exam healing through the four body model.

CHAPTER 9

HEALING – THE 4 BODY MODEL

Intro

The purpose of this book is not to elaborate specifically on the many methods, which exist to perform healing work. There are wonderfully written books and workshops available to do this already. It is designed to provide an overview of the process of healing and bio-spiritual transformation, so you may better understand the various elements, in choosing what is appropriate for you or those you assist.

I will reference sources of which I am experientially aware throughout the discussion but it is not a complete list. There are many others available, surely as excellent as those I may propose, and you must follow your inner guidance to know what is right for you. If you are searching for a tell-all-tale of energy based healing techniques, I would recommend the most resource-laden book I discovered many years ago, written by Dr. Richard Gerber, entitled *Vibrational Medicine*.[26]

We will next examine healing from the perspective of the various energy bodies, which we explored in the last chapter. This will provide a cohesive understanding of what healing implies at each body or level. From this broader perspective, unique tools that exist may then be more conscientiously and appropriately applied.

Etheric Healing

Fig 9-1
Etheric Body

The etheric body, as we discussed earlier, can be viewed as a dynamic living blueprint of the physical body. It is an energy-form body, as well as a field of circulating energy. It encompasses the etheric level of the chakras, the etheric energy forms behind the organ systems in the body, the meridians, and the many nadis of the human energy field. (Fig 9-1)

The etheric body is thus a living bio-field that serves as an inner blueprint for the development, and subsequent healing of the human physical body. During human development the energy of the etheric body is seeded in the developing embryo, and continues to grow as a living field of energy as a child develops into adulthood.

As an adult, once fully formed, the etheric body is energetically maintained to provide a living field that supports the health of the body. It structurally organizes dynamic energy, just like the electromagnetic lines of a magnetic field, into our living bodies of form.

The energy to sustain the etheric body is derived from the physical world through food and elements from the environment. It acquires energy from the etheric element of ingested food materials in the process of digestion. It is also nourished from energy absorbed through the air and sunlight in the atmosphere, termed prana, or chi.

All living things, including the foods we consume, require an etheric counterpart to exist. An etheric energy field exists within the foods we consume, just as it does within the human body. When we ingest foods, such as fruits or vegetables, grains or meats – there is an etheric energy inherent in the food. Our body, to support our own etheric existence, absorbs this invisible energy.

In a healthy, unencumbered etheric body, the energy form is strong and the flow of energy is unrestricted and free flowing. Life force energy will be able to flow through the nadis to the organs and tissues of the body. This sustains health in the body systems at an etheric level.

If structural blockages or congestion develops in the flow of energy within this system, the health of the etheric body will be impacted. If the etheric body is impacted, the physical body, which it supports, is also impacted. The etheric body can thus become weakened. Damage to the etheric body can deform, congest, obstruct or crystallize it. This will have a disease-producing influence on the physical form.

Weakness in the etheric system can occur for many reasons, but key among them are the influences of poor replenishment and excessive devitalization. And as strange as this may first sound, this may be due not only to nutritional issues, but also psychological issues and genetic influence.

Replenishment requires consumption of high quality etheric nourishment – as well as fresh air, exercise and other physical care such as stretching and breathing.

The etheric body may be affected by energy *depletion* when energy is being over expended. This can be due to simple excessive physical work. It can also occur in response to psychological stress. The etheric body will be drained due to excessive or prolonged mental or emotional activities, without allowing proper revitalization of the etheric energy through rest, exercise, meditation and so forth. Lastly, when illnesses develop, they can also lead to etheric devitalization and leakages of energy that will need to be healed or repaired.

Energetic *restrictions* in the etheric body can develop in response to both mechanical and psychological issues.

Restrictions can occur due to mechanical contractures in the system, i.e. posture and structural tension. They can also occur due to energy congestion in the system, which may arise from improper etheric nutrition. This means consuming too much dense or artificial etheric food. Drugs and excessive alcohol can also lead to a restriction on the etheric flow of energy. If such devitalizing or restrictive influences are held in a consistent or prolonged fashion, it will progressively impact the energy flow in the etheric body.

The etheric body may be visualized as a web or lace of light channels or fibrils. Chronically, any impediment to the flow of energy in the etheric body will affect our outward health. This can have a deleterious influence on our human bodies in an infinite number of ways. Hence, appropriate openness, balance and flow are all essential elements of etheric health.

Issues in the etheric body can also arise under the influence of mental and emotional bodies in the "adjacent" energy field.

One can conceptualize that if a person keeps a chakra "closed" due to a psychological pattern, it will affect the flow of energy at each level of one's energy system. For example, if one is constantly fearful and self-protective, one may "pull in" energy at the solar plexus and/or root chakra. Retraction of energy in this fashion, if it becomes a chronic pattern, will impact circulation of energy in the etheric body and the whole of the energy system.

◉

Healing influences upon the etheric body correlate with the above understanding. These are activities that will promote optimal energy charging, balance and restoration within the etheric framework.

Such activities can be "therapeutic" if there are weaknesses or illnesses embedded in the etheric energy that are leading to disease states. The same processes can also be used to "promote and maintain" health and vitality, when one is unencumbered by a limiting disease process. If the energy in the etheric body is so maintained, the possibility of becoming ill is greatly diminished.

Breath and movement are fundamentally therapeutic to the etheric body, in the many forms of exercise that we use. This includes exercise programs which are both traditional and non traditional in nature.

Breathing, particularly conscious breathing, will charge the etheric body with dynamic life force energy. Breath can restore etheric energy or discharge excess energy if it has accumulated in the etheric system. Breathing can further be coupled with physical posturing to move energy in very specific orientations within the etheric system. We see this occurring in many forms of conscious exercise. This type of exercise help unblock or remove constrictions in the etheric energy body.

Tai chi and many forms of yoga are based on these principles. Tai chi for example is designed to open, charge and revitalize the etheric channels of energy in the human body. Pranayama is the eastern teaching on breath as yoga. There are many forms of yoga which integrate breathing and postures to open the etheric channels.

If you have ever taken a stretching or yoga class, or simply tried to stretch your body, you will notice areas in your body where there is a restriction or tightness. These will typically be areas of energy tension in the etheric body – as well as the correlating connective tissues and muscles of the human body. Of course, we do not normally think in these terms. We normally think of "tight muscles" or tendons. It is however not simply muscles that are tight or contracted. It is also the subtle energy field or etheric body that is underlying the physical elements.

During a class in yoga or any stretching program, you may have been advised to "breathe into" tightness in the body, and relax the area consciously. This is an example of working physically to open up the energy channels by energizing focal areas of restriction in the etheric energy. This is a very powerful way to work with the etheric aspect of our energy. As you progress through such exercises, you are working to stretch and strengthen the flow of chi or energy through your etheric system.

Many excellent classes are available in tai chi and yoga today – at studios worldwide. There is a great resurgence of these techniques because people are becoming innately aware of how good they are for our health or when in need of healing. For those who do not live near a studio or place of instruction, or are pressed for time with many commitments, there are online and DVD instructional programs available that may be used anywhere, including at home.

To become a little better acquainted with the etheric body, let us stop for a moment and do a simple breathing exercise to become more aware of its existence. You may want to read through the full instructions first, to be able to do the exercise with your eyes closed:

BREATHING EXERCISE:

Close your eyes and take 10 deep slow breaths – breathing in and out through your nose.

Try to do this exercise using only your nose to breathe. If it is too difficult or if it is congested, breathing through your mouth is okay.

As you breathe, fill the chest and lungs with air, but continue with the breath as if you are opening your abdomen and pulling the air into your belly.

Hold the breath in for 3 to 5 seconds at this full inhalation, and then slowly exhale all the air in your lungs.

Pause for a few seconds between each breath.

When you have completed 10 breath cycles, stop and pay attention to any sensations or awareness you have in your body.

Take a few moments to register what you are feeling or perceiving in your body before returning to the text.

Follow Up:

What is your experience during this exercise? Do you feel an energy charge or tingling in your body? Many of you will feel a subtle tingling with completion of this exercise. This feeling is prana or energy charging the etheric body. If you are feeling this – you are feeling the etheric body consciously at this time!

Reflecting on your experience, at which point in the breathing cycle was it harder to breathe? Where did you feel natural restrictions in your body? Pay attention to the sensory feedback you have through conscious self-awareness. You can use this awareness, to more deeply focus your breathing into these areas of restriction to help unlock or open the etheric energy.

☉

Let us continue examining healing influences on the etheric body. The etheric body will not only require energizing, it will also require *rest and relaxation* to maintain its health. Relaxation allows a natural de-contraction of etheric energy, allowing it to relax, recharge and rebalance.

Relaxation, particularly in an environment that has a high level of life force energy available, is deliciously reinvigorating. This includes many places in nature including forests, lakes, oceans, or, the beach. Everyone knows that rest and recreation are very beneficial to our health, but the why or how is not so obvious. It is actually due to its influence on the human energy system. It calms the mind and emotions and charges the etheric body.

It is an interesting observation that when people spend time in such environments, they innately or intuitively recognize the benefit of it. People navigate to these types of environments for vacation and recuperation. People may in fact get very tired and sleepy in these environments, which often occurs when the body is going into "healing mode". It is the body's way of "shutting down" so that healing may occur. It is infinitely valuable to take time in a park, or in a forest, or near a body of water. Be conscious of the fact that it is a healing endeavor.

Nutrition will have a strong influence on the etheric body. The foods we eat, like our bodies, are also composed of energy. We are aware that all food has energy in the form of calories. Food also has etheric energy as part of its make up. Healthy ripe organic local food might be viewed as having the highest level of pranic energy. This food is likely closest to its source of development, so the etheric energy has faded less. It is closest to fully ripened when harvested, so the etheric energy is strong. And, lastly, it is nearly untainted by potential chemical poisons.

Highly processed and refined foods are not as vital in their composition. Now, don't overreact, you are not going to die if you eat Kraft Dinner, Smarties, or, a peanut butter cup! It is just helpful to be aware of the difference, to help make conscious choices.

Living biological systems have a self-balancing tendency — and I believe the human body will adapt to food and eating styles. I would not advocate a strict dietary protocol for anyone — for there are innate differences between people that account for different food likes and dislikes. The most important and sensible thing for each person to do is to get in touch with what foods make you feel enlivened, healthy and energetic, and which ones lead to digestive difficulties and feeling unwell. This is the actual best way to know which dietary regiment suits you best — but this takes greater self-awareness.

If you listen to your intuition around this, you will find an appropriate diet for you. Not everyone needs to be vegetarian for example, but it is a healthy choice for some. Other people intuitively live well including denser protein in their diet, and this does not necessarily reflect a level of spiritual enlightenment. The consciousness with which you care for and eat your food is very important. If you bless your food with gratitude and energy, you can actually charge or channel energy into your food. And, paraphrasing Christ, it is not what you put in your mouth but what comes out of it that is most apt to be harmful! Admittedly though, these words predate our time of processed, chemical laden foods, toxic chemicals and the like. When you start to pay attention to your body, it will become clear what you should avoid and choose for nutritional choices.

Fasting and internal cleansing can also have an important healing influence on the etheric body. Fasting is based in ancient spiritual principles, and was widely practiced among many religious and spiritual groups. Fasting gives the body, and in particular the etheric body, an opportunity to liberate stagnant energies which may be obstructing the energy field.

Our western culture is not habituated to fasting. Although this is changing now, we do not collectively understand the energy composition of the body, so we do not see or appreciate the rationale for fasting. If it is done or practiced with any regularity, however, it should be done with a great deal of common sense.

Rather than just cutting out food and water completely, or drink only water, to rapid fast - it makes a great deal of sense to eat highly "etheric" foods. This would include less bulk and congestion producing contents, such as starches, root vegetables, meats and grains and processed elements. One simple approach to giving yourself an "etheric break" is to eat apples, grapes or juices from fresh fruits for a few days, or to drink prepared organic juices. This can be amazing in helping the body lighten up" — not strictly "calorically" — but "energetically" speaking.

If you have particular metabolic issues such as diabetes, or are taking medications that require food for example, you will need to do this with appropriate monitoring to avoid a health crisis. If you take insulin, and do not eat, you can precipitate hypoglycemia and would assuredly want to avoid that! In these specialized situations you may well require supervision or support from an able medical care provider or naturopath to be able to do this type of process.

Certain herbs are also known to have a direct influence on specific organs and their functions – people often integrate the use of herbs in detox practices. Milk thistle for liver cleansing, or uva ursi for the kidney are examples. There are many products today with a combination of herbs used to promote or stimulate cleansing available at your local health food distributor.

Use of such products must be done with awareness of the precautions and potential risks of combining herbs with other drugs you may be taking, disease states, pregnancy and other potential side effects. People need to self inform or follow the guidance of a trusted knowledgeable practitioner to do this safely.

Best advice: Don't overdo it, but do it. Try it once and evaluate your experience to know for yourself. Not allowing the body to detoxify in natural or supported ways does lead to a build up in etheric energy, which can contribute to a vast array of medical problems.

Epsom salt baths are a very useful way to help clear, anchor and rebalance the etheric energy. Why this is so effective is mysterious. Perhaps it is due to the creation of a subtle current in water as the salt dissolves (being an ionizing compound) and the reaction this has with the current in the etheric field. I can say personally that there is no quicker remedy to feel realigned when I am tired or feeling unwell than to take a 30-60 minute bath with Epsom salts and essential oils. Too good to be true? Just try it.

There are specific therapies, which have a direct and specific therapeutic effect on the etheric body, and are used more commonly in the setting of a specific health issues. This would include processes such as *acupuncture, prescriptive herbs or essences.*

Acupuncture works on the basis of understanding the meridians and specific surface energy points on the skin surface. By stimulating subtle current, the meridian is activated or discharged. Acupuncture can serve as a tool for healing in the hands of an intuitive, skilled and knowledgeable practitioner. It can be used to therapeutically manipulate the etheric energy. It can stimulate energy flow, and help push or flow though restrictions in the acupuncture meridians. It can charge the meridian or release energy that has accumulated in the meridian or corresponding organ. "Tapping", a process that has become common in conscious healing circles, can also work at this level.

Massage therapy is also very beneficial in etheric healing. Massage works primarily to take tension out of muscles and soft tissues, and promote lymphatic circulation in the body – but also has an effect, through the release of tension in the etheric system.

Direct energy work can also have a strong healing and restorative effect on the human body in ways that include the etheric body. By "direct energy work" I mean processes such as Reiki, Therapeutic touch, any form of "hands on healing", and the many other types of energy based healing processes.

These therapies do not work only on the etheric energy – they often work on multiple levels of energy to heal things that may be draining or restricting the etheric flow. Hence they may have a direct or indirect healing influence on the etheric body. People who become a little more sensitive to subtle energy and are aware of their meridians will often feel energy currents in these areas during energy healing sessions.

In the process of direct energy work, there may be damaged elements in the etheric body, which will restructure. When this occurs, the health of an organ affected by the etheric changes can improve.

One should also be aware that there may be a period of provoking symptomatic changes in the physical body, when this happens. For example, rashes may appear on the skin, pustules may form to release debris in the meridians and so forth. But ultimately, the clearing of the energy field will have a very positive influence on health. When the etheric body is restored to a healthy state, it provides the proper internal framework for a vital healthy body.

☉

All of these ideas can be used regularly or intermittently with awareness of the healing influence they provide. They can be used as part of developing a health conscious lifestyle to optimize health in our body. They will also be implicated in any strategy when dealing with acute or chronic illnesses. In this setting, healing and recharging the etheric body become critical to develop or to maintain overall health.

An Etheric Albatross?

Part of caring for the etheric body also means to become aware that there are many things, which have a negative influence on the etheric body, and learn to make wise choices around them. This implies simply learning to be more "conscious".

One of the greatest challenges in western culture is *loss of harmony* in our overall activity. In our modern world we are an achievement-oriented society. We value work, productivity and goals.

People who function on full steam, and do not take time to stop and smell the roses, invariably get into problems due to its effect on the energy system. The importance of creating an authentic balance in our lives cannot be overstated.

We are in many ways a culture that tends to drive itself beyond normal levels of activity for perceived success. This type of autonomic stimulation can be very deregulating on the energy system. It will deplete energy, and the sympathetic part of the nervous system is in constant "overdrive". Hence it is impossible to relax and restore completely. The body will endure this for an adaptive time, but it will eventually lead to some kind of imbalance, weakness or disease. The concept of correlation between stress and disease is becoming more and more familiar to us in our culture.

As mentioned earlier, intense mental and/or emotional activity also has a depleting influence on the etheric system. This may be positive, negative or neutral mental or emotional activity. For example if I am mentally engaged in work constantly it may be very "productive", but eventually it will be exhausting. If I am emotionally engaged in a lot of stress or drama, it can wear down the etheric energy reserve.

In this light, chronic stress has many negative influences. It affects the mental body, the emotional body and drains the etheric body. People living in chronic states of stress can become weakened etherically - and when the reserve of vital energy wears down, illness can result. People often notice they are more susceptible to common ailments such as colds and flus when they are tired or worn down, but do not necessarily think in terms of energy. Understanding healthy principles of self-care becomes paramount.

Understand that if the etheric energy is weak, it is more difficult for the etheric body to supply energy to keep the body healthy. It is incredibly valuable for a person to create a period of conscious sacred time and space each day. This can be in meditating, walking in nature, yoga, breathing – time to really be present with one's self. This is like taking the time to plug in your cell phone – it recharges your system.

People often claim that they cannot find this time in their lives. Truth being told, it takes both consciousness of value, as well as reorienting a few things in life by making a few informed choices, to make it happen. The time is there, if the priority is there – for everyone I have ever met. It is obviously helpful to understand why it is important to help make it a priority. We have already discussed responsibility in context of healing and energy self-regulation.

⊙

On the flip side, some people have adopted the "couch potato culture" of inactivity. Not only can the etheric energy be depleted - if the etheric energy does not move enough to "recirculate" in the body - it can become sluggish. This is equally imbalanced.

Different people have different "constitutions", so different people will be able to tolerate different levels of physical or life activity and be healthy. Some people are greatly inclined to athletic activity and will be healthiest if they do an adequate amount of physical exercise for their constitution. Other people are less inclined toward physical activity, and this will be more challenging for them – but *everyone needs to move*. Each person will need to find an appropriate healthy balance in this regard.

If you are very de-conditioned you will need to start to exercise a little, to support your health. This can be done with a great deal of self-support and respect, and with medical supervision where required. Gentle or restorative yoga, walking, breathing, swimming or any type of activity that supports energetic circulation may be considered.

Poor diet. Eating specifically low nutritional foods or a lot of food of poor nutritional value weakens our etheric energy. This is a particular challenge to one's health if there are many other things such as stress, mental over engagement, limited physical activity and so forth contributing to devitalizing the etheric energy. Making a conscious effort to eat healthy nutritional food and avoiding junk food is very helpful in maintaining health.

Toxins and some drugs. Many drugs, particularly street drugs have a terrible influence on the etheric body. Cocaine, heroine, even cigarettes – all devitalize, and even can do worse damage on the human energy field, when used chronically. There are also many harmful toxins in these products, which pose many levels of challenge to the human body and energy. The body has to deal with the negative influence of these products and excrete them.

When people overcome chronic drug usage or addictions, a "clean out" of the affect of the drugs on one's energy will occur. Yet a person has to understand that it is a damaging activity and want to heal. This can be very difficult in addicted frames of reality – but still possible to accomplish. In this regard it must be understood that we are each ultimately responsible for the choices we make and the consequences it produces – and aim to get on the healing track in a sincere way.

So What's Right for You?

By becoming aware of our etheric body, activities that promote health in the etheric body, and elements that weaken the etheric body – we are well on our way to restoring and optimizing etheric health. Reflect on these factors now, and ask yourself the question: "What do I need to terms in of diet, activity, rest, balance and specific healing options - to optimize the health of my etheric body?" Listen intuitively to your own body to decide what you need.

Do you need to fast? Change elements in your diet? Address any bad dietary "habits"? Exercise more? Or less? Or differently? Try yoga or Tai Chi? Learn to breath deeply? Find more time to relax? Have a vacation? Try energy-based therapy?

Pick up a pen and make list to review later and make a plan for steps you can take to enhance your health or healing. It is all part of becoming more conscious!

⊙

The last ingredient in establishing etheric health is to understand that its well-being is influenced by the "rest of us". Next we will explore the other energy bodies, to conceptualize how healing may occur at these levels. Sometimes etheric healing means healing there – for many of the behaviors, which directly affect etheric healing are influenced by emotional and mental attributes.

As a human being, since all the energy bodies co-exist and interrelate, the health of one body greatly influences the health of the other bodies. If the etheric body is not healthy and balanced, it can impact the adjacent emotional body and mental body in unhealthy ways. The reverse is also true. So we need to think "holistically" to develop a lasting healthy framework.

If we learn to take care of our etheric health, it supports health or healing, in all of the bodies - the mental, emotional and spiritual levels of our being. If we heal at other levels it will support the creation of a lifestyle that also promotes etheric well-being. Let us continue to explore wellbeing by examining psychoemotional elements of healing.

Psychoemotional Healing Work

Intro

As we discussed, to use the word healing in everyday language typically conjures up the idea of the treatment of physical diseases or trauma. Healing of a fracture, or healing following any type of surgery, or treatment of an infections are some examples. Treatments used, such as drugs, surgeries, and many alternate therapies can be easily conceptualized as real and beneficial. Why? Because they are physical and tangible in nature.

However, healing can also indicate overcoming psychological conditions. It includes healing of mental and emotional attributes that promote states of un-wellness or disease. Such conditions can create tremendous personal suffering or psychological grief. They can also produce physical symptoms and even physical disease manifestations. Support with these issues falls into the spectrum of psycho-emotional healing work.

It must be stated that this element of healing work requires a reasonable degree of insight and the capacity to process psychological information. It is not well suited for people suffering from cognitive impairment or psychotic conditions where insight is impaired by delusion or a serious break from consensus reality. People in these situations may be better helped by more traditional supportive healing programs – but may not be in a position to begin insight oriented and responsibility guided personal work.

For those who are suited to insight oriented personal development, it is important to understand that this is an essential part of the journey to achieving whole body wellness. Psychoemotional issues can manifest with many challenges that a person must "work through" in their individual development. But remember, due to the energetic nature of the mental and emotional bodies, and the interdependent function of the bodies – physical and etheric healing will almost always imply a level of psychoemotional healing as well.

The concept of energy healing in the emotional body becomes easier to appreciate when we think in terms of "energy bodies" rather than strict psychological function such as thoughts or feelings. When a condition "appears" in the physical domain - it will have correlation with the energy of the etheric body. It will often, however, also have correlation with the mental and emotional levels of our being. Much today is written about how mental and emotional patterns have strong correlation with some manifested physical disease states. [15,31]

When a conscious healing process begins with the healing of physical disease, the experience of restoration of the physical body through traditional and non-traditional medicine may be the first step. This might be supported by many physical and energetic elements such as traditional healing methods, nutritional support, exercise and restorative techniques, direct energy work and vibrational remedies as a few examples. It can also be supported by life modifications including diet and lifestyle that are personal and appropriate. It might also entail letting go of habits that are destructive and restrictive in terms of energy.

However, as people process through such healing, they will often surface deeper connected emotions and psychoemotional issues that will also need attention and healing. This will then evoke a mental and an emotional element even in the process of healing what appear as physical conditions.

At other times, psychoemotional energy patterns do not manifest as disease, in the classic sense, at all. They manifest rather as "issues", "conditions" or "patterns of personal manifestations". Conditions such as anxiety and phobias, or patterns such as recurrently picking an abusive partner might fit into this description. When conditions such as these occur, it becomes important to understand that there are energetic patterns, on a mental and/or emotional level, that are present and are contributing to these experiences. Most often, they are reflective of deeper mental and emotional programming, or perhaps significant personal wounds.

Mental and emotional "wounds" lay behind much of what may be understood as "patterned" within our energy bodies. Experiences which are painful often leave a seemingly indelible mark on us, energetically at least, until healing is brought the situation. They create true energetic printing and are "recorded" in our energy fields. Although it can be very challenging to get to the root of them, they are usually seeded in prior conditioning, or specific experiences of significant trauma and fear.

In energy based healing processes, memories may surface, and emotions that have been deeply buried in one's subconscious, may surface. If we think energetically, work that is done will seem to "push up" or "reveal" these patterns. This can include such things as repressed emotions (from conscious or subconscious prior experiences), resentments, anger, guilt, shame, or, a sense of limited worth – just to name an important few.

When these emotional patterns are embedded energetically within our energy signature – they will have a pervasive influence on our lives. We can appreciate how these manifest in destructive ways in our lives and relationships, and even lead to physical illness, during a healing journey. Hence surfacing and spiritually re-integrating them, may be necessary to access restorative healing.

Uncovering these "buried" energy patterns can be a challenging process. One will need a huge amount of patience and self understanding, and often, external support. If you speak with anyone who has endured great wounds and subsequent healing, they will likely share that it can be very difficult to expose one's deep wounds – and allow for healing and spiritual restitution to occur. Yet, it is richly rewarding.

These patterns represent embedded vibrational forms, which remain present in our mental and emotional bodies, as energetic patterns. They consciously or subconsciously influence and often distort our lives in painful or limiting ways until healing is achieved.

Although not seen energetically by most people, patterns are very easy to conceptualize - because they manifest quite clearly in one's life. For example, one may be highly defensive in character, one may be very controlling, anxious, self-diminishing, chronically depressed, victimized in view, constantly in need of external approval, manipulative, and so forth. These are just a few among many potential examples.

If we examine our lives with a love based honesty and insight, we will each have the opportunity to see the patterns we personally carry, those that are based in historical conditioning, or, reactive fear.

When we begin to examine patterns that we hold, there may be a reasonably understandable point of development in the context of a person's life. For example, it may be possible to recall particular events that have seeded a pattern. Every one of us has lived experiences that can scar due to psychoemotional trauma. Traditional psychology has been very helpful in exploring some of these patterns, and developing awareness and helpful treatments.

But a greater challenge exists, when the patterns we carry, have no meaningful basis in the conscious history of our life. It is hard to "source" the original wound – because it does not exist in our conscious awareness or memory. Yet, in context, the pattern does exist *energetically* within our fields and influences greatly what we create, and do not create, in our life – through its influence on our overall energy signature.

This may be the case, for example, when there are "repressed memories" of early traumatic experiences. However, even if we fully review our known life, it might not explain many of the more mysterious, or even "neurotic" tendencies, we may carry as patterns. For some of you, this idea may get a little strange ... but such patterns may have roots in experiences that do not originate in our current lifetime! It is a pattern we carry with us from another lifetime – a karmic or akashic experience. No amount of historical review of one's life will expose the root of the issue.

In this scenario, it is hard to reconcile the pattern on the basis of psychotherapeutic insight, because frankly it makes no sense. Deep unreasonable anxieties, phobias, defense reactions, and so forth may be embedded from experience, which originates in prior incarnational experiences – or even carried through familial genetics! They may require unusual forms of support, forms that are not typically addressed by conventional psychology or psychiatry.

And lastly, as we probe deeper into healing, we begin to discover that some of our patterned behaviors and psychoemotional attributes are not based in a directly wounded consciousness – past or present – directly. They are based on the fall-out of a faulty or misinformed human belief system – that falls into the domain of the "human ego".

The ego, as we will explore, defines attributes of human nature that keep us "divided in perceptions" from the truth of our spiritual nature. The ego's perception of life is based in fear and separation. Its perceptions produce anxieties, worries, guilt, defensiveness, pride, shame and guilt based tendencies – all of which are founded in a faulty understanding of our spiritual nature. This too must ultimately be encountered on the spiritual journey.

In some cases these ego-based patterns are so familiar or ingrained they are culturalized as normal. However, they must be overcome to grow in spirit. There will be some overlap between healing from personal wounds, and the great wound of the human ego. But we will dedicate Chapter 10 to "taking on" the ego, and its pervasive grip on our spirit, to task!

☉

So stepping outside of traditional psychiatry and psychology into an energy inclusive and consciousness based paradigm – we can begin to understand that psychoemotional issues have an energetic form, or pattern, within our mental and emotional bodies. These patterns, in true energetic terms, exist – and are influentially creative. They produce energetic configurations that can influence the ways energy does or does not flow through our systems, as well as the experiences we attract and manifest.

These patterns mold our creative process, acting like a filter or a film in a projector, through which the light of our spiritual nature must pass when manifesting in the world. They are also creative in a magnetic sense – or by energetic attraction and manifestation. These patterns can have a very big influence on our present lives until they are recognized or resolved.

For many of us - life, through experience and conscious relationships, or through traditional psychotherapy, will help uncover some of the beliefs, mental patterning and emotional conditions that are important for us to transcend. As one becomes aware of the patterns they personally carry, and work within their own experience to grow and transform, they can manifest healthier potentials.

However, even in people with an ardent and honest intention to grow spiritually – and have deep personal insight – these patterns can sometimes still elusive. This is where non-traditional methods of healing support such as energy work or past life regression really become so valuable.

Energy-based healing support becomes particularly helpful. Such energy processes will often stimulate and release points of deep energetic patterning, which are embedded in the various bodies of the human energy field.

"How does it work?" you may ask. Energy work serves as a "catalytic boost" to help move energy. Energy can *vibrate* and loosen tightly bound patterns in our energy fields to help us release them. I can also *shine* a little light to help us see them! This is not as metaphoric as it would first appear!

In addition to direct energy work other tools exist. Troubling emotional patterning may be embedded in a prior life experience as we discussed above. It is deeper than this "lifetime" which makes it challenging to heal in strictly psychological terms. Healing of such patterning is sometimes supported by the work of past life regression therapy.

People who experience past life regression work are often led to remember experiences that demonstrate a revealing influence on one's personal psychological or emotional based troubles. The interesting thing is that as people make contact with such memories, there is the potential to bring both great understanding and healing to the causative experience. Such work not only adds insight, but also provides a true energetic release of the energy pattern.

This evolving work of past life regression has been very effective in helping people uncover grief, phobias, anxiety states, sexual repression, relationship issues, life altering fears, and many other patterns of strong emotional issue.

Some of the most fascinating pioneering work in this arena has been done by Dr. Brian Weiss. Dr. Weiss is the chairman emeritus in psychiatry at Mount Sinai in Miami and was astonished in his work as a psychotherapist when patients began to have inter-life recall of events that became instrumental in helping those overcome anxieties and various psychological states.[53]

The vibrational influence that arises through the support of energy work, or through hypnotic access to inter-life memories - may be seen to "shake loose" deeply congealed emotional forms in the energy field.

Interestingly, when one engages in such support – healing may occur with *or* without conscious awareness of the pattern, memories or causative experiences. And it may occur in rather mystical ways.

One poignant examples of this was a story reported by a lady who had just received an energy healing session, which clearly surfaced a lot of grief and anger. The experience was sharply focused on a unique experience in her earlier life. She had spent a great deal of her life "hating" the perpetrator – which had an enormously influence on her life in so many ways. She was little shocked to find a phone message to contact this person (after 25 years) when she returned home that very day after the session. She knew she was being challenged in a very conscious way to get on with the healing and find her liberation! And, with a little support, she did!

It is equally fascinating when during the process of vibrational supportive work – psychoemotional experiences may surface and pass away easily. Sometimes effortlessly! There may not be an important memory or event to process – but suddenly things in a person's are just "different". I remember a lady who told me she felt no "anxiety" after a healing session – for the first *time* in her entire 58-year life! What "let go" in that work, or the issue leading to chronic anxiety, is still a mystery today! In such encounters, it as if grace has befallen and simply taken away an energetic burden, to bring freedom.

It must also be appreciated, however, that sometimes deep patterns can be a little more tenacious. This is perhaps because we are more tenacious in holding on to them. This may be due to their familiarity, or the apparent "protection" they provide. For example, a person who is emotionally defensive might hold on to the energy posturing of defensiveness, because it has been learned as an adaptive technique of emotional protection. It is very fearful to let this posturing go – particularly if a person has learned it as a means of self-preservation.

There will come a time however, when the limiting influence of the posturing may be sufficiently apparent that a person will begin to open up in consciousness and appreciate it's limiting influence on their life. With gentle compassion, strength and courage it can release – and the liberation of one's spirit that ensues will arrive.

⊙

As a person unshackles from the psychoemotional patterning, one begins to feel freer in spirit. As these deep wounds unlock we are left to deal less with "unconscious patterning" and "energy distortions" – and live more consciously as co-creative beings with wings of spirit.

Again, the multiplicity of patterns that may arise in psychoemotional healing work is vast and beyond the scope of the overview provided in this book. We will, however, present some resources and tools that may be useful in this domain of healing as we look more carefully at the emotional and mental bodies and healing.

EMOTIONAL HEALING

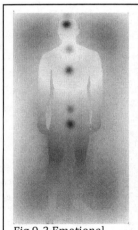

Fig 9-2 Emotional Body

Why do we have an emotional body? What does it mean to be emotionally healthy? Or, to emotionally heal?

Our emotional nature is vital to our relationship with the world around us. It has both a sentient function and an expressive or creative power. It is through our sentience that we are able to feel and register the experience of the world around us. And, it is also through the expressive capacity of the emotional body that we are able to passionately engage in the creative expression of our lives.

To have a healthy emotional life, like a muscle, we must first have a well-developed emotional energy body and the capacity to use it. (Fig 9-2) In other words, our emotional nature must be "allowed" to function and have developed strongly enough to function well.

Secondly, we must learn to be aware of *how* we use our emotional nature to sense and evaluate the world around us, and also to energize our creative efforts in the world – as we fuel and empower experience with the energy it provides. "Healing" issues can exist at any or all of these levels.

The Big Picture

Emotional energy may be viewed like water. It is a powerful life giving force, which has many functions. Water feeds, softens, vitalizes, and dissipates wastes. Unbridled, however, water is a powerful force.

I am about to grossly oversimplify our emotional complexity, in an effort to create a foundation. Life is not really as black and white as I am about to make it – but there are three basic foundations on which people may find themselves standing when they begin "emotional healing".

Developmentally speaking, if the emotional body is not allowed to develop, or is tightly controlled mentally, the emotional body may be weak or underdeveloped. Mental logic, or enforced belief systems, with the repressive fear and control they may imbue – can override, stifle, judge, repress, distort and even ridicule emotional expression.

If a person has been generally emotionally repressed – one may have to begin healing by learning to "allow" emotional energy into their life. So many people alive today have been discouraged from feeling – and taught to distrust their sentient self.

Emotional healing, in this setting, will involve a stage of emotional "permission". A person will need to give himself or herself the space to feel, to discover the feelings they have, to be allowed to express their feelings, and to have feelings honored. This occurs in the process of finding honor of the emotional nature within one's own being. This process can, of course, be supported in a healing or therapeutic relationship. But it must be personally integrated into one's life and one's circumstance in order to support emotional development. This defines a very important element of the emotional healing process for many people.

Secondly, if a person has learned to be aware of, to honor and to express emotion, but lives a life that is ruled only with emotional energy, there will need to be period of development of emotional maturity. This may mean the development of a supportive (i.e. spiritual congruent) mental and logic-based framework around the strong emotional nature that has developed. For example, one might need to learn to establish boundaries, to learn respect for oneself and others, to experience consequences of hurtful or impulsive emotional expression, and learn to make *wise* as well as *sentient* decisions.

Thirdly, the emotional body may be reasonably well developed and reasonably balanced, or not – but remains influenced by specific wounds and attributes that have developed through time.

Everyone has been affected in some ways during our personal development. This may lead to self-importance, self-neglect, and a whole host of limiting or destructive behaviors. These will need conscious attention and realignment in a journey of personal growth and spiritual development. Patterns of defensiveness, aggression, manipulation, lying, fearful living, self-repression, and so forth might fall into this domain. Some of these attributes will fit nicely into the concept of ego, which we will examine in detail a bit later.

If life is lived void of emotional energy it is dry and uninspired. If life is lived only from a self-centered emotional framework it is destructive to one's spiritual well being and to one's relationships. Once a person is well grounded in emotional expression – one can take on their personal issues, and the job of ego integration. Hence we can see three big categories in healing – development, balance and issue specific healing. There you have it, the huge topic of emotional healing in a very small nutshell!

DEVELOPMENT OF THE EMOTIONAL BODY

In a healthy developmental paradigm, as children grow, it is important to allow emotional expression and to teach boundaries and respect as the emotional body develops. This is a vast topic unto itself but we will briefly examine it from the point of understanding energetic development.

If emotional energy is honored and allowed to flow freely with the appropriate structure to contain and support it, a child generally learns to develop the emotional body in strength and self-awareness. As children grow and take on an emotional identity, they will pass through development milestones that are inherent in emotional development. It is important to provide honesty, and to allow feelings to come through in an open and trusting way.

Telling children not to feel, or to feel differently than they do, is silly and damaging. Teaching children how to process and manage the feelings they have, provides a healthy emotional foundation.

As children develop an emotional body they are learning about emotional energy and expression. As the emotional body develops, one is ideally learning to be aware of one's feelings and emotional nature. Becoming aware of these feelings, and the choices and behaviors that follow, is vitally important. Through this, children can develop a mature emotional nature. This development is reflected in the strength and vibrancy of a healthy emotional body.

If this development is not achieved as a child, it will have to take place as an adult ... and this encompasses a large area of emotional healing.

Healing the Development of the Emotional Body

For many reasons healthy emotional nurturance may have been weak or absent during our own childhood experience. If this is the case, one will require healing attention to help us develop and heal.

If emotional energy has been repressed or tightly controlled, healing will involve developing the simple permission to feel. This may sound a little trite – but in reality many people were raised in an emotionally repressive way. This may involve becoming more consciously aware of the existence of one's emotional nature, greater insight about one's feelings, greater permission to honor the feelings one has, and greater emotional freedom to express them.

For someone who has been repressed in emotional energy it can be very intimidating to "open up" emotionally. To achieve this will take some honest personal effort and practice. There will be a few "awkward moments" for sure! It will often require support, understanding and the willingness to live some the consequences induced by including emotional energy in our life!

This can a very challenging task when introduced upon a foundation where this has not been present. It can certainly be unsettling to the norm of one's personal environment. It might involve taking risks and inspiring deep transformation in the relationships we have forged with our family, friends and colleagues at times. But for many, it is a critical step to take on a greater spiritual journey. For those who take it on, it can be tremendously liberating.

There are many excellent healers, therapists, books and workshops based on connecting with our emotional nature and allowing greater permission to honor one's feeling nature available today.[3] If this idea resonates as important to you personally, I would encourage you to investigate.

☉

Meanwhile, if one has been nurtured in an environment that less repressive, and has learned to manage one's emotional energy with some degree of success – one will usually still possess some emotional "issues" to process.

These issues will invariably arise as we take on serious healing. They will be implicit in how we are using our emotional body and emotional energy. They will also affect how we engage emotionally in our world.

We have each been programmed or wounded in emotional ways. If we have not healed or processed this wounding, it will carry forward as emotional patterning. Restrictive or distorted emotional patterning will encumber the function of our emotional nature. It will greatly affect our ability to have a life that we feel deeply connected to and to have healthy emotional relationships with our partners, our families and other human beings in various ways. Specific patterns or wounds we carry may distort how we see or perceive the world and the people around us, the beliefs we hold, our reactions and attitudes, the choices we make, and the choices we don't make. In other words, they can "interfere" in our life as we strive to create a life that matches our "dreams".

If there are deep-seated emotional patterns that preclude healthy emotional expression, or lead to distorted or exaggerated emotional expression – they will affect our "energy signature". The emotional body will contribute in creating difficult life experiences – directly related to this patterning it contains. This can lead to a great deal of personal and interpersonal drama.

What kinds of emotional patterns may this include, you might ask? It would include habitual anger, constant negativity, self denial, self deprecation, shame, guilt, victimization, blaming, issues of worth, withdrawal, over zealousness, controlling, obsessiveness, avoidance, fears and phobias, aloofness, detachment, addictive and compulsive behaviors – just to name a few. Racism and religious bigotry are examples of fear-based emotional and mental programming that would also taint one's entire worldview. Self worth is another fine example of emotional programming that may be diminished by a series of painful emotional experiences during formative development.

In short, these patterns can block or distort emotional perception and expression – leading one to shut down, disconnect, overreact, defend, manipulate or even shatter – within one's experiences of life.

Energetically speaking these patterns become programmed into one's energy body – and often, in what one defines as one's "personality". It can, however, become very challenging to see these attributes with any sense of objectivity – because we carry the pattern within our own energy structure or signature.

Since these patterns are "hard to see" but "present in our energy" they will mysteriously show up in our lives through our relationships and experiences. One may not clairvoyantly be able to see the patterning in our energy body –

but what one will encounter is the out-picturing of the energy pattern in one's relationships and experiences.

Now, what is very helpful to understand, is any energy pattern that exists can be assisted to transform. One will see the experiences that are created, or perhaps "not" created in one's life, due to personal energy patterns. Healing implies the becoming more aware of these patterns and the influence they impose on our manifested life. It also implies a have a sincere intent to support ourselves as we transform them.

This introduces the concept that we are not limited to who we think we are based on history or experience. Human beings are always able to open up to new ways and new possibilities. We are each able to grow and to transform. If one is open and willing to "shift" the energy – one can also shift "reality".

In the natural journey of life, we will each learn to come to terms with the emotional behaviors, and their associated consequences. This happens quite naturally in the process of living and relationships – particularly if one is open or seeking to grow and learn. It is however, in my experience, greatly accelerated or facilitated by both intentional self-development and energy-based healing work.

These types of emotional patterns may be so embedded in one's personality – that one simply views them as the "way I am ", or, "who we are"; that is, until, one begins unraveling the patterns through personal work. From a healing perspective, when these patterns are highly developed or engrained, it can indeed be very challenging to break through them. This is particularly because of the inherent "ego" nature, which we will explore shortly.

Yet, spiritually speaking, to be limited by these patterns is never the "way we are" – no matter who we are. Not really. These are patterns that develop on the basis of often negative experiences, fear, and a lack of consciousness of our core spiritual being.

Everyone will have personal emotional patterns or issues to face in this life. I have never met a person who could not benefit from greater self-insight around several emotional patterns. Yet to try to make a list of all potential issues and how to fix each one of them is an onerous task – not to mention impractical!

You will be happy to hear that you do not need to know of very conceivable emotional pattern – and decide which ones you carry! You simply need be more aware of the process as a concept – and pay attention to your life. Life will show you what you need to see, if you sincerely intend to grow.

So let us pose a few insightful questions to get you thinking about your own story.

Do You "Need Some" Emotional Healing?

First, are you aware of your personal issues when it comes to emotional expression, or perhaps specific patterns you have in term of our emotional life? Just reflect for moment on what you already understand about yourself.

Now, before we continue, stop and set a personal intention. As we continue, ask you higher self to "join in" this exercise. Ask it to help you see what might be of value for you to understand about yourself, in your efforts to grow or heal. Ask your higher self to "turn up the light" and allow it to help your "see"!

All set? Here are a few pointed questions to stimulate your insight:

> What were you taught about feelings as a child?
> How were you handled when emotional as a child?
> How do you handle your children when they are emotional?
> Can you laugh out loud?
> Can you cry when you are alone? With others? Who specifically?
> Do you allow yourself to feel?
> Do you honor your feelings?
> When, or where, are you afraid to show your feelings?
> What makes you feel insecure?
> Do you express your feelings when needed in your life?
> Do you do this in a way, which supports understanding?
> Do you repress feelings? When and why?
> Do you show your feelings to others when you are happy, sad, frustrated or upset? Which ones do you control or limit?
> Do you overburden others with your concerns?
> Do you impose your feelings on others when they disagree with you?
> Do you listen?
> Do you hear?
> What are your buttons?
> How do you defend yourself when challenged emotionally?
> Do you have healthy relationships?
> Are you able to displease your partner, family or friends?
> Do you answer honestly when asked how you feel?
> How do you feel about yourself?
> Do you permit your sexuality to be expressed?
> Are you trusting of others? Elaborate on this.

How would a friend describe you emotionally? Would you agree?
Do you balance your finances?
Are you an emotional spender or consumer?
Are you emotionally available to your family and friends?
Have you discovered habitual patterns in your life that bring disappointment or recurrent experiences?
Do you commonly say things you later regret?
Do you have any addictions? Drugs? Sex? Smoking? Drinking? Gambling? Spending? Exercise? Eating?
How do you handle disappointment?
Do you ask for help when needed?
Do you manipulate others for your own perceived needs?
How do you react to confrontation?
Can you show affection freely?
Can you tell those around you that you love them?
Do you freely love yourself?

These are some tailored exploratory questions to stir up insight. Your specific answers will be very helpful in allowing you to identify attributes of your emotional nature, and areas where a little personal work may be of value. Insight is always more valuable than advice – for it is personal to you! It might also provide signposts to follow – as you explore tools for support that are valuable to you.

If you see things you would like to "improve", I would encourage you to take it on! Do you see patterns, attributes or behaviors that you know are limiting to your happiness and wellbeing? Let this insight direct you in taking guided steps to support your own growth and transformation. As you become more aware of what you see – ask for the support and guidance, and even synchronicities to show up in your life – to help you on your journey. You might be amazed what shows up to help you along! You will find greater and greater freedom in being courageous and authentically loving yourself!

Let's Not Forget Sentience

The emotional body is also "receptive", and works in a "sensory" capacity. Through our emotional nature, we are sentient to the world around us. We feel so much in our world, and we can discern a lot of information through this sensory capacity if we permit ourselves to use it.

Through our feeling nature we care capable of reading situations, environmental circumstances, people's intentions, and safety. It is also through our sentient nature that we can relate with other people, feel compassion and hold empathetic understanding – towards other people and life.

Logic alone is very limited in navigating the terrain of life. One can only be expected to make wise and balanced choices – if one is able to relate sentiently to life. The concept of "emotional intelligence" has been introduced and developed by several authors such as those referenced here for the curious among you. [28,42]

Many people have been taught to override a healthy functioning of sentience by social custom or suppression. It is essential to give oneself "permission" and to trust one's feeling nature. Sentience will provide us with information about our relationships, people and all experiences we encounter in our life. The information it provides can be factored into processes of personal decision making. If this is not how you live your life you may find it useful to explore this topic in your healing process.

Healthy sentience is also a precursor to opening up to the faculty of our intuition, which is a higher sensory function. Use of intuition is a process we may learn about, and practice, as we explore holistic healing. In our *intuitive* ability, we are not only sentient to our emotions or feelings and the world around us – we are also sentient to a transpersonal awareness, which includes non-logical awareness, and direct knowing. Hence it is not strictly confined to the emotional body, but it can involve the emotional body.

When the faculty of intuition is developed – people learn to function by its guidance implicitly. Personally, I would never want to make a logical decision that is intuitively incorrect to me. One comes to understand that intuitive function is intensely personal and tailored to one's own life and wellbeing. I have come to trust intuition more acutely than any other aspect of conscious awareness in my life.

Pathways to Healing

I have seen people experience direct healing on the emotional body in many different ways. Many of them are very familiar and quite natural to life. This may be through family and relationships, traditional counseling or psychotherapy, personal learning, or experiential workshops focused on emotional healing. Evolving approaches are also now found in the domain of energy psychology practices and direct energy healing work. This work can have the capacity to energetically "dig in" and help surface emotional patterns that need to come to conscious awareness or are ready for release.

Yet the patterns can be deep, strongly familiar, attached to our personality, and reluctant to let go. The more challenging of these are those related to deep personal wounds from our earlier *life*, or as we discussed, earlier *lives*.

In this setting, I know both energy based healing and past life regression work can be very helpful. This is particularly true when someone has undergone intense personal therapy and cannot unlock the core dilemma to find healing. If this resonates as important to you personally, tap into your intuitive level awareness, and ask yourself if this would be helpful to you.

That being said, people do not necessarily have to do hypnotic regression experiences to tap into deep emotional insight about personal issues. If we are on a conscious path of spiritual development, experiences will often present to us in our current life – to support our efforts heal. Regression therapy is only one way to tap into and release of the emotional charge around formative memories and emotional patterns. Through regression or any experiential process we undertake, tapping into the emotion pattern and releasing emotional charge, will always serve as the touchstone of emotional healing.

Also during times of healing, the use of other energy-based remedies for energetic support can be very helpful. This includes things like direct energy healing, homeopathy and flower essences, which is discussed in a later section of the book.

I would also re-emphasize that a great deal of emotional healing occurs in the context of relationships and the life experiences that we manifest in our lives. This is particularly true if we develop conscious relationships in our life. They are crafted for our growth and development – because they occur as projections of our inner energy posture or signature. This is particularly true if we seek to learn from our life experiences and are open to grow from the experiences we live with people around us.

So, whether we use tools to support our healing, or simply rely on the school of life - the emotional body and its energy can eventually be freed up from patterned reactivity. This allows us to function more openly and more in alignment with our deeper spiritual nature. As the emotional body is freed – we are more able to sense and feel, to energize our inspirations. This adds a creative stimulation and joy to our lives - and our world around us.

Stepping into Co-Creative Alignment

As a person encounters and heals wounded emotional elements within one's psyche, one begins to feel freer. As one awakens to one's spiritual nature and power - one also learns that we can be much more conscious of our emotional state and learn to master our emotional expression. As expressed in New Age verbiage, we can "choose".

Learning to be more conscious of our emotional experiences and understanding how we nurture certain emotional states is a key to healing and well-being.

To become aware of our emotional experiences takes an element of strong self-awareness. But, as we become more conscious of our emotions, we can also become more masterful at allowing, processing and even transforming these experiences with spiritual wisdom. Okay, but what does that really mean?

We are each aware that there are *higher* and *lower* vibrational emotional states of experience. But perhaps we are not always aware that we have an ability to redirect emotional experience by choice, and in healthy self-respect. To better understand, let's do a short exercise.

Exercise To Connect with Shifting Emotional Energy:

Reflect for a moment on the vibrational quality of the following emotions, one at a time. Take a moment to really focus on each emotion, and feel its resonance.

Let's start with anger. Connect with the emotion of feeling anger and become consciously aware of the experience it evokes, within you. Permit yourself to really "feel" it.

When you have tapped into this emotion, let's move on to another emotional state. Focus on the experience of hatred. Again, pause and really connect and feel this emotional experience in a sentient way.

Now try resentment, then guilt, anxiety, impatience, shame, and doubt.

What do this experiences create within your as you focus on them?

Let us shift gears now. Focus you attention, for a personal experience, on the vibrational quality of the following emotions one at a time: gratitude, happiness, joy, peace, compassion, wonder, tranquility, faith, bliss, and love.

Again, do not rush ... stop and resonantly connect with each one and feel the specific emotional vibration.

Conscious focus on each emotion will help create a real emotional experience. Do you realize you are capable of changing or creating your emotional experience by conscious intent!

⊙

As human beings we actually have the ability to align our emotional nature with whatever state we "choose". This is not meant to be a means of *denial* of emotion. To deny emotion is to live as if an emotion does not exist. That is a type of self-betrayal or dishonesty with a sentient reality. However to transform our emotional experience is consciousness *processing* of emotional energy. This ability is a very powerful tool. It is implicit in the emotional healing process.

Emotional patterns can be thought of as being "fed" by the focus of our attention or consciousness. One can "feed energy" to the creation of lower vibrational emotions if one remains focused on them and direct one's energy there. One can also feed energy to higher vibrational emotions if one channels one's attention and energy there. This seems simplistic but it is actually a highly conscious activity.

As we become more insightful about our own emotional experience, and our personal patterns, learning to do this is recognized as an incredible tool of transformation. It is a tool of "emotional mastery" – and we can use it to help shift our emotional reality when we are "stuck" in dark and difficult emotional spaces.

As we learn to shift, we can become more and more conscious of the emotional experience that "nourishes" our spirit - emotionally speaking – and also what "drains" us. It is all based on a vibrational reality that we create. We can learn to focus our energy in this higher vibrational orientation rather than feeding the lower vibration states - by learning to be more aware of what we are doing.

What brings you joy? What sooths your spirit? What helps you feel aligned with your spiritual truth? What enlivens your creativity? What lifts you up when feeling down? In what ways do you use our emotional energy that you believe honors your life?

One can learn to work with one's emotional body to constructively and honestly raise one's emotional vibration and channel the energy into personally relevant channels. One becomes co-creative with one's spirit and wisdom, as one learns to transform one's emotional life.

There are many excellent resources today available to help guide a person through a process of emotional healing and work with emotion intelligently. But for those who are inspired, some excellent references to work with emotional healing are included to support your efforts! [3,15,31,32]

BACK TO THE ENERGY PARADIGM

To bring context to "energy based" healing in the setting of emotional body healing — we can conceptualize that emotional forms can be patterned in our field. This has occurred through the assimilation of conditioning programs, and the influence of both conscious and subconscious wounds. These may originate in obvious ways in our life, or be more subconscious — even across the veil of lifetimes. These embedded patterns provide a true energetic influence that will impact the health, balance, vitality and creative function of our emotional body.

One can work through many of the emotional issues by gaining greater self awareness — and processing this growth with insight, in conscious ways. But, in addition to, "talk therapy" and other forms of insight development, there are also energy-based processes, which can be engaged. These cannot only support the healing of emotional issues, but also the sustaining a healthy and healed emotional body.

Energy based therapies work primarily by bringing energy and light into the restrictive energy patterns in the emotional body, which may be leading to manifested emotional issues. It can sound a little hocus pocus — but it is a very valid concept. Such therapies may help to "surface" the pattern, so it can be then dismantled. They may provide just the needed illumination to better see the pattern, and begin a conscious process of transformation from greater insight. Let us take a closer look at how this works:

First, energy can be introduced which can "dismantle" an energy pattern. When healing energy is introduced, the energy that is restricted or congealed in the emotional body can be vibrationally lifted, loosened and transformed. Yes, I realize this sounds mystical — but energetically this does really occur.

In my experience, when people first engage in energy healing work, this often occurs with limited awareness or conscious processing for some patterns. It is as if something is just washed away energetically speaking. This is particularly true when someone is carrying a limiting pattern that serves no useful purpose, but stuck for some "reason".

Two, it can "enlighten" such patterns by "raising" energy around the pattern. When patterns are catalyzed as such, it is as if they vibrate. By doing so — they become easier to "recognize" and witness. This may be necessary so we can actually recognize a pattern we carry within ourselves. This helps us see it – so that we can consciously work to transform it. In recognizing our patterns, we can participate consciously in their transformation. This may be important – perhaps to help us process an important or valuable life lesson or wisdom.

I would encourage you to open your mind to this experience if it is not already part of your personal journey – and "see for yourself".

Spiritual Growth in Emotional Healing

Lastly, I would be remiss not mention that learning to align with deeper spiritual wisdom is an important key in releasing powerful energy wounds – and it plays a role in healing at the emotional level and at each level or energy body.

We will discuss this important topic later in chapter 10 in the framework of ego-based healing. There we will examine the practices of compassion, peace and forgiveness – spiritually rooted strategies that help us heal our deepest wounds – as we foray into the world of love-based ego transformation.

Ultimately these practices, founded in spiritual wisdom, provide the greatest force of healing of our emotional and mental bodies. They point to a well-worn path of freedom and healing; one, that only a deeper connection with ones spiritual nature can provide.

☉

If you know that emotional healing is important at this point in your journey, I would encourage you to check out some of the resources referenced, or those available at local healing centers, bookstores, or, on the internet. There is a vast array of tools and techniques available to support emotional healing adding detail and practical ways to implement what we have discussed. If you want to understand the power of energy work to help you in your healing, you will need not simple to learn but also your own personal experience. But now that you have a framework to understand how it all fits together … maybe you will feel more comfortable in taking such a step, or going more deeply into this potential, if you already have some experience.

Let us turn our attention now to the concept of mental level healing.

Mental Healing

"A calm mind releases the most precious capacity a human being can have: the capacity to turn anger into compassion, fear into fearlessness and hatred into love."

Eknath Easwaran

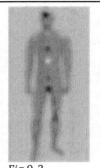

Fig 9-3
Mental Body

At the level of the mental body, we can once again reflect on the nature and purpose of mental energy to see how healing is implied.

The mental body can be viewed as a structural energetic vehicle. It is a body of energy that exists as a "tool" for the spirit to exist in this world – and be able to function or operate in the "mental domain". (Fig 9-3)

The mental body is capable of creating or storing thought forms. It can form thoughts, hold onto thoughts, absorb the thoughts shared by others and project thoughts to others. Thoughts can "solidify" into organized programs of belief. Our thoughts and beliefs, to large degree, define or model our relationship with life, and also what we choose to create as our reality experience. These beliefs can also greatly *limit* what we create as our experience. Belief systems, and the programming we contain in both our personal and collective mental field, have a huge influence on what we manifest both tangibly and experientially in our lives.

The mental body, as a structural and functional body of energy, can be understood as analogous to the hardware of a computer system:

As a structural body of energy, the mental body functions like the hard drive in a modern computer. The hard drive contains an operating system into which we install programs. Similarly, in the mental body, we can install programs, beliefs, thoughts patterns, and so forth – that define its capacity.

The mental body, like a computer, once it stores programs, can process information on the basis of the quality of the system and type of programs that are installed.

Then, the mental body "interfaces" with the brain and human nervous system in a quantum way - sort of like a Wi-Fi connection!

The mental body, like the emotional body or a computer, is neutral to content.

It can be uploaded with any kind of programs – healthy or unhealthy – constructive or limiting. This can be anything that we choose, or assimilate, through conditioning and experience. Like any tool, it will simply operate according to its programming which in many ways is defined by the degree of consciousness of the user. In fact it can be used very little at all, if we so choose.

Just as a computer program defines the capabilities and the limitations of the computer - our thoughts and beliefs in so many ways define the same abilities and limitations in our lives. And the good news is – it can always be upgraded!

◉

The *mental body* and *consciousness* are not the same thing. Consciousness is "awareness" and is a function of our spiritual nature. Consciousness lives *through* our mental, emotional and human expression. It is not simply defined by the mental body. Consciousness lives through the function of each of these bodies in our sojourn as a human being.

Consciousness, rather than existing simply as the mental body, works through the mental body. Consciousness is bigger that the mental body, and is actually *limited* through it's structure, function and level of development. Consciousness is vast and infinite. It is perhaps limited, as a human being, so that we can relate to and function within the world of earthly form through a mental framework – and not "overwhelmed" by its vastness. The mental body can be viewed to form a structural framework through which consciousness can create and experience within the world of form in which we live.

So as a spiritual being, consciousness is much vaster than we can comprehend as a "simple" human being. We might accept that the mental body serves as "a tool" – a tool of "spirit" to allow us to experience and relate to the world of form.

So the first step, but the most essential step, in mental level healing – is overcoming a belief that our mental body, despite its capable mental function, is the true definition of "who we are".

In the words of Descartes, "I THINK therefore I am" has been a popularized concept that demonstrates humanity's reliance on thought as a sense of identity. Yet, it is a very limiting concept.

"I AM, therefore I think" is more accurate depiction of the human condition. It is through consciousness that we exist – and our mental ability is simply a function we possess – largely through the capacity of the mental body.

The function of the mental body is highly valued in our western culture. Intelligence and academic accomplishment are prized attributes in our society. Certainly, there is nothing wrong with intellectual development; in fact it is quite important. But the time is evolving to understand the difference between identity defined by our mental attributes, and identity defined as spiritual beings.

It should be very clear to us all that a strong mentality without a heart can be a devastating force of destruction. We cannot approach life through our mental nature only, and expect to understand the deeper nature of life.

So much of our lives and our identities are defined by mental attributes. We commonly express statements like I am … a man, a Christian, an American, a French-Canadian, an athlete, a nurse, a parent, and so on. From a spiritual perspective – these do have a form reality. They are, however, better viewed as "roles we play" or "attributes" than a true "identity". We form these roles, as appropriate as they may be, through our mental and structural framework – but they will never define the totality of what we represent.

We are actually spiritual beings, who have a mental body – and that body can be used to serve the spirit within us. If we better understand our mental nature and the mental body, we realize we are more capable of transformation than we might first believe, or dare to imagine. This opens a doorway for highly transformative healing.

To understand the truer role of the mental body, and the capacity for transformation, requires an awareness and acceptance of our spiritual nature. This window provides the ability for consciousness to reprogram and heal the mental body in any way it may not function in alignment with greater wellbeing, or simply betrays our truer spiritual essence. Through it, we can loosen the grip of our mental nature as an identity – and free it up to operate under the guidance of an expanded consciousness. This simple idea encapsulates the whole essence of mental healing.

Mental Body Healing

Healing of the mental body implies learning to bring both the *content* and the *function* of the mental body into alignment with our essential spiritual nature. Now we are not talking about the potentially stifled ways of a distorted spiritual programming. We are talking about the ways of mature spiritual self-responsibility and love.

The mental body is indeed a powerful tool and organizes life force energy to manifest things into form. If we utilize this ability with greater conscious awareness, we can adapt the world we build through our thoughts and the actions they inspire.

This healing can involve developing a greater awareness of the *core beliefs* we have integrated about ourselves, other people, and the world around us. It may expose how these beliefs are creative and how they can be limiting, illness producing, or distorting to a truer spiritual expression.

It can also imply a much greater awareness of how we *utilize* our mental function in our lives. We can develop insight into how we are inspired or impaired by our thoughts; and, how they may distort or interfere with wellbeing; by the way we use our mental energy on a day-to-day basis.

Through this aspect of healing, we begin to truly understand that we are not simply the conglomerate of thoughts, beliefs, ideas and conditioned states of being that lie currently in our mental bodies. We can each learn to "consciously" examine ourselves – to grow in self-awareness. This can help us understand how the beliefs we hold about ourselves and about life may be very limiting, destructive or based in ego consciousness and fear. It will also provide the ability to change and to grow.

The mental programs we carry can be strongly correlated with energetic imbalances, which drain or negatively qualify the energy we carry – our energy "signature". This can lead to the manifestation of both psychological and physical disease.

Through awareness one can transform the mental body. As mystical as this may first appear, this process is actually a natural function of human development even when we are not aware it is occurring – part of the evolving consciousness of humanity. It is, however, a process that is greatly accelerated in these transformational times. Exposure to consciousness-based healing and energy based healing practices is one element of this awakening. And, through this process we are learning to be more conscious, masterful and responsible – about how we use our mental body – and the subsequent manifestation that occurs by energetic resonance. By being more conscious, we can be clearer on what we want to create, live and manifest in our personal and collective lives.

The Formation of Structured Thoughts and Beliefs

As we grow up in our world we are exposed to many different thoughts, experiences, beliefs and systems of beliefs. Through this exposure, and our relationship to this exposure, we develop our own beliefs and patterns of thinking.

Some of the thoughts and systems of belief become embedded in our mental body as formed thoughts. These thought forms are like crystallized mental patterns that resonate in us, and form a great deal of what we call reality. They define how we view our world, relate to others, and dynamically create our lives and interactions.

Some of the thought patterns or "software programs" that get installed in our mental structure are simply cultural. Others arise from experiences or educational transference from those around us. They can be derived from education and conditioning by a parent or teacher, and people with whom we interact. Personal experiences we may live, also lead us to form core beliefs and patterns of thinking.

In an overview, this can lead to assimilation of a healthy mental framework. However, if our beliefs are derived from traumatic experiences, or experiences of great fear and limited awareness, they can also lead to a "wounded" system of beliefs. Sometimes the source of instruction (parent or teacher), or the players in our experiences, are wounded in their own right. As we form our core beliefs, there may be many things that lead to us produce core beliefs that will require healing transformation.

The mental body, which contains the energy patterns, serves as an organizing force of creation. Our thoughts and beliefs are very powerful forces that tailor our creative intentions and efforts, toward their essential patterning. In other words, the beliefs you hold and the way you think, contributes enormously to the way your life takes shape. The challenge here is – the quality and content of our mental body defines to a large degree what we can and cannot create in our lives.

Unhealthy mental function can therefore lead to psychological issues in our life, the relationships we hold with others, the relationship we hold with ourselves, and the choices we make in our lives. It can also lead to physical disease because of the impact such energy has on our energy fields and the way we use our mental capacity.

Let us take a look at a straightforward example to better understand some of these concepts:

Imagine while growing up, a child lives under the care of a parent who is very anxious and fearful. As a child is exploring the world around them, the parent may be setting up many excessive boundaries and invoking fear at every turn. They may say to the child "you cannot do this or you will get injured", or "if you do such and such, you will hurt yourself", or simply overreact at every gesture.

As a child, living in this environment, one will be exposed to the core belief that the world is exclusively an unsafe, threatening and dangerous place. But, there are a few options open to the child in terms of "relating" to this psychological environment.

One option that the child may experience would be to become very concerned and fearful. This will create a certain mental patterning – not of safety – but of mistrust, fear and uncertainty. A process of repeat exposure and assimilation will instill this program. Once these corresponding thought forms "take up residence" in the child's mental body – they will, of course, affect the child's energy expression.

As this child grows up, they will learn to see the world as a very fearful place. In such a scenario, the impact may be that the child will learn not to follow their dreams and inspiration, because of all the fears they hold from this deep patterning. This would lead to a great restraint in the child's life, and perhaps an inability to move forward in many ways toward a productive and satisfying future.

In such a case, where a strong passive transference of a wounded belief system occurs, healing would certainly involve an unshackling of this deeply embedded influence in the mental body – to liberate the restrictions it imposes.

This is a simplified but poignant example. Each of us has been indoctrinated in different ways as we grow up. This represents one of thousands of potential examples that could be introduced. There are elements of parental conditioning, peer conditioning, social conditioning, patriotic conditioning, political conditioning, positive and negative experiential conditioning, traumatic conditioning – that combine to help us develop into the people we each know ourselves to be.

Through such processes, distortional beliefs can form around a whole host of issues, such as one's intelligence, athletic ability, personality, likeability, career potential, sexual expression, religion, and culture. The list goes on. It can be an arduous task to uncover or rectify deep conditioning to help a person find a truer self-expression.

Yet, magically, deep limiting beliefs will usually present themselves in a very tailored way if we are open as individuals to personal and spiritual growth. How? Well, they will be found at the root level of problems or "issues" that may manifest in our personal lives. If we take the time to reflect and learn from our personal experience and manifestations, we will see very well some of the deeper programming that we may carry.

◉

Now, of course, it is truly not responsible to place the origin of all such programming on parents, family and culture. These arenas do source many of the beliefs systems we build around us, but from a spiritual perspective we may have "chosen" certain conditions and environments, as a soul, by design. Meanwhile, other deeply embedded mental attributes may be karmic or transpersonal in nature – bleeding over from another incarnation.

Some mental attributes do seem to come with a person "across the veil of lifetimes". We can easily see in children how a particular temperament or way of approaching life is inherent in the child from the moment of birth. Through this we know it is not simple "parenting" and early childhood experience that defines some of these mental and psychological attributes.

That being said, when a person embarks on a journey of healing or spiritual growth, deeply held patterns of mental function will come up for cross-examination. The "reason" this occurs is – beliefs are highly formative in the life a person creates – or sometimes, does *not* create. If there are aspects of one's life that are not working well or leading to illness – they need to be reconciled. And when we are ready to grow and expand in consciousness, some of our old beliefs will simply need to be dismantled.

When there is a spiritual prompting to move forward, we will each encounter some of these highly programmed beliefs for they will be directly or indirectly contributing to both the quality of our lives, and many of our disease states or personal experiences we manifest as human beings.

EXERCISE TO EXAMINE SOME CORE BELIEFS:

What are some of the deep belief systems you hold in your life? Here are few poignant questions to help you observe some of the important attributes of belief that may or may not serve your health or spiritual development:

How do you define yourself?
Are you safe and supported in life?
Are you strong and secure?
How do you view the world?
Are you able to create what is important to you?
Are you able to handle challenges that present themselves in your life?

Can you handle constructive criticism?
How do you perceive conflict?
How would others describe you? Ask them. Do you agree?
What triggers you to become defensive?
How do you handle rejection or disappointment?
Are you worthy of love?
Are you able to be vulnerable?
Are you capable of loving those who hurt you?
What can you not forgive?
What do you believe about other people or groups of people?
Can you heal?
Can you create a life, which reflects your personal integrity?
Do you believe you are a spiritual being?
Do you allow others to control you?
Do you control others?
What do you judge in other people? ... other cultures? ... religions and religious people? ... the media? ... politicians and government? ... health care?
Where do you have difficulties with other people? What are the thought forms that stand behind this?
What do you judge in yourself? Be specific and complete.
Do you believe you have a spiritual purpose?
Are you fulfilling it? What gets in the way? Can you reach a core belief?
What would your life be like if you could manifest your dreams? What gets in the way?
Where do you encounter the greatest challenges in your life? Your family? Your relationships? What are some beliefs you can identify that may be contributing to the issues you may face?

These are just a few interesting questions to help you probe into your core beliefs. These beliefs might impede or support your spiritual expression. As people grow and heal, they will encounter issues that have a strong mental attribute or belief that is central to the issue.

If we think in terms of *energy*, rather than simply *beliefs*, we can conceptualize that these beliefs represent well-formed patterns in our mental energy field.

The patterns that exist in our mental body will influence or affect our overall energy signature. Our energy signature is like a magnetic force of creation – and the contributing influences will define what we manifest in our lives. If we can think of belief patterns "energetically", it makes it easier to grasp how we can deconstruct them, and vicariously their influence on our overall energy signature.

THE MISSING PILL

As we each examine our own personal lives, it is possible to see some of the core beliefs we have assimilated. Through insight, one can progressively learn to transform negative, restrictive, or distorted beliefs. Freedom from mental patterning that has ensnared one's life in self destructive, ego laden, diseased, or, potential limiting patterns – can be "unearthed" and transformed.

The topic of core beliefs is really well examined in a supportive and awakening book by Tara Brach entitled "True Refuge: Finding Peace and Freedom in Your Own Awakened Heart."[4]

DEALING IN REAL TIME – THOUGHTS IN ACTION

The mental body not only deals with holding belief systems or thought patterns. It is also a *processor* of thought. Our beliefs will have a strong influence on how we relate to life and other people - but our mental body is also capable of forming, storing and receiving new thought forms in its interactions with life. *How* it does this, is subject to some degree on the consciousness of the individual who "owns" the mental body.

For example, in my capacity to think, I may choose to form a judgmental thought about another person. The thought may be triggered by some core belief I have about a group of people, for example – but it is "formed" or "made" from my own mental energy body. Think of how we can store information digitally on a CD to conceptualize how a thought may be "stored" as such.

By doing this I will form a recorded pattern in my mental energy field. As I focus my attention on the thought I am activating and empowering it in my awareness. I will "energize" it. And, as the focus of attention grows in power, it grows in creative strength.

Can you conceptualize what I am creating in my energy field as I do this? Think of our discussion earlier about cymatics to conceptualize how this actually occurs. By focusing attention through consciousness, this focus works the way sound works in a medium, to structure mental energy into form patterns. The patterns can be metaphorically crystallized and stored.

Hence, the mental body has the creative capacity to *form* thoughts. These thoughts are like little energy "structures" that form within the energy field of the mental body. You can visualize them as little geometries that develop in the field. When we hold such patterns in our field, they will actually influence the overall vibrational quality of our energy.

Remember, it is the patterning in our own energy field that becomes a force of attraction – and magnetizes many experiences and many manifestations. Just imagine what happens if one is full of judgmental ideas?

Once a thought is formed, I can then even "share" the thought with another person – by expressing it in words.

Through this, we can understand that our mental body can *resonate* with thought forms that someone else has created. If someone shares a thought that I accept, or if I "buy into" a thought form or an idea – I will form an energy signature in my own mental body to correlate with it.

Can you see what you would be accepting into your mental body if you accept all kinds of negative thoughts from other people, in your mental field? Yet, the saving grace is … it is equally true of higher vibrational patterns!

This helps explain why it is so important to be aware of how we use our mental function. Imagine for a moment that I am engaged in gossip or witness to an attack on another person's character. Remember, regardless of how true or false the statement might by – most of what is expressed in this setting will be based on either the wounds, or the limited consciousness, of the speaker. We have all been told, in spiritual teachings, that this type of activity is hurtful and to be avoided. Now it becomes clearer as to "how" and "why". You see, if you are taking on these patterns – you are forming them in your own energy which will "lower your vibrational signature" – and subject you to the consequence of your own energy patterning! There is a great truth in the concept – what you do to another you do to yourself!

Part of spiritual growth is to become conscious how we use our mental capability, as well as the thoughts we accept and harbor. This is not to be lived fearfully, but rather conscientiously. It is important to fill one' self with thoughts that are life affirming, loving, kind, tolerant and wise. The foundational precepts of every religion and spiritual teaching are better understood with this simple awareness.

It is from this spiritual perspective that people may successfully use affirmations, or neurolinguistic programming(NLP), or mindfulness techniques as examples of tools form mental healing. We may, however, have to weed some mental patterns out of our mental body if they are deeply rooted in it – an important element of transformational healing. We can also consciously learn to introduce thoughts into our mind, which powerfully supports our wellness and wellbeing.

Exceptional work on affirmations has been provided by Louise Hay in her book *You Can Heal Your Life* and many other wonderful authors.[31] Of course, if someone is just randomly inserting a few ideas superficially and thinking they will "take on life" in a new way, this may not work so easily. This is particularly true if they are in competition with many other thoughts that are already well rooted in your psyche. This garden will grow better if it is first weeded and prepared. But "practice makes perfect" – and all things spiritual must be practiced.

Do Thoughts Create "Reality"?

Thoughts that a person accepts, and holds strongly in the mental body, grow in power. If you hold thoughts or beliefs in your mental body, they do hold a creative influence. This awareness is the basis of statements like, "Your thoughts create your reality."

Strongly energized thoughts create energy forms that begin to order or magnetize energy around them, to make them happen or "materialize".

Hence the creative power of our mental body must be respected and understood with wisdom. We must learn to be responsible and spiritually mature in the use of mental energy. It is important not to energize negative thoughts about others and ourselves. It is equally important to nourish the mental body with high vibrational thoughts of kindness, encouragement, courage, empathy, faith, and love.

What are the Implications on Healing?

Healing work involving the mental body may involve deep exploration of beliefs and patterns of thought, which lead to "life issues" and spiritual "limitation".

This can occur in many ways. First, it occurs often simply through the insight gained through our life experiences and our relationships – particularly if people are open to grow and to learn in their life. It can also occur through self-help work, psychological support, or coaching. These processes can involve the development of greater insight and transformative self-awareness. And, we can work energetically to support this.

When a person develops the intention to heal or to grow spiritually, one will energetically initiate a process to "push up" and expose the mental patterns, which are energetically embedded in one's energy field. This occurs to bring them into greater conscious awareness. From a healing perspective, this helps us see, examine, recalibrate and realign our life with a healthy reality. This can involve exposing beliefs and patterns of all types. But clearly, patterns that have occurred through painful wounds, as well as simple habitual mental patterns that are interfering with spiritual well being, will need to arise. And, it might not be "fun".

In addition to examining core beliefs and mental patterns, the work of healing will involve becoming more conscious of how we use our mental force.

At the mental level of healing, thoughts and beliefs that promote hatred, judgment of self or others, worry, control, fear based choices, and ego drama start to be exposed. Thoughts and thought patterns that inflate or deflate our individual significance are challenged. Thoughts and thought patterns that promote victimization and disempowerment are challenged. Developing a more conscientious approach to life and use of our mental energy, we will unravel many of the thought forms and beliefs that influence our personal lives in unhealthy ways.

⊙

Eventually this process will involve an encounter not simply with thoughts and beliefs, but with what we come soon to explore as the "ego". The ego represents the aspect of self-identity that is founded in fear and based on a belief in separation from our spiritual origin and nature. It is the aspect of the human experience that is separated from a greater awareness of the love-based nature of reality.

This will take on greater meaning in Chapter 10, but for the moment we will introduce the idea that ego "uses" the mental body and emotional body to "survive" by invoking fear. The work of healing the ego is essentially a spiritual instruction to the mental and emotional bodies. This understanding will provide a reliable compass to navigate our efforts at spiritual realignment and recalibration. By developing this understanding, our higher self is better able to guide and override the ego-based tendencies we each carry.

As we take on this healing challenge, we begin to realize that not only are our beliefs and thoughts flexible and impermanent in nature – we can learn to be more responsible and wise in how we engage mentally with life. And as we find freedom from the ego tendencies, we find greater freedom in expressing our truer being.

Understanding Surrender

Healthy mental development and healing may be arbitrarily divided into three segments, although they overlap.

This first level is developing a very healthy sense of one's own worth, value, strength, and capability. The second initiates the task of encountering and dismantling limiting or destructive beliefs we have incorporated into our lives. It might entail becoming aware of our personal wounds and how they have altered ones view of reality. The third, is surrendering the last of our ego based mental qualities so we can mature as spiritual beings.

When we begin to understand the function of the mental body, we realize that we must learn to be "in charge" of the mental body from a spiritual level of consciousness. Ironically, this is part of a process often termed "surrender".

Spiritual surrender is not a "giving up". It is a purposeful surrender of the use of the mental body to our spirit, rather than our ego nature. The ability of an "unruly or fear filled mind" to ultimately destroy peace is encountered in all of its forms – so we can find and manifest the deep peace of spirit within our own being.

We need a mental body and healthy sense of individuation, self worth and self-responsibility entrained within us, to take on the ultimate task of ego integration or deep spiritual healing. The mental function is gradually sublimated or integrated in its function to the mastery of the soul, albeit sometimes, with a bit of resistance!

Now I often tease people, particularly spiritually inclined people, by saying, "You cannot surrender what you do not have!" Spiritually oriented people sometimes get caught in the process of becoming "empty" and "free of ego". An important part of our lives involves the development of a healthy sense of self-awareness and responsibility. We must develop ourselves as individuated beings of value and spiritual significance. We must develop our mental and emotional bodies so they are developed and strong. But as we mature, we must learn to surrender a strict sense of personal isolation, as we understand the spiritual workings of life.

Our soul will have the job of getting rid of the mental and emotional attributes that are based on limited ego perceptions. To surrender in this sense is not to become insignificant or invisible. It is to give up what is false within us – so our spirit may shine forth. I find that this is a concept is often misunderstood by spiritual seekers. It truly does not mean to become irrelevant or subservient to another person or even an organization. It is to become spiritually authentic, unencumbered by the sense of spiritual isolation this perception breeds. It is to surrender our creative abilities to an alignment with the way of spirit and path of our soul.

The soul and higher self learn to be "in charge" of the mental body. Through this we learn to extract beliefs that are damaging or hurtful, tame its unruly restlessness, let go of restrictive or hurtful patterns of thought, and plant seeds that are inspiring, life affirming and rich in potential.

Meditation as a Path To Mastering Mental Energy

People often first begin to encounter the active and sometimes unruly nature of the mental body when they try to learn to meditate. If you sit to meditate, you will begin immediately to see mental activity. As you sit in stillness, you being to see thoughts come and go across the screen of your mind or consciousness.

Thoughts arise about everything. You think of things you need to do, the people you need to speak to, events which happened this morning, what you should have said to so and so, your next trip, what made you upset yesterday, and so on. The mind jumps from thought to thought – and you are taken along for the ride.

You also become aware that you can "latch on" to the thoughts that arise, and energize them by your concentration or focus. When we do this, certain thoughts may then trigger or lead to other thoughts, or to subtle emotional reactions. This can eventually lead to a whole dialogue and inner experience. They can stimulate whole discussion in our head and create little soap operas of experience.

If we focus our attention on a particular thought, the thought is energized. We can feed our thoughts with energy, which empowers them. It is as if they get bigger. As thoughts get "big" in our mental body, they get bigger in energy or vibratory resonance – and become stronger in creative potential. This is one mechanism by which thoughts are turned into experiences.

As you continue to practice in meditation you may become aware that the consciousness that is witness to, or "observing" the thoughts, is distinct from the thoughts themselves. *You* exist separately from the thoughts, and you are able to be aware of them and witness them. The thoughts in your mind come and go – but you start to grasp the difference between thoughts and your observing consciousness.

In this realization, you discover what we can term your witnessing consciousness. Your "witnessing consciousness" *is* your spiritual being.

You also become more aware of the impact of thoughts that are entertained in your mind. You begin to realize how the thoughts you engage can affect you emotionally and mentally and even physically.

As you progress in developing a witnessing consciousness, you also learn that you are able to witness but *not* "attach" to the thoughts that enter your consciousness awareness. Thoughts can be allowed to pass by like a breeze, and you do not need to attach your conscious focus to them. In doing so, you also learn that you can attach or detach from these thoughts by *conscious* awareness – which is a very critical step in spiritual liberation. They can even be consciously "dismissed".

This experience is very powerful for it is beginning to teach conscious "detachment" from thoughts, as well as the feeling which they inspire. Learning to recognize the transient or impermanent nature of thoughts and feelings is an important insight gained in our spiritual growth.

This process gently allows us to become aware that so many of our experiences are products of our subconscious or even conscious patterned thoughts and emotions. It also teaches us that we do not need to be living life as the experiential product of random or subconscious thoughts and feelings. We can become directors of them.

The reason this is so powerful is that we spend a great deal of time living under the influence of our thoughts and emotional patterns, which we have assimilated during our life or lives. They can completely control us – until we become a little more conscious of our spiritual power. We can feel blatantly powerless to them, and frankly disconnected from our spiritual power – until we "awaken".

At this point in our spiritual journey, we awaken to spiritual sovereignty. If we blindly follow our thoughts and feelings without greater consciousness – we are at the mercy of their character. As we learn to identify with our witnessing consciousness – we are starting to awaken and identify with our "spiritual core". From this position, we are able to relate to thoughts and emotions in a more conscious way. We can learn to identify, dismiss, dismantle or reconstruct thought energy at will. We can also learn to neutralize emotional energy, which is hurtful from a spiritual vista.

Beliefs and established thought forms that we have integrated into our mental and emotional energy bodies are simply highly patterned thoughts and feelings. Although it seems a bit mystical at first, they are highly subject to transformation when we awaken to our spiritual nature.

As people take on the task of self-examination, they will undoubtedly become very aware of the habitual thoughts that they harbor. One then becomes progressively aware of the more deeply buried thoughts and emotions that are present in their mental and emotional fields.

As a person encounters highly negative or limiting thoughts about themselves, other people, or, about life in general – one is able to recognize them, choose not to engage them, or consciously transform them. We can learn to "replace it" with a thought of greater potential or vibration.

As a person learns to bring this awareness into real life, or "non-meditative" moments, one can learn to live "transcendent" to the mental and emotional patterning of one's life. Thoughts arise in the mental body, and feelings in the emotional body – but you can learn to relate to them without energizing attention.

☉

Also, at this time in the journey of spiritual awakening, when the power of thought is consciously recognized, people may become essentially afraid to even think! People do not want to have "negative" thoughts and feelings – fearing they will create bad things in their life.

Please understand, it is absolutely *not* important to be perfect or afraid – it is important to become more conscious. Spiritual aspirants or people on a healing journey often struggle in this process. To suppress and deny thoughts and feelings or to be afraid of thoughts and feelings that pass through us is "silly", and perceptively self-destructive. Learning to witness thought does *not* mean suppressing or denying thoughts (or feelings). It means not to be "snared" by them!

As negative thoughts and feelings arise – you are learning to separate yourself from their power, not deny they exist. It is important to clarify that a conscious relationship to your mental and emotional experience is not the same as the act of denial. It is simply learning to manage thoughts and feelings with greater conscious attention.

Everyone has negative thoughts and feelings! If they are present in your mind – do not empower them with attention. Thoughts of judgment, worry, guilt, and general negativity may continue to arise – but you will learn to choose how to disengage from them. You can learn to be "aware" of thoughts and feelings you may not like to have – but remain "undisturbed" from a perspective that they are not "you". In progress, one will still encounter many patterned thoughts and feelings, and you will be more and more aware of the experiences. Most importantly, one can make more conscious choices from this vantage point about one's "relationship" to the experience. This begins to free us from reacting in habitual patterns so familiar to ourselves. You can learn to fill your mind with life affirming thoughts, positivity and good will.

As you grow in witnessing awareness, you can see the foibles in yourself and others with greater ease. And importantly, you learn to see them with the eyes of understanding, compassion and forgiveness. And, you see them, with the strength to transform.

Living Meditatively – Getting Down to Earth

"So how does all of this 'ideology' translate into a practical experience?" you may ask. Let us look at an example:

Imagine for a moment that you feel really defensive in response to something that someone says or does in your presence. Someone has been perceptibly offensive or has pushed "your buttons".

In the state of a conscious witness, you will recognize the defensive posturing that is arising in you, and the thoughts that arise along with it.

As a witness, the defensive attitude does not need to overtake you. Yet even if it does, you remain in a state of both experiencing the pattern and observing your reaction simultaneously. You recognize the thoughts and triggered emotions, but you remain "aware" of the event as an experience.

Recognizing the defensive posturing - you can make a choice to more *consciously respond* to the experience. Rather than reactively responding in "anger" you may remain centered and calm. You may even be able to recognize the pattern arising, but learn to communicate the experience through words. You may be able to share that you disagree or see things a little differently, without developing an extremely defensive posturing or becoming angry.

Taking it to the next level, you may begin to realize that defense is a response to an internal perception. You may begin to loosen the sense of "blaming" someone else for creating it. Regardless of how "reasonable" it may be – you recognize the experience has made *you* defensive.

You may come to understand that such defensive reactions are based on a perception of a fear, or a threat that we hold within ourselves. We sometimes say that is our "ego that is feeling threatened". The perceptibly hurtful, annoying or accusatory actions of others may be recognized for what it is; but they do not have to take over or destroy one's personal wellbeing. As we mature in spirit, it becomes rare to react to such a provocation with little other than deep compassion.

It will also begin to make sense that the person, who has "stimulated" this anger, potentially has "control" over you in some way if you allow yourself to be drawn into the experience, and are not self aware. This leaves us completely at the mercy of our own "buttons", and the people who would care to exploit them – until we do our personal work of healing.

As we become more aware of the nature of our mental and emotional bodies, we can learn to consciously relate to patterned behaviors in a more self aware way. Equally importantly, we begin to realize the power we hold to add thoughts and create belief systems that support health, wellness, peace, and any creative intent. These are thoughts we can "empower".

Eventually through conscious spiritual integration, one begins to learn that our truer nature is not defined by our thoughts and beliefs at all. We learn first hand that we are really conscious spiritual beings who have a mental body with the capacity to think and hold beliefs, which we ourselves can consciously manage. We are creative forces of life that can bring healing into any mental or emotional pattern.

This is a simple, but huge transformation to make – for up to this point in a persons journey, the programmed and patterned thoughts and beliefs we each carry are entirely in charge of our lives – like we live on "autopilot".

We begin to understand that thoughts, and even whole belief systems, can be viewed as fixed – but "transient". Belief systems can be retained as crystallized forms in the mental body. This is not a bad thing at all – these systems provide a foundational framework of experience. But when we outgrow limiting beliefs it is time to allow them to transform to allow us to grow. We can have more conscious relationship with the beliefs we carry.

We also begin to understand that the thoughts we habitually hold on to are energized. They are "fed" energy and grow in power. They vibrate throughout our energy field and can serve as organizing force of creation. As this is demystified, we can unravel patterns of belief that serve to suppress, dishonor or misappropriate energy in our lives – and, of equal importance, we can consciously utilize this ability in a very life affirming way.

So healing at the mental level will help us encounter some of the crystallized energy patterns that form part of our personalities, our beliefs systems, and what we will examine as our ego identity. It will free us up from such patterning, piece by piece, and allow us to use our mental power in a spiritually conscious way. This forms the foundation of so many strategies for self improvement in our modern self help paradigm – but an understanding of ego function, the spiritual element of our being, and the concept of self mastery of the mental function must be introduced to really grasp the power of programming and mental healing.

Tools to Support Mental Transformation

Many tools can help energetically support this release work. It is important to realize that tools do not "do" the work of consciousness – they "support" it. The human journey is one of becoming a conscious co-creator – as a spiritually realized being. This means learning to operate our mental body, and all of our bodies, with greater conscious awareness. Mentally speaking, the deep mental patterns that contribute to spiritual limitation, and various disease states, simply have to be released in order for healing to occur and to be retained.

Many tools are available to support the process of mental healing, expansion and transformation. This includes:

1. All forms of work in psychotherapy, counseling or coaching that work to raise awareness of core beliefs, heal deep personal wounds, and support our general personal development.

2. Processes such as core belief engineering, neurolinguistic programming and working with affirmations are very useful, and make positive contributions to healing the mental body.

3. We have already discussed meditation. Meditation is a process of entering into a communion with your spiritual self. There are many forms of meditation that are practiced. People may like a less structured way to practice and that is certainly okay if it suits one's temperament. Other people are attuned to more disciplined practices. I would encourage you to make time daily for sacred space and contact - in a form of meditative practice that is personally suited to you. For those who would like to learn about meditation, there are many programs which introduce and teach mediation available through many authors and publishers, spiritual organizations, and new age groups in all cities as well as online.

4. Processes that work with direct energetic stimulation of the mental body *through* the physical body also have a strong ability to release crystallized energy in our systems. This can include, for example, massage, Rolfing or deep bodywork.

Mechanical processes will often trigger the release of actual crystallized energy patterns that sometimes is referred to a "cellular memory". Wounds and congealed mental and emotional energy in one's system may be released in the mechanics of this work.

It is not uncommon that following such therapeutic interventions people may encounter the release of emotional energy, or memories and thought forms that contribute to restrictive energy posturing or illness. All therapeutic processes, including the many forms of yoga, and yoga based healing work, which have a direct effect of opening the structural energy of the body, can produce this phenomenon as well.

5. Direct energy (non physical) healing work is also an extremely powerful catalyst to promote mental transformation. Energy work may be conceptualized in very simple terms – as consciously allowing light and energy to flow into our bio-energetic system. This means light actually enters into our mental, emotional and etheric bodies.

What does light do? Light first shines and then exposes – like a burst of sunlight through the clouds or an open window in a shuttered up house – light enters a space and reveals what is there. Energetically, this light has the power to "open up" crystallized or congealed energies in any or all of the bodies. It can lift the vibratory quality of the energy embedded in the energy bodies, and even release stagnant energies.

This may sound "poetic", but it defines a real event in energy healing. It is always incredibly satisfying to see the self-awareness that develops, the release, and the deep healing that people experience when they open themselves spiritually to energy based healing. It can help "reveal" the pattern producing the energy restrictions, which burden them. Light brings conscious awareness. Through consciousness we can grow, release, heal and transform.

An example may help illustrate how "energy work" functions:

If a person has been perceptibly wounded by a person who is close to them, and they do not allow (or know how to allow) healing to occur – they may protect themselves energetically. This usually means closing down an element of the energy field. This closure will be supported by mental and emotional power. This occurs perceptibly in an effort to protect one's self and one's "vulnerable" spiritual core.

The outcome of this energetic posturing may manifest in different ways in a person's life. Imagine for example, in the setting of a relationship, a wife or husband has cheated on a spouse. This can be a very painful experience as a human being, and often leads to a deep sense of mistrust and betrayal. The partner may "shut down" energetically in response to the wound.

If the relationship dissipates, the partner may fear falling in love or getting close to another person. Mentally and emotionally, thoughts and energetic emotional defenses are created internally in the process of shutting down – to protect one's self from this eventuality. We now understand that these thoughts and energetic defenses are also actual "energetic constructs" that develop in the corresponding energy fields.

A period of healing will always be necessary following a painful event like this, but if healing does not progress – eventually the patterning in the energy field will begin to create new problems due to the posturing or the energy and the creative signature it produces. The issue is, this will limit or distort the flow of energy in one's energy system. Can you see how this transpires?

When this person presents for an energy healing session or program, the light that enters into the energy system will stir up, energize and enlighten these energy constructs. The healing energy can engage the pattern and the energy that has accumulated around its creation. This can help "clean out" the crystallized or stagnant energy - but memory of the experience, emotions related to the experience and beliefs formed around the experience may also surface in an effort to heal and restructure the energy field.

Energetic cords of attachment to the other person may need to be severed. But the thoughts and feelings that surface add an element of conscious awareness to what has occurred and what one must do to "open up" or "heal".

This is a highly simplified, perhaps overly cartoonish, demonstration of how "light" can stimulate the awareness and release of energy patterning. Yet, it is an accurate description of what occurs. Energy work can bring both conscious awareness and healing to such wounds – in a rather mystical way. In such scenarios, not just simple release – but actual conscious awareness of the patterning is very important. Why? If one does not adapt to the healing – one can simply go right back into the old pattern of energy and recreate the old energy configuration.

As issues surface there will often need to be a mechanism to explore the awareness of what is being awakened. This may involve some discussion, therapeutic sharing, journaling or psychotherapeutic counseling. This can help to clarify or add concrete awareness to the process in healing, and help in overcoming these patterned issues.

As the consciousness and insight emerges – a great release of restrictive patterning occurs. This is a liberation of sorts, one common in healing

34processes. Progressively, through such work, a state of peace and presence emerges as such issues are truly healed. Your spirit begins to shine, ever so brightly, through your thoughts, words and deeds.

☉

Any or all of these elements listed may contribute to healing of the mental body. It is important to recognize that we do not necessarily heal the mental body in one sitting or through one healing event. It is vast, and an enduring process for most people. It is simply valuable to be aware of the essence of healing, and to develop practices that utilize the power of conscious thought as a routine practice in one's life. It is also valuable to be aware of the tools or methods that may be implemented to support us as we heal.

Progressively, we come to really understand that our mental body is a functional body or vehicle, which we are responsible to operate. Your thoughts do not control you – you are capable of defining your thoughts and beliefs. You are able to relate fearlessly to thoughts and feelings that arise within you – understanding your spiritual power and responsibility to define your life experience.

This is where spiritual "wisdom" and elements of spiritual healing becomes of paramount importance in our lives. So let us journey forward in to the next level of healing – that of the spirit!

Spiritual Healing

On a level of pure spirit, it can be argued, that no one actually needs "healing". If you expose yourself to profound spiritual teachings you will inevitably be told, "you are perfect" or "you are love". And, these statements are true! So why is so much more complicated?

These statements, to our everyday level of awareness, may appear grandiose and frankly silly. The paradox is that there are different levels on which we each exist. Such statements are issued as truth from the spiritual level of your existence where they are true. Yet, frankly speaking, as a human being we do not always feel or experience ourselves as quite so loving or so perfect! Am I right ☺ ?

This is at first a puzzling issue, for we could argue that if we are already perfect, why is life not perfect, or, why do we need healing at all? Well, we are all perfect in our spiritual nature; yet, in our human nature we are limited in our ability to recognize or manifest our spiritual nature, because we are veiled in consciousness of this understanding. We are *limited* in consciousness of who we are – and hence we are living our lives at a different level of awareness than from which these statements are issued.

Spiritual healing thus implies an "awakening". As we become conscious of this essential nature, we experience an integrative process – we come to know and experience our self more and more consciously as a spiritual being. As humans we can therefore understand that each of us is involved in a process of learning, growth in consciousness, and remembering (or awakening) to our spiritual self. Spiritual healing defines this process.

Life, from this perspective, may be viewed as a *spiritual school* – one based on experience. In our efforts to learn we have experiences, we make choices, and we witness ourselves. We have successful life experiences, and we make mistakes. Mistakes, as well as successes, become lessons or opportunities to advance or grow in our spiritual awareness. This becomes particularly true when we seek or *intend* to learn and to grow in spiritual wisdom.

As an awakening being, we appreciate that we are each born with both purpose and potential. As spiritual beings we are beings of greater consciousness – and we begin to awaken to, and integrate the meaning embedded in this statement. The consciousness we express in human form is simply limited.

What creates this limitation one might ask? It is produced by an energetic veil. The veil is of spiritual design. Yet, simultaneously, it is in part created and reinforced by the energetic patterns in our mental, emotional and spiritual bodies. These patterns work to keep us in doubt and disbelief of our spiritual heritage, and enmeshed in various states of ego-laden fear. The act of spiritual awakening is often defined as piercing this veil.

Some of the energetic patterns we each carry are formulated by spirit with a specific spiritual purpose. Others are patterns we have developed or accumulated through our human experiences, or karma, through time. The journey of life, from a spiritual perspective, becomes an opportunity to take advantage of our experiences, to grow; but ultimately, this leads us to awaken to our spiritual nature. This allows us to realign our lives with our deeper spiritual nature. Through our personal connection with spiritual wisdom and power, we grow in consciousness and manifest greater healing potential.

The lessons of life are many, but can be arbitrarily grouped into two over lighting categories:

First, they may relate to overcoming issues in our lives that are spiritually founded or programmed by spiritual design. This would include such things as *karma* and *life lessons*.

Secondly, they will also involve becoming more conscious, and overcoming the fear-based ego attributes and allow love to become the foundation of our life.

Healing or integrating the ego is the great moment of spiritual development that can teach us to assimilate profound spiritual growth and bring deep healing into our emotional and mental bodies. Understanding the nature of the ego and our capacity to "transcend" it, we are brought to learn about the mastery of balance that we must achieve in our mental and emotional bodies.

Spiritual healing is therefore the process of awakening and integrating a spiritual consciousness into form. This is sometimes termed, in energetic language, as "raising our vibration". The process implies opening to our spiritual power, energy, wisdom and love. It also implies the integration of a spiritualized wisdom into all elements of our lives; with the healing it brings to these elements. This has "energetic implications" in the energy bodies we have previously examined.

Spiritual healing is essentially restitution to our truer nature and an awakening of the healing potential this creates. Healing at this level is not about fixing our spirit — it is acknowledging our spiritual nature and reality — and letting it emerge into our lives in a rich and healing way. Healing can in this way be seen as a means to overcome — what are "blockages" or "distortions" — to individual soul expression.

When the experience of life is distilled, human experience will show individually and collectively, where love is present and where love appears absent. This is the great compass on the wheel of life.

☉

On the level of spiritual healing there are a few important contributing factors that are helpful to understand. They can have implications on our healing journey.

These elements will be integrated into our life through our spiritual "set up" so that we may process them in the journey of life. These influences include:

1. Personal and family karma
2. The set up for our personal life lesson(s)
3. The influence of our spiritual history, purpose and potential through our higher self

4. The overall influence of the human ego and its limiting influence on our development.

We will explore the significance of the first three items in this chapter, and we will reserve point 4 for Chapter 10.

To do this, we will discuss a few spiritual elements of the human story that are vital to assimilate, in order to proceed in an understanding of healing in spiritual terms. First, we will look at reincarnation. It is an important concept to begin to understand life beyond the simple view of our one mysterious lifetime. This provides the foundation to be able to understand the mechanism of other important influences. We can then examine karma, grace and our "higher" spiritual nature – our higher self.

Reincarnation

To discuss "spiritual" healing, we need to remove a veil of understanding that exists for many westerners. This is an awareness of reincarnation.

Our life as we know it is an "incarnational experience", but it is does not represent the totality of who we are, nor what we have experienced as spiritual beings. Reincarnation implies that life is not a single event.

Human life on planet earth makes little to no sense, without a broader concept of life than the traditional western view. The idea that life is a random act of non-intelligent evolution, or that a soul is created and born at birth as a fresh being, and then has the potential to live eternally in only one direction if they are good, seem shortsighted.

It also does not make sense that God would make one person – to give them loving parents, every comfort, and incredible support – while exiling another to life of abuse, poverty, misery or hatred – and expect the same thing from them. What "kind of God" would that be?

We can see all the inconsistencies in life – but are told we are all "equal"! How are we equal when people are born within such a vast spectrum of privilege and suffering? Life simply has no logic or meaning unless there is a real explanation for such observations.

Life is frankly absurd, until we realize there is an order, purpose and potential – an intelligence – in the way things are designed. Life must be more complex than the simplistic view in which we are indoctrinated. The concept and conscious experience of multi-incarnational life begins to explain a lot of mysterious things.

Perhaps we are all different because of differing types of prior life development?

If a human being happens to be born with a pre-existing incredible talent – such as with music or the intelligence to develop incredible gifts for humanity through science, engineering or art – we tend to view them as gifted. They are indeed gifted and proved their gifts to humanity. Yet is it conceivable that such ability exists also because of prior experience? Imagine for example if Beethoven were "born again" today – what passion and ability he (or she) may have in music?

Furthermore, why do some people face particular challenges that have no merit or understanding on the basis of their current life. Is it karma, or a purposeful spiritual challenge? Is it part of a greater plan or design? Have they even taken on the challenge as an act of service to one's family or humanity? Perhaps.

There is reasonable logic in the concept that if a human being lives not once, but through a series of many incarnations, each person will have lived many different experiences, developed many talents, developed lessons and karma. These prior experiences would surely have an impact on one's current life. Perhaps we have each gained a great deal of wisdom through prior experiences, and also created obstacles to our own progression? They show up in our current life and form part of our overall learning and spiritual development. There is "bleed over" of influence from one lifetime to the next.

In our current life today, like many of you, I believe we are a composition of the influences from many of these past life experiences. These influences could explain many things. Personally we are each so unique in attributes and tastes, likes and dislikes, fears and "issues", and general interests. It makes great sense that these qualities are due to the "history of the soul".

It is not difficult to conceptualize that we may carry forward such talents and attributes. It is also feasible that we can create some consequences from one life to the next – and leave "unfinished business". This could show up in the form of both karma and spiritual life lessons. By virtue of this, it would have important ramifications on our personal life and spiritual journey, as well as healing endeavors.

The story however does not end with reincarnation. In emerging quantum understanding, time itself is held to be illusory – part of a construct. We do not live in the past and future – we live in an eternal now. The now is a point of probability and focus. This stimulates discussions around the likelihood of "alternate" lifetimes, which occur simultaneously in time – but we are very linear in consciousness and it is easier to think in terms of past, present and future. An interesting question is raised, if we do live a series of incarnations, becomes: "What are we moving toward?" What is the idealized goal? What is our higher potential being? Who is your future self? An intriguing question indeed!

Karma

Karma is a spiritual principle that may be understood as a universal law – the law of cause and effect. It is based on the understanding that there is right (love perceived) and wrong (fear perceived) action. In the setting of universal law, our thoughts and actions create consequences - by setting into motion a probable future experience that is defined by the nature of our present thoughts, words and actions.

If we set "bad" or "hurtful" things into motion, we must also personally endure experiences to demonstrate to us the nature of these actions. For example, if I lie or steal – I must also live an experience of the consequence of these actions to understand the nature of such choices. It is not punitive like earthly law – it is purposed to teach or to "enlighten". Karma in essence teaches about our spiritual creative responsibility.

Karma, as a principle, doesn't make much sense in the context of one lifetime. If we look at the panorama of life, it is difficult to understand why one person is happy and another suffers, why one is healthy and another ill, why good and bad things happen out of the blue during our life, why some people have great bestowments of ability or gifts, why someone may die young or old, and so on.

Karma implies there are mysterious influences in the present that arise from the past. Past actions influence the present – and present actions influence the future – so it is important to live "rightly". By living rightly we can negate past karma and create good karma for the future. But note that karma is neutral – it is not bad or good it is simply consequences of action and one determines its positivity or negativity by our own choices.

When we face certain experiences in our life today it can be valuable to understand the principle of karma. But when karma befalls us – it can also be understood to represent a moment of opportunity to realign the consequence through right response. This is where spiritual teachings have always served to help us. Kindness, patience, understanding, forgiveness, generosity … are signposts we may follow to greater self-realization.

Karma may be personal, familial and even cultural – and all of these can bare influence on us – until we learn to walk the path of personal or spiritual liberation.

As we learn through karma we rise in consciousness and we can exercise the activity of manifesting positive karma by right action, and by enduring suffering in the right attitude of learning and growing, as spiritual beings. The purpose to karma is simply to teach right living – don't lie, cheat, steal, covet, judge, dishonor, and treat people well. In short - embody love.

Karma may be considered as the fire which refines a soul. It helps a soul dismantle the mental and emotional patterning which keeps it separate from our more noble nature. As a soul processes or neutralizes its karma, it may recognize itself in the light and higher vibrational reality from which it emerges – while in the form of a human being.

Now, although karma plays an incredibly important role in our early spiritual development, if we were left to decipher and learn from our lessons it would inevitably take an infinite number of lifetimes to grow and "get it 100% right". If life ended with the concept of karma, it would be pretty safe to say that we would be on the wheel of karma for a very long time!

The role of karma is to prepare a soul to refine itself enough to awaken. At this point in time, humanity is preparing, and many are ready, to step out of the karma paradigm, into our spiritual role as sovereign co-creators with spirit. When we align our intention to grow spiritually we are supported in infinite measure to grow, to heal and to advance in the journey of awakening.

Karma loses its necessity to teach, and is released – so a soul may become a responsible co-creative force of nature! This is the concept of "dropping karma" – an experience, which is actually an incredibly important part of the shift we are living today. The spiritual response to this creative effort can be understood, in part, by a comprehension of spiritual grace.

Grace

With the advent of the "new energy" there is an incredible opportunity provided for humanity to process spiritual development a "little" more quickly – or to awaken in a catalyzed way. Humanity can achieve great progress in a very short time. Humanity has actually *created* this event – by it's collective spiritual progress. The spiritual response may be understood in terms of *grace*.

Grace, metaphorically, may be thought of as a spiritual intervention. Grace is like a gift from spirit to provide something beyond the scope of merit or karma. But remember, we too are *spiritual* beings. It is a gift that comes *through* our higher self and our relationship with a greater spiritual reality!

Grace is a divine providence to stimulate faith, progress and potential. Yet humanity as a whole has merited it – because we have *collectively* chosen, and attained a level of spiritual vibration, to support the gifts it bestows as we proceed into a new collective reality. It is a spiritual gift, but we too have created it by our growth and efforts – and by collective choice or intention.

Grace occurs in many forms as human beings. We are all given infinite blessings by "the universe" to support us in our lives. Yet, uniquely at this time, there is an incredible outpouring of grace being provided to support humanity, particularly in the realm of healing.

This grace arrives, in part, through a large-scale collective awakening knowledge of the energy structure of the human body - just as we have been discussing. It also provides support through new traditional and non-traditional techniques of healing. And, ultimately it occurs through an awakening "upshift" in our DNA.

It is important to understand that even with grace, nothing precludes our development of consciousness. If we want to grow and evolve at this juncture – it is on the basis of free will *intention*. A person must decide individually, if they want to move forward in healing. We must also each do the personal processing to understand important elements of our own unique life experience, to develop in our own spiritual potential.

To be blessed by grace does not mean we are no longer responsible for our actions in the sense of karma. As sentient beings it will always hold true that we are responsible for our actions and choices. But grace will assist us to "drop" past karma – to *facilitate* transformation into a new way of being. Making karma becomes much less attractive from this awakened stance of inner peace. We must however become conscious of our choices, our use of energy, and handling the forces of the ego. Whimsically, this supports our growth from "karma based autopilot style creation" to responsible "co creators with spirit".

As a person makes a conscious choice to move forward in this way, spiritual changes do occur within us to support our personal choice for transformation. It occurs in response to our personal sincere intention and the mechanism by which this occurs within us, is through our spiritual DNA.

Spiritual DNA

Our spiritual DNA is a mysterious energetic connection we each hold to the spiritual realm of existence. When it first presented itself to me, it was in the form of a giant cosmic helix of light. It was tangibly "connected" with my physical body and my energy field.

One way to conceptualize our spiritual DNA is that it is like a quantum-based interdimensional supercomputer – one that can store an unfathomable amount of information – and one that interfaces between the domain of spirit and our physical DNA.

The spiritual DNA governs the degree to which we have communication and energetic connection with our spiritual self. It has many functions, one being a "regulator" that controls energy, which can be shifted or transferred safely into our physical nature from the domain of spirit. If any one of us were to totally incarnate the energy of our greater spiritual nature, it would likely burn up the physical body in a zap!

Our DNA through this quantum interface provides a "wiring" – in fact a mechanism of communication between our body and our higher dimensional nature. Of course, this sounds a bit "fantastic" from our everyday level of awareness, but it is possible to conceptualize that our DNA is influenced this way from a higher dimensional perspective if we simply open our minds a little.

The interesting thing is that this connection is now being adjusted and strengthened. And the energy provided to as human beings, through this personal connection, is expanding. This is part of the mechanism to explain how we are "raising the vibration" on the planet earth. It is much easier to heal and to develop new ways of healing in this higher vibrational reality. But this connection itself is the act that greatly facilitates this spiritual development and healing potential.

Our spiritual DNA contains information. In DNA, information or programming that is important spiritually is conceptually contained in a system that is referred to as "layers" or "dimensions". For example, information that governs our "life lesson" is coded as information. Personal attributes, skill developed in prior lifetimes, and even karmic issues in our personal life and families, are coded in the spiritual DNA. This produces energetic influences that give rise to probabilities of life and experience.

Grace, as introduced above, can work through our DNA to "elevate" our vibration and lift programming that is outdated as we step into the healing paradigm we are discussing. People who engage in energy healing practices and DNA rewiring processes are experiencing this today.

Consciousness can work though our DNA system – to help us clear old patterns of energy and karma that are encoded and have influence on our life. These patterns in our DNA are "programs" that influence our personal consciousness. They produce attributes, probabilities, and in some cases patterns of illness in the mental, emotional and etheric body due to karmic restriction.

As we awaken to a greater spiritual understanding and allow this DNA expansion to occur within us, we are literally opening ourselves to this healing grace. For people keen to learn about our quantum or spiritual DNA I would again refer you to the book by Lee Carroll and Kryon.[12] You can learn to work within your energy system intentionally to promote this transformation. We will examine one way to do this in Chapter 11.

Life Lessons

The concept of life lessons is important to understand for it will have an important influence on our lives. Our life lesson, like other spiritual information, is coded in our DNA.

The easiest way to conceptualize a life lesson is to understand there exists one, or perhaps a few, very important things we hope to develop or come to understand during the present incarnation. It is probably simple to realize that there is, or perhaps a few important things, for you to master in your current life.

As a human being, we each possess attributes and a defined set up of circumstances that are particularly suited to supporting us in our unique lessons and spiritual development.

This list of lessons is vast, but if you review your life you will likely see themes that are very personal to you. Some examples of life lessons would include, trust, integrity, forgiveness, courage, finding your voice, healing and teaching, compassion, mastering a talent, parenting, or healing family karma. This names but a few, from a very long list of possibilities.

The environment we choose, the attributes we hold, the choices we make, the family we chose, and the challenges we face in our lives will support our life lesson. Life lessons are not so much karmic, but important to our spiritual development. They are opportunities to master important understandings and capabilities, because they are meaningful to your souls development.

Life lessons are often tied to our individual potential or "purpose", and are intimately tied to the spiritual healing process. As we break through barriers or pass hurdles that are important, we are able to manifest new possibilities. They are stepping stones in spiritual development.

FUTURE LIVES AND POTENTIAL

An interesting concept exposes itself in the context of reincarnation. If we have past lives, do we have future lives? And how is this all connected?

Reincarnation implies there is a state toward which we are growing as spiritual beings through incarnational efforts. What are we becoming?

If we are developing towards something - what is the idealized state as it manifests through each member of humanity? It is clear that the past can influence the present – by choices and so forth. But can the future influence the presence? Is there a calling from a future potential that guides our footsteps and our choices in this world? And, can healing in the present change the past or future?

People who engage in past life therapy sometimes are surprised to encounter not a historical lifetime but a future life! Can we conceivably see the future, and how would it influence us in the present moment?

Exploration into the quantum nature of reality potentially adds a little insight to help us understand this concept. We are told that these lifetimes are not really past or future – but in a quantum soup of probabilities. The intriguing thing to consider here given the quantum nature of reality is that we can also have a consciousness influence from an alternate realty, which can influence this "focus of time".

Just as the past can influence us – perhaps the future can affect us. An interesting concept – but fun to think about! How is the future taking you? When we understand we are a creation in constant refinement – it is perhaps through connecting with our future potential that we can "bring it into reality" in this moment.

Yet, perhaps we are not only tapping into our "future" potential – we are actually tapping into the spiritually expanded realty of who we are. This is where we discover "the higher self" who is conscious of our past, present and future. Is it possible that through its guidance that the future unfolds?

THE MISSING PILL

The Higher Self

Life isn't about finding yourself. Life is about creating yourself.

George Bernard Shaw

When we accept that we are spiritual beings, we begin to view the physical world, as an experiential realm. To paraphrase a common concept – we are not a physical being seeking a spiritual experience; we are spiritual beings having a physical experience. We can conceptualize that our soul emerges into the world from a higher consciousness.

Human beings have long lived in a limited consciousness state, seeking to experience a spiritual or divine connection. Most of humanity believes in some sort of spiritual after-life, angelic support, or a religious system of spiritual realization. In fact over 80% of North Americans believe in an afterlife. However, the step of re-identifying with oneself *as* a spiritual being is a remarkable shift in paradigm. It means you yourself are of divine origin and nature. These are no small words.

For many, these words are not easy to assimilate or digest. In fact it could appear arrogant or simply foolish to say we are "divine beings". But central to every spiritual teaching, and at the origin of any religion, is the precept that there is something greater inside of you that you can aspire to realize – or make real. The key word here is *inside*. And, the issue might be perceived that there are simply many mental and emotional obstacles, as well as a host of ego based detours that exist - which seem to be in the way of this self-realization.

Imagine if you were 100% confident in the belief that you are a spiritual being. Imagine you knew and accepted that this is – with no trace of doubt – absolutely true. What would this mean? If you knew the power of spirit lives in you as love and healing, what would you be capable of being or manifesting?

Well you are indeed a spiritual being. To make the transition from being an "un-awakened human being" to a "spirited being incarnate" implies to awaken and subsequently integrate one's truer spiritual nature and the healing potential that lay within this realization. This does not happen overnight for most of us – it arrives as a process.

"Who" or "what" is this spiritual self? As an individual, when we begin to open to the spiritual and energetic nature of reality – we are opening a doorway or portal. More than conceptual, through this aperture we have greater communication and communion with a higher vibrational aspect of ourselves, which many people refer to as our "Higher Self".

The higher self is not simply your future self – it is your *idealized* self. It is you – in the way you are made by the creator – as an aspect of that creator. It is you as a "piece" of God. It is the I AM presence within your being,

Our higher self may be viewed as our most spiritually realized nature. The higher self is more than just one's "conscience" – it is our vibratory origin – and our true self. It exists at a "higher" or "interdimensional" reality – but it is you. The higher self over lights us, and is constant rapport with us. It is aware of our souls journeys, and the state of our lives.

The higher self expresses itself through our human nature – but is potentially limited by patterning embedded within our human nature, and our free will alignment. These patterns may be understood as energetic patterns that exist in our mental, emotional and etheric bodies. However, as formed energy patterns, they contribute to our energy signature – and hence attractively manifest form expressions in ways we have discussed. The flux between form and energy at each of these energy bodies can be understood to represent the interface between matter and spirit or consciousness.

The higher self is aware of our strengths weaknesses, lessons, purpose, potential and everything about us. It knows our energy state and how to heal it. It also knows how to support us, guide us and help us thrive. The light and healing that can come forth through this aspect of our self is nothing short of miraculous.

When a human being opens in consciousness to their higher self or spiritual nature, one is opening to a reconnection with one's true, higher vibratory spiritual state. It is through the influence of this aspect of yourself that healing may be brought forward into the world of form expression.

The higher self has the capacity to "download" energy into our lower body energy systems that will support healing processes. This requires openness to this potential and sincerity in our intent to manifest healing changes. This will occur through the mechanism of our spiritual DNA and directly through our energy system as outlined.

When we invite healing assistance, the higher self can comprehend our life from a broader or greater perspective than is possible through the limitations of our current personality and state of self-awareness. It is also not limited to a single lifetime of understanding. It is like the all-knowing part of us. It sees the potentials that lay before us – but is aware of the "choice" factor we each hold with free will as a human being.

The higher self knows why we are living certain experiences whether they seem bad or good, it knows about our unique potential, it knows about our prior experiences (or past lives) and future ones too. Through our higher self we can mature in spiritual awareness and find the support to make great progress on the spiritual aspects of the journey of life. Importantly, we can also access healing.

Many people, who are interested in energy healing and the awakening consciousness in these times of transition, are what are referred to as *Old Souls*. This means that one has had a long series of life experiences – all of which are understood in your higher self nature and your spiritual evolution. The long-standing experience of life in human form is why old souls are so ready to take these monumental steps of transformation.

Appreciating the higher self is important in understanding spiritual healing. Healing is a process that is governed by the wisdom and integration of your higher self. By allowing a spiritual influence of our higher self nature into our lives, it can support the mental, emotional and etheric healing and balance so that each and every one of us may benefit from in tailored and specific ways.

We can then understand that we are conscious spiritual beings who are living purposefully on the planet. We hold the potential to truly awaken to our own spiritual nature and potential, and more deeply understand our interconnectedness with all of life on the planet, the universe and with each other.

Revisiting Spiritual Healing Through Energy

The higher self may be thought of as our spiritual self – a higher state of consciousness. And remember, consciousness governs energy.

When we discuss biospiritual integration, a conceptual way to consider energy-based healing might be to ask, "What is it that limits, blocks, forms or distorts this internal light of our higher spiritual nature from emerging in the form world? What are the potential obstructions within the various energy bodies? An equally interesting question is to ask, is if the light of one's truer spiritual nature were to shine *unencumbered* through our mental, emotional and physical/etheric bodies - how would one "be"?

Life itself is animated by a flow of spiritual light. The light that shines through each of us emerges from the deepest spiritual aspect of our self and is "processed" or "influenced" by the patterns we contain – particularly within our emotional and mental bodies. Life is energy – and we use it according to our level of consciousness and the programming we contain.

A simple analogy is to think of an old style movie projector in which the light, sourced by the projector, passes through patterns on a film to create a projected image. Our higher self may be seen as the point source of light, our "patterns" create the mental and emotional configurations, and our life is in essence "the movie"!

The fears we hold, the beliefs we carry, the thoughts we manifest or accept – are all reflected in the way the light of creation shines through us individually and collectively. When we think in these terms, we easily conceive of how the mental and emotional patterning in our energy fields and our chakra system would "qualify" the life energy that moves through us to produce the "movie" of our life.

This patterning will qualify the light, but it may also interfere or alter the light, potentially "getting in the way" of fuller spiritual expression. Such patterns, as we have reviewed, may be formed from prior wounds, ego, karma, life lessons or Higher Self development. Hence this concept is an apt illustration to discuss healing.

If there is fear based restrictive mental and emotional pattering in our bodies – we can lose sight of our soul's potential expression. Healing can be appreciated as learning to overcome such patterning and the ways it influences our human experience. Unblocking etheric, emotional and mental restrictions is this key. It is, ideally, teaching us to get in alignment with our spiritual potential. This helps us grasp how all healing is essentially spiritual in design.

◉

Earlier we introduced the ego as a fear based driving force in human consciousness. It is based on a core belief in spiritual separation - that one is separate in nature from a spiritual reality. In this state of limited awareness, one is shrouded from the reality of our spiritual origin. Before a point of spiritual awakening, one can imagine that we are divided from a more spiritual reality or "less than spiritual being" – and hence live like it is true.

When we are open to the healing influence of spiritual reality – we begin strengthening a connection with our spirit. This is not a metaphorical expression – it is a true energy and consciousness connection to a spiritual level of reality. This defines an act of illumination. The light or energy it provides will stimulate healing. It will teach us to see where fear and ego based influence is still present in our life – and help us transform issues that are personal to us.

This process will begin to reveal where spiritual resistance may persist even though we are spiritually open. It will show us, through the journey of ego integration, what within us does or does not align with love and spiritual wisdom as a way of life.

Healing at the level of spirit thus implies a willingness to overcome the ego and a willingness to take on the challenge of our personal issues and life lessons. This will mean a systematic undoing of patterns of energy in the mental and emotional nature of being that keeps us divided in consciousness from this spiritual awareness. It means developing the courage, patience, strength, kindness, tolerance, honesty, integrity, perseverance, forgiveness, and love to be in this alignment all the time.

Spiritual healing is thus really a personal reunification with our spiritual nature and the love based nature of universal life. It does not change our spiritual nature – it unfolds it. It occurs through integration with the higher self nature through energy and consciousness – a transformation that lends itself to becoming progressively more healthy and whole.

You are Not Alone

People who opt to heal or grow spiritually are supported in this endeavor by tools and the many gifts being provided to support the process of a global awakening. This implies everything from knowledge about spiritual growth and personal development, processes for emotional and mental healing, and direct energy processes which work by the mechanisms we have discussed. These energy processes span from the largely familiar hands-on-healing to some of the new quantum modalities being provided by gifted healers around the world.

Some of these new processes defy description – simply because we do not have yet the true capacity to understand them. But people who experience them, understand within their own experiences that they do indeed work. This is where Energy Medicine and Energy Psychology really enter into the modern healing paradigm.   It has been my personal experience, and the experience of millions of people, that they do work. Their success involves both a huge energy transformation in the human body as well as a huge shift in consciousness.

Energetically speaking, energy can transduce or transform – as it passes through chakras and the human energy system. As these centers become more highly functional and clear within a human being – one's consciousness of life grows profoundly. Energy from higher levels of our being can move into our bodies, into our awareness, and into our world. As we become aware first of our energetic nature and our energy bodies, and secondly of our spiritual nature as sentient beings – we can really begin to understand the flow of energy from a spiritual plane of reality into our energy system and our world. Through this we better understand our bio-spiritual continuum – and how to invoke healing in brand new ways.

As energy is transduced through layers of our energy bodies, it moves through blockages in the etheric and parallel energy systems. The energy is more accessible to provide healing and restoration to our subtle energy bodies. This energetic restoration can present in our physical bodies and lives as greater balance, health, joy and exuberant well being – or any combination of the above.

When life is better understood as a spirit-energy-form continuum, it becomes much easier to understand how spiritual growth and vibrational healing strategies have the strongly positive healing influence that so many people now report to be true. It is also easier to appreciate why certain lifestyle choices, psychological attitudes and the practice of wisdom teachings are so complementary in supporting the vibrational framework that supports healing and balance.

When a person enters into a more conscious relationship with one's spirit by intent, or by any form of an energy healing session, they are opening to the energetic support that may flow through this channel to allow a healing and restorative influence into their lives. Because this is an auspicious time on the planet, a greater window of opportunity exists for people to make a deeper connection with their own spirit. The energy that is flooding the planet is here to support this transformation. People are rapidly opening to grow in more balanced self-expression, and a greater spiritually conscious state.

By bridging our intention, with self-responsible action, we learn that we are supported in spirit to embody the peace and healing, the courage, the kindness, the joy, and the love that is our truer spiritual nature. The mask-like filters that impede this expression are slowly unraveled, as we learn to trust the spirit within ourselves to guide us and heal us from the inside out. Through this interface of spirit with matter, we are slowly and assuredly restored to our divin birthright as spiritual human beings.

So let us together take a focused look at the most challenging aspect of spiritual healing – ego integration. In this discovery we find a tool that can unravel so much of what ails us in the magical experience of being human.

CHAPTER 10
DEEP BIOSPIRITUAL TRANSFORMATION

It is wonderful how much time good people spend fighting the devil. If they would only expend the same amount of energy loving their fellow men, the devil would die in his own tracks of ennui.

Helen Keller

INTRO

We established that the term "healing" could be used to describe a very large spectrum of concepts. It can imply the simple healing of a cut, healing from a cold, healing a broken heart, or, overcoming a serious life threatening illness. It can involve the process of overcoming psycho-emotional wounds, or even beliefs.

Yet, above and beyond the consideration of specific conditions, as we are discovering together, healing can imply a more comprehensive process. It evolves into a spiritual process – a transformation by which the Higher Self aspect of our human nature awakens and tangibly integrates into our lives through our bio-energetic continuum and spiritual DNA.

Spiritual intelligence is involved in any healing, no matter how physical or how spiritual the healing involved appears. It is true, regardless of the traditional or non-traditional means used to achieve it. However, when people consciously engage in personal growth or energy-based healing, they will progressively become more aware of the spiritual construct of life.

The initiation into healing at the spiritual level may *or* may not be understood for what it actually represents, when it first occurs in a person's life. It occurs in several different ways – for different people.

Some people, for example, are "thrust" into a spiritual healing crisis by a major life event such as an illness, or a life altering accident. Others may enter through a family crisis – such as a marital breakdown, death of a family member, or dealing with addiction. In these cases healing often begins with a search for support to process or heal through the immediate experience – a healing which may be physical, psychological or both.

The quest to find healing, for many people, creates an opportunity to explore more deeply the nature of life. One begins to ask big, significant questions – about meaning, purpose or related spiritual matters. Through this opening, a person is led by the hand of spirit, toward knowledge, experience and processes, which can reveal a larger healing paradigm than the immediate event. When this happens, one is led from the immediate healing of illness or a psychological crisis - to the healing implied by deeper spiritual integration.

Other people, who are lead to spiritual development, do not live a 3D healing crisis at all. They encounter some type of experience, which simply dismantles their worldview. This may be an event such as a near death experience, a spontaneous kundalini awakening, the awakening of a special ability such as clairvoyant sight or other clairsentience, or any type of spiritually expanding experience.

This event, or series of events, also prompts a person to begin a search for answers to understand the events they are living. And this, vicariously, leads one on a journey of spiritual awakening and healing.

Finally, some people are simply drawn, by an innate drive or inspiration, to seek for greater understanding. There is no earth-shattering event – just a quiet awakening heart.

As a person crosses any of these thresholds, they are potentially being led toward a spiritual opening. When a spiritual awakening does occur, one will have the opportunity to integrate a spiritually conscious foundation into one's life. When we use the term "spiritual awakening", for some people this might imply an element of religious affiliation. But for many people - it is more of a "spiritual realization" than a "religious conversion".

Spiritual integration ultimately leads to the instillation of a wise, balanced, strong, gentle, healed, loving attitude – one that is inherent in a spiritually awakened human being. The process, however, also involves becoming more consciously aware of the elements and behaviors in our life that are "not so aligned".

This process is perhaps best termed spiritual growth rather than simply healing. However, in essence, it is *the true* healing process – for it represents the healing of the soul. It is a process of spiritual integration that has a transformative effect on both our energy and our consciousness. It can bring the strength to truly heal anything in our life as an expression of our energy and consciousness – in a powerful and unlimited way.

Through the labyrinth of this spiritual journey and awakening, we are each guided to learn of the attitude and attributes that are essential for each of us to uncover a greater healing power. This includes access not only to knowledge and energy healing processes, but also to understand the power of peace, conscious presence, and the ability to love more unconditionally in our lives – all of which are foundational to spiritually integrated life.

Through this, we come to understand, that we are all spiritual beings who are not limited or confined to pre-exiting patterns present in our mental and emotional natures. We learn the attitude of "spiritual sovereignty" that is inherent in an awakening heart. We also begin to better understand and recognize the ego's influence and the manifestation of fear based persuasions in our lives.

These precepts are not new. They fall into the domain of spiritual teaching that has been provided by many enlightened beings over time. However, they become *personal*. The spiritual drive and power to dismantle unhealthy belief systems, emotional patterns, mental patterns and social arrangements begins - so that a person can assume a sense of spiritual authority in their own life. This is an awakening of spiritual responsibility for ones health and one's experience of life.

Truth teachings in every religion point us toward this very goal. Living with integrity, kindness, honesty, wisdom, peace, generosity, non-judgment, and compassion, as examples - all become integral to our development in the healing journey. These values take on greater personal significance and meaning.

As we encounter some of our less noble traits, we begin to recognize the perceptions of fear that dwells within such behaviors. We become more and more eager to find and maintain a conscious wellness. We will inevitably face the last vestiges of ego-based behavior in our nature, which must at this time come forth for healing.

Concurrently, for many people in our modern day, this also includes developing an awareness of the energetic nature of reality, the human body and truly all of life. When we think not in terms of "behavior", but rather in terms of "energy" and our energy fields – it is easy to appreciate that ego-based behaviors and perceptions, as we will examine, are perceptibly destructive and disturbing on our energy state. This will begin to make a great deal of sense. The wisdom of these perennial teachings becomes transparent. For example hatred, judgment, hostility, worry, guilt, bigotry, shame, denial and repression are blatant forms of fear; and they have an obvious restricting or disturbing influence on our personal energy. We truly begin to grasp the deeper message hidden in the statement, "What you do to another, you do to yourself."

Life affirming and self/all loving behavior until this point is something we are *supposed* to do. When we begin to learn about our spiritual being and the energetic impact of certain behaviors, we can grasp that these spiritual attributes are something we would *choose* to do. They describe the attributes that are necessary to heal our mental and emotional bodies, and keep them healthy, unencumbered and well aligned. They become essential in the quest for health and wellbeing.

Such choice sounds simple, but to truly give up the self-destructive ways of the human ego is a dedicated de-conditioning practice! It becomes very transparent that our ego nature, when properly understood, is the big rate-limiting step in our healing and overall wellness. We will inevitably encounter the last vestiges of our ego – and at this point in one's journey it becomes very important to understand what the ego really is.

Although this step can be greatly facilitated, it cannot be bypassed or handled exclusively by an external healing process. It is a process of deep *conscious* personal inner transformation that brings one's higher self nature into the forefront of one's reality. The ego is recognized, encountered, processed and surrendered – through conscious responsible choice – step by step.

All Things Ego

The Ego

Ego is a word, understood by many different people, to represent many different things. The term ego is often used in a traditional psychological sense to represent the "functional and mediating independent self". It exists between forces of instinctual behavior and higher moral nature. This is not, however, the connotation implied when discussing the ego in context of spiritual healing.

The ego, in spiritual context, is better understood to represent a false or illusory component of our identity. The ego is not a person's true identity or true nature. It is a mask or force in human consciousness, which operates due to a limited understanding of the spiritual design of life.

The ego operates as if life has no true spiritual foundation, or a very distorted view of spiritual foundation, and, as if our true nature is simply human and unequivocally not divine.

We could conceptualize the ego as a force "manipulating or limiting" our consciousness. The ego functions exclusively in its own "separate" perception - separate from the spiritual construct of reality – and it simply fights to stay relevant or survive. The ego is not the human mind, nor our capacity to think or feel. Rather, the ego can be seen to *use* the mind and emotions – to serve its own perception of reality or existence. Yet the ego behaves as if it is really who we are.

The psycho-spiritual issue of the ego is simply that it is based entirely on a false premise. The ego is sourced in a deep fear of spiritual isolation and annihilation – because it believes it exists separate from the spiritual construct of reality and the power of love. In subversive fear of death and being eradicated, the ego creates a fearful psychology of life and existence, inspiring us to follow its fearful premises. The ego hijacks the truth and creates a twisted series of perceptions that inspire human beings to believe in it, and its vast array of contorted perceptions, rather than one's inner light and true nature.

The ego's real focus is to preserve the state of limited consciousness in which it resides. If you discover your true nature, the ego begins to dissipate in power. Yet it is the proverbial "tempter" or "wolf in sheep's clothing". So it doesn't mean it is easy! The ego is pervasive, occult, sneaky and often bypasses conscious awareness – at least until we begin to become more aware of it existence and presence in our lives.

As a person awakens spiritually, the ego is sublimated in the healing process. It will sometimes do this with a little (or a lot!) of kicking and screaming – at least in my personal experience! However, as a person works to liberate one's self from the ego framework, it does gradually lose its power. A person becomes more and more fully immersed in the light, energy and consciousness of their own spirit. The ego "dies", so the true spiritual nature of a person may be "born". This is a true archetype of being "born again" – a process that defines a true spiritual awakening. Yet, in simplest terms, it represents a *perceptual* correction.

The ego is an inherent force in every human being to some degree or another. Its influence in our lives can be both conscious and unconscious. When the ego is in operation we are not operating from the level of consciousness that our higher self nature would provide, and this has perceptual consequences.

The foundation of this correction can be expressed in the idea that in our very core nature, every human soul is founded in love. In all ways that we do not create or honor love in our world, or our lives, you can be sure the ego is in action. The world we see at this time on the planet is based on this ego structure in so many forms and activities. Hence it becomes necessary that people in a healing process become more aware of its presence, nature and ways – or you stay enmeshed in the ego's grip.

Piercing The Veil

Perhaps, the most straightforward way to really begin to grasp the nature of the ego, is to begin to understand what it is not. Simply speaking, the ego is not love.

If you were to image yourself as a highly evolved spiritual being, what would you envision yourself to be. Peaceful? Tolerant? Wise? Strong? Joyful? Kind? Honest? Inspiring? Playful? Balanced? Loving to self? Loving to others?

These attributes would obviously well describe someone who achieved a degree of spiritual attainment or healing. These attributes are a fundamental part of our truest nature as human beings, when we have achieved a strong degree of spiritual integration.

When can ask the question: "What gets in the way of a person's ability to manifest the above attributes?"

The answer, as we will explore, is always some primal fear. None of the above attributes listed manifest readily in a person who is fearful, or who perceives the world through a fearful perspective. It is only in a state of peace and spiritual fearlessness that these attributes become possible. Fear in its many forms creates a veil to this truer perception of our nature. And it is sneaky!

Fear is manifested through attributes that define the ego's nature. Behaviors such as judgment, hatred, worry, shame, guilt, pride, defense, and anger all manifest in response to fear based perceptions.

THE MISSING PILL

Why do we judge? Why do we hate? Why do we puff ourselves up? Why do we get angry? If we probe deeply into these situations there will always be an underlying perception of fear at the root of these behaviors. If we understand the fear embedded in these attributes, we can begin to see the ego in action – and unravel its control.

Unequivocally, it is true, that you are a spiritual being who has journeyed to the earth. It is important to grasp that it does not matter whether a person believes in a spiritual reality or not – they are still a spiritual being. No exceptions. That does not imply however that everyone chooses to manifest his or her best spiritual nature – consciously or unconsciously. And it does not imply we remember this at all times.

If we *really* understood ourselves – it would be impossibly difficult to play the games that the ego likes to play. In a state of unconscious forgetfulness, however, one can easily get caught up in illusory states of experience that are fear founded. One does, however, always retain some of the qualities of this spiritual nature.

Look around you and within your own story. You will see a great deal of love, compassion, good will and kindness in our human nature. Yet in many ways, one can lose trust, faith and belief in a deeper truth and power, because of fear and its perceptions. One can indeed live as if one is divided and non-reliant on our spiritual nature and design.

As long as one lives enmeshed in an ego perception of reality, we cultivate a false reality in which we are ensnared. In this state of limited awareness, we too are capable of great fear and its many creations. We can manifest an endless array of anxieties, judgments, doubts and worries. We are also capable of very dark and hateful thoughts and feelings, even life extinguishing thoughts and feelings, which surface because of our "spiritual ignorance".

As we mature in spirit, we come to understand that no matter what appears in the world of form, it does not show the reality of a human being or human nature – unless what we are seeing is based in love. This sounds somewhat utopian or unrealistic to the ego because it cannot grasp any understanding outside of its own nature. Yet – *you* – can come to accept that it is true.

The ego is understood to represent any thought, feeling, action or perception that is not based in love inclusive consciousness. When we grasp the profundity of this statement, we realize how much of the world we know is based on ego detail. And remember, what isn't love, isn't real. As far as spirit is concerned – it doesn't even "exist"!

Yet to us as manifest human beings, it does perceptually exist, and we must learn to relate to it in a healing and transformative way.

Profound wisdom teachings have always introduced us to the power of this healing. "Turn the other cheek" and "Be in the world but not of the world" are statements that guide us in this orientation. As one learns to practice forgiveness, exhibit strength, kindness and understanding toward the deluded ego's manifestation – one finds indeed, the key to the heart. The perennial wisdom that has been taught over and over again reveals itself as true. You are love.

Love And Fear

It is often said by spiritual teachers, and recorded in innumerable scriptures, that the whole fabric of creation is based on love. In fact, it is reported that God *is* love. This may be difficult to accept, as a human being who witnesses a world that appears filled with not only loving expressions of life, but also chaos and destruction all around us. How do we reconcile this conflict?

The hatred, chaos and destruction that exist in the world are not to be confused with "God's intention". The earth may be understood as a school of free will where human beings get to choose the way they will participate. The challenge is, as a human being, we do not have all the information we need to understand. We can see the world around us as "reality" but it is not "reality" – it is a simple projection of human creation. It is primal life force qualified by human intention.

Human beings are shielded from the whole understanding of the nature of life. We must aspire to learn about it, or through experience have it revealed. The world we see – full of things like sickness, poverty, lack, or racism – is not a creation of spiritual intention in its purest form. It is a creation of universal energy; manifested through humanity, partly because it has forgotten or is unaware of its spiritual nature and heritage.

From a spiritual perspective – the loveless creations found in the world are made through the human ego. The ego, believing it exists independent of spirit, is a false player. It therefore is not "real" – it is an illusion. And, it creates an illusory world.

It is in this gap that we better understand the nature of the human ego. If humanity as a whole retained consciousness of its true nature, while existing in human form, we would not be creating the world as we see it today. It is only in a state of forgetfulness that the ego is capable of doing its tragic-magic.

Love is the foundation of reality, it is the way of spirit, and it is the way of humanity when it is not distorted by ego-based lack of consciousness. Anything within us that is founded in fear or distorted by fear is essentially false when seen from our truest nature. There is only love in truth, and when we surrender our ego nature, it is what remains of us. Fear, in the form of the ego, simply veils us from our true nature. FEAR is even sometimes noted to be an acronym for the phrase *False Evidence Appearing Real*.

Everything within us, based on fear, is potentially a source of energetic distortion and disease. Even disease can be viewed to exist in this domain of ego making. Many diseases arise from the impact of energies on the human bioenergetics system – and the ego is a key player in making this so. It can however, be transformed through an open heart.

One of the wisest and most direct courses of instruction that has been provided, to teach the "western mind" about the nature of the ego, is a program entitled *A Course in Miracles (ACIM)*.[43]

The program teaches us that there are basically these two primal forces governing human life – fear and love.

Fear opposes love. But love, unlike fear, has no opposite. Fear rebukes love. But love, is capable of including fear in its embrace. If one could instantaneously internalize and assimilate this wisdom – one's spiritual healing would be done. But alas ... it requires a little more work than that for many of us.

From the introduction to ACIM:

> *This is A Course in Miracles. It is a required course. Only the time you take is voluntary. Free will does not mean that you can establish the curriculum. It means only that you can elect what you want to take at a given time. The course does not aim at teaching the meaning of love, for that is beyond what can be taught. It does aim, however, at removing the blocks to the awareness of loves presence, which is your natural inheritance.*
>
> *The opposite of love is fear, but what is all-encompassing can have no opposite. Nothing real can be threatened. Nothing unreal exists. Herein lies the peace of God.*

When we examine our lives, we are aware of many influences that contribute to healing. Time, medicines, natural remedies and conventional remedies of all types are known to help provide healing – but we are told again and again that the greatest of healers is love.

From a spiritual perspective, love is the foundational nature of life and creation. This is expressed in many ways. "God is love." "Love heals all wounds." "Love is the nature of reality." "All things that are enduring spring from love." "When all else passes, only love remains."

What do statements like these really mean? Not everything we create as human beings is based in love. Hardly news right! Human beings are capable of incredible hatred and provoking incredible suffering. We begin to understand that it is through the perceptual nature of the ego that this arises. The spiritual work of life is in our personal realignment – toward love-based existence.

The struggle of good over evil is paramount in importance when we look at any great story in life. Yet when it comes to deep spiritual healing it is not a struggle of good and evil that takes place – it is an integration or an adjustment in perception towards only that which is "real" in spiritual terms. The rest is left to fall away.

Every spiritual sage who has lived on the planet has attested that humanity is capable of a much greater potential than what history reveals. And we each know this fundamentally, within the core of our own being, to be true. Yet, in order to arrive at this elevated existence, humanity must rediscover its own true nature. Yet, this occurs one person at a time.

In context of our discussion, this simply means that a human being must learn to surrender the human ego through the power of grace, and empowered awakening. True spiritual teaching has provided "a recipe" to help each member of humanity live according to the directive of a love-based consciousness. It is not represented by a fire and brimstone theology – it is the story of the emergence of our deepest spiritual being, and its desire to empower our lives through the magic of our journey. It is destined to reunite humanity with the oneness of itself, and its oneness with all life – nature, the planet and the universe.

Yet again, these are special times. The ability to overcome the fear based ego and release our personal and planetary "karma" through grace inspired awakening is here and available. The time to learn to live as self-responsible, love inspired, conscious co-creators is upon us.

This simple understanding vicariously exposes a few very important ideas:

1. Humanity is not universally aware of its spiritual nature and potential.

2. It is possible to realize this, and make a personal effort to live in a more conscious, empowered and loving way.

3. Doing so creates an important healing on both an individual level and a collective level – but it is only through the healing of *individuals* that this occurs.

So what is this loving way? Is "to love", simply "not to hate"? The idea of *hate* as the opposite of *love* is an incomplete idea. We can do many non-loving things to our selves, to others, to animals and the natural planet – without expressing frank hatred. Hatred, as a concept, does not really encapsulate the spectrum of non-loving manifestation.

The opposition to love is really better understood as *fear*. Hatred, and any of the non-loving (separation based) behaviors we manifest, can be seen through a distortion of fear in some way. In addition to hate, there are many other forms of fear.

Fear may be understood as the aspect of human consciousness that does not understand the universal, interconnected nature of life and energy. Fear is the patron of the ego. It believes life can be destroyed or extinguished because it exists apart from the source from which it arises. Fear blocks, distorts and/or suppresses the expression of light and energy.

Although this later statement may appear metaphoric, when we understand the workings of the human energy system – it is an actuality. Consciousness controls energy. Fear and love interact with, and ultimately greatly influence, the human energy bodies.

As a simple exercise, pay attention to what happens when you become afraid. You stop breathing, or breathe in a shallow fashion. You "pull in" your energy. You "elevate" your defenses. You "pull away", or get "defensive" or "aggressive". In such responses, one is simply reacting from a fear-based point of view. Yet, importantly, your energy bodies are implicated in every one of these activities.

What happens when you are angry, worried or judging yourself? Just pay attention to your energetic posturing as you concentrate on each of these potentials, and reflect on what it reveals.

Now pay attention to how your energy is influenced when you are safe, peaceful, relaxed, inspired, or simply being kind. Again, just pay attention to your energetic posture and each of your energy bodies in each of these states of being. This reflection provides a key to understanding why ego integration is so critical to healing success.

Fear stems from the primal belief in separation of our human consciousness and our human experience, from our spiritual nature. It has the consequence of suppressing or deforming our energy expression – through its influence on our energy bodies.

Fear is however far reaching in its power and implications. We have to learn how fear shows up in practical ways, and also to recognize, honor and integrate our spiritual nature to overcome fear. It is at this juncture that energetic healing becomes undeniably spiritual in quality.

Fear is very powerful force that can manipulate human consciousness into many behaviors. To overcome such fear based reality is the cornerstone of spiritualized existence. To achieve this, it is essential to learn to live in ways where our energy is open and free – and able to permit healing into the deeper wounds in our lives.

Let us take a deeper look at some "real" life attributes of the ego to understand its nature. This will also expose its "energetic" influence. Ultimately it will lead us to appreciate both the value and process to transform fear based tendencies – to help us progress on the path of healing.

Ego in Action

In our truest nature, we are wise, loving, peaceful and joyful beings. Anything that takes us out of this state of being will reveal itself to be an activity of the ego. To explore what actually takes us out of this level of self-awareness, we need a compass.

The question to ask becomes, "What are some of the things we do that destroys the peace of our spiritual nature?" As we will see, the attribute of peace becomes a great barometer of how deeply we are ego enmeshed, at a moment in time.

Well let's see. We judge. We blame. We get angry. We shame. We worry. We impose guilt. We are defensive to condemnation. We are arrogant. We fill with pride and self-importance. We deny. We can engage in a vast array of activities - that are simply "tricks" of ego consciousness to keep us from greater "self" realization.

None of the activities or attributes listed above is truly a loving quality. Nor, in general, do they represent a human being's truest nature. But importantly, they are also states of existence that preclude the presence of peace. We are so familiar with them, in many ways we "assume them" to be in our human nature. Perhaps in some ways they are – but they are founded on a shortsighted level of consciousness. If we look a little deeper they are ego behaviors that originate in the belief of a "separate" human existence from a greater spiritual reality. They separate us as human beings, in perception, from the great web of life.

Let's examine an illustration of the ego in action:

Imagine you are driving down the street one-day, and someone cuts you off and causes you to brake your car. You start to get very close to the car in front of you, and have to pull to the side of the road to avoid hitting the vehicle.

You are startled, and upset. As the shock settles, you realize that no one is hurt – but you have to process the experience. Take a moment and imagine how you would personally react.

Let us look at this same experience through the eyes of ego and then through the eyes of spirit.

Through ego perception, one would likely be upset that the other driver cut you off. You might become angry and call the other driver some derogatory name. You might curse or swear. You might judge the other driver's ability to operate a vehicle. You may say how you were wronged, and perhaps how well you responded to the crisis. If you have an encounter with the other driver, and you may have the chance to share all of your views with him or her in an inflammatory conversation. Later that day you might tell someone else all about the event – perhaps even a little embellished by the further thoughts and feelings that subsequently transpired.

Now just stop – and pay attention – what happens to you energetically through such an encounter? What do all of these thoughts and feelings create inside of you?

Would you be shocked to know that this whole reaction, although it is very "understandable" as a human being, is totally ego-based? And, more importantly, all of the mental and emotional activity invoked through this ego state, is temporarily quite disturbing to your energy system.

Do you blame the other person for these thoughts and feelings, or do you own them as self created? How does blaming *feel*? To what have you surrendered *your* peace, personal power, and alignment? Is it *truly* worth it?

Eventually people who do react in a strongly ego oriented way, are likely to let go of the experience – by letting go of the thoughts and emotional energy. Some will do this quickly and others slowly. As the experience dissipates, one's energy is restored to a more balanced state. Importantly however, it can, at any moment, be re-created with a simple reminder – and you can live it all again. Yet, eventually, it will fade away, and the energy of one's system will be restored to balance.

Imagine however, if we do not "let go" of such an experience. What then happens? Well, it remains stored as an energy pattern in our overall system and is subject to reactivation at any time. If a person lives many such experiences which are imbued in the energy field – and they build up an energy formation – one can develop a certain "posturing".

Do you know anyone who is "angry" most of the time? How about "defensive"? Do you know anyone who "worries" or is "anxious" all the time? How about "arrogant"? It is easy to see how the ego can infiltrate our minds and emotions and become so routine to us that we think it is our personal nature or personality. If we try to make excuses for how we react, that too is ego. Yet, ironically, as much as we are each capable of any of these attributes, they do not define anyone's true nature. And this is true, even if we believe they do!

How often do you hear people say things like: "I am just a worrier." Or, "That is just my personality." Holding on to the influence of such activity is actually very disturbing to one's health and wellness – by virtue of its influence on our energy fields. This is an essential concept to grasp.

◉

Okay, let us revisit the experience through a "non ego-based" perception. Through spiritual eyes, we might handle this experience very differently.

People sometimes ask the question, "What would Jesus do?" or "What would Buddha do?" Whimsical as it is – it is a great question! They would likely handle this situation and many things in life, a little differently than the way we witness things happen in our everyday world.

A person who is more "integrated" would likely experience a little shock or surprise by the event - but they would likely hold themselves together. They might realize first they are not injured and no one else was injured either. They would recognize the danger in what had occurred, but be most aware of the safety afforded them in the experience.

They might spontaneously wonder what is happening in the life of the other driver to have them behave so erratically. They would not be inspired to attack or condemn them. They would harbor no angst or hostility toward the other person – even if they have acted tremendously irresponsibly.

They would not likely be inspired to share the story, unless perhaps it was to share a story of how a mystical source of protection has operated in their life to inspire faith in another person. Peace would be retained.

As idyllic as this may all sound, it is obvious that the influence of an *external* experience holds much less power to affect this person's internal alignment. A person, as such, is living from a state of internal self-awareness and conscious "energy management". One is choosing to live and react in a way that is spiritually conscious.

This provides a glimpse of what is required to maintain energy composure and not surrender to the ego based tendencies in one's life. The term "personal empowerment" is often used in self-help or spiritual literature, and although there is some confusion around what it means spiritually, it is really describing this power to live from a spiritually conscious perspective. Are you ready for this kind of responsibility? This is how valuable your peace has to become to you when you are challenged by life, the ego in yourself, or the ego in another being.

The Point of Power

We can see that if we are to live in the nature of our spirit, there is a huge shift in awareness, or "perception", that will take place for many people.

Frankly, the ego will not want to do this – and the spirit within us will. It can create a tension, and in the day-to-day events of our lives we will need to consciously align one way or the other.

To do this, we have to become more aware of what the ego is and what it is doing. We also have to become aware of our spiritual nature. We have to recognize the potential it provides us to manage our energy responsibly, in such a way that greater balance is available to us.

The ego-based attributes will bring one into struggle, conflict, negativity, righteous superiority, blame, judgment and so on. Consequentially, one will become very "twisted up" in one's energy fields by this choice. If one follows the attitude of spirit, it will undo these tendencies ... and it will always lead one back to peace.

We come to understand that we are constantly in a state of choice between spirit and ego. One can be at peace, or, one can be in ego – but one can not do both simultaneously. It is at this point, *the point of power*, where we learn that we can choose.

To choose a spiritual posturing can be made to look silly, weak, stupid or ridiculous to the eyes of the ego. Yet it is hardly weak. It takes great spiritual strength and courage to do this – for one is overcoming strong tendencies embedded in one's own personal energy, as well as the ego pressure from the external world.

When we reflect again on healing it is useful to ponder:

Where will the ego lead you and what impact will this have on your mind, your emotional body and ultimately your etheric and physical body?

Where will your spirit lead you and what impact will this have on your mind, your emotional body and ultimately your etheric and physical body?

It becomes more obvious why ego integration is so important in overall healing – particularly when we begin to think in terms of the "human energy system".

The Shape Shifting Ego

As we explore the core attitudes of ego based posturing it becomes more obvious how pervasive and nebulous the ego can be. The ego also has an ability to shift from one quality or attribute into another – in a very sneaky way. Blame shifts to anger, anger to judgment, judgment to defense. It becomes a merry-go-round of suffering – and not so "merry" at all!

Earlier we discussed how thought is a vibrational force that functions like sound – and can pattern energy. Similarly, thoughts create energy patterns in our energy body. As focus is applied to these thoughts, they are further energized.

As thoughts are energized, they grow in power, and they vibrate. This mental energy stimulates the emotional body to react in kind. In the emotional vibration that is created, the mind can be influenced and the pattern shifts to another thought. Then new feelings arise. This can very quickly build up into quite a psycho-emotional state. This cycle will continue until something happens to break the sequence of events – or a new event distracts the ego's focus.

In this cycle, the sequence of thought might go something like this:

"Oh, that person is so annoying. (Judgment). "Oh, I shouldn't be so judgmental." (Guilt) "Oh I am not really judging, just observing in this case." (Defense) "And, they should know better." (Defense again) Yeah, but I am the one judging – I can be so stupid. (Blame and Judgment).

The ego's influence can slip from one attribute into another attribute - to hold attention. The ego slips from righteous to victim, external to internal, all in effort to keep itself relevant. Meanwhile, because we are "not at home", the ego is using the mental and emotional body to its own avail, but at our expense. Yet we are subject to the vibrational reality!

We will discover that we surrender our ego, or, we surrender our peace. There is not much in between – in fact they are "worlds" apart!

Projection and Triggers

Deeply embedded beliefs and wounds serve as trigger points for the ego. When we personally hold certain thought forms in our energy field – arising from prior conditioning, experiences or traumas – they are quite easily triggered by any perception of fear that we encounter in our lives. This is a mechanism that explains how something may evoke or "trigger" certain reactions.

The magnitude, and sometimes even the presence of such a reaction, does not make sense in the context of what is happening in the moment. The reactions could be either positive or negative – and sometimes lead to psychological "projection".

Here is an example, which I can share from my own life experience, to help illustrate: When I tell someone I am a physician – people will have variable responses depending on their prior conditioning.

If people hold being a physician in a high regard – they will view it as honorable or impressive. If they have had negative experiences in their personal health care or the institution of medicine – it will trigger a negative reaction. But – I will be looped into their perception.

If they "hate" doctors – they will hate me. If they "admire" doctors – they will admire me. I have nothing to do with either of these responses really – these are triggered reactions from a pre-established view or belief.

Conditioning we each carry will have a strong ability to create triggered experiences where the ego could fly into action. We have to become very self-aware and learn how to step out of the ego's framework when we find ourselves enmeshed or triggered by events in our lives.

If it were all as innocuous as such perceptions life would be easy – but alas it is not always so simple, and can get a little messy …

DR JOHN G RYAN MD

IT CAN GET REALLY UGLY ... BUT STILL

Now we have looked at some relatively simple and straightforward examples to see the ego in action. But the ego is also capable of being quite sinister and outright hateful when in full swing.

Racism, violent attacks on innocent people, torture, ethnic cleansing, and environmental assault – the list of horrific human actions that we can trace back to fearful and dis-spirited living can be very long! All of these hold ego-based perceptions in common. The ignorance at the foundation of such activity, which propels people to justify these behaviors, can certainly be disheartening to an awakening being.

When human beings are exposed to such devastating things, the healing to overcome the damage may be deep and intense to get to a place of ego transcendence. When it affects us personally, this may require incredible patience, support, love and compassion on many levels to process, heal and thrive.

However, the paradox or challenge that lies in the ego and its foundational wounds - is this. No matter how we have been hurt, mistreated, judged or neglected in our lives – we are still ultimately energetically responsible for *our* life. We are responsible for how we manage our own energy – an activity that requires great consciousness. We are also always responsible for what we do within ourselves, and what we do to others – energetically and in behaviors – regardless of past events. This is why it is so important to grow in consciousness, and to heal all wounds, old and new.

Remember, the way you think, feel and act influences your "energy signature" always. You lower your overall vibration if you act in ego based ways. This is devitalizing to your energy state. You act in ego; you hurt yourself. You respond in ego, you hurt yourself. You follow your spirit; you change your energy. Healing brings freedom from the ego – the freedom to live in the truer balanced, healthy, peace-filled nature of the spiritual self.

GETTING ACQUAINTED

Let us take a closer look at the common attributes of the ego. These are the disempowering fear based behaviors that pull a person out of peace, the core alignment of our spiritual nature.

The list includes judgment, defense, worry, guilt, shame, pride, denial and fear itself in nebulous ways. Let us examine them one by one.

Guilt is a great force in human life, used mostly to control. The only real value of guilt is to be aware in our lives when we have done something hurtful to ourselves or to another person - to begin the process of correction or restitution. But guilt is used pervasively by the ego; both within our own thinking, and in the way we try to manipulate each other.

Parents, children, bosses, friends, lovers, and co-workers, in trying to manipulate each other, often use guilt. Guilt can also be used internally to manipulate the choices we are making or not making. We make ourselves feel guilty through the guise of the ego – for things we do or don't do.

Guilt is a deeply indoctrinated force in our cultures, our religions and society. But guilt is neither the way of love, nor our true spiritual nature.

The ego protests to this understanding are many, and highly logical – but they are shortsighted. The ego would attest that without guilt people would not "behave". One might not be responsible in one's jobs, or do what is expected as a family member, or partner – as some examples.

Well, if you want to stay embedded in the ego this is all very reasonable – but if you want to heal you must begin to leave guilt behind. To live aligned with our spiritual nature, one must become self-responsible in one's attitude. One must learn to not be influenced or manipulated by guilt, not to use it on others, and not to use it on one's self. Guilt as a form of manipulation, through greater conscious awareness, has to be transcended. One must release the attitude that we are not making conscious choices in our lives.

By learning to be more aware of guilt, we can learn that if we are acting on guilt, we need to stop and align ourselves. If we are being propelled by guilt to do something – we need to give ourselves permission to evaluate the choice. If we really do not want to do something – we need to give ourselves permission to say no. If we choose to do something, we need to take responsibility for the choice and live it whole-heartedly. It is incredibly devitalizing to do something in a victimized and guilt-ridden attitude, and it simply creates a lot of problems and disease.

Guilt is also used to suppress our spirit. People often live under the veil of guilt for a great portion of their life. This often occurs due to mistakes that were made, and experiences that were naïve or hurtful. To live in guilt is an extremely devitalizing state. If mistakes are made in our lives, there will need to be forgiveness and atonement, which we will examine shortly – but to stay in guilt is an ego state of existence, and this will need healing attention.

Worry is a great companion of guilt. To worry is to conjure up thoughts and feelings that there is loss of control, or focus on the perceivably bad things that may happen, and the fear it induces. Remember that one's energy will follow one's attention. If we are using our energy or channeling it into worry, we are not only wasting or misappropriating energy, but also sometimes even creating the focus of our energetic attention. By focusing on our worries, we are energizing and potentially manifesting them – or bringing our worries "to life"! What spiritual avatar ever taught – go forth and worry!

You can worry all you want, or learn to be at peace – but you will never be able to do both simultaneously. You have to give up one to know the other. We will see shortly that to align with peace or to align with any ego attribute is a choice we constantly have to make. It is a theme – and a key to healing.

If you have a propensity to worry, what would your life look like if you relinquished worry? Would it fall apart? Would you become irresponsible? Would you not be a loving person? Would you not take care of your family?

The ego will often attest to the value of worry, and justify it as a state or attribute that is "normal". "To worry is normal as a parent" is a common example. You see, it is not really worrying that makes you a good parent – it is your ability to love wisely.

To worry is an attribute of ego – for it takes you away from your essential nature. To overcome worry, we are learning to have faith in the spiritual design of life and trust in the universe as a supportive and loving place. We learn to rely on our intuition and wisdom to make good choices or create safety – but not use worry as a propellant. To align with our spiritual self, we will learn to relinquish worry, but this will require practice for many of us.

Worry takes credit for things, which do not belong to its merit. It is not the act of worry that makes anything better in our lives, or in the lives of those we love. To act supportively, to encourage, to share or teach, to listen and accept situations as they occur in life while responding wisely - will have value. To do something for ourselves, or others – because it is important or of conscious value – is honorable. But worry – it is never the action that makes life better. Worrying simply energizes negative thought forms and energy.

When you begin to understand the energetic nature of your bodies, it is easy to appreciate that worrying involves the process of thinking. Thoughts are energy structures that are created in your energy field. If you are filled with thoughts of worry – do you believe this is a healthy state? Of course not. How about the influence on the emotional body? Healthy? Of course not! And the greater challenge is that these thoughts and feelings contribute to a creative energy state – and they actually support creating the outcome on which the worry is focused.

To overcome worry implies learning to let it go, but it also implies the development of faith and trust. We gently acquire great faith in spirit, and trust in the process of life. We develop greater detachment of outcome in the journey of healing – and by letting go we learn to flow in the river of life. You begin to accept that as you play your part, you can have faith in the highest appropriate outcome. To worry is simply to have little faith in spirit – and little faith in your own spiritual power. When faith and trust are absent – we are disempowered, energetically speaking.

Worry is a doorway through which fear enters and makes itself at home in our lives. Close it, and be at peace. And, let's not worry about it anymore! Let's move onward ... to defense.

To understand *defense* as an ego attribute, it is helpful to first understand the strength of true spiritual alignment.

When we are falsely accused, for example, there is often a great urge to defend ourselves to protect our integrity. Our defense here is to protect a perception of honor or reputation.

If we are rightly accused of something, but do not want to hear about it – we can also propagate a defensive attitude. We do this in an effort to deny or hide from the accusation. Our defense here is to "spin" a story or to "conceal" something, in order to maintain face.

This is not how the higher self would deal with things that occur in our lives. The higher self understands the energy distortions produced in our mental and emotional bodies by this defensive ego activity.

In a state of spiritual alignment you may or may not choose to correct a misperception, but you will refuse to enter into a struggle with the ego-based perception of the other person. If you have done something wrong or hurtful, it is an opportunity to "come clean". If there is nothing to confess or take responsibility for, you will remain at peace – despite the ego challenge.

If someone is hurtful or foolish, or convinced of some maliciousness in your nature, and feels the need to attack or accuse you of something – it is hard at first not to act defensively. But to act defensively is to take as "real" the illusion of the ego attack. To overcome this – one must stay centered in spirit and "see through" the ego-based attack and illusion.

The ego of course will object to this notion of defenselessness, call it weak, and declare that you must stand up and defend yourself. As difficult as it might be to imagine, this is not true of our spiritual nature – which will overlook such ego-laden nonsense.

For each of us, it is helpful to consciously understand what happens when we become defensive. Think of a time in your life when someone accused you of something or blamed you for something. Reflect on the immediate reaction that occurred in your "energy posture". Did you become "defensive"? Compare this a time in your life when you did not react defensively to an accusation. Again pay attention your energy posture. It is a very different experience, when you peacefully accept the truth in you.

The point in this example is first to understand the difference in outcomes. Secondly, it is to awaken an understanding of the concept that you always get to "choose" how you react. If you choose "wisely", which implies a surrender of your own ego-based reaction, the outcome is very different – for you.

As you learn to step out of ego based programming, you will proceed to discover that it is exhausting to hold up defensive posturing and totally devitalizing to your energy system.

The spirit sees through ego in us, and in each other. When you "see", you can choose wisely. This wisdom forms the foundation to understand the famous teaching – "you must turn the other cheek". To turn the other cheek is the act of seeing through an ego attack with wisdom, compassion and understanding – and not getting caught in the drama that it is trying to evoke.

Denial is another ego attribute that keeps the light of ones spirit from shining brightly. Perhaps we are confronted with an experience that is hard to digest or accept? Maybe we receive an insight into something that is part of our mental and emotional programming that we don't "like"? Maybe we are brought to an awareness of something we have done that is hurtful, but we refuse to see it or accept it? These are some scenarios where we may be in "denial". Denial is strategy of fear and the ego will always want to hide and conceal its nature. We have all experienced denial in our lives. Right? Don't deny it ☺!

Denial is encountered in the simplest events of our lives when we do not want to come to terms with the nature of an aspect of our lives. It is also really well appreciated in context of deeper patterns of behavior with which we are familiar such as addictions, self repression, patterns of irresponsibility, martyrdom, and passive aggressive behavior – to name a few.

The higher self within us is not afraid to look at our experience. It is present to evaluate and to help bring healing in ways we have been actively hurtful or repressively neglectful towards ourselves or towards other in our lives. The ego will not want to do this, of course – and it aims to control its upper hand through this repression, denial and sometimes attack.

A good example of denial lies in the familiar pattern of "enabling" another person in the setting of an addiction. This is common in an environment of alcoholism, when a spouse or family member may try to mask the severity of problem, to avoid conflict. It may involve covering up the problem to other members of the family or community, or making choices that look kind and supportive - but essentially allow a person to cover up the severity of the problem.

When you look deeply into this behavior, there are many issues and fears that are part of the scenario. However, at its core – this behavior is a form of denial. Until the issue is addressed in an open way – the denial actually supports the disease, rather than healing.

Spiritual growth requires an attitude of openness. It requires a willingness – to bring to light anything we encounter in ourselves and in our experiences, so that we may correct or realign elements in our life based on developing insight. Every human being has said and done things in their life, which they learn were hurtful to themselves or to others. And everyone has at times repressed or denied what is authentic within themself. To deny is to repress healing. It is much better to be open within yourself, to learn from your mistakes, be free to be "imperfectly perfect", and grow.

Judgment is a pervasive attribute in our modern world. TV and social activity is full of judgment in so many ways. To the ego, judgment is a way to be relevant. But what really becomes relevant in this action? You see, to judge, is to completely misunderstand life.

From a spiritual perspective, when we judge, we are examining the world blindly. We are imposing a mental energy on someone or something that we do not completely understand. By doing this one is separating one's self from something or someone perceptually. If we judge our self, we are again separating – this time ego from our "spirit".

Judgment and discernment are often confused. Discernment is an intrapersonal awareness with no sense of judgment toward someone, something, or some event. Discernment allows us to understand our own relationship with people and things around us. It is an inner awareness about things that helps us decide what is right or appropriate within us. It is a tool of insight.

Judgment involves imposing or projecting an opinion, a self-imposed value, or ridicule on an other human being for something one doesn't like, agree with or understand. It often stems from ingrained beliefs, fears or from wounds that one carries in their own make-up. Insecurity, fear of being judged or ridiculed, playing "superior" to hide our inner "inferior" self-perceptions of weakness and worth — are all ego motivations from which one tends to judge.

When we judge, we are declaring a relationship with something we perceive as external to ourselves. As we explore the nature of spiritual reality, we recognize the separation is an illusion. In reality, more than defining someone or something — we are actually defining our own relationship with life. It is a statement that says, "I am totally in my ego when I look at you!" No matter how we dress it up with intellect or words, we are expressing our own fear and insecurity through the judgment. This explains the wisdom in the statement — "live and let live".

If we find ourselves being judgmental, we are always better off looking within and doing the internal personal work that would allow us to live freely, and let others live freely, without judgment. Let yourself be free to open and live with the same spirited attitude toward yourself. Let judgment go. To live and let live is very wise indeed.

False *pride* is a similar attribute of the ego. This is essentially taking your false self — that is the ego-founded aspect within ourselves — as real!

In our spirit there is strength and comfort that doesn't come from an idea we hold of our self, or from accomplishment. It is an inherent spiritual worth that is not inflated or deflated by earthly accomplishment. To honor oneself, or take pride in doing an excellent job in service to another person, or acknowledging another person's wonderful contribution is surely noble — but to inflate or derive worth from this honor becomes an ego orientation.

Someone who has made many great achievements does not necessarily demonstrate pride. It is possible to be highly accomplished in many different ways and still be humble and full of spiritual integrity. Pride is simply demonstrated in someone who feels superior or more important because of their personal achievements — or sometimes in a reverse flip — lack of them.

Pride can get in the way of admitting "weakness", or the need of support in our life. We see this perhaps when we are "too strong" or "self sufficient" to need the help or kindness that might lighten our journey in some way.

Pride can get in the way of honesty, respect, dignity, fairness, generosity and all things that are inherent attributes of love.

If pride is a strong component of our "personality", life in magical ways will step in to help relinquish it. It might look nasty when this happens – but there is a spiritual salvation hiding in the crash. Perhaps you are familiar with the phrase – "pride before the fall". True humility, not ego founded humility, is the antidote for false pride.

Shame is another ego attribute used to evoke control and suppress power. Shame is evoked to have our self or another person feel diminished in the eyes of ego. It is also a technique of false superiority. Shame and guilt often go hand-in-hand and we will look at undoing both of them in the practices that follow.

⊙

The ego, operating through these attributes, is understood to create a false but perceptible world. It is a world of spiritual isolation. The ego struggles to keep itself safe and pertinent.

It is the world of the ego that forms the foundation for "comedies and tragedies of errors" that are inherent in human life. It is the ego, in it's many forms, which creates the suffering of humanity. The ego has been depicted in all great literature and art – time and time again – as the source of human drama. But, it is undone by spiritual grace.

The ego basis of human life is often presumed to be the "way humanity is". Meanwhile, avatar after avatar of enlightened consciousness has come forward over the centuries to show us – actually to remind us and inspire us – to unravel the ego's illusory power. Undoing the ego – expressed in a thousand different ways – has been the foundational teaching of every religion and true form of spiritual teaching – since the "beginning of time"!

In simple terms – at the core of such teachings – the world of the ego is completely undone with the stroke of love. The concept is very simple. It is made, however, much more complex by the nature of ego, and all of the things the ego sets into place. In the world of the ego – it is very easy to find ways to not trust and believe in the power of love.

To reintegrate spiritually, there is a choice we each must make within our own being. It is to align with the ego or align with our spiritual nature. No one can do this for another person – and no one can force another to do it. It is a self-chosen alignment, and ultimately a practice of conscious awareness.

Spiritual growth and integration implies learning to overcome the tendency to act in ego-laden ways. To achieve this, we first need to be more aware of its nature. As we become more aware of its manifestations within our own lives and experiences, we can then learn to transform them.

As one progresses, frankly one must become quite vigilant about the ego – because the ego is a great "trickster"! It can manipulate thoughts and feelings, often without our conscious awareness unless we are paying close attention!

Love is the true power of creation – an omnipotent force of light and energy. Fear is everything in our make up that operates without love. Even loving actions that are tainted by ego qualities get distorted or destroyed to some lesser or greater degree. Everything that serves to restrain love, bind love, twist love, veil love, and suppress love – is essentially ego. And this can create no shortage of human confusion – because love in a spiritual sense, and love in an ego sense, are not parallel.

When you are present in the moment, connected with your spirit and radiating your spiritual energy, witnessing without objective, experiencing gratefulness, peace and joy – you are in your true nature. When you step into the world of human "reality", this can be lost very readily, until you learn about your own power.

Most of us have been so embedded in human life that we have assimilated deeply engrained energy patterns in our mental and emotional bodies. We might not even realize they are operating. They will become clearer to us as we develop an understanding of the ego, and how it does operate in our life. By doing this we can begin to use tools to help us regain our spiritual core alignment when we manifest ego reactions and behaviors. This will require a conscious effort, and we will examine them shortly in the practices of atonement, forgiveness and peace consciousness.

The ego can serve to create many "energetic distortions" in the human energy bodies. These distortions often bear heavy consequence on the human spirit through its ramifications on the human energy system. In energy-based healing work, the work can stir up the patterned energy, and loosen the crystalized patterns in the mental and emotional bodies. These patterns have been founded in the lower vibration of fear based perceptions – familiar to us all.

Energy healing processes will liberate energy around these old patterns, which have been contributing to holding the deep "fear based patterning" embedded in one's personal energy bodies.

Healing work will also at times greatly challenge the human ego. The ego will resist healing – often unconsciously - while the higher self will be working to support it. As the patterns of restricted energy are loosened vibrationally, the potential for healing is greatly facilitated.

Let us look at healing illustration to better understand:

Imagine that a person holds a restricted throat chakra due to prior experiences that have occurred in their life. Perhaps this was through being raised in an environment where there was no space for them to express themselves in words or creative expression. Perhaps they were judged and ridiculed, or simple told to be quiet and not let themselves be heard.

It would conceivably be very difficult for this person to trust and "learn to speak". If the energy of the throat center is closed however – the ability for verbal and creative expression in all its forms, is restricted. This restriction will have huge consequences on ones ability to express themselves – through words or any form of creative expression, in their life.

Now imagine during an energy healing session, the energy of the throat center is stimulated, and is opened. The ego may want to step in – in an effort to keep the center protected and closed.

Fears of being ridiculed for speaking or expressing may arise. Thoughts of self-judgment may echo in one's head, to try to suppress the opening. It is fear, hence the ego, which would be supporting this restriction.

If however the throat center is truly supported in opening, and one musters the will, courage and spirit to learn to express oneself, one will begin to release the obstructing energy pattern that is blocking the chakra. Aligned with healing, one will become present in a self-supportive, courageous and loving way - to "open up". Through this alignment, one can have the experience of a great healing.

In this over-simplified example, the "mechanics" of healing are again introduced. It implies an energetic transformation, but also an attainment of consciousness. This is essentially why we need to learn about "fear and the ego nature" in the healing process.

Taken again from Chapter 4, of A Course in Miracles, p 53:

> *"Spirit need not be taught, but the ego must be. Learning is ultimately perceived as frightening because it leads to the relinquishment, not the destruction, of the ego to the light of the spirit. This is the change the ego must fear, because it does not share my charity. .... Teaching and Learning are your greatest allies now, because they enable you to change your mind and enable others to change theirs.*

Surrender

So if the ego is a force that is based on separation from love, spiritual growth implies ego transcendence, relinquishment or integration. This is often spoken of as ego "surrender". What is it – to "surrender"?

Surrender, in the "*ego* warrior's" lexicon, infers weakness. It is the triumph of the *strong over the weak*. To "surrender" is simply perceived as "weak".

Surrender in the "*spiritual* warrior's" lexicon is actually an understanding of the triumph of *strength over weakness*. It understands the tremendous force of courage and strength required for the soul to sublimate the energetic force of the ego. It implies surrender of the ego – with which we can all identify – to the strength of the soul.

Spiritual surrender is not surrender of one's self, one's worth, one's value, one's power or one's important ability to spread love in the world. It is a letting go of patterning and content in the mental and emotional bodies, which are based in ego, and keep one separate from one's spiritual potential.

Tenacious patterns in our mental and emotional bodies will sometimes need a great deal of encouragement to let go. It takes vigilance, consciousness and will to let the spirit within us "take over" – when ego patterns arise – so that they may be "surrendered". Hence, surrender is not a placid giving up, it is a conscious and effortful practice: one requiring dedication, effort and courage.

Spiritual surrender can be a very confusing concept for many people. "Overcoming", "surrendering", or as I prefer to say, "integrating" the ego - is the practice of realigning with one's spirit. You do not "lose yourself". You lose what is perceived to be yourself that is founded in ego confusion. You actually "find yourself". It is not a loss of mental or emotional capacity – it is perhaps more like an *upgrade* of them.

It can be challenging to recognize the "subconscious" factors that pervasively interfere in our lives. When one begins to explore ego integration, it becomes easy to see how pervasive and elusive these types of patterns can be. Worry, shame, pride, defensiveness, competitiveness, denial, guilt and limited spiritual empowerment are ubiquitous in our culture. They are "expected" of us. So it takes a willingness to be different than the norm. The words, "Be in the world, but not of it" take on a deep personal significance.

Yet, if we tried to individually pick and identify every pattern ever created that is out of alignment with our divine potential – you might imagine that we would be very busy, for a very long time! Fortunately, it is made a lot simpler by learning to align with guiding principles that facilitate a re-attunement with spiritual alignment.

We shall take a look at practices that facilitate this process of surrender. These are the practices of *forgiveness* and *peace consciousness*. But first, to prepare, let us take a look at the challenges we commonly face when taking on the task of ego integration.

EGO INTEGRATION – SOME CHALLENGES

In truth, no spiritual being is an evil entity. This may be incredulous to accept or imagine as we look at the world around us. You might think it is even foolish to say this. Yet this is a world where human beings are able to express both an authentic spiritual nature, as well as a limited ego nature – and all the things a limited ego consciousness might dream up. We are all capable of betraying love, due to the ego influence we carry.

So if we look at the world for evidence – we see both good and evil, or love and fear. This creates a great struggle of understanding within humanity. How often have you heard the idea, "How would God allow this?" or "How would God allow that?" as we witness human actions on the stage of life.

What an awakening human being begins to realize is that it is not God who is creating evil and hatred and injustice – it is the human ego through its perceptions. Yet, the human ego does it because the soul's power is not developed enough to overcome its sway. The ego does not grasp or understand the truth. It is the human ego's perception – that we can exist apart from love – which creates the potential for an evil or "fear based expression" to exist.

The challenge before each of us – is to personally work to examine ourselves. It is our task to examine our lives, our behaviors and our choices. It is our responsibility to see where fear is in control of our "reality" and where ego has nestled in at home.

As we come to understand the premise and existence of the ego, we can then become aware of how the ego works within us. Then, we can learn to make adjustments. We can more readily become aware of the expressive nature and presence of love within us – we can reorient our life in wise and healing ways. You heal – the world heals. One person at a time!

However, that does not mean it is easy. When the force of the ego is strongly in control of a person's life experience – great illusions develop. The perception of the ego manifests in the thoughts and feelings and choices.

These perceptions lead to constant fear, isolation and suffering – all of which are self-evident in the world around us.

We come to understand that the reaction of humanity to atrocity is also often based in ego perception. As we witness unbelievable things happening in the world, we do not always understand it is the working of the ego. We do not yet have a full grasp of "Truth", so what we witness or experience as manifested life is perceived to be the nature of reality. To a tender and compassionate heart, or to anyone personally affected by such experience, it can be overwhelmingly difficult to process – and this is where a spiritual understanding becomes imperative. It can be very challenging to bear witness or experience heart breaking suffering, and still maintain a higher consciousness view. It requires a greater understanding – but humanity is becoming ready for this understanding.

Energetically speaking, when we are capable of transcending the attributes of ego within ourselves – we are healing both humanity and ourselves, simultaneously. This adds credence to the very wise words, "Be the change." This takes a great deal of compassion, courage, strength and forgiveness. One must learn to rise above it, and live from a different plane of consciousness, yet still be present, to heal.

We begin to grasp that our individual "struggle with fear", in the form of the "ego", is essentially the great struggle of spiritual life. One can align with the ego or with a wiser spiritual awareness. If the ego assumes the role of central importance and value – it aims to keep us safe by preserving its sense of separation through it's evoked thoughts and feelings. However, it vicariously separates us from our own higher nature. In keeping us "safe", it keeps us away from our essential self. There is no true "safety" in this illusion.

As one takes on the spiritual task to move past fear and ego as the creative foundation in one's life, one encounters a few challenges, common to all travellers on the spiritual path:

1. Until one begins to learn about the ego, most human beings *identify* with attributes of the ego as their "self".

This shift in perception is a monumental adjustment. It is perhaps one of the greatest challenges in facilitating healing work. As a person begins to understand and "awaken" to the ego nature, and learn about it - deep spiritual work is really just beginning.

2. The next challenge of the spiritual awakening process is learning to *recognize* the ego within our own being.

As we awaken more and more to the spiritual light within us we can begin to witness our lives more clearly. In what ways do we live fearfully? Where do ego's attributes manifest in our lives? Do we recognize it? Can we adjust it?

This involves the development of greater self-awareness – a consciousness that can witness the ego at work. From the perspective of "witness", we can work more consciously to transform.

3. As we encounter ego attributes within our own personality, we must learn to *overcome* the ego attributes.

The ego aspect of our own nature becomes our "adversary". It is the tendency to identify with the perceptions and manifestations of ego attributes that must be overcome.

Yet from the perspective of a wiser spirit founded in love, one holds no "adversary" – simply the healing view of reality that love purveys. Love sees through ego – and embraces it.

This takes wisdom, discipline, courage, strength, honesty, patience, support, kindness, compassion, and forgiveness. It takes love in all its attributes. We learn to love others and love ourselves authentically in this phase of the journey. We love ourselves "back into balance and alignment".

4. The fourth challenge we come to face is the *nebulous and ubiquitous quality of the ego*. You cannot wrestle with the ego and win – you must instead identify with your true nature, surrendering the ego attributes to love.

The ego is a great masquerader. It will shift endlessly in its expression to stay relevant and in control of our lives. It can work through every attribute in its fearful arsenal as a "tester" and tool for transformation. When people begin to really learn and assimilate spiritual concepts, the ego can be strongly engaged in usurping the process and preserving itself in anyway possible.

As you encounter a personal experience that is a manifestation of ego, it will shape shift from one form to another. When you worry what happens? You start to think negative thoughts and create anxieties. These thoughts and anxieties lead to frustration – which becomes judgment. You judge the situation, yourself, other people, an institution, and so forth. This becomes anger. Anger becomes righteous. Righteous becomes defensive. It goes on and on – until the *entire* ego process stops.

Engaging the ego, and reacting to ego through more ego attributes, is an activity that ensnares us in grief. Guilt, shame, pride arrogance, worthlessness, self importance, victimization and vengeance are its strategies – all to keep a soul bound in its tendrils of control so the luminous nature of our true self can not shine free. Fear can even masquerade as love!

5. The fifth challenge is coming to terms with how deeply the ego is embedded in our civilization. Qualities that are purely ego based in nature are part of every system of conditioning we encounter as human beings. It is in our family structures, our educational structures, our social structures, our commercial structure, our legal structure, our religious structure and even our relationship structures.

Overcoming the ego, in many ways, is overcoming the world, as we know it. One can feel like a salmon in its fateful swim upstream. Yet, the world around will not *seem* to change.

In actuality, the world does change – slowly and incrementally by each person's progression – but this will not always be measurable or easy to see in a day-to-day way. You must understand your growth is personal and your healing is personal – so the satisfaction of progress must come from within. The external world will not necessarily support you; in fact it may greatly challenge your perception in all of the egos capable ways.

If one is strong in connection with one's spirit - one lives quite differently. One learns to release the thoughts, feelings and choices that are strongly under the influence of ego fear. We cannot change the external world to change this orientation – one must work within one's self. One changes the perception and relationship with the world around us.

Spiritual growth cannot be forced – it must be self-chosen for that is the nature of human life. Each and every human being must choose their path and own alignment. Each one of us must simply choose for our self. So people around you may not support you – simple as that!

As an awakening human being you cannot change the world directly. In fact, if you react to the world externally, you are bearing witness to its real nature, when it is not "real" in the first place. To try to change the world is a false place to begin the healing journey. If you step out of the ego perceptions that are continuously remaking this world and learn to see with a unified consciousness – you start anew.

This transformation is the process of surrendering the ego. It must be learned and practiced. But, it is in this process that a deeper healing of authentic self-awakening emerges, and healing occurs.

THE TESTY LITTLE EGO

People will sometimes get defensive or testy, when you bring up the idea of sublimating or surrendering the ego in the process of healing and transformation. This reaction is often based on a misunderstanding of the ego nature. Humorously, this sometimes actually represents an ego reaction itself.

It will also be said sometimes that we need to preserve a "sense of ego" in order to live or exist in the world. This is not really true – but perhaps semantics a little. You need to preserve the ego for *it* to survive, but you do not need to preserve the ego as we define it, for *you* to survive. The ego is not you.

You can certainly preserve an identity, assume many roles as a human being, and continue to live a full, rich and rewarding existence. In fact, you "should". You do not become a mindless buffoon. You do not surrender your power to some spiritual, political or social authority. As one comes to understand the nature of the ego and higher spiritual consciousness – one realizes we are learning to think, feel and operate in alignment with this higher consciousness. This is very different than the way the ego would witness, perceive and react. You give up the ways of the ego, but you do not give up your life!

Your ego is not your intellectual and mental function, nor your emotional capability. It represents the "misuse" of these functions based on a limited understanding of life. Just as the ego uses thoughts and feelings to evoke fearful discord, the spirit can equally utilize the mental and emotional body to instill healthy, supportive, power laden beliefs, integrity, balance, conscious choice, peace and joy.

To surrender the ego also does not mean that you will turn your back on your family or the world, and stop caring about life where love is alive. The world, and sometimes one's friends and family, may choose to do this if they judge your path. If so, it is encountered with the same love that begins to pervade one's life. But to integrate ego does not mean any of these things will happen.

It also does not mean that you will have to work in the world to bring betterment, in the way of a selfless "martyr". It means that you will bring betterment to the world by becoming "*better*", or actually "*real*", within yourself. It means you can bring love into everything you do – by becoming who you really are – in your core nature.

One must be cognizant of the fact that the ego tends to "go on high alert" when it recognizes that you are at a point in healing where you are ready to take this magical leap. It will perceive it as a direct threat. In an effort to preserve its importance it will rebel – so expect it.

One might easily hear thoughts be conjured up: "That is nonsense." "What, does this mean you just drop out of the world?" "Do you let people walk all over you?" "Do you stop taking care of your family or responsibilities because you are 'spiritual'?" "Do we let terrible behavior go unpunished?" The prerecorded and familiar thoughts are ready to go.

The answer is of course not. You learn to relate to all of these things in a different way. You begin to allow the veils of perception, which keeps these types of things in place by ego involvement, begin to melt away.

Ego Integration and Energetic Healing

As we each begin to examine our own lives, we will become aware of the ego-based behaviors embedded in our psyche. The automated responsiveness in our characters based on wounds or conditioning becomes much more transparent. The impact of these patterns on our energy, health and manifested reality is gently but powerfully revealed.

If we examine, how as human beings, we surrender or lose our peace – we will understand its implication on health and healing. In healing, it can be understood that peace is a compass and your greatest prize. Ultimately, everything that seems to threaten your peace may be understood to originate in ego awareness. Let us look again at an example:

Imagine you are at home and feeling very relaxed and at peace, and you receive a phone call. The person on the other end of the line is agitated with something you have done.

How do you see yourself reacting? You might begin to feel hurt by the other person's behavior. Or, you might feel guilty. This could lead to defensiveness in your posturing. It might lead to an angry response. You might start a series of thoughts about how crazy or silly they are. This might inspire a little pride or arrogance in your attitude. There is a spectrum of possible reactions.

Now while any of this is going on, you have transiently surrendered your wellbeing. But, how would you act if you refused to surrender your peace? Just think about it for a few moments. This is the shift in perception that must occur, to step out of ego based living. Learning to do this is the practice of ego surrender and spiritual peace. If this is foreign to you, not to worry. We will look integrating peace consciousness as a practice very shortly.

As we examine the experience, we might see readily that peace-stealing attributes of the ego are choices that we make without being consciously aware of what we are doing. The anger made by ego responses, the rigidity of ego defensiveness, the judgments we make of ourselves and others, the anxiety and worry we nourish, the folly of hatred and revenge – all become a little more transparent in their nature to the spiritualized mind.

We can also, however, begin to realize the real impact that ego based behavior has on the energy construct of our "bodies". When we posture ourselves in a particular way energetically – we are "becoming" like that – energetically speaking. I cannot get angry, without becoming angry, for example. This, ultimately, is a choice I am making. We are going to live out the consequences of the choices we make, ego-based or not, within our own energy field.

The quality of our energy signature is directly correlated to the way we manage our energy in this regard. This is where an appreciation of the human energy fields, the chakra system and the spiritual nature of our true self become so important and so valuable to understand. Ego based activity "messes up" the mind and emotions in true energy terms. This impacts our mental body, our emotional body, our etheric body – and even our physical body.

The mental and emotional bodies can be viewed in a highly simplified fashion, to be following the directive of either the ego or the higher self. Chronic patterning produced by the ego creates an energy patterning in the mental and emotional body that becomes a formed part of the "personality" one expresses.

For example, if a person is habitually withdrawn, afraid, angry or hostile – these attributes are patterned in the energy field. The more affected one's energy field becomes through the energy and vibration of these ego-based activities, the harder it is to acknowledge or "believe in" our spiritual essence.

As one stays enmeshed in ego distortions, disturbances in the energy field take on a greater and greater ability to limit our perception of who we really are. If you think in terms of an energy field – it is "clouded" by disturbing vibrations – at least until the energy is cleared and healed, or restored to its natural state. These distortions *disempower* us from the potential to "truly" see our self.

Disturbed by the ego, it is as if we are looking at life through the surface of a lake on a windy day, when the surface is disturbed by activity. When the surface calms, we can see more deeply into the water – even to the bottom of the lake. We can also see a perfect image of the lakeside environment in its mirrored reflection. As our energy calms – we too can see through the ego and into the loving nature that is every human being's foundation.

Healing can be supported both by consciousness practices *and* through energy processes. But as our energy is supported in its transformation, we have a progressively conscious role to play. By better understanding our energetic bodies – we can see that we need to be much more conscious about what is taking place in them. We begin to understand that we are spiritual beings who must be conscious how we are using our mental, emotional and physical bodies. We become more conscious of our spiritual nature and power.

We can use this strength to regain sovereignty over our self and the world we perceptibly manifest. We do not need to be obsessed or "worried" about it – just conscious and self-responsible.

We can learn to witness our personal thoughts and feelings. We can become aware of what we carry as habitual thought and feeling patterns. We can learn about the nature of ego and how it manifests in our lives. We can witness our ego, and learn to surrender. As spiritually conscious beings we can learn to more consciously engage in our lives.

We begin to understand that the way we think and feel, the programs we carry, the wounds we hold from prior experiences, and the thoughts and feelings of others toward us – are entangled in the ego nature. But – they do not define us. These mental and emotional constructs simply create an energy pattern that can that block or distort expressing our truer being – the wisdom, power and love of our true spiritual nature. Importantly, we can understand how wellness is promoted if we become responsible guardians of our own energy bodies.

As one dismantles the ego, one will continue to live with a rich panorama of both mental and emotional capabilities, but the priority changes from one of ego preservation to one of spiritual integration. It represents a huge transformation of consciousness.

Biospiritual transformation implies the process of merging with our spiritual consciousness to reveal, teach and heal. The story of this integration will be unique and different for each one of us. Yet, healing at this level takes on a common but transpersonal expression. It is a process of learning *a way*. It is the way of love – and it brings enormous healing into our life.

Freedom

We can now understand that the ego is not simply our thoughts and feelings, nor the ability we have to think and feel. It is a limited consciousness that arises with the false precept of spiritual separation. The ego can "use" the mental and emotional body toward its own objective.

The challenge for us is that the ego is so entwined in human conscious, we can confuse it for ourselves. We often do not realize that we are acting or reacting from the ego. The ego is not our real nature – but we do not necessarily feel "free".

When the term awakening is used in a spiritual context, it means experiencing an awakening to one's truer nature as a spiritual being. This implies to live less under the tight control of ego. This is the mechanism by which a spiritual awakening brings what is viewed as authentic freedom.

Spiritual liberation is not really liberation from the world or anything external to our self. It is also not simply being free to do or behave in whatever you want. These are important personal freedoms, but often ego-based freedoms. So even though we are free to behave as we wish – we are not free from the constraints of our own ego issues. True freedom is liberation of the control of the ego aspect within our lives.

As the ego is integrated and we learn to operate our lives from the greater peace that arises within us, we come to understand that peace is an aligned internal choice. By aligning with peace, we start to loosen the ego's grip and control, and discover an expanding spiritual freedom.

As we become free of the ego, a great sense of peace arises in our lives to replace the mental and emotional wrangling induced by the ego. To be unshackled from the thoughts and feelings imposed by ego alignment exposes the "pearl of great price."

In the process and practice of ego integration, one must be willing to consciously surrender the mental and emotional habits the ego relies on to control one's life. The great spiritual struggle for freedom is won by recognizing one's truer nature as a spiritual being – and use the love, wisdom and power we hold to help unshackle ourselves, and our energy fields, from the ego's entanglement.

Ego Integration – Atonement

The process of ego integration is also sometimes referred to as the atonement. Atonement can be defined as a conscious relinquishment of ego through greater self-awareness. It implies the practice of ego surrender through forgiveness, and the practice of peace. It is not an *acquiring* process; so much as it is a process of *letting go*. Surrender, in this true sense requires a tremendous force of strength, wisdom and self-love.

Atonement may be viewed as the correction of the misperception of one's separation from spiritual reality. It carries a "heavy tone" because of the strong religious connotation implied in the understanding. It is stated, for example, that Christ died to atone for humanity's sins. Yet, in the teaching of ACIM, atonement is viewed more from the perception of restoration. This occurs by not only forgiving ego based perceptions, but also by grasping the ego is based entirely on a false premise.

Our personal task is to understand how this false perception has become part of our own character – and atone – or return to be at-one – with our spiritual potential. Atonement means seeing through the falsity of ego and restoring a state of peace and unity consciousness in our lives. As the ego fades in relevance, the higher self becomes more influential in one's life. It is a return to love.

In an ideal world we could imagine that the higher self within would direct our life experiences. We would live from this level of unity awareness – not from the polarizing views the ego uses to preserve itself.

As the higher self communicates and flows through the mental body, our thoughts become energized by, and aligned with, a greater spiritual understanding. Our thoughts learn to uplift our emotional body. A greater consciousness is present at all times – to support or advise. It can neutralize ego-based reactions. It can maintain balance when confronted with internal or external forces, which usurp the mental and emotional bodies into states of disharmony or disease. Our physical manifestation begins to reflect this ideal state of awareness.

When one looks at another human being they also begin to see them more *truly* – not from the ego perception of either person. People in an ego transcendent state would uplift each other. Yet, no matter how someone is behaving or appearing – you will always be aware of the divinity in both of you. No matter what thoughts and feelings that arise within your bodies, or what the external world subjects us to as we face our relationships, our interactions and our day to day lives – this "presence" is always "present" and will provide the experiential stabilization to maintain personal harmony as a living force. This allows God to be within us and come through us – as spiritual teaching has always truly professed.

This spiritual journey between these two worlds – the world of peace and the world of ego perception - implies conscious ego integration or atonement.

As you learn to recognize the ego within your own character, your relationships with others, and your relationship with your self – the way will be made clearer to find peace. Moment by moment, the choice for peace will always remain with each of us – so understanding ego integration through the practice of forgiveness, and the practice of peace, is invaluable. I believe, it is requisite, to find a healing that endures.

Atonement can involve the release of energy encapsulated around deep and painful wounds. As these wounds are healed, atonement becomes a day to day practice as one learns to overcome the ego based behaviors and reactions that contort our energy, and lead to the energy distortions which produces the innumerable faces of disease and suffering. It is a constant practice. And though I write these words, I assure you, I still practice this everyday of my life.

◉

The ways of a spiritually conscious being will often look silly to the ego. In fact the ego uses this to discourage honoring the spiritual nature within. Healing work can take on a very challenging nature when the experience of harsh ego behavior has impacted our lives.

For example, if someone who has been raped, brutally abused, neglected or diminished to worthlessness by the experiences of life, it can seem an impossible task to begin to view the past as "nothing" or "unreal". It is imperative to realize the difference between what happens in the construct of ego-based consciousness, and the truth of human nature. It takes an incredible courage to overcome this type of history and regain a sense of spiritual nobility and peace – but many have done it.

Those who are able to walk through such a healing journey find an end to the suffering that plagues their lives because of history, and put an end to the spiritual rift that would allow such a manifestation to occur in the first place. In fact, this is very often a healer's journey.

The Concept of Mastery

Some also view this process of ego integration as the "practice of mastery". Spiritual mastery, unlike the worldly concept of a master, is to become masterful in one's self. A spiritual master is masterful toward sublimating the ego within him or herself – and is spiritually realized in their self-expression. A true master is able to manifest a spiritual authenticity that is founded in wisdom and in love.

True spiritual teachers have always taught attributes such as gentleness, kindness, forgiveness, and peace. These are not taught to make victims and slaves of good people to the ways of ego or external authority. They are taught as natural to the process of ego liberation and enlightenment. These are the attributes of spirit, which can unravel the ego and its perceptions, in its very cunning ability to veil the light and energy we each carry.

It is said that the "meek shall inherit the earth". In the wake of the old world, and as a new one is born before us, this is the "time of inheritance". Truly the meek will inherit the world, as this one comes to pass, for the meek are those aligned with the nature of this new energy. Who are the meek? Meek does not imply powerless. In fact, it is a path perhaps not well suited to the faint of heart! It is those who are willing to follow the way of love. Love is the master!

The ways of the ego will gradually lose power in the world. In this time of transition, unity consciousness will become the foundational understanding, as the new way of life. Although the ego may flail in the passing, in the next few generations we will surely witness this transformation. Humanity will look back at this time of world conflict, greed, war, hatred and spiritual negligence as a chapter in history, which was overcome by the rising vibration of a masterful humanity who discovered the power and love of spirit within themselves. It will change, because of you.

Practice of Atonement

So how do we practice atonement? It implies "transcending ego consciousness". It may mean forgiveness or practicing peace. Yet, what does that mean in practical terms? To make this discussion a little more tangible – let us look at a demonstration of "atonement in action" in a simple daily encounter.

Imagine for a moment that someone is "getting on your nerves", and you say something hurtful to this other person.

It is probably easy to grasp that we could hurt someone's feelings and cause great damage in our relationship by an impulsive emotional reaction. The reaction might seem justified – since it was the "annoying behavior" of the other person that "triggered" the reaction. However, regardless of how we try justifying our reaction at first – when we step into a state of spiritual alignment – we will see this ego-based behavior. We will understand that it is the ego in us that has stepped forward to create this damage or wound - because we have to step out of love's nature to act this way. It is also the ego that wants to protect this reaction, to preserve its existence.

So now, let us assume the "damage has been done". Whether one can admit it or not at first, spiritually, there is an awareness that this is not one's "higher behavior". As one becomes aware of what has happened, one might feel guilty or shameful in the reaction – because these are outcomes of ego activity. If one is not aware of ego – one will spin in the confusion of ego activity – deny its relevance or beating one's self up. So how does one reconcile this energy?

If one can see that they have been hurtful it would be natural to apologize. This is an action to acknowledge to the other person that you have not been loving in nature. You are admitting it – both to them and to yourself. This appears humble to the ego but is ultimately an act of spiritual strength if it is authentically expressed.

You might ask to be forgiven for having acted hurtfully. You would not step into self-judgment, for every human being is capable of ego-based behavior but you would atone for the action due to its spiritual merit. Simple enough, right?

Now, if you are on the receiving end of such an attack how do you handle it?

If one reacts from one's own ego, it would likely involve a defensive posturing. One could insult, attack, start an argument of defense or struggle – and so forth.

If this occurs, the higher self can be restorative to a person - by coming to terms with an understanding of one's ego involvement and following a conciliatory course.

To atone in this setting – you would own up to the "foolishness" of your response – and apologize for reacting hurtfully. You would accept responsibility for your reaction as a spiritually conscious being, one who knows you were acting destructively toward your own energy and toward the other person energetically by the choice you have made. You were taking the ego as "real" by reacting to it as such, and manifesting ego yourself.

If one can attain this level of awareness of experience, one will atone immediately and restore peace, love and truth in this setting. In this situation, it is an attitude of forgiveness and compassion that keeps a person free from ego entrapment.

In truth, one human being, through ego folly – cannot hurt another person *spiritually*. But one can bring injury through assault to the mental, emotional, etheric and physical bodies, which challenges the presence of spirit! One must learn to be strong in one's own spiritual presence not to succumb to the energy of attack. When we begin to think energetically we can begin to see that it is our energy signature that is most important in maintaining our wellbeing.

On the receiving end of this assault, if one remains centered in one's spiritual core, we would not allow the thoughts and feelings of another to penetrate and hurt so deeply - and the energy, compassion and love that emerges from our higher self nature would keep us free from inflicting pain and hurting ourselves.

The higher self is not confused by the inappropriateness of the hurtful attack – but it knows how to handle it. It sees *through* the ego.

It should also be clearly stated that the higher self would also not "endorse" the idea of keeping a person in a hostile or hurtful situation – when enduring the presence of someone whose ego is unrelenting. The setting of an abusive relationship might serve as an example of this. It would guide a person to become free of such an entanglement – through the power of self-realization and development. It will teach and support any one of us to move through the experience — by owning it, and the power of one's own worth and divine nature, to become free of this perceived spiritual entrapment.

Atonement occurs by the process of giving up the ego to restore peace within one's own being. Atonement is an act of conscious awareness and it has energetic consequences upon our being. Compassion provides understanding of the human predicament. Forgiveness restores the truth. If we can grasp the deep significance of these two ideas, the concept and outcome of atonement becomes vibrantly clear.

Forgiveness

Forgiveness is an essential element in spiritual development. It is a key to unlocking the ego's challenging stance on many perceptions.

Forgiveness is essential internally — for things you have thought, said or done which are hurtful to yourself or to others. It is also true externally, for the actions others have done towards you.

> *The practice of forgiveness is our most important contribution to the healing of the world.*
> Marianne Williamson

As we grow in consciousness and begin to understand the higher self "perspective" — we realize all human beings have an element of ego perception and are capable of wrongdoing to some degree. When we are holding others or ourselves in contempt, we are ultimately being bound by our own perceptions to the ego level of creative vibration.

Forgiveness is "a tool" for shifting perceptions to facilitate the release of ego entrapment. It is a mechanism to restore spiritual freedom. Forgiveness is a conscious action that has the potential to liberate a human being from an ego-based creation, or one's reaction to an ego-based creation.

Forgiveness may be oriented towards one's self or towards another. Self-forgiveness becomes important in all the ways the ego has influenced our life in spiritually unconscious ways. The higher self understands the ego's creations are not one's real nature — and that making ego-based mistakes is part of the human story.

Yet, the act of forgiveness does not ignore the lack of consciousness that led to the experience, it allows for a shift in perception that brings freedom to the soul. Through authentic forgiving, one does not react in the patterned ego ways that perpetuate ego control. Rather than wallow in guilt and grief toward some wrongdoing – the higher self acknowledges the pain inflicted by such activities – and works to reconcile past wrongs and to restore peace by overcoming the ego's responsive ways.

Forgiveness offered to others is important in all ways that others may have acted unconsciously – in terms of ego manifestation. As a human being, it is not without great challenge to forgive someone when they have acted horrifically towards us, or another human being. Yet, to forgive is not an activity of our ego – it is a natural choice of spiritual realization. Forgiveness is not something that occurs simply at the mental or emotional level in isolation – it occurs through the awakening and expression of true love, compassion and mature spiritual wisdom in our heart.

As we grasp the wisdom in forgiving, we realize the power that true or authentic forgiveness holds to release human beings from fixed states of suffering. Anyone who has ever offered or received heart-aligned forgiveness will comprehend the power of this realization. True forgiveness is of the spirit – and dissolves the ego's manifestation. Forgiveness doesn't simply change the past; it changes the future, and the most powerful point in time that exists – the "now" in time.

Forgiveness offers the opportunity to step away from the ego's manipulations and perceptions to a state where peace and freedom are found through a freer energy flow within our own being. If we restrict our energy by thoughts and feelings that impact the movement of energy in our personal energy field – it impacts greatly our personal wellbeing.

Forgiveness may come to the forefront when we are hurt in simple ways in our lives and our relationships. But, forgiveness will also become essential when we are dealing with deep psychological wounds that we may carry from prior experiences. Healing from heavy psychological wounds is indeed a great human challenge.

Forgiveness must also be whole hearted. To mentally forgive is not sufficient – true forgiveness must come from one's spiritual being. I can say for example, "I forgive you" – but if I do not reconcile the experience in my spirit, I can still harbor resentment or animosity towards you. To truly forgive, I will release the mental and emotional energy I am harboring in response to the experience, and in this action, let it go. It loses its influence on my energy and in this I become free. Authentic healing will always involve making amends with the past, to be free in the present and transform the future. To forgive, is, to heal.

To hold on to these past experiences in a strong and unforgiving way will bind us to the experience and will bind our creative energy by its existence. How do we ever forgive when we are subject to personal or collective ego atrocities?

The Case Against Forgiveness

When someone hurts us deeply, or hurts someone we love deeply – whether it was intentional or unintentional – it is often very difficult to step into a stance of forgiveness.

If we have hurt another human being – the guilt and shame can also be overwhelming. It may be very difficult to think of self-forgiveness in such times. If someone hurts us – forgiving may seem impossible.

When we face such challenging experiences of forgiveness, the arguments against forgiveness by the ego become obvious.

The ego will pull on any or all of its attributes to keep us snared in its perceptions. It will insist that if you allow yourself to be hurt, you will become a bigger victim. It will insist on suffering and retribution. It will insist on vengeance or shame.

But pay attention to what happens within one's own energy when living in such energy postures. Does it seem in any way healthy? Does it seem that one could feel free? Of course, the answer is no. Yet, there must be a way to realign this energy. This is where forgiveness enters into the picture – irrespective any argument that might be raised.

It is essential to grasp that living in forgiveness does *not* imply the endurance of suffering, or the perpetuation of malicious behavior. Forgiveness does not condone hateful behavior. It does not dispel the need for corrective action, or even legal action, upon a perpetrator of a crime.

For example, a dangerous person may need to be imprisoned, or an abused partner should be assisted to get out of their abusive circumstances, and children need authentic protection by conscious humanity in many ways. It may be very important to stop the hurtful actions around you – or to speak the truth about them to begin healing.

It should also be understood that when an injury occurs, forgiveness might require time. In the aftermath of a tragic experience, it is often not the time to process or expect forgiveness. In such a time of emotion – it is a time for compassion. The time will come for forgiving when we are capable and ready. But when we do, we will let go of the creative impact of this energy in our lives.

Forgiveness will simply dispel the ensnaring quality of the ego that would keep any human being in hatred, condemnation and energetic self-destruction. There will be no argument to forgiveness that will veil the power of love when one is ready to move through the process of healing – and forward in their lives.

☉

As we mature in our understanding of forgiveness, we begin to realize that it liberates us from the entanglements of ego and the creative influence it holds on our energy signature. If one forgives transgressions, it might certainly look foolish from an ego perspective. Yet, if we do not forgive, we stay entangled. If we stay entangled we suffer energetically. This is a simple but challenging principle – but it is emphasized to say that forgiveness must be authentic and it is in forgiveness you will set yourself free.

If you know that in your own life there are important things that will need to be forgiven – I would encourage you to begin the work of forgiveness, to open to heal, and let go. If you have made amends with the past then practice forgiveness as often as you need to, to remain free. Practice it daily and in all ways you encounter the ego – and you will find a greater peace, joy and freedom in your heart.

It is in the words of Christ, as he surrendered the totality of his human experience to the hands of his fear filled prosecutors, that action of atonement and the expression of true forgiveness is supremely modeled: "Father forgive them, for they know not what they do."

Ego Integration – Revisiting Healing

So it becomes much clearer why ego integration is so integral to healing.

The ego is hidden in thoughts, beliefs and emotional patterns. These patterns create fear based energetic changes in our energy bodies. This can have important consequences on the human bio-energy system and what we term our energy signature.

This energetic distortion, like a veil, can obscure the ability to perceive the truth of our spiritual design. However, it also impinges directly on the life we manifest in this world in ways we have discussed.

Ego based patterns in the human energy field – fear based thoughts and emotions – are creative. There may be an infinite array of mental and emotional patterns that exist. They not only impede a more direct awareness of one's own higher self-nature, but also the energy, which flows creatively into our life.

The ego is a force of endless distraction, misperception and misguidance. It will need to be reconciled for deep healing to occur. At some point in the healing journey, a person comes to grasp that fear of the ego has usurped one's truer nature, and it is an unreliable ally. Atonement is the process of forgiveness and release, allowing elements of ego to rescind in value, and allow the light and the energy of our spiritual self to emerge with peace, joy and healing in its wings.

It is ultimately the light within us as energy based spiritual beings that emanates through us. It has the power to reveal, and ultimately to heal our fear oriented attributes. This inner light is a force, which can reveal and dismantle these energy constructs we carry. When we grasp this simple energy principle, it is obvious why energy work and conscious spiritual integration, which is based on this spiritual precept, is so powerful.

When higher-self integration occurs, the ego is slowly sublimated to one's higher consciousness. The lower energy bodies are progressively cleared and held in balance and alignment. As all four bodies we have examined learn to operate in alignment or in harmony with ones Higher Self nature – a strong biospiritual integration occurs.

Ego integration will restore an open circuitry, clearing blockages and energy distortions, liberating the vital energy in our lives. Through pure intention, when a person chooses to grow spiritually and to heal – a whole new dimension opens up to assist us. The higher self is there always, silently waiting and watching – ready to step in to teach, to heal and to inspire. It is through this higher self connection that we can access the energy, power and love to heal - anything.

Ego Integration – A Living Testament to its Healing Power

I recall an experience I had the privilege of witnessing one day, while attending a spiritual conference. It will forever rest with me as a testament to the power of atonement. It is a simple but powerful story. It demonstrates the pervasive power and potential of love to heal all of our ego's transgressions.

As the audience was taking its place to hear a well-known speaker, I took my seat. As I settled in, I noticed in the row in front of me, that a lady weaseled in between another lady and the seat behind her, and took the seat! I watched – admittedly a little bewildered and in awe – for this was a "spiritual conference". But as events unfolded, I watched these two ladies encounter a marvelous synchronicity about to take place.

The lady left standing turned to the lady now sitting and declared softly, "I'm sorry. This is my seat". The sitting lady replied, "It isn't anymore." She looked her in the eye, and she continued, "It is now my seat, I am sitting in it." An awkward silence filled the space. Eventually, in a nearly apologetic tone, the lady sitting continued to speak, "Look, I have spent my whole life putting myself second or third or fifth. I want to be close to the stage today, and the energy of this conference. I am learning to love and honor myself. I sat here first and this seat is mine."

The standing lady, seemed to reach inside herself for composure. She took a breath and let down her defensive posture. She looked lovingly at the lady sitting as she said, "Please take the chair. If it means you are able to love yourself a little more deeply, or be closer to the energy of God – it is yours." There was no tone of arrogance or dismay. She continued, "May I give you a hug"?

The original tension slowly began to dissipate in this turn of events, but an awkwardness remained. The lady who was sitting slowly stood up looking nervously at the standing lady. The standing lady held her in her arms and you could feel the love in her flowing and embracing them both.

The lady who aggressively took the seat began to cry. She cried for several minutes, with momentary gushes of deep emotion coming to the surface and releasing. It was a magical moment of healing. As her waves of tears began to settle, she was visibly shaken and slowly composed herself.

"In all of my years as a wife, a teacher and mother – I did constantly for others. Partly, this was because it was simply my nature to do that, but somehow, my sense of worth also seemed to depend on it. I could never do enough or be enough to deserve being loved the way I wanted to be loved. Today I behaved in a crazy fashion – nearly hurting you to have what I wanted. It was so wrong in so many ways – and you gave me in response, what I have always craved the most. I came here to be close to the energy – but I realize I came here to experience a love I had never known, and I have witnessed it today, in you".

She dried her eyes and stood up straight. "In all my years of healing ... searching ... workshops, I have learned so many things – all fascinating and all inspiring. But today in your response to me, I have seen love, spiritual love,

God's love – the love of universal cause. I saw it in your eyes and felt it in your touch. In this gift you have given me, and I have felt this love *in* me. I have been foolishly trying to love myself - but today I am aware consciously of the love that *IS* myself. I do not need to love myself, I AM love. I have been offered a glimpse that this love is who I am. I do not really have words. This is simply who I am."

As she spoke, deeply and sincerely from her heart, the magic continued to unfold. The standing lady also began to weep. She cried a few solemn tears and she began to speak. "I have always known love is the way. I have always tried to be loving and kind to the best of my ability. Today in you I see mercy and the magic of love's grace. For so long I have been asking, "Spirit what am I to do?" I was deeply disturbed by the fact that I could not see or find my purpose – like I was missing something.

Today I understand with my whole heart, I will never find a greater purpose than to love. That is also who I am. Thank you for this lesson. Thank you from the bottom of my heart. Today, you have brought me to the threshold of peace."

As the scene ended and the speaker was about to take his place, a third lady appeared. She had placed her things in the adjacent chair long before these two ladies arrived. She began to accumulate her things and was obviously planning to change her seat. As if scripted by the hand of divine grace she attested, "My friend has saved me a seat on the other side – if anyone needs a chair please feel free."

The two ladies who were standing began to laugh in disbelief. They nestled in beside each other and enjoyed the conference together – as newfound friends. Such is the healing that allies with grace.

◉

Healing through ego awareness and integration will have many phenomenal outcomes – both in the quality of one's personal life, and in overcoming the psychological and energetic patterns that promote disease states. It can restore peace, and a sense of presence. It provides an ability to cope smoothly, playfully and joyfully in life, with a sense of healing compassion. It allows us to willingly let silly little ego-based perceptions fade away in one's relationships. It awakens a great disinterest in drama and a much greater awareness of the subversive tendencies of the ego to snare or trip us up in the world of ego form. You see, it will return us consciously to love's embrace. What more could we really wish to become?

Peace Consciousness

> "Peace has to be created, in order to be maintained. It is the product of Faith, Strength, Energy, Will, Sympathy, Justice, Imagination, and the triumph of principle."
>
> Dorothy Thompson

The Practice of Peace

One of the most relevant spiritual teachings that I have encountered personally is the practice of peace consciousness. Peace is not a concept – it is a practice. For me, understanding the "practice of peace" has not only been a great tool, which has provided me with countless opportunities to stay true to a core spiritual alignment; it has also shown me the truth of our spiritual power to step out of ego perception, heal old formed patterns embedded in one's personality, and remove countless hours of suffering from daily life.

People who are inclined to healing are often "spiritually oriented" people. They are often sensitive, open hearted and aware of deep potential of the earth to be a much more enlightened and wonderful place. They pray for peace through all of the struggles we see manifest between people and the nations of our world.

Yet, what one comes to understand is that the only effective way to promote peace in our world is to become it. It is in this wisdom that the practice of peace becomes essential. The practice of peace is a process in which one can steadily undo the ego nature.

So, let us explore the practice of peace. But first, there are three things to realize upfront as one begins this practice:

1. You will be spiritually supported in this endeavor. Anyone who endeavors to do this will be very much supported by his or her higher self.

2. You will be challenged in this endeavor. In many ways this will be a challenge posed by your own ego. It will also be through the manifestation of ego in the world around you. Hence, the challenge of the ego will perceptibly come both internally and externally. But as you learn to center in peace, and call upon the support of your spirit to

aid in this transition, you will find great progress in your practice – and in your life.

3. Peace comes at a price. The price you will pay - is greater and greater surrender of the ego nature. But as you will discover, it is a small price to pay and the rewards far outweigh the investment! To surrender the attributes of the ego, those that weaken the manifestation of one's spiritual power and love, is not a high price when you can understand what you are doing.

In no way will you surrender anything of *true* value. You will discover that you are allowing spiritual nature, your beauty, and your incredible creative strength and ability – to flourish. Of course, you must be willing to let go of a lot of drama, a lot of the familiar ways to the human being, if you would like to mature in peace.

⊙

The key element in the practice of peace lies in the acceptance of one very simple realization: Peace is a choice. Being conscious of this, and applying this wisdom in the form of a practice, provides a "tool" for healing and growth.

A choice, however, does imply that we are making a conscious decision. To *choose* peace means having to make a conscious choice to leave other options behind. "What does one have to leave behind, to be at peace?"

Well the answer of course is … all of the things that take peace away. If we were to construct a list what would it include do you think?

The major components can be shortlisted into the following attributes, with which we are becoming very familiar! We reviewed them as attributes of the ego: worry, guilt, shame, pride, denial, judgment, hatred and defense. Each of these represents a behavior we exhibit as human beings that destroys a peaceful countenance. And, each and every one of them is founded in a primal human fear. When you examine these attributes one by one – you will realize that one cannot participate in any one of them and remain peaceful. One must surrender one's peace, to engage in them. Understanding this, we have found a compass!

Let us look at an example. If you begin to think about something that is provoking worry, it is perhaps now easy to grasp that there is *fear* lurking beneath the worry. If you are very worried about something – you cannot be at peace. Through this simple illustration we can realize that every time we begin to worry, we have vicariously surrendered a peaceful countenance.

Now, if you are actively engaged in thoughts and emotions about something that triggers fear and worry, are you able to stop? If someone tells you to stop worrying, are you able to do so?

If you are like most people, you will admit that this is very challenging. It is hard to stop these forces, because of the occult nature of the ego. The ego will likely step up and explain why worrying is necessary, or potentially fruitful, or even required. The ego will make itself look like it is even doing something noble — that worrying is a useful activity to engage in. The ego has a "grip" that makes it very difficult to let go.

The simple point is — to worry you must absolutely, unequivocally have to ignore your spiritual power. You cannot maintain peace, and continue to worry. You cannot maintain worry, and be at peace. One precludes the other, and at some point one must consciously choose. (Fig 10-1)

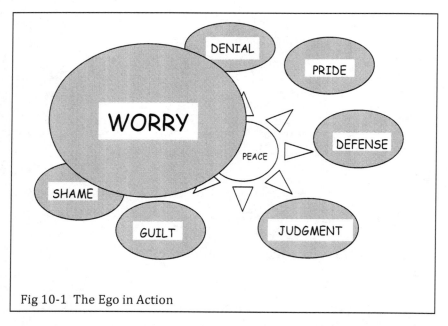

Fig 10-1 The Ego in Action

In this understanding we realize the most direct way out of an ego pattern such as worrying, is to "simply" choose peace in response to its prompting. As we understand the attributes of fear and ego — we are more able to recognize them, or in spiritual terms, have greater "awareness". As one becomes more aware — one becomes more able to change or transform.

When you begin to recognize an attribute of the ego, and you also become aware of your spiritual sovereignty — that is "your power to choose" — you have a powerful tool for personal transformation.

Let us look at a few of the other attributes. If you are full of shame in your life, or experiencing shame about something you have said or done, or perhaps not done – can you be peaceful? If you are full of judgment about yourself or about others – can your really be peaceful? How about if you are defensive or arrogant? You see, the same principle will carry through for each and every attribute of fear and ego.

Now, from a healing perspective, what is important to understand, is that each of these ego activities will create or amplify a "distortion" in our own energy bodies.

We have learned that what we empower in our mental and emotional bodies contributes to our energy signature. Our energy signature then has a magnetic way of drawing energy to manifest what we are empowering. It begins to "show up" in our life to reflect our energy back to us. We have also learned that the idea that "interference" in energy created by integrated patterns and ego attributes serves to create a veil of consciousness, one which keeps us even more perceptibly apart from knowing and manifesting our higher spiritual nature. It is hard, for example, to "recognize" your divine nature when you are enraged, lying, or defensive. And, although the ego may deny it, such action certainly is keeping us apart from feeling peace.

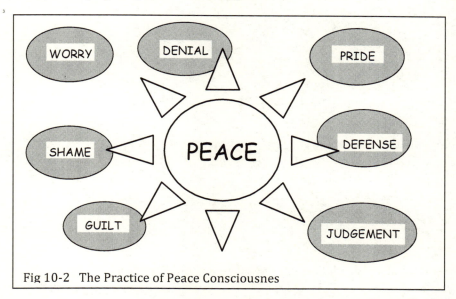

Fig 10-2 The Practice of Peace Consciousnes

One can examine each attribute outside of peace in Fig 10-2, and realize it is not possible to be at peace while we are engaged in it. As one realizes the truth in this, it is a little easier to recognize the fear-based tendencies one carries, and also to become more conscious of how we choose to align our self as we journey through the experiences of our life. How you align – with ego (fear) or with spirit (love) – is completely up to you.

Moment by moment, we are faced with the option to align with a peaceful countenance, or with ego drama. Through any given day, one will encounter an infinite number of experiences that test one's patience, challenge one's fears, and evoke insecurities. Even while alone, if one sits still and let one's mind wander – it is capable of creating a series of thoughts and feelings that can be disturbing. We are constantly faced with the choice – between love and fear.

As one sees events occurring in one's life, and becomes aware of the disturbing influence imposed, one can learn to deal with the disturbance by consciously aligning with peace.

Moving from concept to practice, you can begin to work with this simple but profound understanding in real life situations when you see the ego and fear at work in one's life. As you encounter the force of ego attributes, the items listed outside of peace in Fig 10-2, you can begin to practice by aligning with your spiritual nature, as you say to yourself:

I can be at peace, or I can   (i.e. worry) , but I cannot do both.

I choose peace. I am peace.

Peace, being a choice, provides a point of power. It is the point of reversal – one where we learn to step away from fear as the foundation on which we build our lives.

Moment to moment in our lives, we can be in the presence of peace, or consumed by the ego's fearful tendencies. To be at peace implies a willingness to let go of the ego struggles we each face in the form of worry, guilt, shame, pride, judgment, anger or defensiveness. These attributes are so "pervasive" in human nature that we have to develop an understanding of how and why they are so limiting and hurtful to us – and how we can begin to transform them. As we do this work, the influence they have on our lives begins to fade.

It is probably not difficult to imagine that this requires both vigilance and practice. Imagine all of the types of life experiences, thoughts and feelings that we may experience in the run of a day that may pull one away from peace. In discussing the concept, we use the word *practice* with great specificity – for the most humbling thing we encounter when we begin this practice is a discovery of how deeply ego tendencies are embedded in us, and how challenging they can be to overcome. I still to this day see things I want to judge, find worries that I think are important enough to entertain, and find a brewing frustration and anger over things I know are of ego's design. And when I do – what do I do? I practice.

When we begin to entertain the idea of releasing ourselves from the drama of the human ego – it may at first appear that life would become a boring and complacent activity. The ego loves drama. Yet, an integrated, undisturbed, peace filled person is highly capable, full of joy, wonder, awe, compassion and creative self-expression! Life is not boring in a state of peace consciousness – it is full of wonder. We have the power to realign with a greater spiritual wisdom, a power revealed in the practice of peace.

Peace as an Exercise of Healing

Healing implies the work of regaining spiritual sovereignty over the focus of consciousness, and the constructs we build in our mental, emotional and our etheric bodies. It follows that the choices we make, and experiences we manifest, become less and less controlled by the ego and the energy distortions it would create. This process reveals the ability of our spirit to step in and begin to unravel these tendencies. It restores sovereignty of the mental, emotional and the etheric bodies – to the consciousness of the soul.

Hence, the practice of peace brings healing. Healing may be implied on the mental, emotional and/or physical-etheric level. Such healing will support the correction of energetic changes, which have led, or will lead, to a manifested disease state. Such practice can lead to mystical healing experiences of mind and body, as so many people have experienced today. Or it can lead to the "non-manifestation" of probable diseases or experiences that would otherwise have been part of one's life experience. It begins to make sense how this all "fits" together.

⊙

So, are you ready to do a little work together? Let us take a few minutes to do and exercise to put some of this into a more personal context.

EXERCISE:
1. Take a pen and paper and write down three things you judge or dislike about yourself. Leave a few blank lines or space.

2. Write down three things you judge or dislike about others. Leave a few blank lines or space.

3. Write down three situations where you see guilt has made you do things you resent or regret. Leave a few blank lines or space.

4. Write down three things you stanchly defend about your character when people judge you. Leave a few blank lines or space.

5. Now go back to item number 1. As you reflect on the three items one by one – what do you *feel* inside of you? What *thoughts* do you have? Are you truly at peace in these moments or are you disturbed in some way? Write down anything you find important to remember.

6. Now take the statement "I can be at peace or I can judge, but I can not do both. I am peace." What does this statement bring to your awareness? What resistance do you feel? What thoughts arise to negate its power or influence? Write down anything you find important to remember.

7. Now go back to item number 2. As you reflect on the three items one by one – what do you *feel* inside of you? What *thoughts* do you have? Are you truly at peace in these moments or are you disturbed in some way? Write down anything you find important to remember.

8. Again, take the statement "I can be at peace or I can judge, but I can not do both. I am peace." What does this statement bring to your awareness? What resistance do you feel? What thoughts arise to negate its power or influence? Write down anything you find important to remember.

9. Now go back to item number 3. As you reflect on the three items one by one – how does guilt control you? Do you make conscious choices *or* guilt inspired choices as a matter of habit. What happens inside of you when you act on guilt and not from a conscious point of view?

10. Now take the statement "I can be at peace or I can be guilty, but I can not do both. I am peace." What does this statement bring to your awareness? What resistance do you encounter in letting go of guilt? What would you need to do to truly appease any guilt you may have in your awareness? Write down anything you find important to remember.

11. Now go back to item number 4. As you reflect on the three items one by one – what is it about yourself that you need to defend? Are you

truly at peace in these moments or are you disturbed in some way? Write down anything you find important to remember.

12. Now take the statement "I can be at peace or I can be defensive, but I can not do both. I am peace." What does this statement bring to your awareness? What resistance do you feel? What thoughts arise to remain defensive? Write down anything you find important to remember.

13. As you reflect upon the exercise, are you more aware of the egoic tendencies that keep peace at bay? Did you encounter the transformation from one ego attribute (i.e. guilt), to another (i.e. judgment)?

14. How do you see yourself if your ego was dissipated, and you lived with a greater and greater sense of peace? To anchor this thought, write down some of your ideas. How do you want to live? Do you realize the great power you hold inside of you to "choose" this more and more?

As one becomes aware of the difference between ego, and the natural state of spiritual being, one can begin to put this awareness into practice in one's daily life. Each day as you become more aware of your own ego based tendencies – you can also become more aware of the ability you have to shift your perception around them – from fear to love. When you see yourself worrying, getting anxious, judging, condemning, hating, angry, defensive and so on – you can "intervene spiritually and remind yourself:

"I can be at peace, or I can be _____ – but I can not do both.
I choose peace. I am peace."

I would encourage you to select one of the ego attributes each day for the next few weeks – and ask your spirit to help you become more aware of it's presence in your life. As you see the attribute manifest, such as worry or judgment, step in to realign your consciousness with your spirit. Understand in this exercise that you are aligning with you spirit, and you have the power of choice!

As you put peace consciousness into practice in your life, you will surface or encounter deep ego tendencies that are personal to you. Do not judge these tendencies, but do not deny them. Let them surface and let yourself be honestly aware of what you see. Let your higher self nature work with you to dissipate the control they have on your mental and emotional energy.

If you encounter memories of remote experiences, or memories that trigger strong emotional and mental reactions, it may require some processing. It may be useful to solicit support of a wise friend or counselor in this process to help you.

For those who would like to deeply immerse themselves into this awareness, the program of *A Course in Miracles* is available to establish a daily practice that can greatly assist in unraveling the ego influence in our lives. Some find the content of ACIM a little overwhelming and I often recommend a beautiful book by Marianne Williamson – *A Return to Love*, as a primer to explore the idea of a love vs. fear based reality. [55]

Peace Plus

In addition to the practice of peace there are a few additional attributes or practices that will move you light years on the path of healing. They are all conscious actions that will serve to loosen the bind the ego will hold on ones mental and emotional expression. This includes the practice of *forgiveness* as we have already discussed, the practice of *compassion*, spiritual *faith*, *perseverance* and honest *gratitude* for both the blessings and the challenges that life has brought to your experience.

Compassion

As we grow in spiritual awareness and we encounter our own healing experiences, it is natural for the heart to open in expanded ways. We really grow in our realization of the challenge created by ego perception in a world where many people do not really understand the ego nature. We begin to realize that all human beings are ensnared in ego tendencies in ways they do not recognize or understand. This awareness softens our view of ourselves and other people, and it opens us to compassion in a greatly expanded way.

As human beings we each carry ego tendencies that we do not at first appreciate. It is difficult to recognize the degree of suffering imposed by the ego - and it is even more difficult to transcend because of its occult and nebulous nature.

As a person grows stronger in spiritual awareness and biospiritual integration – ego becomes more obvious. Through the lens of greater understanding - it is easier to hold greater *compassion*. Instead of judgment and condemnation – with an open heart, one adopts an attitude of greater and greater compassion towards life, toward our self when we are struggling, and toward others, when we recognize behavior that is greatly enmeshed in ego.

This is not compassion born of spiritual arrogance, or in an ego effort to feel superior – but compassion of heart. Compassion develops as a way of life towards any and all types of human suffering – personal, racial, national, or environmental. Compassion is a natural expression of a well-integrated being.

As a loving parent may witness the naivety of a child with great tenderness – a person who has been blessed with a greater comprehension will look at the world a little differently. This again echoes through time, in the statement: "Father forgive them for they know not what they do". This is Christ talking to the ego laden humanity around him, who were acting in ignorance and violence to the beauty and majesty he carried as an awakened spiritual being in "Christ Consciousness".

Before you judge, understand. With a compassionate heart great healing will emerge.

Faith and Perseverance

Faith and perseverance are also attributes of our Higher Self nature. Everyone who is engaged in a process of healing or spiritual growth will face success, triumph, defeat, ego resistance, and many fears. It takes a courageous and enduring spirit to walk through these challenges and obstacles – and not lose faith. You will receive all the spiritual help you need if you are sincere in your effort and intention to grow.

You will also be provided with all of the experience you need to see yourself and to liberate yourself spiritually speaking. This can be very humbling to the ego. That is the way of things. But a humble ego and a triumphant spirit go hand in hand!

It is important to not allow the humbling of ego to cloud the majesty of your spirit. Your spiritual worth and your ability are beyond measure. To "walk the pilgrims journey of healing" – you will need to know that you will be given all you need – energy, support and experience – to find your way. Have faith, and carry on ...

Gratitude

Gratitude is also an attitude that strongly supports our healing endeavors. As one continues to grow spiritually, one will develop an increasing gratitude for one's life. We become thankful for the teachers who present in all forms – from supportive friends to soul adversaries. We become grateful for the blessings afforded us, and the challenges that made us grow. We are thankful for all the lessons and experiences that have played a pivotal role in shaping or leading us to an awakening experience.

As we step away from ego-based drama and misery, we find a growing peace and freedom. We find a greater natural expression of joy and gratefulness – just for being alive. But why wait? Be grateful for all you have been given, and will continue to receive, each and every day. Make it a practice!

THE SPIRITUAL EGO

This section would not be complete without a short discussion on the spiritual ego. The spiritual ego might be viewed as the element of ego - which develops when people begin to walk the journey of spiritual healing.

As people make progress on the spiritual and energy-healing path, they will inevitably learn many things about energy and spiritual consciousness. It is easy for the ego to sneak in and vicariously try to control spiritual attainment and spiritual growth. It becomes critical to understand the nature and workings of the ego at this time for it can be a challenging passage.

People who awaken to energy and spiritual healing are usually drawn to it because of their soul work in prior lifetimes. They will often quickly step into the role of teaching because of the overall development of their soul. Other people who awaken and pursue healing knowledge may just continue to learn and learn and learn and absorb great quantities of information - but do not integrate the teachings into practical growth and change. Either of these situations can present spiritual challenges, potential for ego manifestation, and sometimes a spiritual danger. A "danger" - because they will implicate karma when they have been provided the tools to live in grace.

In this time cycle of awakening we are being given great gifts – both as knowledge and as tools. This is purposed to facilitate the development en masse of a more enlightened humanity. This attainment is the potential to experience a spiritual mastery that we have seen only in avatars, gurus and the spiritual masters among men and women. Yet this attainment, this enlightenment is a birthright of every human being if one so chooses to grow and develop towards this ideal.

THE MISSING PILL

As people step into the role of teaching, one needs to understand also that the ego loves the idea of spiritual importance. It wants to jump in and create a hierarchy of enlightenment, and judge itself superior or inferior to another being to understand where it lies in this hierarchy. It wants to establish itself as the intermediary of God and spirit, and not as its humble ambassador. There are some teachers in the world of emerging spiritual knowledge may have to face this correction in time.

The higher self nature is aware of its inherent value, and the value of all beings. Self worth is an attribute of enlightenment. Yet, it is not lofty or arrogant. It is not puffed up or self important with knowledge or accomplishment. It is truly humble – because that is its true universal nature. The ego is not so lucky.

The ego is always trying to be unique, important, distinct, separate, divided, superior, different, etc. When a teacher, a student or any human being is manifesting these tendencies, it will be an element of ego that is manifesting at that time. It is important for people in teaching roles to be very self aware and correct tendencies for ego inflation or derailment. It is important for those taking on this important role not to be misguided.

The reason this becomes so important is that many people awakening to energy and consciousness today, are destined to share the knowledge in some form of teaching, and will need to be very aware of the ego to avoid its pitfalls in their development. It is important to nip this spiritual ego in the bud at the beginning and stay vigilant as you grow. Keep it real, down to earth and humble in truth.

This being said, in the role of a teacher, it is also very challenging to stand in face of another person who may be exhibiting their ego nature – disguised in a desire to learn and grow – and remain in a spiritual alignment. This is probably the greatest challenge in front of someone who takes on this role. You have to be prepared for it as a teacher of any type. When being challenged and confronted in such a way it is very easy to step into an ego defense mechanism rather than ones spiritual core.

This is also important to realize as a student. You may see your ego manifest in judgment, attack, ridicule, and so forth. If a teacher presents a concept that rattles your ego's cage – you may find yourself reacting equally. At other times, you may see a great ego in a teacher and have the discernment to steer away legitimately from the teacher or teachings. This is a lesson in personal discernment that you will have to encounter, to learn to trust the spirit within yourself.

A seeker quickly learns that circles of spiritual teaching are not void of the same ego tendency that may perceptually poison life in general – but you will find many good natured, evolved, loving, kind people with a good deal of knowledge that can help you on your journey, and help awaken in you, your latent spiritual nature, abilities and talents.

To me, the clearest, simplest model and teacher of this advanced bio-spiritual attainment was Christ. As enlightened, grace laden and love radiant as this man was – his teaching was simple – you are both human and divine. Give up your ego, you are more than that – your goal is to love.

> *The ego has built a shabby and unsheltering home for you, because it cannot build otherwise. Do no try to make this impoverished house stand. Its weakness is our strength. Only God could make a home that is worthy of His creations.*
>
> *A Course in Miracles*

It is often stated that to grow spiritually is to grow in love. At the core of our existence love is who we are. This love reveals itself as the veils of our ego's tendencies are effaced one by one.

In a world greatly constructed on ego perceived vision, it is obviously challenging at first to accept love as the foundation of reality. Yet it is shown over and over to be true. It is in personally living through the deep transformation stimulated by love's healing presence, that deep healing is found.

When we think of altruistic love we often think of selflessness. But, the paradox is that to become love aligned, and surrender ego tendencies, one must identify and align with one's true worth. You will hear this expressed in the idea - learning to love one's self.

One must learn to love and honor one's self; to treat one's self with respect, kindness, understanding and support; to allow creativity to blossom; to allow curiosity to inspire, and inspiration to elevate. One must learn to permit love to flow so profoundly through you, that you become one with this essence.

With courage, compassion, perseverance, integrity, kindness and love – you will find the efforts you put forth to grow will be rich and fruitful. As you release the ego, you will find your most authentic self. It is truly through this self, that healing may flow.

COMING HOME

A question I am sometimes asked is, "What happens in one's life as people engage in biospiritual transformation? Or, what does it look like when people heal?"

Healing for many people begins in an effort to overcome an illness, or deal with a psychological crisis. So first, of course, people may experience a profound personal healing. There is an infinite array of physical, mental or emotional states that may accompany transformation during a healing process.

At some point along the journey, which may be in the beginning, middle or end - there will be a growing awareness, an awakening that will demonstrate the reality of the one's spiritual and energetic nature. This awakening will stimulate a desire to grow in knowledge and experience, and to manifest the secret potential held inside.

Although each person will travel a unique path in the form of their life and awakening – there are a few common elements. Certain key attributes and attitudes develop. A curiosity to grow and learn strengthens, but an interest in drama fades away. A sense of inner peace and power grows, while the need to control, manipulate and deceive dissolve. Peace becomes a cornerstone and a touchstone – it is the rock of existence. Value, presence, and joy blossom – and infiltrate all you do.

Yet, healing does not produce a bunch of cloned specimens. Healing is a spiritual restoration. From a spiritual perspective every being is remarkably unique. No one will be exactly like his or her neighbor in manifestation. But each person will have in common, is the love they manifest in their own unique way.

So although unique to each person, love does manifest in some common attributes, which we can attempt to define. We will review them here to have a good understanding of the healed or "new" human:

1. Self Responsibility
2. Gratefulness - for one's life and experiences past, present and future
3. Acceptance of one's self and one's worth
4. Authenticity
5. A humility born of true self worth
6. An attitude of love toward one's self and others
7. Gentleness of approach to life

8. A grounded presence in the moment
9. Patience born of understanding - an acceptance of the flow of time and of life.
10. Tolerance
11. Honesty and Integrity
12. Compassion
13. Kindness
14. Disinterest in drama
15. Disinterest in gossip, belittlement or judgment
16. Strong interest in activities that nurture the spirit, mind, emotions and body
17. An awareness of prior mistakes and transgressions and ego based creations, with a desire to heal them.
18. Release of shame and guilt
19. Release of worry
20. Active listening
21. A willingness to see, understand, admit and pardon
22. A willingness to forgive, release and grow.
23. A greater sense of intuitive awareness
24. A greater flow in synchronicity
25. A deep appreciation of life, family in all its forms, work and nature
26. An awakening of a new vision or purpose
27. Peace
28. Joy
29. Love

Now, although this process is highly personal, we can begin to see that attributes do not so much describe a *behavior* or a *religion* – but rather a *way*. It is our greatest potential to manifest these attributes and this state of inspired wholeness. It is our destiny. And, it is – the way of love.

THE BODY AS A TEMPLE

The human body in science and in modern culture receives a lot of attention. In popular culture the body is despised, revered and everything in between. To some it is the foundation of reality; to others it is a prison of consciousness.

It is time to refresh our understanding of the "human machine". The body is an incredible work of art. It is a functional system of an unimaginable intelligent design. It houses one of the most complex organizational feats of systematic cooperation, and provides the vessel to live on this amazing planet.

But in the most profound of terms – the body is the abode of your spirit. It is the true temple – the dwelling place where the sacred resides.

When we view the body not only as a physical vehicle – but also in expanded terms as the "anchor" of multiple bodies of energy. It is a vehicle of consciousness expression. Each of the bodies is interrelated and function as a system. Each one of them is a vehicle to create and experience the world of form.

The temple is, however, transient. The consciousness dwelling in the temple is not. It is divine and eternal. The ultimate goal of life is not to live forever in a body – the body by nature is impermanent. It is to manifest our spirit while in the body to a greater and greater degree. It is to care for the body as a spiritual vehicle and allow our spirit to manifest more fully through it. That is our greatest gift and potential.

As we grasp this understanding – we can perhaps more easily accept that our relation to our physical body (and our many bodies) - is one of guardian rather than identity. The body temple is provided to us. This occurs through many elements including the genetics of our parents, the earth and the sacred elements that go into its creation, and the soul from which we emerge. The body is a gift to us to experience life in the world of form. We are its caretaker and custodian.

The body is not simply a "possession" – it is an extension of our spiritual self. In simple terms, if we think in this way, we are responsible for how we treat it and care for it. We are in charge of what we let into it and how it is cleaned. We are responsible for the way we use our minds to think and to create, and our emotions and feelings to energize and inspire. The question becomes - do we use it to honor the spirit of love, or do we lose our way?

As we learn to view the body as a continuum of energy, emanating from our spiritual self, we can appreciate it is a portal or access to the knowledge, wisdom, light and love of our spiritual nature deep within. By letting this light into our lives, we allow for a transformative healing to take place. We will retain the responsibility for guardianship, but a level of light and intelligence that can do the unthinkable will support us. It can reinvigorate, restructure, realign, reorganize and restore. It can heal.

To heal is to invoke our spirit into the temple. Safe to say, that all of our temples have been a little beaten down by life – yet the ability to heal lies within our inherent spiritual design. As a person opens up to energetic healing and transformation they are opening up to the continuum that exists between these domains – human and divine.

By invoking the spirit within us, we are calling upon the divine consciousness within us to return to the temple. We are preparing a place for the love, inherent in this consciousness to dwell. In this invitation we are bringing back the spiritual wisdom, power and love that is our essential nature – forces which chase out discord and disharmony and restore a sacred space.

We are asking to more fully incarnate our God granted divine nature – and in doing so we become more like that divinity itself. This healing is a light of higher vibration. It is energy. It is consciousness. It is love. All wounds heal in the return of love.

Let love and wisdom into your temple. Echoed in the Vedic prayer of peace –
Om shanti, shanti Om – may peace be with you and in you.

CHAPTER 11
UNITY FIELD HEALING

Intro

In this chapter, we will take a step forward into a mystical potential. To some, it might appear that we are about to foray right over the cliff of common sanity! Alàs, that is okay ☺. I am about to introduce you to some concepts that have little foundation in 3D reality, at first. They will however take root in understanding, and flourish through your personal experience. Are you ready to encounter a deep and profound reintegration with your own spiritual nature? If so, let's explore an evolutionary way to achieve this together.

We have already discussed that this is an auspicious time on our planet. Through the advent of the new earth, humanity is being given special tools and special knowledge to introduce new paradigms of healing. *Unity Field Healing* is a new and unique energy modality, developed through a series of visionary experiences, to support healing and transformation. This work involves first creating an intentional connection with your spiritual DNA, followed by the use of a special light energy pattern which is called the *Unity Field Healing Template* – and the magnificent potential this combination provides.

I will begin by first reviewing how it came into being. We will then invigorate a conscious connection with your spiritual DNA, and work with the light pattern, in the form of an exercise. This will introduce you to "the energy" of this work.

Unity Field Healing

Unity Field Healing is a simple but powerful energy process, intended to support and facilitate the healing integration outlined in this book. The first step of this work involves a process to assist strengthening a conscious connection to your spiritual DNA. With this in place, we begin to use what I refer to as an "interdimensional living-light geometric template" or "light template" to facilitate healing work within the quantum DNA paradigm.

Your spiritual DNA exists in a quantum interdimensional reality. This spiritual DNA is poised "to connect" more completely with any member of humanity who expresses sincere intent to develop spiritually at this time. Understanding that it is time of great awakening, this DNA connection and integration is a fundamental part of the mechanism by which people will participate in this transformation.

This form of DNA first presented to me in a visionary experience around 15 years ago. During this experience, a "cosmic DNA" helix appeared to me in a meditative vision. A luminous filament of DNA made a literal "interdimensional descent" and connected with my energy field.

As the DNA connected, it first appeared as long cord or rope-like structure composed of light. It connected to my crown chakra and created a luminous energy throughout my energy field. The luminous cord subsequently opened or expanded – into the form of a luminous double helix strand.

Through this personal experience I was introduced to the idea that "DNA integration" is not simply a poetic concept – it is an actual "event". Now whether the visionary experience was meant to be symbolic, or, was meant to demonstrate the actual mechanics of the process, it is difficult to know with certainty. As human beings, we are limited in our understanding of quantum energy processes and spirit will communicate with us in a meaningful way. Yet this vision was very "real" to me. Its influence was more than tangibly "suggested" – as highlighted by some of the subsequent changes that it produced in my life.

Although I lived this experience personally, I know whole-heartedly that the process of DNA integration is certainly not unique to me. It is open to anyone with sincere intention to grow spiritually in the new energy paradigm. This process, in my understanding, defines a first step in the expansion of what I refer to as "the axis of Spiritual DNA". I believe I simply lived this experience personally, with a visual "confirmation" that it was taking place. "And everything has a reason, right?" he says, as he sits here writing these words ☺ !

This direct DNA connection literally expands a person's potential to connect spiritually to a higher vibratory reality. Supporting this energetic expansion is the focus in the first one of three sessions that comprises *Unity Field Healing*.

Consciously connecting with our Spiritual DNA greatly facilitates healing work. Why? Well because it reconnects or rewires us to a much higher level of consciousness and understanding than we are accustomed to experiencing. This alone awakens a tremendous new healing potential.

The second level of this work introduces the use of the *Unity Field Template*. The template is an organizational field of light and order. From the way I have come to understand it, this pattern is a catalytic light pattern that gently but powerfully facilitates the re-ordering, or recalibration of the quantum level DNA. This is purposed to support us uniquely in the process of higher vibratory integration.

The template, as it was presented to me, represents the fundamental quantum pattern that is mystically behind the human process of DNA integration and recalibration. When your spiritual DNA connection is strengthened, and this pattern is made "active", it can support a process of recalibrating the connection you have with your spiritual nature. Through this, the information that is delivered to your human DNA is potentially transformed.

By activating an awareness of the template within our Spiritual DNA axis, I believe each one of us supporting our own personal bio-spiritual transformation. It is a quantum process, which means that as this reordering occurs, I believe it can facilitate an expanded communication between the spiritual DNA and your human DNA molecules.

As this occurs, it will theoretically have an important influence not simply on your human DNA but also the bodies of energy that manifest through your DNA as a human being. This introduces the unique way that this evolutionary energy work can stimulate healing within your physical body, your etheric body, your emotional body and your mental body in a direct and powerful way.

Facilitating your process with the energetic support provided through *Unity Field Healing*, and gaining knowledge to support the integration of your spiritual power and balance – you can accomplish wonderful things. We are poised to heal in a new and profound way. Ready?

The Origin of Unity Field Healing

The first important element, that is integral to this work, is an understanding of Spiritual DNA integration. I believe this DNA reconnection is the foundation of humanity's involvement in the large-scale transformation upon us – and is open to anyone who expresses sincere intention. As we noted above, it is a real event and it is foundational to the work of *Unity Field Healing*. It is encapsulated in the first level of attunement (Session 1) of this healing work – in which a strong alignment with your spiritual DNA is developed.

The second precept of this healing work came to me in a series of visionary experiences beginning late in 2011. The first experience occurred while participating in a spiritual gathering, entitled the "11-11-11" event hosted in Little Rock, Arkansas by a wonderful gentleman and friend James Tyberonn and his lovely wife Anne.

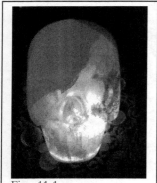

Fig. 11-1
Max the Crystal Skull

During the conference, I experienced many wonderful exchanges and experiences, and the privilege of working together with a group of kindred *earth keepers*. Energetically, this was a very powerful gathering – and the energy throughout the four-day conference was high.

I have learned over time that such gatherings of conscious awakening are incredibly supportive to help us in our process of growth and integration. During highly conscious events, it is as if we are creating a higher vibrational reality during these gatherings – which creates a tangible energy field. This field energetically catalyzes new insights and transformative possibilities for those participating. For me, when in the presence of such an energy, my inner vision becomes highly activated, and I can experience things in meditation which seems very hard to do when on my own.

During this particular event, two things will forever stand out as personal highlights. The first is that I was introduced to a crystal skull named Max. (Fig 11-1) The second is the gift that was given during that experience ... the arrival of the *Unity Field Healing* Template.

Now, I will have to tell you up front (in case you have not figured it out) I am quite open-minded. I am, however, also very discerning and appropriately skeptical about some new age ideas and philosophies. I have to experience and discern things for myself. It is important for me to know how I feel and relate to things through experience. It is part of a process of personal discernment that we should each honor in ourselves.

So the "crystal skulls" phenomenon, for me, fit into the arena of skeptical folly. When I heard people talk about crystal skulls I thought it was silly, or fantasy thinking. It seemed like Hollywood hoopla – one to create fascinating drama.

Spiritually speaking, I believe tremendously in the power of the human spirit, and the wisdom and love it can access and manifest. I do not rely heavily on amulets, icons or external objects to provide me with what I need. I have used a few things, many listed in the subsequent chapters, which have been tools that are very useful in healing. But I was reluctant to add significance to the concept of the healing power of a crystal skull to my world!

When I sat in meditation with Max, I was impressed with the energy I felt radiating from this crystal. It was truly a remarkable experience. As I closed my eyes, I was not sure what might happen or what to expect – yet I remained in a state of openness. Perhaps it was the energy of the conference, or the crystalline field supported by Max, or simply my own readiness – or, perhaps all three together – the scene was set to unfold a new potential. I began to have a vision.

The Inaugural Vision

A Note on the Experience of Visions

I have at several points in my life had vivid dreams and visions. These do not seem to occur under my "conscious control" – but are guided by a larger process of consciousness. They have, for me, occurred at pivotal times of personal growth or understanding.

In my understanding, they seem to occur when "the time is right", and often in what I would term a "high vibrational" state or environment – such as at the gathering described.

I have noted two distinct types of visionary experiences that occur. First, important or symbolic visions arise that may contain content which is familiar to anyone in the 3D world – but the composition of the vision has a deeply symbolic meaning. This may include elements such as scenery and people that are familiar to one's everyday consciousness. The symbolism, and inferred awareness, in these visions carries both meaning and guidance.

Secondly, the content of other visions is founded in a "setting" that has little 3D correlation. These visions are purely composed of energy but also contain elements that have a deeply symbolic significance. It is as if they are occurring in another plane of reality – like a field of geometric light. I have experienced several of these interdimensional visions during my life, and it is this type of vision that took place in this meditation.

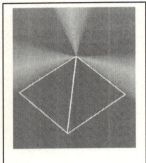

Fig 11-2 Light Pyramid

There are consistent elements in these visions when they occur. They arise on what I would describe as a dark blue backdrop, like a "cosmic sky". On this backdrop, a point of light will appear. The light serves as a "nexus" to allow something to pass through from one level of energy into the next level of vision. To visualize this, you can imagine something emerging through a surface of water, or an interdimensional barrier of energy. However, each time before anything appears through the point of light, consistently in the center of this point of light a pyramid will form. It begins as a ray of light fans out in four directions, like rays of laser light, which form the sides of a luminous pyramid – forming a translucent pyramidal shell. (Fig 11-2)

Then, through the pyramid of light, another light form or object will descend. When I experienced the "Spiritual DNA" vision many years ago – the filament of light I observed came through a pyramid and descended to connect with my crown chakra. (Fig 11-3) This is also what first occurred when the *Unity Field Healing* Template first appeared.

Fig 11-3 Cosmic DNA

I believe the reason the vision presents in this way, is that the energy is importantly presented as an "interdimensional" process. It is demonstrably emerging from "another level or dimension" of consciousness, into this plane of conscious awareness. I realize this can sound a bit sensational. It is however an honest expression of what happened for me.

THE INAUGURAL VISION OF UNITY FIELD HEALING

I will explain next specifically the vision that inaugurated *Unity Field Healing*, exactly as it first unfolded.

THE MISSING PILL

The vision began, as noted above, with a scintillating dot of diamond white light appearing on a dark blue backdrop or "cosmic sky". From this dot there descended several lines of fire white light – to form the shape of a translucent four-sided light pyramid.

As it formed fully, a short ray of light then descended through the center of the pyramid, ending first in a dot. It then began to unfold a second interlocking pyramid, which formed below the first one. Then a third pyramid formed - all in a similar fashion – creating a stack of translucent light pyramids, one on top of each other.

Next, down through the third pyramid came another small dot of light. This dot expanded like a controlled explosion of a firework or a supernova, to form a ring of light. The image appeared flat or "in 2D" as this was first occurring. When the ring was fully formed, a series of four smaller rings developed in a descending fashion, aligned from top to bottom, like pearls appearing on a string. (Fig 11-4)

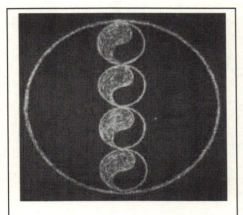

Fig 11-4 Unity Field Healing Template

As the pattern took this form, it stabilized. It then appeared to be "activated" by a light that came from within the form itself. The inner rings began to scintillate. As this occurred, the symbol was activated from a flat 2D template, into a 3D series of scintillating light spheres. (Fig 11-5)

As the energy moved through the pattern, it created the visual impression that energy within the central spheres was circulating and spinning. The pattern became alive with energy and light.

These smaller spheres were so alive with light that they began to take on the appearance of a scintillating or luminescent yin yang symbol. This reminded me of the way a wheel appears to be rotating backwards, when a car is travelling very fast. The yin yang symbol is the famous symbol found in the I Ching Spiritual teachings. This appearance was like an "optical illusion" created by the speed of the moving energy, as the light spun through them.

Once it appeared to me in this way, for the remainder of the weekend, each time we sat in a meditation group meditation or when I would close my eyes, the template would reappear.

At the time, I had absolutely no "logical" idea what this pattern represented, or what it meant. I knew, however, it was *important* - hence I wrote it down and saved the memory of the experience for a later date. For several months that followed, that was the end of the story.

The Story Evolves

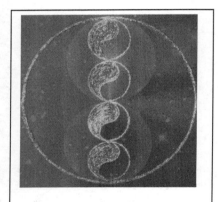

Fig 11-5 UFH Template

The story continues after returning from a trip to Egypt in February of 2012. This trip for me was a very powerful connection with what I perceive an "ancient personal history". I made a deep connection during this voyage – one that served to stimulate a deeper awakening.

After returning from this voyage, I was meditating one day after a yoga session and without thinking about it, or focusing on it, the template returned in my inner vision "out of the blue".

As it happened, I could feel a very strong energy presence "above" my head. It was so strong – and the pressure was so great on my head – I was not sure what was happening. I tried to relax, but the energy was intense, and I began to see light inside my head. This was a little difficult at first to endure but eventually my body seemed to accommodate it. The pattern first appeared in the form I saw months earlier, but as it appeared, I realized it to began "to work".

As it "activated" I could feel the template of energy interact with my energy field. It did not seem to "enter into" my body or directly into my energy field. It stayed above, or adjacent to it. It is difficult to describe this experience, for there is no true sense of perspective. The clearest description I can provide is that I "interfaced" with the pattern. The energetic influence of its action, however, became evident to me directly inside of my personal energy field.

As the template began to "work" I could feel "adjustments" occurring within my energy field. It felt as if it were pulsing energy. I could also feel a sensation as if it were pulling on filaments of energy in my body. I became aware of oscillations of energy passing down through my body, into and through the meridian system in my etheric body. Little jerks and twitches occurred as the energy continued to work on me.

As this occurred, I began to see a field of iridescent light. It contained all kinds of translucent colors – oranges, purples, yellows, blues, greens, opal, silver, gold, fuchsia, and blue. The colors were not opaque. They were translucent or crystalline in nature – like the light that would emit from a jewel or laser. Embedded in the colors were luminous tendrils of light – light filaments that appeared to be arranged quite randomly.

Through the experience, it was obvious that the light pattern was "activated" – and it was having some sort of influence on my energy field. It was as if the energy process was creating a push-pull effect to help release restrictive energy patterning in my system. I could perceptibly feel a gentle pulling as if it were aspirating energy, almost like a vacuum pulling released energy out of my system. Subsequently there was a flushing of my energy system with pure unqualified high vibration light or energy. It was a pretty remarkable experience.

It was through this second experience that I was first able to appreciate that the pattern that I was shown earlier represents a new healing "light template".

I slowly began to realize that the vision I experienced was more that just a vision … it represented a spiritual gift. It is one of many gifts that are arriving on our planet for healing and for transformation at this incredible time. I started to understand that it could be used to promote healing and transformation – and that it could be shared. Admittedly though I was not at first, sure how!

⊙

Reflecting of this experience, in the months that followed, it became clearer to me that the pattern represents a light template, and the template is a spiritual "symbol". A symbol, unlike a simple *sign*, is a pattern that not only represents a communication – it "embodies" a whole field of consciousness.

For example, the color green in our world may be used as a *sign*, meaning to proceed forward such as traffic light on the road. In Tibetan Buddhism a Vajra is a spiritual *symbol*. It represents the entire male principle in spiritual enlightenment and activity. A symbol embodies the fuller consciousness of what it represents.

The *Unity Field Template* is a light template, but to me it is also *symbolic* of a consciousness principle contained in the essence of the *unity* principle. *Unity*

Field Healing is the ultimate process that birthed through this experience. It is meant to support reintegration and recalibration to a unity state of consciousness, and the healing this implies.

I began to work more consciously with the pattern over the months that followed. There was first a period of time to further personally "integrate it" into my own being. As this took place I experienced a graceful shift in energy that promoted both further deep release and deep healing in my own personal energy fields. If it happened too quickly it would be overwhelming and I knew it could be as fast or slow as I wanted to live it – so I chose a graceful speed of medium! As this was occurring, things became a little clearer in my mind …

NEW INFORMATION ARRIVES

Several months later, in a third meditation I asked consciously for more information on the pattern – in an intent to understand its potential and purpose. Following this meditation, I was aware that I was to sit and begin to write the information that was about to be provided. However, you would like to define this process, here is an edited version of the information that was received:

> *This is a pattern of universal alignment. It represents the unity of energy inherent in both universal and human design. When all elements of energy are returned to the point of balance that exists at its point of origin, it can recreate itself anew. Herein lies a clue to the power of its potential.*
>
> *This pattern is a symbol and living field of consciousness. A symbol both represents, and conceals a vaster consciousness that is inherent in its design. Within this symbol is a living way, as well as a transformative power of healing, balance and transformation.*
>
> *You cannot control spirit, but you can invite it through intention and your gratefulness, to promote the potential for healing and reunion. Through an open heart this light can emerge, but an open heart is a healed heart or a heart with intent to heal.*
>
> *Resonance with this pattern can catalyze the restoration of energy to one's*

Higher Self alignment through one's Spiritual DNA. This is supported by the rebalancing of energy to find and maintain alignment with a universal consciousness of unity that is inherent in every awakening being.

Those who are drawn to it are those who will benefit from it - because of their nature, their history and their level of consciousness. Some will appear to be highly conscious energy beings, and others will appear novice in terms of energy understanding, which will not be so. Do not imagine that great knowledge is needed to manifest great healing – for humility of spirit or nobleness of intention are keys to the kingdom of universal design.

The catalytic benefit will occur by a unique or tailored process for each person – for it works not to create, but to restore. In this restoration lies conscious memory of a healed alignment with ones own spiritual being. You might say that it opens the channels to promote healing energy from ones own higher self into ones life and incarnational experience.

The pattern represents also the perfection of 12 in 1. The unity of 12 attributes into one total unit is found over and over in universal design. 12 apostles surrounded Christ. 12 signs in the zodiac. 12 layers or strands implicit in your evolving DNA. This harmonic is inherent in the perfected 12 "layered" DNA.

It is also a pattern whose time has come! Bring it forward to share with those who are inspired to heal. May it bless one and all.

The Sharing Begins

During the year that followed, I had the opportunity to begin working with the pattern both in guided meditative work, and hands on healing sessions, with people who were open and interested in the experience. People registered a variety of experiences in working with the influence of this pattern.

People sensitive to energy, often noticed a strong healing energy and an awareness of energy working through their chakras and energy bodies. People felt energy move though the spine and unraveling restrictions in the energy around the spine. People felt chakras pop open and energy release during sessions. Others heard sounds, and others saw light. Some people felt strong physical reactions in their body, with involuntary movement of limbs as energy worked their personal energy system. Yet despite the strength of the energy people always told me they felt incredibly safe and supported.

I was greatly reassured as people began to have positive and potent healing experiences under the light of this work. It gave me the courage and the reassurance to continue with the development of the program.

Synthesis

Fig. 11-6
Spiral Galaxy/NASA

Approximately one year following the arrival of the template, in December of 2012, I had a fourth meditative vision. This experience further consolidated the information I was given and helped me better understand.

This vision opened with a view of a galactic spiral. (Fig 11-6) The spiral "dissolved" and I was looking into an energy form, which was modeled on the structural pattern of the DNA molecule. (Fig 11-7) I had seen a similar image of DNA previously, in scientific information on DNA, but this was not a solid image – it was an "energy form" of the molecule. The molecule was scintillating with pastel colors of iridescent light.

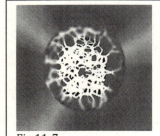

The image transformed from a cross sectional orientation into an upright or elongated form. This allowed me to see clearly that I was looking at the double helix form of the DNA molecule, an image familiar now to all of us. It was still a translucent energy form, however, and it emitted the same glow of light.

Fig 11-7
DNA in "cross section"

Within the helix, I could see the Unity Field energy template. It was floating around inside this huge energy molecule. I chuckle as I recall this vision, for the pattern looked like a scrubbing bubble from a familiar TV commercial for a toilet bowl cleaner! (Fig 11-8)

THE MISSING PILL

To me, it was expressed this way symbolically – for it represented a means of communication that I could clearly grasp or understand. It is a symbolic language used to convey a concept. In visionary experiences, information is usually expressed in such a way – so that it will be specifically meaningful to the viewer or recipient.

I knew intuitively that the vision was demonstrating "Spiritual DNA" – not simply the chemical DNA molecule, as we know it in form. The message inherent in this vision – is that the pattern of the Unity Field Template is working within the "spiritual DNA" to heal and promote bio-spiritual integration. As unusual as it all sounds – it really did begin to make some sense!

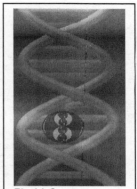
Fig 11-8 DNA with Template

This element of the vision began to fade or transform. The next element to appear was a crystalline staircase floating in a cosmic energy field. The staircase went straight up but ended in the "sky". The view was oriented from the perspective of looking up the stairs, as if it were an invitation to ascend, at least in consciousness.

Fig 11-9 Ascension Stairway

In a flash, the vision "refreshed" and a symbolic pattern of DNA now appeared on the stairs in this vision. It was expressing to me that the stairs represent "steps of DNA transformation" – not "footsteps" in the traditional sense. DNA transition represents the mechanism by which these stairs are to be taken. It was clear to me that changes in DNA configuration represent the steps by which this process occurs. (Fig 11-9)

The vision seemed to represent a spiritual message that we ascend these stairs through modification of the spiritual DNA. Yet, simultaneously, I knew that we are not simply "going up" the stairs; it is an invitation to bring this consciousness from spirit into form. We are raising the energetic vibration of our DNA – down through the spiritual DNA axis. Why is this point so meaningful? Instead of simply ascending to a higher state of vibration, we are birthing a higher state, as it descends from spirit into form. This vision was essential to my understanding. It was truly at this point, that the purpose and potential of *Unity Field Healing* work became crystal clear.

The Workings

When asked how Unity Field Healing works within the DNA, it is a very challenging question to answer. I cannot "prove" what I believe about it. It is a difficult concept to explain in a 3D sense – because its effect is energetic and interdimensional – like all energy healing work. But, I can share a few ideas however, which I honestly do believe will help explain its mechanism.

Its level of influence is directly upon one's spiritual DNA. Some of the energetic properties we reviewed earlier can be used to help explain the process, and how it works on our energy system.

Let's begin with the understanding that DNA is not simply a chemical molecule; it is a quantum molecule, with a multilayered field of information around it or "within it". This energy field and its information serves as a quantum bridge to our spiritual being. We reviewed this concept earlier, but for those who are interested in this esoteric understanding of DNA, again I would suggest reading the book by Lee Carroll and Kryon[12]

Based on this esoteric information, our DNA expression is currently very limited – operating at ~ 30% capacity of its potential "power". Hence, the communication between our human cellular DNA and the spiritual DNA is very "limited". There is obviously some room to grow and develop.

Now understand that it is not inappropriate that our DNA has been "limited" – for the DNA limitation serves us simply to create experiences that reflect developing human consciousness. This involves a process of a much greater spiritual design, one that leads us collectively to the threshold of a spiritual awakening. However, following this premise, we are simply operating as human beings without a "full powered" connection to our spiritual DNA. And it follows that if the DNA is not fully engaged, we are not fully wired up to the greater potential of our spiritual DNA expression.

The mechanism of *Unity Field Healing* is perhaps best expressed in the concept of a quantum *entanglement* process. In quantum physics, quantum entangled particles have a communication that occurs beyond time and space. In the UFH process, there is an intentional focus placed on the "entanglement" between one's spiritual DNA and one's human DNA molecule.

The template itself appears to work as an intermediary, a catalyst if you will, which is present to assist in rewiring or restructuring the human DNA linkage. The entanglement exists naturally as a natural communication or relationship that exists between our human and spirit nature. This linkage is not created by the presence of a template – the template is "just" an energetic catalyst. As a catalyst it promotes or accelerates the exchange between the entangled elements of our DNA.

Hence, the *Unity Field Template* is a *catalyst* for the process of DNA transformation. How might that work?

In Light of DNA …

Human DNA has recently been shown to have a bio-plasmic radiance, and it is also capable of storing incredible volumes of digital information.[60] To add to the mystique of DNA, it can even be shown to be teleported under precise conditions! These scientific explorations are beginning to provide scientific evidence that point towards an understanding of DNA's quantum nature. Suffice it to say that DNA is a magical molecule of which we have a very elementary understanding!

If human DNA is impacted by greater communication with one's higher vibrational spiritual DNA – it will conceivably be able to carry or "radiate" more energy. Personally, I believe that the energy and quality of vibration within the spiritual DNA, and it's degree of calibration with our molecular DNA, will impact one's overall health and healing capacity.

Genetic expression, typically thought to occur by the simplistic pre-ordained expression of genes, is actually highly variable and influenced by many environmental as well as consciousness influences. Again we refer to the new field of study - epigenetics.[14]

Why some genes express and why others do not, is essentially still a mystery. Yet, it is becoming better understood that much of what controls gene expression is tied up in a mysterious regulation, one which occurs through non-gene coding components. This aspect of DNA was originally called "junk DNA" because it was so poorly understood. Yet the question then becomes, if genes themselves are not in control, "What feeds information to the DNA to know how to "behave"?"

The recent hypothesis of DNA as a "quantum molecule" will help us begin to understand this mystery.

One important idea that has emerged in the midst of epigenetic and DNA studies – is that our DNA expression can indeed be modified. This, alone, is a very mind opening realization! Consciousness is being shown to have a role in genetic regulation!

The information that is relayed to our DNA can be potentially programmed by many influences or elements of consciousness. Some of these are "human" and some of them are "spiritual". In other words, it can respond both to our human consciousness and our spiritual or "over lighting" consciousness.

This implies that our DNA can really respond to our human state of consciousness! You can learn to "talk" to you DNA. As a field of information, the quantum field of energy that supports our DNA appears open to transformation.

Although this might be laughable to modern medicine and standard science, this is what many believe is the basis of spontaneous healing. It is conceivable that if the internal "vibration" of the DNA is raised, or made coherent – simply through the power of consciousness, or through recent esoteric quantum rewiring and activation processes – it could potentially clear "disease expression" that occurs within us as human beings, through genetic deregulation.

DNA can be understood to represent the blueprint which patterns our human structural form, as well as the formation of the energy bodies we have discussed. If we had a more "connected" DNA we would manifest greater health and healing potential than we would imagine possible today. You see, in appreciating a quantum understanding of DNA, and the influence of consciousness on DNA, one begins to grasp how transforming the information held in the DNA field could positively influence one's genetic expression.

What would be the impact of piercing through energy veils that block the fuller expression of our spiritual DNA, and allowing the light and energy it carries to transform its expression? Might this enliven the energy around our structural DNA? If the energy and information around the physical DNA was enriched in this way – could our DNA be "informed" to produce healthier expression? Could we overcome genetic probabilities to manifest nasty disease conditions, or heal diseases that were once though irreversible? Well, this just may be so!

New healing systems are being introduced, and understood to help us in our rewiring and recalibration with our source or spiritual DNA – the DNA that exists above the level of influences of mental, emotional and etheric programming.

If we connect with this higher vibrational blueprint – we can invite an energetic healing through our DNA axis. It is my understanding that the *Unity Field Healing* process is simply one powerful catalyst to help this occur.

THE MISSING PILL

HOW IT ALL "SHAPES UP"

Let us revisit a few energy concepts that were introduced earlier to gain a deeper conceptual understanding of how this type of energy healing can work.

Everything physical is energy – energy that is patterned into form. The forms are built upon energy blueprints, or templates. Templates are etheric patterns of form, which exist outside the visible spectrum, and like the visible electrometric fields, they serve to provide a living organizational field upon which the physical form arises. The etheric body, for example, may be viewed as a living template for the human body. These templates are patterned from "invisible" etheric energy – yet perfectly guide the construction of life and the repair of life form patterns in our world.

Patterns of energy, through the science of cymatics, can be understood to be created by sound and vibration. Therefore, inherent within every geometrical pattern is a sound or vibration. For example, when the sound of "Om" is passed through a medium, a special pattern is produced. It is the ancient "Sri Yantra" pattern.

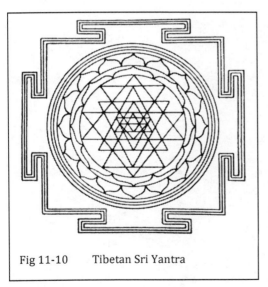

Fig 11-10   Tibetan Sri Yantra

The Sri Yantra (Fig 11-10) has long been revered as a sacred yantra. A Yantra is a tool of "containment" – kind of like a *symbol*. They are often expressed as geometric mandalas which are representations of spiritual power. The Sri Yantra is composed of 9 interlocking triangles. It is believed to represent the most powerful and intriguing of all yantras and is declared to contain the primordial manifestation of unmanifest consciousness. What did the ancient seers know?

Sound, or vibration, represents a creative principle of the universe. This is not limited to "eastern" spiritual disciplines. Even in the words of John the Apostle, it is expressed that "In the beginning was the word, and the word was with God, and the word was God."[1] This is a testament to the power of word or sound as the primordial influence on creation.

In yogic teachings, when this sound "Om" passes through the human energy field – it is believed to carry a healing potential, because it carries the capacity to "reorder" energy within the body. Sounds based on spiritual forms are viewed to have this capacity to "reset" the energy state within a human being – toward an original spiritual alignment. Now this all might seem very esoteric to a westerner, but there is a great deal of profound understanding present in this ancient wisdom.

When we begin to understand sound and sacred geometry – it is not a great leap to conceptualize that sound or enlivened sacred geometry can have an ordering influence on the energy of our body or the physical world.

Earlier, we also introduced the phenomenon of crop circles. This, I believe personally, is a manifestation of the energy transformation that is taking place on the planet. You can now realize how these complex geometries represent a highly coherent energy patterning as well – when you simply appreciate the vibrational order created by sound. Imagine for a moment, that we could bring this potential of energetic order into a new consciousness healing process. Could this potentially have an influence on the energetic order within the DNA? I believe this helps explain how a process such as *Unity Field Healing* may work.

In *Unity Field Healing* we are linking in consciousness with a coherent light geometry. It is conceivable that work based on conscious connection with a quantum energy pattern could facilitate an ordering of the vibrational harmony in our DNA system. This occurs through "resonance" and through a process of conscious facilitation.

A light pattern or template can be understood to represent an energy structure that exists trans-dimensionally. It could be defined as higher vibrational or spiritual in nature. Personally, this is highlighted in the way that the template first presented itself to me - as a "trans-dimensional vibrational gift".

Putting this all together, one could conceive how an "ordering template" could *resonantly* influence energy at the energetic level of form – by "sounding" or "vibrating" a coherent vibration. In this case, energy is sounded is through one's DNA axis. (Fig 11-11)

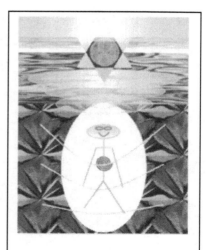

Figure 11-11 Interfacing with an "Interdimensional Template"

In my experience, when we begin to work with this pattern, and it is "activated" – the "catalyzed recalibration" it first influences an internal state of energy – but it ultimately does have an influence in the world of form. The impact is felt through the bio-spiritual continuum of energy and consciousness. It influences us holistically – through its transformative influence on the energy within our bodies.

Is This For Real?!

When people begin to work with this template, they sometimes report actually seeing the template or seeing energy "interdimensionally" in their "third eye". But most people do not see energy. Please understand that it is not imperative to see it – for success is not contingent upon vision. It follows your intent. However, everyone I have ever worked with will somehow *feel the pattern* as it works. As one is attuned to this process, the experience of feeling palpable energetic shifts is common. This is exciting and intriguing when people live this – especially if it is a brand new experience. Yet, perhaps even more importantly, one can begin to notice vibrational shifts in their life.

In working with the template, I believe that one is in a state of entanglement with this light form, and one's spiritual DNA. As a "universal pattern" and "an inherent organizing field of energy" it simply will "sound" or "activate". Like striking a tuning fork, this will send coherent high vibratory radiations throughout one's DNA, and the spiritual axis of our energy bodies.

Here are some of the conceivable "effects" upon our "personal" energy and consciousness:

1. The energy provided may assist in the "breakdown" of patterns of crystallized or congealed energy within our energy bodies. These may be in the form of etheric crystallizations, memories and thought forms, or embedded emotions - stored in the energy bodies. This has a liberating effect on the human energy field in ways we have discussed.

2. As a spiritually inspired harmonic pattern - it helps recalibrate the vibrational signature or "foundation" upon which we are built – our DNA. By rewiring and recalibrating the communication between our spiritual DNA and our physical DNA – it opens a channel for clearer and effective communication.

3. It "reminds" our energy bodies of the vibrations of a higher

consciousness reality! This may feel incredible as waves of love and recognition begin to flow through our bodies. But is also serves to create a new vibrational foundation.

4. As we are energetically supported, it facilitates personal growth and transformation through adjustments in consciousness. It is our job to learn to keep our energy system in the best possible balance. Learning and exploring information about wellness, healing and support as biospiritual transformation becomes so valuable to us. If we know how to make choices that support our spiritual growth, healing and transformation – we can manifest great healing indeed!

SESSIONS

Currently the work of *Unity Field Healing* involves one, two or three distinct sessions. These sessions are provided in sequence up to any level.

Individual sessions can be performed in several ways. A session may be performed in a typical setting, on a massage table, through a guided energy process. It can also be performed equally effectively, at a distance, through a silent or vocally guided consciousness process. It can be provided in a group setting through a guided meditative experience. This format invokes the power of group consciousness! And finally, in an effort to make it more accessible and economical for people to access this work – the first two sessions are also now provided through a meditative guided audio session. The third session is available only as a personal session at this time.

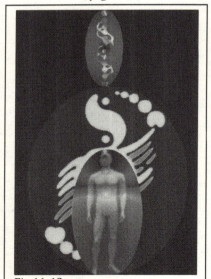

Fig 11-12
Quantum Energy in Action

SESSION 1. SELF-ATTUNEMENT SESSION

The first session is intended to reinforce the connection with your own spiritual DNA. Like each session, this one may be done in the form of a table based healing session, or, a meditative attunement process. This session is provided to intentionally attune to your own higher self nature through your spiritual DNA axis.

This session will open a tremendous portal of healing and may be performed exclusively, without continuing the deeper work in session 2. The attunement will however prepare you energetically, and is in fact a prerequisite, to work with the *Unity Field Template* in session 2.

The Self Attunement session is focused on consciously developing a restorative connection with your spiritual DNA blueprint. By opening to this attunement, one is establishing a much stronger connection with one's own spiritual nature and power. It is this connection that provides an enduring support for healing in our lives.

This session is a "spiritually honoring" healing process – and it is essential to understand that it occurs under your own spiritual sovereignty. You could say that it is "supervised" by your higher self.

Work with this session may result in the release of restrictive energy patterns according to your own inner spiritual wisdom. It can "catalyze" the release of patterns that are not useful to your spiritual growth at this time. It may also facilitate a greater awareness around these patterns so that you may grow and manifest in new ways as an awakening human being.

If you are drawn to this work, it will be under the guidance of your own spiritual being. If you are curious about it, I would suggest that you tune into your own awareness and see if it resonates with you. If you do feel aligned but are apprehensive, realize that the effect of such an attunement will be totally under the "surveillance" and "appropriateness" of your own spiritual being. This integrity will always be maintained in this work.

The principle of DNA activation is to bring your growth into alignment with your intention, as you step into the new energy paradigm. This type of work will support you further in your healing and spiritual development. It is a powerful catalyst but not a causal influence – for the power and responsibility to grow spiritually and in consciousness is an inner process that must always be respected as sacred and sovereign. I consider it more like a cosmic helping hand ☺!

Session 2. Unity Field Healing Attunement

The second session is an attunement session to begin working with the *Unity*

Field Template. This session is intended to work through your spiritual DNA axis that was awakened or strengthened in session 1 – by adding the catalyzing resonance of the *Unity Field Template.*

This work is intentioned to further accelerate or support your personal healing and biospiritual transformation.

The template, in my understanding, works to resonantly support the DNA axis in ways earlier described. Strengthening the connectivity and communication within one's spiritual DNA axis, one is creating a stronger channel between the spiritual DNA and one's human expression. This effectively opens the energy field for the experience of a much higher vibrational state; a state in which healing resides.

The outcome of this process can once again involve healing changes in any of the energy bodies under the influence of our spiritual DNA instruction. This includes the mental, emotional or etheric – as well the physical body and its DNA expression. These effects are highly personal, for they depend on the pre-existing state of one's energy bodies and spiritual state.

I do not want to program too many ideas of what an individual should expect – for each soul is as unique as a snowflake, and has its own perfected potential to manifest. I prefer you to have your own unaltered experiences. I will however share a few events that commonly arise so that you may have a better understanding of what to expect.

As the energy works through DNA into manifested form, the crystallized or congealed energy held in patterns, is released. Physically and ethereally, this process will work to open the channels of energy of the body. During and after the process, one can encounter transient sensations in these energy fields. These are a natural part of expanding energy in our spiritual axis.

As energy is opened and cleared, there may sometimes be more energy adjustments that follow a session. Experiences like transient aches and pains, sensory sensations, or transient rashes can occur. These are all part of energy adjustments, and will pass spontaneously. It can also stimulate an organ detoxification when necessary, and people sometimes experience a flu-like state for a short period of time. This can include such things as mucous clearing, frequent urination or diarrhea – if these are needed to support one's healing process. Headaches, transient surfacing of symptoms related to chronic conditions or old injuries can occur. These are due to the augmented vibration created by this energetic process – as it works to stimulate an energetic healing environment within one's energy configuration. Use of the support tools listed in the next chapter can be enormously valuable in facilitating personal transition through this process.

So why would you want to endure any of that you may ask? ☺ Well, as the adjustments settle in – there is a greater freedom in the body and spirit that develops – as it is freed up from its ingrained limitations.

Psychologically, the process can also have some important influences. It can facilitate a clearing of patterns that are sustained as memory, emotional repression, or fear based patterning, which are embedded in one's energy system. People sometimes experience long forgotten memories, memories of prior life experiences, or surfacing of unresolved psychological conflicts – as they arise to heal.

Psychological patterns can also be "illuminated" as such, raised in consciousness and supported in transformation. This would lead to a greater awareness of the psychological patterns or issues one is experiencing – particularly patterns that may be causing "problems" or "imbalance" in one's life. This awareness surfaces however with greater insight. This is a mechanism to support the recalibration of such patterns – particularly those which do require conscious awareness and participation to process a transformation.

At other times unexplained emotional states seem to "surface" and pass away without any significant conscious memory. Patterns that serve absolutely no purpose but are limiting - are free to release.

The activity or catalytic influence of the second session will continue to work with you long after the work has taken place. People have reported back to me many months or even a year later with transformative moments that they attribute back to changes catalyzed in the energy session. I know it will continue to support you in your process as these layers unpeel.

Since there is a timeline involved in an un-layering or growth process, there is a patience, self-compassion and understanding that is needed following the work in this session – attributes that are inherent in state of wellness.

As a person progresses in the work of biospiritual integration, a sense of inner peace and well being genuinely emerges, as a reflection of an accelerated spiritual development. As the energy around mental and emotional wounds are released, and ego patterns are re-integrated – there is a progressive freedom of being that settles into one's mind, one's heart and one's life. Often, a renewed sense of purpose and potential awakens in this balanced state of self-expression. Creativity blossoms and inspiration flows. What you dream of spiritually, becomes more accessible to you personally – and that is what this recalibration process is truly meant to evoke.

Session 3. Targeted Intentional Support Session

As a person makes progress on their spiritual journey, experiences may arise where an individual feels intuitively that they would benefit from a helping hand. At such times, with a sense of self-responsibility, we are inclined to request further support around very specific patterns or experiences, to enhance our growth and transformation.

This session is a targeted support session with specific intention to bring healing and greater awareness to an identified personal event. It is available to go more deeply into a difficult pattern, to help process. This may imply a disease, a psychological pattern, an ego based resistance, or a crisis event in one's life.

This is a focused support session, using the energy awareness of our spiritual DNA and the support of the Unity Field template. It aims to invoke the inherent support found within them – during such moments of personal or intense transformation.

An Exercise of Introduction

As part of this introduction, I believe it will be beneficial to offer an exercise to experience "the energy" of *Unity Field Healing*. This exercise has been created to give you opportunity to connect with the resonance and energy of this work. If a picture is worth a thousand words, perhaps an experience is worth a million of them!

First, read through this exercise to have a sense of what you are preparing to experience. You can then read through the exercise step by step, taking time to re-center in yourself with your eyes closed after each step in the exercise. However, I encourage you to listen it in a guided audio mediation available on the website at: www.drjohnryan.org/missing-pill.html. Simply go to this link and imply scroll down to "Guided Meditation – Introduction to Unity Field Healing" and follow the instructions.

EXERCISE

To begin this exercise, find a comfortable place sitting down – in a chair or in a mediation position:

1. Center. Take a moment to consciously honor the divinity, the light that lives within you, and has brought you to the planet to experience life in this amazing time. Honor also your body, an incredible vehicle of light and consciousness, always in service to your presence. Breathe and release any tension you may feel in your body.
2. Acknowledge the presence of your Higher Self. This aspect of your being accompanies you at all times, but is consciously present within you, as you embark upon this exercise.
3. Now, bring your attention to your feet. Allow the energy centers in the soles of your feet to open, and allow energy to flow into you. Feel it move up your legs, and into your pelvis. Visualize or feel it rises up through your chakra system and spine, and out through the crown of the head.
4. Next, begin to rotate your pelvis in a circular pattern. Begin by rocking it first to the right, then push your lower spine backward, then rock toward the left, and then push your spine gently forward. Continue the rotation for at least 10 cycles. Repeat in the opposite direction for 10 full cycles. Stop now and breathe.
5. Now simply move your chest forward as your head relaxes backward. Then reverse the movement by arching your back gently while your heard moves forward and faces down toward your chest. Repeat back and forth 10 full times. Breathe in as you move forward, and out as you move backward. This will open your spine. Breathe deeply and relax.
6. Rotate or gently spin your chest around the axis of your spine. Rotate you shoulders first clockwise to the right as the right shoulder moves backwards, and the left should rotates in front of you. Then reverse the rotation toward the left. Repeat several times, slowly and deliberately, while breathing.
7. Now, rock your head back and forth several times. Then, tilt your head from side to side. Next rotate your head around the axis of your spine from side to side if this is comfortable for you. Repeat several times. This is to loosen and open your energy. Breathe
8. Relax deeply. Now feel or imagine another wave of energy come up through your feet and body. Feel it filling your arms and passing out your fingers. Feel it move up the neck and out the top of head.

9. Now, bring you awareness to your heart center. Imagine a luminous ball of light in the center of your chest, or heart chakra. Feel the heart with each pulse if you can, and visualize the radiant energy emerging out through your heart like a pulsing sun.
10. Feel the energy expands to encompass your entire body.
11. Allow the love and energy you are receiving to flow outward and arch around your body. Feel it return to you amplified and uplifting.
12. Next, visualize the image of the *Unity Field Template* in your mind's eye. If you don't see it, connect mentally with the idea.
13. Allow the symbol to come to life for you. Allow yourself to feel the impact of the energy radiations. You may feel dizzy or a little lightheaded – which is normal. Don't be alarmed; just allow the energy to move through you and around you.
14. You may feel this energy moving, to push or pull in areas of tightness or restriction, within your body. If you are aware of this sensation, gently breathe and imagine drawing your breath deeply into your body and allow it to relax. Breathe.
15. Stay in this meditative space for as long as you would like.
16. As you return to a wakeful state, pay attention to any thoughts or feelings that formed part of your experiences. What physical or energetic sensations did you experience? Notice any ideas or feelings that come to you in the next few moments. Just allow.
17. Now bring your consciousness back into your body. Feel your arms begin to tingle and your legs. Take a deep invigorating breath and let it charge your body.

As you awaken you may want to register or record the elements of the experience that you know are important to you.

This is a simple exercise just to introduce you to the resonance of this work. I hope you enjoyed this guided introduction to the energy of Unity Field Healing. For more information on this work, and access to guided audio sessions of Session 1 and Session 2, you can visit the website at www.drjohnryan.org/unity-field-healing.html .

CHAPTER 12

SUPPORTIVE TOOLS, INFORMATION AND GRACE

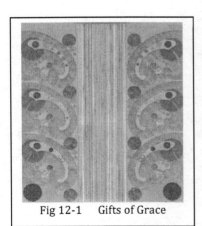

Fig 12-1   Gifts of Grace

Bio-spiritual transformation is a process which will invariably bring energetic changes into the energy bodies at all levels. This includes the mental, emotional, etheric and physical levels. At each level, you will encounter adjustments, which are a natural part of the healing paradigm.

As you learn to find harmony within your own spiritual reality, and you progress in your healing journey, you will find not only "healing" but also experience an energetic expansion. This expansion process occurs as a natural integration, as you are learning to carry a greater energy in your physical form.

Understanding some of the events or experiences that may occur - can be tremendously reassuring. It will also be helpful at times to have certain tools to turn to – to facilitate or assist you. In this section we will review some things to understand, and tools you may experiment with, to support you in your personal process.

Many of these suggestions are intuitive really; activities, which you know, are good for you. Others are more specifically "therapeutic" in orientation. The list is by no means comprehensive, but it represents a collection of what I know personally be very useful. You will discern for yourself what is of value to you.

1. COMMON MANIFESTATIONS THAT REQUIRE SIMPLE UNDERSTANDING

There are a few peculiar effects that are common to experience during energetic transformation. Many people encounter them when they begin to work with energy therapies or spiritual stimulation. We will review them below.

The challenge is that some of these can mimic bona fide health conditions – which can be unsettling. So for a few reasons, some reasonable caution is required.

If such experience is not understood, these transient changes may be mistaken to represent a disease presentation. They can also be inappropriately treated or medicated by well meaning health care providers, who are unaware of such phenomena. So it is important to be aware of them to keep a clear perspective and make conscious choices.

Alternatively, I must caution, that an important symptomatic disease presentation may be ignored if one assumes that such symptoms are simply transient energetic related phenomena. This could delay the diagnosis and treatment of a medical condition when may be detrimental to one's health.

For this reason, when these phenomena occur, it is advisable to have a health check up to diagnose or exclude certain medical conditions. If medically nothing is uncovered then reassurance may be in order.

In this category of experience, I would include:

SLEEP CHANGES

Changes in sleep patterns may include difficulty sleeping, frequent awakening in the middle of the night, multiple awakenings, periods of deep very unconscious sleep, and a need for rests or naps.

Many such sleep changes are seen during energy transforming activities.

They are, however, also experienced in psychological conditions such as depression and anxiety. Hence it can be confusing to experience them as part of a healing process or spiritually transformative journey.

If the changes you are experiencing are very disruptive, or part of a psychological condition, it may be important to treat them. However, understanding they can represent an expected phenomenon as part of healing and energy transformation can be reassuring. If changes are distressing or prolonged review it with a health care provider. If there is nothing more serious occurring, this awareness can help endure the changes without becoming overly anxious or stressed.

Balance Issues

There are intermittent periods when people will notice a loss of balance, a sense of rotation, and a perception of spinning or even falling down.

These symptoms also may also be seen also in certain medical conditions such as inner ear infections and other problems with the vestibular system. These types of medical conditions can lead to vertigo, tinnitus (ringing in the ears) and related phenomena.

If you are experiencing perceptual balance disturbances that are dangerous or concerning, it is wise to have a medical check up to uncover or exclude serious or treatable problems.

It is again valuable however to understand this can occur in energy integration, and may not imply a medical condition. In this case it will usually pass with some time. At all times, if you are noticing orientation problems, be appropriately cautious – avoiding activities or maneuvers that could lead to injury.

Head Aches

As energy expansion occurs, many people experience burning, headaches, pressure and tightness in the head. This can also occur in areas of the body that correspond to any of the energy centers or chakra we have discussed.

In the head, these are of course also symptoms of many medical conditions such as tension headaches, migraine headaches, high blood pressure, metabolic disorders and tumors.

If you experience new or uninvestigated neurological symptoms like these, it is prudent to have a medical check up. If testing is normal it may be reassuring simply to know you are "enlightening"!

STIFF MUSCLES AND JOINTS

Many people will experience migratory aches and pains in their body and trigger points of tenderness. The same principle applies – rule out endocrine, metabolic diseases and electrolyte problems, or other cause of generalized or specific pain with a medical consultation. If all checks out – understand this is common to experience.

PRESSURE, PULSATION AND TWINGES

It is not uncommon to feel energetic phenomenon in the body. This can occur in the form of pseudo-electrical pulses in the arms and legs, pulsing feelings in the body, twitches, jerks, tingling feelings, and so forth.

Again many disease conditions can produce these kinds of sensations so it is generally advisable to discuss them with a physician or allied practitioner, and undergo an investigation where appropriate.

If there is no underlying disease state, such as compressed nerve or aneurism, you can find assurance in the understanding offered.

LIGHT PHENOMENA

Many people will note transient sensitivity to light. People will also sometimes notice they see or sense unusual light activity. People may see haloing, sparks, light flickers, energy fluxes, or occasionally other energy bodies or beings. Best advice – stay cool!

Again, some medical conditions can produce similar phenomena such as migraine headaches or central nervous system disorders – so use discretion and be investigated medically where strange experiences may indicate illness.

MOOD SHIFTS, EMOTIONAL LABILITY, AND CONFUSION

People will commonly notice an increased flux in mood changes. This is true for men and women – so not a gender based consideration. People may experience transient periods of deep sadness, or overwhelming joy, and everything in between.

THE MISSING PILL

If you are undergoing large emotional and mood swings, or more sustained states of specific emotions, it is important to discuss it with a health care provider or alternate therapy practitioner. Conditions such as depression or manic-depressive disorder, for example, can manifest such changes – so it is important to exclude a treatable condition.

Just be aware, you are not necessarily ill if this occurs. Support yourself appropriately at these times. If they are part of biospiritual integration, they will pass with time.

DREAMS

Many people experience unusual dream phenomena. This may include intensely vivid dreams, alternate reality dreams, deep memory dreams with recall of prior life events, transformative dreams, guidance dreams, uplifting dreams, dreams of family members who have passed on, and sometimes even violent dreams.

The dream state provides a complex array of memory, alternate consciousness contact and processing. If you are having peculiar dreams try not to be disturbed about them. Discuss or explore the dreams with a reliable counselor or friend.

Pay attention to dreams that have obvious meaning to you, or a sense of supportive love based guidance. You will sometimes receive very valuable information through dream experience.

MEMORY LOSS OR UNRELIABLE MENTAL FUNCTION

People often report days where the brain just seems to have taken the day off. Words don't seem to come out appropriately, or one's memory is not working very well. Then the next day it can be fine.

The challenge here is concern of age related memory loss, or dementia states, such as Alzheimer's disease.

This again may require an investigation if there is concern of true illness rather than a healing related phenomena. Otherwise, go with the flow.

LOSS OF INTEREST OR TOLERANCE IN SOME ACTIVITIES

Most people notice they lose interest in many activities that were once important to them or part of their lives. Hobbies and interests may change.

Conversations may lose appeal if they are negative or low in consciousness. TV shows that were enjoyed may lose appeal.

People simultaneously also notice new and emerging interests, unlike people with a strictly affective disorder. It is a time of deep transition so it is important to get comfortable with your inner prompting and know you will be guided to what is valuable to you.

During periods of intense healing, people will often want to explore new creative possibilities, attend lectures or workshops, read and so forth. The quality of relationships becomes important. Presence is important.

Honor your personal changes, don't judge yourself or others, and be understanding.

Heightened Sensitivity

Many people become more sensitive to sensory stimulation and other people. People may become overwhelmed in crowds or gatherings. People may feel tired quickly or unable to handle the energy of these environments.

It can be difficult to function like this if you are in the world working, or taking care of yourself and family - and you will need to find an appropriate balance for yourself.

This may mean opting for a combination of doing different activities, modifying choices to accommodate your needs, or learning to stay strong and centered energetically in environmentally challenging situations. Eventually you can acclimatize to the environment while learning to hold your spiritual center.

Food Intolerance

People may notice anything from a shift in dietary interest, food avoidance, food cravings and frank intolerance of some foods. If dietary problems occur, a medical investigation is warranted to assess for malabsorption, intolerance, inflammatory bowel diseases or allergies.

If dietary changes are prompted, honor the intelligence of your own innate system to guide your dietary choices. Don't get in the rut that one type of eating is right for everyone. Do your own appropriate thing – but pay attention to your internal insight. People may also sometimes notice transient up and down shifts in weight – weight gain or loss. This may be part of transitions in an energy state as well. To the very best of your ability, keep a healthy diet and lifestyle.

◉

With a greater awareness of these phenomenon, you may find reassurance that what you are living is "normal" in context of what you are experiencing. You can explore ways to support your self as you make adjustments, while you are on your way to a reassuring transition!

2. BREATHING

Of all the vital functions – eating, sleeping, drinking, elimination and breathing – breathing is perhaps the most intimately connected to energy and spiritual vitality. If you stop breathing for even minutes, the damage to the brain and nervous system is tremendous. It is easy to see how closely related breathing is to consciousness and life.

Reflect for a moment what happens when you have a change in psychological states. If you are afraid, what happens to your breathing? How about if you become angry? Or, anxious? What happens when you exercise? Or, encounter a beautiful unexpected scene in nature? You can quickly see, that all of these events, co-experience different breathing tendencies.

It is vital to consciously breathe! Breathing expands all aspects of the energy system – the etheric, emotional and mental bodies - and allows vital energy to flow through the human energy system. It is truly a key to unblocking energies that become stagnant in the system.

There are systems of pranic breathing (pranayama) that are instructed in yoga traditions to specifically charge elements of the energy system. Yet, even if you are not into "complicated" breathing or breath control – you can still learn to breathe fully and deeply! Simply learning to breathe into the full chest and full abdomen is extremely valuable in opening and charging the energy system – helping us to open etheric restrictions and releasing both physical and psychological tension.

Let us take a few moments to breathe together! This will help you anchor an awareness of the importance of your breath.

EXERCISE:

Close you eyes and center yourself. Become aware of your own Higher Self nature. Take a breath into your lungs and release it slowly. Breathe out all the way then gently take another breath in.

Cycle through this breathing for a few times. Each time as you breathe in, do so a little deeper, and a little stronger and let your chest fully expand.

As this becomes comfortable, with each breath in, really begin to let your abdomen relax and expand while you breathe. Imagine the breath is being drawn into your abdomen with the breath expansion.

In doing this, you are drawing vital energy through your lungs and bloodstream into your body. You are also drawing vital energy, or chi into your etheric system and meridians. Together this will charge, clear and vitalize your system.

Relax now and pay attention to how you feel in your body after a short period of conscious breathing. You may be aware of little restrictions that let go during the process of breathing. You may feel a little lightheaded and tingly. You may feel little zaps or pulses of energy in your body.

Whenever your feel anxious, restricted, agitated, or, during any disturbing experience – remember your breath is a tool that can take you back to your spiritual center. Take a few minutes and breathe into your body and let go of the reactive tendencies. It can always take you home.

3. WATER

Water is also vital in the process of both healing and energy integration. Water is the foundational element of this planet and also our bodies.

On a more direct level, water not only is vital to the circulation of body elements, but also a conductor of electricity and energy in the body. Drinking lots of water is essential if the body is receiving more energy through energy and spiritual work. Water helps circulate energies through the system, prevent overheating and promoting the ability to expel or circulate energy.

Water is also essential in the elimination of toxins or other elements that are released in healing work. On physical level water is necessary in extracting toxins released in the energetic stimulation of the etheric and physical body by spiritual energy processes. Anyone who has experienced a good corporal cleansing after energy work, or an energy intensive workshop, would understand directly.

Be aware of the value of drinking water beyond the simple perception of "thirst" while engaging in healing and energy process. It is advisable to drink at least a couple of liters or quarts of water every day.

4. STRETCHING

Stretching the body is important to open up the body, release restrictions, and let energy circulate. If you pay attention to animals, such as dogs and cats, they do this quite spontaneously and liberally.

Stretching obviously elongates the muscles and connective tissues to release built up tension, and tendons so they remain flexible and unrestricted. But when you begin to appreciate that there are actual energy channels in the etheric body, and that keeping them open and clear is important to promote health – the value of stretching takes on a new significance.

Stretching helps to keep the energy fields open and keep them unrestricted. When your body is open, you are more emotionally and mentally open, and ultimately more spiritually open too. When you feel less constrained you feel better. It also allows energy to circulate more readily because there is less resistance to its flow.

When you stretch to open the body you will begin to realize that many mental and emotional patterns tend to constrict the energy fields. You may notice this during stretching exercises, or, you may notice this after stretching when a certain emotional experience has you "pull on your energy" in a constricting way.

When you are anxious, or worried, or enraged, or in tight ego control – the body contracts both through the chakras and meridians, limiting energy flow until it relaxes and reopens. Very tight or habitual restrictions in the energy fields may require longer practice to unravel. However, leaving restrictions in the energy unattended will impact the energy circulation in the energy system and have a consequential impact on one's health.

To achieve this awareness is a wonderful development - for it helps to increase an understanding of the impact of particular mental and emotional activities on the health of the human body. Remember part of healing is greater self-awareness. As we see the positive or negative influences of different activities on our energy we can be more consciously engaged in our own health and wellbeing.

Stretching can be done as a straightforward exercise program. It can also be done through formatted exercises that are specific to promoting energy movement in the body. Exercise programs such as yoga and Tai Chi involve a lot of stretching movement, which is based on an appreciation of the energetic anatomy and function. These practices are not strictly "exercise". They are meant to represent time spent in conscious awareness of your spiritual self, with exercises to promote the flow of spiritual energy in your system. They innately include the consciousness of one's Higher Self and your connectedness with the universal energy field – which is a phenomenal way to exercise. Making this realization was a fundamental shifting point in my own life and spiritual practice, particularly when it came to exercise.

Exercise and movement is fundamental to a healthy body. And, I would add that conscious exercise is fundamental in healing. I have found just about all exercise I have ever done to be valuable for health – walking, running, cycling, aerobic based work outs, strength training, you name it. However, when you begin to recognize the spiritual – energy continuum there is a shift in consciousness around exercise for many people. There is less inclination to sporting activity that is over aggressive and potentially hurtful to the body. There is greater inclination to activity that honors the body and work to improve vitality, flexibility, strength and form. Focus also shifts from "looking perfect" to "feeling healthy" – which for many is a huge relief!

There are many excellent CD and DVD programs to instruct stretching, tai chi and yoga. There are also many studios, gyms and yoga centers which offer any number of classes to those who like to exercise in groups or follow a live instruction.

I encourage you to listen and follow your own body, level of physical ability, and inner awareness in this regard. Just do it – start with any process you may feel inclined toward doing.

5. SOUND, TONING AND CHANTING

The impact of sound in the form of music to create a space or environment is quite powerful. This is reviewed more specifically in the section on music to follow. We will look here at sound as a healing tool within the body.

Sound is a form of vibration. When we vibrate the body we stimulate energy movement within the energy body through the vibration.

When sound is used internally, it has a powerful healing ability. You can learn to make sounds that are not simply sounds, but sounds that vibrate the inside of the body. In yoga systems this falls into the domain of mantra and chanting.

Sages in the past have described specific sounds that emanate from an inner space which correspond to various elements of creation. There are seed syllables that correspond to the chakras, for example.

By learning to tone and sound internally, particularly in conscious communion with your Higher Self presence, the energy can stimulate the energy system in the body to move energy, to open and to heal. Again there are many instructional programs to learn to chant and use sound in healing, but I would encourage you also to simply explore sound within your own body.

Take a few moments and close your eyes, now or the next time you are in a place where you can do this without interruption. Make a few sounds to see if you can "feel" it inside your body. Make a deep bass like Aay sound, a mid range Ahh sound and a higher Uum sound and register where you feel them inside. Play with sounds and see what they do inside of you.

6. GROUP GATHERINGS – THE POWER OF TWO OR MORE

When people are in the middle of a healing process, they are often in a vulnerable place in their lives. When you are attempting to grow spiritually, you can feel quite alienated or judged by people around you. It can also mean being counter-culture in some ways – although this is changing daily in modern times. There is a true need for a supportive environment.

Finding people or groups in person, or even online - can be incredibly supportive in moving forward in your process. Many people form spiritual groups or networks to support each other.

When people gather together, however, particularly in honor of the spiritual in life, there is something very special that occurs. The power of one individual is not simply "doubled" in joining with another – it seems to grow exponentially. You have probably heard the expression when Jesus spoke from an ascended Christ consciousness – where two or more are gathered in my name – I am there among them. Remember God is love and where love gathers, power magnifies.

There is a spiritual force that is present when groups gather to honor the spirit or to heal. I have been astounded over the years how easy it is to experience things in groups, or in spiritual gatherings, that never seem to occur alone. Healings, visions, understandings and synchronistic encounters – all kinds of magic – seem amplified and strongly guided by the hand of grace. Stuff just happens! I would encourage you to join in groups, seminars, in-person or online events that resonate with you and truly support your personal process.

7. NATURE

When you are actively engaged in either a healing journey or spiritual growth – most people will notice both a longing for, and deep appreciation of nature and nature's beauty. During times of change, you will probably not find anything more deeply grounding and restorative than conscious moments with the earth.

Nature lives in a much greater balance, than we tend to as humans. Anyone can attest to the value of a few days in nature to harmonize and clear the mind, body and soul. This is not always possible – so simple walks, sitting in a park, yard or public garden, walking or sitting at the beach, are all wonderful ways to spend times in the natural elements and valuable to energetic harmonization.

Nature is a living dreamscape. It is full of vibratory patterns that are part of the fabric of nature's creations, as well as high-energy states of prana. It is very restorative to spend conscious time in such an environment. You may recall, the first experience I ever had of "seeing" energy was restfully sitting in the middle of the earth's four elements – Earth, Water, Fire and Air.

The nature based spiritual traditions have always had a deep awareness of the sacred elements. Healing ceremonies consciously honor these elemental forces in their design. Ceremonies are created with a spiritual call upon the elements, for purposes related to the consciousness of the element, to support healing ceremonies. For example fire is archetypally invoked for burning away restrictive or disease-laden patterns, water to calm, soften or nurture when needed. To the western thinker these may be seen as poetic or metaphoric but to the Shaman these forces are quite real.

Regardless of the depth to which one develops a relationship with nature, one will certainly benefit from presence in her embrace. Honor your prompting to spend time in Nature or learning about human relationship with nature in the ways that are self-appropriate.

> *The best six doctors anywhere*
> *And no one can deny it*
> *Are sunshine, water, rest, and air*
> *Exercise and diet.*
> *These six will gladly you attend*
> *If only you are willing*
> *Your mind they'll ease*
> *Your will they'll mend*
> *And charge you not a shilling.*
>
> ~Nursery rhyme quoted by Wayne Fields,
> What the River Knows, 1990

8. MUSIC

Music is a vibrational and healing treasure house. The power of music to alter moods, environments and mental states has long been appreciated. Above and beyond the obvious beauty of music, and the appreciation of music as a social and environmental stimulus – it is a therapeutic instrument. This is becoming increasing recognized by conscious musicians and healing arts practitioners.

Sound is vibration. Harmonic sound carries a complex vibratory nature, which is very easy to appreciate if you look at cymatics. This helps us to understand the vibratory patterns formed by various sounds or music. When we understand our energetic composition and see how music affects our environment – it opens a window of consciousness. It helps us to understand the potential of sound to influence the human being, as an "energy based" entity, in supportive or healing ways.

If you reflect, I am sure you will recognize the power of sound and vibration to create or change an atmosphere, uplift your mood, release emotion, or elevate your spirit? Sound can also be used in other ways to induce specific states of consciousness. Theta wave induction to induce deep relaxations and altered state experiences, or drumming by shamanistic practices to induce a shamanic journey are some examples.

You can also learn to make internal sounds, which have the power to move energy within your own body, as you experienced earlier. The science of Mantra and chanting uses the knowledge and influence of sound to enter higher states of consciousness, which is very powerful.

Music is a medicine. I have always believed in the use of music therapeutically. Personally, if I need to relax, or want to feel uplifted, I use music directly to achieve this. If I am doing creative work, I will often play non-lyrical music or soft music in the background, for its power to create a vibrational space. I also use music in meditative work both in exercises such as yoga, and in healing or consciousness expanding meditation work.

Personally, I have also used sound intuitively in doing hands on healing work. This does not always happen, but sometimes I am guided to sound certain unusual tones over the body or chakras centers, or hum in an unusual way when doing hands on healing work. I know intuitively this sound is supportive in the work being done.

What I would suggest is that you explore the use of sound and music in your healing work. You will be drawn to different music for different times and different needs. Choose music intuitively in any energy work you may be doing, or simply while enjoying your day. Play music in the background to support your creative activities. Explore some of the therapeutic practices of sound. Follow you intuition to do this and you will be amazed at how supportive it is. Feel the healing, balance and beauty that you experience when treated to the "right vibrations".

For those who are interested to learn more, there are many references and audio programs available such as the work by Jonathan Goldman.[27]

9. LEARNING

Learning is very important and usually spontaneously inspired when people begin to explore the world of energy healing, or begin to spiritually awaken. There is an infinite array of books, articles, websites, journals, workshops, retreats, DVDs, CDs, and computer downloads to promote learning.

The quality of information available is highly variable so some discernment is necessary when exploring information. As always, one should ultimately base one's own beliefs on what one is personally experiencing and what one innately or intuitively discovers.

For example many different systems of energy healing now exist – and all have strengths and limitations – based on the clarity, the experience, and the understanding delivered. Extraordinary claims are made, and conflicting information is sometimes presented – so it can be a challenge to decipher what is accurate or trustworthy. Do not "worry" about it – but be present with yourself and simply find what works for you. Do not get caught up in ego based experiences.

Some very trusted authors today have written wonderful books and explanations of the emerging field of energy and spiritual medicine, and new consciousness. Authors like Barbra Ann Brennan, Caroline Myss, Donna Eden, Eric Pearl, Peggy Pheonix Dubro, Bruce Lipton, Gregg Braden, just to name a few. [7,8,32,35,39]

Follow your own interest and guidance in what you would like to learn about. Understanding that what you are most inspired by is best realized from within your own nature. Visit online bookstores such as HayHouse.com or Amazon.com, or visit a local bookstore particularly one that specialized in holistic healing or new age content, and let your spirit guide you.

Sometimes life-altering books will seem to pop off the bookshelf or "light up" in some special way to catch your interest. Your intuition will prompt you towards material that is useful to you personally. Trust this. You will be surprised what you may find.

10. DIET/ FASTING/CLEANSING

When people begin to work with energy healing, it is typical to become a little more conscious of diet. There is infinite advice on what you should and should not eat. There is also tremendous judgment from both spiritual and moral points of view.

It is not necessary to eat a specific diet to heal or grow spiritually. Period. There is however good common nutritional sense and personal intuitive awareness that will truly support you if you honor it. For me, I function best with a diet that includes a little meat and fish, lots of grains and vegetables and fruit. My body feels best on this diet. If I eat strictly vegetarian I get weak. If I eat excessive red meats, I get sluggish – so these are very limited in my diet. I also enjoy a good glass of wine.

Nobody can tell you what is best for you – BUT – *YOU* will know best if you pay attention to yourself.

What most people do notice, in my experience, is an inclination to eat a little less in terms of portions. Many people also find a benefit in doing sessions of light fasting and herbal detoxification. This must be innately navigated individually.

I had learned of a 4-day fruit fast a few years back, which serves me well. If you feel inclined to try it, and your health does not contradict doing so, this is how it goes:

4-Day Juice and Fruit Fast:

On day 1, the only food you will eat is grapes. Select a grape variety that you enjoy. The quantity is not necessary to measure – eat as much as you want. Organic grapes are the best choice to limit pesticides and toxins.

On day 2, you will eat only apples. Choose a variety of apple that you enjoy. You can eat any number of apples, as many as you would like. Again, organic apples are ideal, if possible.

On day 3, you will only consume grape juice. Drink at least 1-2 liters, but more if you like.

On day 4, you will only consume apple juice. Drink at least 1-2 liters but more if you like.

<u>Drink also lots of water each day during this time for cleansing of tissues.</u>

This daily choice provides a small variety, and the process provides a short but wonderful chance for the body to clear. Again, drink plenty of water and do not stop on day two or three because you feel 'yucky' – this is the clearing that is occurring and if you persist with it you will be grateful.

Personally I will also usually do a herbal detox program once or twice a year. There are many natural or herbal preparations today that are designed to clear the colon and internal organs, clear yeast, or treat parasites.

11. Counseling and Personal Process

When you are engaged in healing and transformational work, you may encounter various types of personal psychoemotional experiences, or the awakening memory of old mental and emotional injuries. There will be times when you are experiencing things that you do not understand.

You may find you benefit from some assistance to help process the impact of such events. It can be particularly helpful to have an understanding person to help navigate such times. This must be a person you trust and feel aligned with in your spirit. This may be a clear headed and openhearted friend, or an excellent counselor, or personal coach.

Sometimes you need someone just to listen to you a little, while you process these events. You may need someone to point out ego based tendencies that are limiting to you – and need to be placed in conscious awareness so they may be assimilated in your process. Whatever is occurring, it is important to reach out in ways that support you – but do not disempower you, spiritually speaking.

The notion of psycho-emotional support is especially important if one is working with past trauma, inner child issues, abuse issues, abandonment issues and challenging events of forgiveness related to very difficult life experiences.

It is important equally, that you do not become counselor "dependent". You have your own innate spiritual nature that will walk you through life and provide insight, intuition and support. External guidance is simply to reinforce this awareness as it develops. Walk away if you know someone is attempting to control you, with or without your personal wellbeing in mind.

One size does not fit all. You will be led and inspired to what suits you – if you pay attention to what "feels right" in you.

12. Rhythms

You will probably note a change in personal rhythms.

Almost every person I know who has undergone energy work or spiritual healing has encountered changes in personal rhythms.

For example, we discussed sleep patterns. This can be experienced as less sleep, more sleep, or variable sleep when compared with what was "normal". Move with the rhythm.

Interests wax and wane. The need to rebalance personal vs. social vs. family time may arise. You will probably experience a conscious need for "personal" time. This may be to do "nothing", or simply do what is important to you as a spiritual being. Honor this! People give lots of reasons why this is not possible – it just doesn't help with the energetic need to achieve balance that one may require. This is really possible if it is understood and integrated as an *important* element in ones life. If life is really too busy to find a small amount of time that is dedicated to your personal development, it will be time to reflect on why.

Finally you may notice shifting personal interests in the world. Things that were extremely important may fade and new interests develop. Allow yourself this freedom to discover who and what you are. Do your best not be disturbed by the changes. They are an expected part of growth and transformation.

13. MEDITATION AND RELAXATION

For most people, it will be very important to spend time in conscious relaxation or meditation. Different things work best here with different constitutions, so it is hard to give general advice.

Learning to recognize the "busy nature" of the mind, and its ability to agitate and stir up emotional responses, is greatly enhanced by awareness practices. Some people like to use guided meditation and imagery to relax. Some like music without lyric or guiding works. There are relaxation tapes available, of endless variety. If you are inclined to this, I would find one or several to enjoy.

Mediation is a practice that many people find infinitely valuable to center and remain aligned, particularly when faced with busy or demanding lifestyles. There are courses and programs in meditation instruction in every city, online or through electronic instruction programs.

Most important is to take time in whatever form suits you personally to still the mind, be present in the time and space you are in, and open yourself to learn more about your spiritual nature and reality.

14. Creativity

Many people become increasingly aware of a creative presence in their lives and search for outlets or ways to express it. Some are drawn to traditional artistic expression, often for the first time in their lives. Others integrate creative strategies to support healing or transformation. Our spirit is creative by nature and expresses some of its deepest messages and guidance through creative tendencies.

Honor your inner guidance in this regard, and you may be surprised at the abilities that are part of you and ready to awaken. Do not limit yourself. This may be in the form of writing, drawing, painting, artistic hobbies, music, educations programs, business, or cooking – endless ways. Play, have fun!

15. Energy Work

Energy healing is a powerful way to assist one in healing changes.

A healer may be viewed as a conduit through which universal energy may flow or catalyze healing for another human being. It is important to understand that the healer is not the source of the energy. A healer serves as an instrument for a greater healing force to work through, and make it available as a support to you.

Healing involves the assembly of at least two people who unite in an intention to create healing. It is a little different than the medicine we are used to - where you may specifically and intentionally treat a problem in a specific way based on knowledge given by the healer. What is important to understand in energy-based forms of healing – is that the outcome is based on intention, but it is not strictly under conscious human control. It occurs in conjunction with your higher self-awareness, and it is balanced with your experience, so that your healing will be supported in a complete way. Healing will be inspired in such a way that you may grow and assimilate the lessons or teachings that are important to you on your life journey.

There is some obvious potential for ego to enter into a healer's thinking - if they see themselves to be a "powerful healer" or "master". A true energy master has moved completely beyond ego-based reality and would never take ownership of something they know does not belong to them. They understand grace, and do not want to engage ego thinking into the mix. To put this in context, think of Christ or Buddha. When did you ever hear them say, I am such an excellent and powerful healer? Just didn't happen. They were of such high and pure consciousness they did not ever speak from ego based reality. Always be aware of the source of healing and one's role in service to the divine in all of life.

Here are few things to reflect upon when engaging in energy work:

1. Intention is important. Pure intent. You and your Higher Self nature are always in control of a healing process. Although I invite this awareness into every moment of my life, I would never begin a healing session without invoking the over lighting wisdom of the higher self of both the healer and the healee.

2. Healing must be viewed beyond the physical domain – the goal of healing from the spiritual eye, is reintegration with the spirit. Healing is often to overcome the consequence of ego-based separation in consciousness. It is to restore the truth of your being, which includes elements of etheric, emotional, mental and spiritual realignment.

3. There may be spiritual important reasons why certain things exist. From a spiritual perspective, some "problems" are the key to some further important "realizations" - and will heal with time and greater attainment of consciousness. Be patient when things do not unfold the way you think they should, but do not lose faith in the process.

4. Healing may take time to manifest. Synchronistic occurrences may be part of the journey. Personal learning may be part of the journey. For many reasons, the process of energy transformation may be better experienced a little more slowly than our human nature would like, for a multiplicity of reasons. We are wise to honor process and leave ego out of the process.

5. All energy healing is from spirit and from within. It is not external to you. No one heals you – a space is created for healing to occur within you. A healer is a catalyst or conduit but not the source of healing. Energy healing simply supports the healing and recalibration of the energy fields, and a strengthening of your personal connection with your spiritual self.

There are many excellent texts that discuss energy healing in greater detail and complexity, and I would recommend several as reference in the index section of this book. [7,8,32,39]. I would encourage you to explore them. If you have never experienced an energy healing session, give it a try. There is nothing that will replace personal experience to help gain consciousness in this matter.

16. NEW ENERGY MODALITIES

In the new energy of these times certain gifts are being given that are extremely esoteric, but are very powerful to help people heal and awaken.

Unlike simply working the energy fields directly, these modalities work with interdimensional light patterns and an awareness of the spiritual DNA axis. They will have an accelerated ability to stimulate healing within the human body and all of its associated energy fields.

Unity Field Healing fits into this paradigm, joining ranks with such work as Reconnective Healing and the EMF balancing technique. These modalities of healing support are geared towards supporting healing through a spiritual recalibration that is new when compared with older well-established healing processes.

Our DNA is being upshifted, which has the affect of making healing easier and more accessible to us.

17. MASSAGE AND BODY WORK TECHNIQUES

When one is processing healing, the use of massage and body work can be extremely beneficial.

The body's muscles, connective tissues and nervous system can "store" a great deal of tension and resistance. When one undergoes massage work to loosen the body's tissues and unravel restrictions, it also allows energy to flow more unencumbered in the body.

There are many different types of massage work and bodywork available — but what is important is to find a practitioner who can work cooperatively with you, who you trust, and with whom you can relax into healing.

I have used massage therapy both alone and in conjunction with energy work to help move the energy in my body, and to recalibrate to a relaxed and open state. I would encourage you to explore this, if it is not part of your experience to date.

18. Epsom Salts Baths

Whenever I am experiencing a sense of energy imbalance, one of the first things I like to do, is to take an Epsom salts bath. If I experience any type of flu like changes, or am tired from travel or other activities – I turn to this remedy. Use a cup of Epsom salts in a bathtub and soak for a good half hour or more.

Sometimes I will do this in silence, and other times with music. I will sometimes add various essential oils, which I will select intuitively. I have found this to be one of the most profound balancing actions for me personally and I know others who share this experience.

The action of soaking in water is a natural balancing activity for the body in so many ways. The weightlessness tends to promote natural relaxation. The salt content ionizes the water. And it seems there is a healing influence provided through the subtle current created, and by the osmotic influence of the salts which seems "to pull" tension and its associate toxicity out of the body.

Don't worry about the mechanics – I would encourage you to try it for your own experience and anytime you feel inspired to do it for its benefits.

19. Flower Essences

Flower essences are vibrational tinctures that are prepared from the blossoms of various flowers, which subsequently carry a vibrational signature that corresponds to the energy signature of the flower from which it is prepared.

This sounds very esoteric, and it is. It does however become a little easier to appreciate when you realize the inherent geometrical patterns that are present "etherically" in flowers, and the impact of consciousness or etheric printing, on water. The most direct way to really grasp the potential of this is to explore the work and teaching of Dr. Masaru Emoto.[18]

The flower imprints energetic "structure" in water, in correspondence to the etheric imprint of the consciousness to which it is entrained. In the setting of flower essences, these perfected little geometrical signatures that are part of the flowers etheric nature are imprinted in the tincture and create a vibrational support for the human energy system. To better understand flower essences there is an excellent book by Michaelle Small-

Wright entitled *Flower Essences – A Revolution in Our Understanding and Approach to Illness and Health.*[47]

Intuitive people who have worked in essence development have brought forth an understanding of the healing properties in essences developed from many different flowers, plants and trees. A very unique healer in England, Dr. Edward Bach, did the earliest work in this domain. He developed the Bach Healing Remedies.[2]

Work with essences has flourished in recent times and there are several highly conscious producers of essences including Perelandra, Canadian Tree Essences, and Flower Essence Society. I have long used essences and programs produced by such companies. Some excellent resources are provided in the reference section.[2,47]

Essences can be used for specific reasons or you may be drawn to one or several of them to support you in your healing efforts. For example, if you have a tendency to worry or be angry or impatient – these can impact your overall energy balance and health. It can be astounding how these patterns seem to "melt away" with appropriate essence support.

When learning to work with vibrational remedies of any kind, it is very valuable to work with kinesiology or muscle testing. This is illustrated in Michaelle Small-Wright's book referenced above.

Kinesiology can "read" the energy system and bypass the mental and emotional involvement if we don't exert control. It does take a little practice, for the mental and emotional body can be very strong and override the kinesiology so it is important to try to be open, free and relaxed. You will get the hang of it if you try.

You can be creative and learn to adapt these processes to ways that you trust and work for you. When I work with essences I run my index finger over the solutions and feel a little "buzz" when I encounter an essence that would support healing. You can experiment yourself what works for you.

20. ESSENTIAL OILS

Essential oils have long been utilized in healing practice. Pure floral oils have unique vibrational qualities that may be resonant with the healing of certain disease conditions, or for creating an optimized environment for energy balance. There has been a recent resurgence of interest in the healing properties of essential oils, and many of the healing attributes have been catalogued.

There are certain oils, which have specific resonance with the chakra systems and if one is sensitive to energy and can feel or see energy – this is fairly easy to appreciate.

While travelling in Egypt I had the privilege of meeting a wonderful man – Abdul - who works with energy healing and essential oils. His background knowledge of the oils, their preparation and their properties is handed down through many generations. He lists 7 oils, which have direct chakra activation properties, which I have found to be true. The essential oils are:

Root Chakra: Red Amber
Sacral Chakra: Musk
Solar Plexus Chakra: Jasmine
Heart Chakra: Rose
Throat Chakra: Kashmir
Third Eye Chakra: Sandalwood
Crown Chakra: Blue lotus

Many other oils are also noted to have particular therapeutic properties, such as lavender, peppermint, spearmint, orange, lemon, eucalyptus, pine, myrrh, and so forth. Oils may also be worn in place of perfumes or colognes. Many people are sensitive to the modified oils used in highly esterized or alcoholized perfumes - but exhibit no sensitivity to pure oil extracts. One must exercise appropriate caution in the setting of hypersensitivity or allergy – but this has been my experience.

An excellent resource on therapeutic applications of oils is found in a book by Valerie Ann Worwood entitled *The Complete Book of Essential Oils and Aromatherapy*. [54]

21. CRYSTALS

I am not an expert on crystal healing and have some limited experience in healing with crystals. I have found working with and meditating with crystals to be very interesting, and I am personally convinced of the healing properties of crystals and gemstones.

One of the most knowledgeable people I have met in regards to gemstone healing is James Tyberonn, and one of the best references I have discovered on stone and healing properties is entitled *The Book of Stones: Who They Are & What They Teach* by N. Simmons and R. Ahsian.[45]

Crystals are like mini-amplifiers of certain vibratory quality that can help resonantly affect the energy field. I believe certain crystals have innate vibratory qualities that can benefit the human energy field in different ways. They can be used therapeutically, assist in healing and meditative experiences, or worn as jewelry.

Some of my personal favorites are lapis lazuli, emerald, quartz and selenite. There is a vast amount of knowledge on crystal healing being produced, and I would encourage you to approach it with an open mind.

22. Personal Environment

As you go through a personal healing process or spiritual integrative experiences, you will undoubtedly manifest changes in your life and the world around you. Your personal environment may "ask" to change.

You may want to tidy up, get rid of junk, harmonize your space or add other balancing forces to your environment. You may want to change colors of your home or your clothes! Flow with the changes and allow yourself to add or release what is of inherent value to you.

Relations too may adjust. Friendships may remodel or dissipate. New ones will form. Friendships and relationships that were based on pathologic tendencies or meant to "teach" something may become outworn.

Some people will change jobs, homes, cities, or countries – following their paths. Change is an inherent part of growth and better appreciated than feared. Make wise, intuitive, inherently-valued changes. I include this short discussion, because shifting realities is often troubling for people – and it need not be that way if we understand and accept the underlying current of growth that is stimulating the changes. Expect change and flow with it – you will find shifting levels of harmony instilling in your reality. Breathe and flow!

23. Honoring New Abilities

In treading a path of healing or spiritual development, you will begin to learn about the spiritual nature of reality – and learn to function with a greater spiritual awareness. With this, people become aware of the incredible power of authentic intention, the role of intuitive guidance, and the ways of synchronicity.

The role of *intuition* becomes very important in guiding one's life, and one's decisions. When we are trying to listen to our innate wisdom or spiritual guidance, most of us have not been instructed or well versed in how to do this. When we are seeking personal guidance – it will most often manifest through the power of intuitive awareness.

Intuition, unlike the cacophony of everyday life tends to whisper, not scream. When we are trying to make a decision or be aware of what to believe or what to do – the answer is often best appreciated by direct, non-rational knowing. Intuition often occurs in a flash of awareness that arrives in our mind, and is very commonly the first "gut response" to a question. It is a quiet direct knowing, and learning to trust it involves practice and experience.

As our ego tendencies become more and more consciously externalized – and they have less direct control on us – we become a little freer. Past conditioned responses lose power to our spiritual intuition. As we do permit ourselves to make intuition-based choices, the truer "logic" may only become evident itself days or months that follow, when we see the outcome of our choices and how wise this guidance was. This is not a comfortable way to live for many and does require some personal experience and confirmation!

Intention is a driving force of spiritually conscious creation. Intention is the ability to align our lives consciously with our spirit and assume a co-creative role in manifesting our life experience. It is often said, "thoughts create reality". I prefer to say that thoughts mold our creative expression.

Life flows through us, and our thoughts mold the energy of life into the shape of its form. It is, however, the power of consciousness and intention that can adapt our thoughts and feelings toward healing and greater creative self-expression.

Our intention may be blocked creatively by our patterns or ego forces, so it may not always seem to work directly – but there is nothing as powerful as pure intent. If a person wants to manifest healing or positive growth, pure intent is key. Not wishy-washy intent. The real McCoy.

Synchronicity is the improbable occurrence of events, which contribute to shaping our life and our world in ways that could never be fully organized, controlled or arranged. To understand synchronicity, one has to realize that one is a spiritual being living in relationship with others spiritual beings in a connected energetic tapestry of life. We live in a universe that is designed to support our life, our growth and our spiritual evolution.

The chance meeting of a new life partner. The inconvenient distraction, that keeps us safe from harm. Picking up the right book at a moment when you are ready to learn or explore something. This list goes on and on. When we begin to understand this, we learn that we can relax a great deal – for the universe is conspiring to help us. We simply have to relax and follow our intuitive directive. We can learn to listen, honor its promptings and move with the rhythm of the universe - as it responds to our spiritual intention by allowing synchronicity to unfold in our lives.

Through these attributes we become co-creative forces, and move into our role as empowered, connected, responsible creators and as stewards of life. I would encourage you to read and learn about all of these abilities for they will serve you well in your personal growth and healing endeavors.

24. MAP

One, next to last, item that I will include is a reference to a healing program that has been very supportive to me in my own personal journey. It is especially accessible and useful when you do not know where to go for assistance and you do not want to spend a fortune on healing support!

MAP is a healing process introduced in a book to explain the process, entitled *MAP: The Great White Brotherhood Medical Assistance Program*.[46] It was written by Machaelle Small-Wright.

This program teaches you how to connect in consciousness and work with a team of etheric beings who specialize in healing. The book teaches you to work through meditative sessions with this interdimensional healing support. I am aware, like a few other things in this book, this may sound strange – but I can attest to the reality and value of this work.

I won't go into a lot of the detail about this work – for it is superbly introduced in the book itself – which you would need to read to understand it. It is like having a personal healing team on call. The best thing is, once you buy the book, you never pay for an office visit!

25. ACIM

A Course in Miracles was introduced earlier in our discussion of healing. It is a tremendously powerful tool to unravel the limiting and illusory power that the ego holds over our lives. The deep healing achieved through this integration is, as the book attests, miraculous!

The book is a channeled by Helen Schucman, taught by Christ, to unravel the spell of the ego's illusions in our life. It is a systematic undoing of the ego entrapments that keep us divided in perception from our spirit and love as the foundation of reality.

Many people are challenged to relate to the work at first because of the familiar religious terms that are employed in the work. Yet, if you can see past them, and perhaps the ego's reactions to them, the work can take you deeper and deeper into the realization of peace and spiritual transcendence.

More accessible writings are available such as the beautiful book by Marianne Williamson entitled *A Return to Love: Reflection on the Teachings of a Course in Miracle* [55], and works by authors such as Wayne Dyer and Eckhart Tolle. [51,52] They can serve as wonderful reflections in their own right and also open the doorway to better understanding the ACIM material. [43]

◎

As you take your own journey through healing and spiritual awakening you will undoubtedly find many further tools and processes that are helpful to you. This is not meant to represent a complete reference. It is a personal list. If you are looking for resources to explain some forms of energetic healing, one of the most complete scientific references to energy healing processes is found in a book by Dr. Richard Gerber, entitled *Vibrational Medicine.* [26] Most of all, honor your own experiences; follow your inner guidance and your dreams.

CHAPTER 13

IN CLOSING

So let's see ... we have covered a lot together. We have come to understand that this is a unique, unprecedented time on the planet. There is a magnificent transformation that is occurring, which is striking a spiritual impulse and awakening a new spiritual potential in humanity. This is a transformation in which you, through your inspired interest, are a very integral part. We are ultimately participating in a Conscious Biospiritual Transformation – and we are each blessed beyond measure by an awakening grace.

We have learned that there are rich potentials available in terms of healing and transformation available to us – potentials that require us to expand in our understanding of both our spiritual and energetic nature. These potentials will help us manifest unprecedented healing and change. These new potentials, which appear foolish or magical in the old paradigm, are becoming completely comprehensible in the new one – but we each have some learning to do. We are becoming conscious, responsible, spiritual co-creators – learning to operate in a new paradigm of healing and quantum consciousness.

As we pursue healing and spiritual development it is perhaps easy to get overwhelmed by the information available. When you find yourself overwhelmed with information or personal experiences - remember always the journey is quite simple. The compass of the needle always points toward peace and awakening love.

The path to peace is as close as a memory – a shift of perception. It is important to learn, but not to get bogged down in detail and facts as we shift to heart-based living. The perception of love and healing is always as close as your next breath.

It is my intention that the ending of the book represents the beginning of a new healing paradigm. I truly hope that you have found both awakening knowledge, and living inspiration. May it stimulate transformation, in the way your soul beckons, for you to heal and to grow. I have great faith in the process of life. I also have great faith in you, and the part you are playing in this time of personal and planetary transformation.

As we wind up our time together, for now, I would like to take a personal moment to thank you. To share and spend time is perhaps the greatest gift a human being can give to another – so I am conscious of the gift you have bestowed upon me. I genuinely hope it has served you well.

Through this panoramic view of healing and biospiritual integration, I hope a new or renewed passion to heal and become more spiritually aligned has been ignited. I trust you have discovered some of the answers you have been seeking. May your faith continue to inspire you on a path of spiritual exploration and integration, one that will serve you well at this magnificent time on planet earth.

I encourage you with every molecule of my being and strand of DNA - to pursue your personal growth. It is time to become the most inspired love-filled being you can imagine yourself to be. The time is truly at hand.

In closing, may you be inspired, as I have many times in my life, by the embrace of these eternal words. These words are wiser than anything I could have written, and anchor profoundly the truth of these times:

The Way of Love

If I speak in human and angelic tongues, but do not have love,
I am a resounding gong or a clashing cymbal.
And if I have the gift of prophesy, and comprehend all mysteries and knowledge;
if I have faith so as to move mountains, but do not have love, I am nothing.
If I give away everything I own, and if I hand my body over so that I may boast,
but do not have love, I gain nothing.
Love is patient, love is kind.
It is not jealous, love is not pompous, it is not inflated, it is not rude, it does not seek its
own interests, it is not quick-tempered, is does not brood over injury, it does not rejoice
over wrongdoing but rejoices with the truth.
It bears all things, believes all things, hopes all things, endures all things.

Love never fails.
If there are prophecies, they will be brought to nothing; if tongues, they will cease; if
knowledge, it will be brought to nothing.
For we know partially and we prophesy partially, but when the perfect comes, the partial
will pass away.
When I was a child, I used to talk as a child, think as a child, reason as a child; when I
became a man, I put aside childish things.
At present we see indistinctly, as in a mirror, but then face to face.
At present I know partially; then I shall know full as I am full known.
So faith, hope, love remain, these three;

But the greatest of these is love.

1 Corinthians 13

BIBLIOGRAPHY

1. The Holy Bible, King James Cambridge Ed
2. Bach, Edward and Wheeler, EJ The Bach Flower Remedies McGraw-Hill 1998 ISBN 0879838698
3. Bays, Brandon The Journey – A Practical Guide to Healing Your Life and Setting Yourself Free Atria Books ISBN: 978-1451665611
4. Brach, Tara True Refuge: Finding Peace and Freedom in Your Own Awakened Heart Bantam ISBN 055380762
5. Braden, Gregg, Awakening to Zero Point – The Collective Initiation, Radio Bookstore Press 1993 ISBN 1-889071-09-9
6. Braden, Gregg, Deep Truth Hay House 2011 978-1-4019-2919-0
7. Brennan, Barbara Ann, Hands of Light – A Guide to Healing Through the Human Energy Field, Bantam Books, New York, NY 1987   ISBN 0-553-05302-7
8. Brennan, Barbara Ann Light Emerging Bantam Books 1993 ISBN 0-553-354566-6
9. Carroll, Lee, Kryon Book 6 - Partnering With God: Practical Information for the New Millennium, Kryon Writings 1997   ISBN 1888053100
10. Carroll, Lee, Kryon Book 7 - Letters from Home, Kryon Writings 1999 ISBN 1888053127
11. Carroll, Lee and Jan Tober, The Indigo Children, Hay House Inc., Carlsbad, CA 1999 ISBN 1-56170-608-6
12. Carroll, Lee/Kryon The Twelve Layers of Mastery Platinum Publishing House 2010 ISBN 1-933465-05-0
13. Carroll, Lee http://www.kryon.com/k_chanelhandbook01.html
14. Church, Dawson The Genie in Your Genes Energy Psychology Press 2nd edition 2009 ISBN1604150114
15. Delfino, Mona The Sacred Language of the Human Body Createspace ISBN: 1480095702
16. Dubro, Peggy Phoenix and David Lapierre   Elegant Empowerment: Evolution of Consciousness Platinum Publishing House 0-9711074-08
17. Dale, Cyndi The Subtle Body: An Encyclopedia of Your Energetic Anatomy Sounds True 2009 ISBN 978-1-59179-671-8
18. Emoto, Masaru Messages from Water and the Universe Hay House 2012 ISBN 1401927467
19. Feinstein, David et al The Promise of Energy Psychology   Jeremy P Tarcher/Penguin Press ISBN 978-1585424429
20. Ferrini, Paul The Circle of Atonement: The Wounded Childs Journey into Love's Embrace Heartways Press 1991 ISBN 1-879159-06-6
21. Ferrini, Paul Reflections on The Christ Mind   Heartways Press 1991 ISBN 1879159236
22. Ford, Debbie The Dark Side of the Light Chasers Riverhead Trade ISBN-10: 1594485259
23. Galilei, Galileo Dialogue Concerning the Two Chief World Systems University of California Press 1967 ISBN 520-00450-7

24. Gallo, Fred Energy Psychology – Exploring the Interface of Energy, Cognition, Behavior and Health CRC Press ISBN 978-1574441840
25. Gawain, Shakti Living in the Light   New World Library ISBN 1577310462
26. Gerber, Richard, M.D., Vibrational Medicine – New Choices for Healing Ourselves, Bear & Co., Santa Fe, NM 1988 ISBN 1-979181-28-2
27. Goldman, Jonathan Healing Sounds – The Power of Harmonics Healing Arts Prss 2002 185230314X
28. Goleman, Daniel Emotional Intelligence Bantam ISBN: 978-0553804911
29. Goswami, Amit PhD, The Quantum Doctor Hampton Road 2004 ISBN 1-57174-417-7
30. Grey, Alex, Sacred Mirrors – the Visionary Art of Alex Grey, Inner Traditions Intl., 1990 ISBN 0892813148
31. Hay, Louise You Can Heal Your Life Hay House ISBN: 0937611018
32. Judith, Anodea, Wheels of Life - A User's Guide to the Chakra System, Llewellyn Publication's 1987 St. Paul MN ISBN 0-87542-320-5
33. Krishna, Gopi The Awakening of Kundalini Institute for Conscious Research and The Kundalini Research Foundation 1975 0-525-47398-X
34. Lawlor, Robert Sacred Geometry: Philosophy and Practice Thames & Hudson 1982 ISBN 0500810303
35. Lipton, Bruce The Biology of Belief: Unleashing the Power of Consciousness, Matter, & Miracles Hay House 2008 ISBN 1401923127
36. Melchizedek, Drunvalo, The Ancient Secrets of the Flower of Life - Volume 1, Light Technology Publishing, Flagstaff, Arizona 1998   ISBN 1-891824-17-1
37. Michelsen, Neil The American Ephemeris for the 20th century ACS Publications 5th Ed. March 2000 ISBN 0935127194
38. Mirriam Wesbter Dictionary www.Mirriam-Webster.com
39. Myss, Caroline, Anatomy of the Spirit – Seven stages of Power and Healing, Random House Value Publishing, 1997 , ISBN 0-60980014-0
40. Myss, Caroline Why People Don't Heal and How They Can Three Rivers Press ISBN: 0609802240
41. Parks, Joann www.maxskull.net
42. Pert, Candice Molecules of Emotion: The Science Behind Mind Body Medicine Simon & Schuster 1999 ISBN 0684846349
43. A Course in Miracles, Foundation for Inner Peace, Mill Valley, CA 1993 ISBN 0-9606388-8-1
44. Shealy, C Norman Energy Medicine 4th Dimension Press 2011 ISBN 978-0-87604-4
45. Simmons R and Ahsian N The Book of Stones: Who They Are & What They Teach North Atlantic Books 2007 ISBN 1556436688
46. Small Wright, Machaelle, MAP - The CoCreative White Brotherhood Medical Assistance Program, Perelandra, Ltd., Warrington VA 1990 ISBN 0-927978-19-9
47. Small Wright, Machaelle, Flower Essences – A Revolution in Our Understanding and Approach to Illness and Health, Perelandra, Ltd., Warrington VA 1988,2011 ISBN 0-9617713-3-X

48. Stone, Randolph Polarity Therapy: The Complete Collected Works on this Revolutionary Healing Art CRCS Publications Sebastopol, CA 1987.
49. Tansley, David *Subtle Body - Essence and Shadow* Art and Imagination Series 1977 Thames and Hudson, London ISBN 0500810141
50. Tiller, W et al Conscious Acts of Creation – The Emergence of a New Physics Pavior Publishing 2001 1-929331-05-3
51. Tolle, Eckhart The Power of Now New World Library 2004 ISBN 1577314808
52. Tolle, Eckhart A New Earth: Awakening to Your Life's Purpose Penguin 2008 ISBN
53. Weiss, Brian Many Live, Many Masters The True Story of a Prominent Psychiatrist, His Young Patient, and the Past-Life Therapy That Changed Both Their Lives Fireside 1988 ISBN 0671657860
54. Worwood, Valerie Ann The Complete Book of Essential Oils and Aromatherapy New World Library 1993 ISBN 0931432820
55. Williamson, Marianne, Return to Love, Harper Collins Canada 1994 ISBN 0061092908
56. Zukav, Gary Seat of the Soul Free Press ISBN-10: 0609802240
57. Online Ref: http://www.geometrycode.com/sacred-geometry/
58. Online Ref: http://en.wikipedia.org/wiki/File:Health_care_cost_rise
59. Online Ref: http://www.britannica.com/EBchecked/topic/190813/precession-of-the-equinoxes
60. Brown, William Morphic Resonance and Quantum Biology, Nexus 2012:19(2)
61. Dephasing in electron interference by a `which-path' detector Buks, E.; Schuster, R.; Heiblum, M.; Mahalu, D.; Umansky, V. Nature, Volume 391, Issue 6670, pp. 871-874 (1998).

DR JOHN G RYAN MD

FIGURES AND REFERENCES

Chapter 2
Fig 1-1 Health care cost rise based on total expenditure on health as % of GDP. Countries are USA, Germany, Austria, Switzerland, UK and Canada.
http://en.wikipedia.org/wiki/File:Health_care_cost_rise

Chapter 3
Fig 3-1 Precession of the Equinoxes J Ryan

Chapter 4
Fig 4-1 Unity Field Healing Template J Ryan

Chapter 5
Fig 5-1 Atom - Oxygen atoms - Water Molecule J Ryan
Fig 5-2 Polarity Diagram J Ryan
Fig 5-3 Wavelength Diagram J Ryan
Fig 5-4 Electromagnetic Spectrum http://en.wikipedia.org/wiki/File:Electromagnetic-Spectrum.png
Fig 5-5 Prism
http://upload.wikimedia.org/wikipedia/commons/6/63/Dispersion_prism.jpg
Fig 5-6 Magnetic Field J Ryan
Fig 5-7 Magnetic Filings
http://www.fi.edu/htlc/teachers/lettieri/classroomexperimentsandactivities.html
Fig 5-8 Kirlian Photography
http://www.everystockphoto.com/photo.php?imageId=680674&searchId=f0b2621de079bfc3688cd62128f3174d&npos=5
Fig 5-9 DNA https://en.wikipedia.org/wiki/File:DNA_orbit_animated_static_thumb.png
Fig 5-10 Consciousness and the Atom J Ryan
Fig 5-11 Consciousness and Sacred Geometry J Ryan
Fig 5-12 Cymatics Photo Dr Hans Jenny
Fig 5-13 Flower Artichoke and Nautilus http://www.pachd.com/free-images/food-images/artichoke-01.jpg
Fig 5-14 Flower of Life Tree of Life http://en.wikipedia.org/wiki/File:Tree-of-Life_Flower-of-Life_Stage.jpg
Fig 5-15 Crop Circle Schematic – Original image Lucy Pringle - Rybury/Tann Hill 28 July 2011 http://www.lucypringle.co.uk/photos/2001/uk2001cc.shtml
Fig 5-16 Unity Field Template J Ryan

Chapter 6
Fig 6-1 Aura J Ryan
Fig 6-2 Etheric Body J Ryan
Fig 6-3 Emotional Body J Ryan
Fig 6-4 Mental Body J Ryan

Chapter 7
Fig 7-1A Chakra Frontal J Ryan
Fig 7-1B Chakra Lateral J Ryan
Fig 7-2 Chakra Positions
http://simple.wikipedia.org/wiki/File:ColouredChakraswithDescriptions.jpg
Fig 7-3 Energy Flow J Ryan
Fig 7-4 Caduceus J Ryan
Fig 7-5 Christ Photo - J Ryan Taken at St Louis Basilica St Louis MO
Fig 7-6 Buddha Photo - J Ryan
Fig 7-7 Electromagnetic Visible Spectrum
http://science.hq.nasa.gov/kids/imagers/ems/visible.html
Fig 7-8 Planetary Chakra J Ryan
Fig 7-9 Sushumna, Ida and Pingala http://bhajanananda.blogspot.ca/2010/07/pranayama-science-of-breath.html
Fig 7-10 Caduceus
Fig 7-11 Nadis David V. Tansley, *Subtle Body - Essence and Shadow*, (1977, Art and Imagination Series, Thames and Hudson, London)
Fig 7-12 Meridians http://commons.wikimedia.org/wiki/File:Chinese_meridians.JPG

Chapter 9
Fig 9-1 Etheric Body JRyan
Fig 9-2 Emotional Body J Ryan
Fig 9-3 Mental Body JRyan

Chapter 10
Fig 10-1 The Ego in Action J Ryan
Fig 10-2 Working with Peace Consciousness J Ryan

Chapter 11
Fig 11-1 Max the Crystal Skull Photo J Ryan
Fig 11-2 Light Pyramid J Ryan
Fig 11-3 Cosmic DNA J Ryan
Fig 11-4 Unity Healing Template J Ryan
Fig 11-5 Unity Field Template Activation J Ryan
Fig 11-6 Spiral Galaxy   Photo courtesy of NASA
http://www.nasa.gov/multimedia/imagegallery/image_feature_2457.html#.UjG_pxY6LzK
Fig 11-7 DNA in "cross section" J Ryan
Fig 11-8 DNA with Template J Ryan
Fig 11-9 Ascension Stairway with DNA J Ryan
Fig 11-10 Tibetan Sri Yantra http://en.wikipedia.org/wiki/File:Sri_Yantra_256bw.gif
Fig 11-11 Interfacing with an "Interdimensional Template" J Ryan
Fig 11-12 Energy in Action J Ryan

Chapter 12
Fig 12-1 Gift of Grace J Ryan

THE MISSING PILL

ABOUT THE AUTHOR

Dr. John Ryan is a physician, consciousness and energy based healer, founder of Unity Field Healing, and author of two books – *Harp of the One Heart – Poetic Songs of Ascension*, and, *The Missing Pill*.

For more information on his work and trainings, please visit the website:

www.drjohnryan.org

Titles are AVAILABLE on:

AMAZON.COM